Financial Accounting

An Events and Cash Flow Approach

Financial Accounting
An Events and Cash Flow Approach

George H. Sorter
New York University

Monroe J. Ingberman
Late of New York University

Hillel M. Maximon
New York University

McGRAW-HILL PUBLISHING COMPANY
New York St. Louis San Francisco Auckland Bogotá Caracas Hamburg
Lisbon London Madrid Mexico Milan Montreal New Delhi
Oklahoma City Paris San Juan São Paulo Singapore Sydney
Tokyo Toronto

FINANCIAL ACCOUNTING: An Events and Cash Flow Approach

Copyright © 1990 by McGraw-Hill, Inc. All rights reserved. Printed in the United States of America. Except as permitted under the United States Copyright Act of 1976, no part of this publication may be reproduced or distributed in any form or by any means, or stored in a data base or retrieval system, without the prior written permission of the publisher.

1 2 3 4 5 6 7 8 9 0 DOC DOC 8 9 4 3 2 1 0 9

ISBN 0-07-059739-1

This book was set in Caledonia by Waldman Graphics, Inc.
The editors were Robert D. Lynch, Johanna Schmid, and Ira C. Roberts;
the designer was Chuck Carson;
the production supervisor was Friederich W. Schulte.
R. R. Donnelley & Sons Company was printer and binder.

Library of Congress Cataloging-in-Publication Data

Sorter, George H.
      Financial accounting: an events and cash flow approach / George H. Sorter, Monroe J. Ingberman, Hillel M. Maximon.
            p.   cm.
      Includes index.
      ISBN 0-07-059739-1
      1. Cash flow—United States—Accounting.   2. Corporations—United States—Accounting.   I. Ingberman, Monroe J.   II. Maximon, Hillel M.   III. Title.
      HF5681.C28S67   1990
      657—dc20
                                                                                      89-12566

Kierkegaard said that
life can only be understood in the past
and only lived in the future.
This appropriately defines both the role of
accounting and the purpose of this book.

We dedicate this book to our parents and teachers—
who taught us to understand the past,
and to our children and students—
who, by understanding the past, will learn to live in the future.
David, Ruth, and Saadyah.

Contents

Preface   *ix*

PART ONE

The Accounting Model   1

Chapter 1   Introduction: The Nature and Purpose of Accounting   3

Chapter 1
Appendix   Cash Flows and their Equivalents:
             Present and Future Values   14

Chapter 2   Accounting Categories: Assets and Equities   29

Chapter 3   Accounting Numbers   43

Chapter 4   The First Day of The American Grabule Company:
             Debits, Credits, and the Balance Sheet   63

Chapter 5   The Second Day of The American Grabule Company:
             The Income Statement   85

Chapter 5
Appendix   Transactional Analysis:
             The Events Approach to Accounting   105

Chapter 6   The First Two Days of The American Grabule Company:
             The Statement of Cash Flows   129

Chapter 7   Recognizing and Quantifying, Recording and Reporting
             Accounting Events   155

PART TWO

Operating Events   183

Chapter 8   Revenues and Operating Expenses   185

Chapter 8
Appendix   Calculating the
             Uncollectibility Adjustment   203

Chapter 9   Consumption of Inventory:
             Cost of Goods Sold   215

Chapter 10   Amortization of Long-Lived Assets   241

Chapter 11   Income Taxes   271

PART THREE

Financing Events   **297**

Chapter 12   Accounting for Long-Term Debt: Loans   299

Chapter 13   Accounting for Long-Term Debt: Bonds   325

Chapter 14   Financing Events with Owners   353

PART FOUR

Investing Events   **381**

Chapter 15   Accounting for Investments in Long-Lived Assets   383

Chapter 16   Accounting for Investments in Other Firms   411

Epilogue   *451*

Glossary   *459*

Index   *473*

Preface

THE PURPOSE OF THIS BOOK

This book presents a new method of explaining financial accounting. Its purpose is to show preparers and users how to understand financial statements and make effective use of them. But, to understand accounting reports, users must know which events accountants record as significant, and what conventions accountants utilize in describing, reporting, and transmitting these events.

As the title of this book suggests, we stress the **events approach** to financial accounting. The events approach focuses on the events underlying accounting numbers. We will emphasize the cash implications of accounting events because the financial accounting framework is based on cash flows, and thus can best be understood in those terms.

Some textbooks present an explicit set of procedures for readers to accept and memorize. This is not our approach. We aim to foster understanding rather than mere mechanical facility. In our teaching experience, we have found that what is memorized is often forgotten and what is understood is generally retained.

Knowledge of the fundamental concepts and limitations of accounting is essential to the effective use of accounting information. We believe it is equally important to discover that accounting can be an intellectually stimulating and exciting adventure, rather than an arid exercise in procedural drudgery which it is often thought to be. Moreover, this discovery motivates the learning process.

Early on, we explore the myth that financial statements contain all that anyone might want to know about a firm, or that all relevant information about a firm can realistically be expressed by one or more "bottom lines." Instead, we demonstrate that financial statements present a useful history of a firm's significant cash events — events that either have affected or will affect cash — in terms of how these events affect the rights and responsibilities of a firm.

Therefore, the first challenge is to determine which economic events are accounting events and which are not. As the book develops, we demonstrate that the basic accounting task is one of allocation — to classify and separately report those accounting events that will generate future cash benefits, or will require future cash sacrifices, and those that will not.

THE BOOK'S ORGANIZATION

This book is organized into four parts: the accounting model, operating events, financing events, and investing events. This organization is consistent with the classification of cash events in the statement of cash flows, the newest required financial statement.

The discussion of the accounting model begins with the purpose of financial reporting (Chapter 1). To stress the importance of cash flows and their timing, we include a discussion of present and future values as an appendix to Chapter 1. In Chapters 2 and 3, we discuss accounting categories (assets and equities) and the relationship of accounting numbers to cash flows. In Chapters 4 through 6, we introduce the basic financial statements—the balance sheet, the income statement, and the statement of cash flows—using an integrative example. Chapter 7, the final chapter in Part One, abstracts and synthesizes the material from the previous six chapters into a unified accounting model.

Parts Two, Three, and Four provide a closer examination of the operating, financing, and investing events of a firm: how they are accounted for, and how they relate to cash flows. The operating events—Revenues, Operating Expenses, Cost of Goods Sold, Depreciation Expense, and Income Taxes—are discussed in Chapters 8 through 11. Financing events—the Borrowing and Repayment of Debt, and the Issue and Repurchase of Equity Securities, as well as the distributions to debtholders and equityholders—are discussed in Chapters 12 through 14. Investing events—Investments in Long-Lived Assets, and Investments in Securities of Other Firms—are covered in Chapters 15 and 16.

PEDAGOGICAL FEATURES

We pose "Thought Questions" throughout the text. These Thought Questions encourage the student to **stop, think,** and **absorb** the information just presented, and they provide the instructor with issues that can be amplified upon in class discussion.

Each chapter ends with a "User's Perspective." All of the User's Perspectives alert the reader to the uses and limitations of accounting reports so that they can be understood. The User's Perspectives in Chapters 8 through 16 serve two additional purposes. First, they demonstrate how significant information about the amount and timing of cash flows can be extracted from financial statement disclosures, and how substantive changes (changes with cash flow implications) can be distinguished from descriptive changes. Second, they demonstrate the relevance and limitations of using financial ratios in assessing the significance of the cash flows.

In addition to the Thought Questions and User's Perspectives, Chapters 8 through 16 contain examples from actual corporate financial reports, illustrating the discussion of reporting requirements.

The end-of-chapter problems are of three types: objective, logical, and analytical. The short, multiple-choice **objective questions** are AICPA-adapted problems addressing particular concepts from the chapter. The **logic questions** focus on the ability to reason, using the material in the chapter. The longer **analytic problems** are designed to demonstrate **transactional analysis,** a technique for extracting information from financial statements about significant events that have occurred.

Because these analytic problems are more comprehensive and substantive than customary, they require considerable effort and time. Our classroom experience has been that the number of problems provided in this book is more than enough to enable students to comprehend the material. And they are fun, too!

All of the material customarily covered in beginning financial accounting textbooks can be found in this book, if in somewhat less detail and presented in a nontraditional manner. To that end, we sometimes introduce descriptive, nontechnical words that facilitate understanding the substance of financial accounting.

The first time we introduce a new term, either technical or nontechnical, it will appear in *bold italics;* a subsequent occurrence of the term will be in *italics*. All terms appearing in italics will be defined in the glossary and referenced to the text. Eventually, all nontechnical words are replaced by their technical equivalents, but not until the accounting language no longer impedes the learning process.

In addition to italicization, we utilize two other visual aids to foster comprehension: all accounting events are in SMALL CAPS and all balance sheet titles are Capitalized. In doing this, we highlight the effect of accounting events on accounts.

ANCILLARY MATERIALS

An Instructor's Manual/Solutions Manual accompanies this textbook. This manual serves a number of purposes. First, it contains solutions to all of the problems in the textbook. Second, it gives answers to all of the Thought Questions. Though the primary purpose of the Thought Questions is to let the student stop, think, and absorb, they can be expanded upon for meaningful classroom discussion and additional problem assignments. Third, it suggests more detailed discussion of topics raised, but not elaborated on in either the Thought Questions or the other material presented in the book.

Finally, it provides methods and techniques used by the authors in teaching the material to stimulate class discussion, and thereby further the understanding of financial accounting.[1]

Also available is *The MixMax Company*,[1] a comprehensive problem-set. It integrates the mechanics of different accounting and financing methods with transactional analysis, in one continuous problem.

All of these ancillary materials were designed to reinforce, through varied and practical examples and exercises, and bring to life the concepts developed in the textbook.

In summary, this book describes the accounting model from an events, cash flow, and user's perspective, to demonstrate how reports can be analyzed to provide meaningful information about the cash flows of a firm. While highlighting the limitations of financial reports, we show how information in them can be used to generate a history of a firm.

ACKNOWLEDGMENTS

Our teachers and students, colleagues and friends contributed a great deal in making our manuscript a book. To Miguel Angarita, Ross Archibald, William Beaver, Norman Berman, John Bildersee, John Cheh, Sidney Davidson, Haim Dov Fried, Martin Gans, David Green Jr., Charles Horngren, Rohit Jain, Alice Jarvis, Robert Kay, Bruce Koch, Sam Laimon, James Lorie, Stephanie Lovett, Earl Ludman, Kathleen McGahran, Patricia McQueen, Marilyn Neimark, Alain Oberrotman, Raymonde Rousselot, Arie Ovadia, Joshua Ronen, Thomas Selling, Jack Slain, and Roman Weil, many thanks. A special thanks to William Vatter who started it all.

We would like to express our appreciation to the following reviewers who read the manuscript and helped to improve the material presented: Wayne Boutell, University of California—Berkeley; Alan Cherry, Loyola Marymount University; C. William Cummings, Northern Illinois University; Richard Murdock, Ohio State University; and Mark E. Zmijewski, University of Chicago.

We are grateful to the following people at McGraw-Hill: Chuck Carson, Mel Haber, Caroline Izzo, Cathleen Ledwith, Joe Murphy, Johanna Schmid, Fred Schulte, and Paul Short. We are indebted to Ira Roberts, whose painstaking thoroughness and persistency shepherded this manuscript through its final stages; to Mary Rosenberg, whose skillful copyediting shaped this book into its present

---

[1]Hillel M. Maximon and George H. Sorter, *The MixMax Company*, Third Edition, McGraw-Hill, New York, 1990.

form; to Allan Forsyth, who demonstrated the wizardry of a true word magician; and to Robert Lynch, who had the vision and courage to be tolerant and supportive of the nontraditional aspects of this book and its authors.

Some things appear trite, but only because they have enduring validity. This book has had a long odyssey. The journey started more than twenty years ago, but could never have come to a conclusion without the continuing support, sacrifice, and encouragement from our families.

George H. Sorter
Hillel M. Maximon

Financial Accounting

An Events and Cash Flow Approach

PART ONE

The Accounting Model

Introduction: The Nature and Purpose of Accounting

INTRODUCTION

This book reflects our conviction that *accounting* is an intellectually stimulating and dynamic discipline, well worth the effort necessary to master its intricacies. Throughout this book, therefore, we examine the conceptual origins of accounting rules and explore their continued relevance in today's ever-shifting economic environment.

Accounting has been the subject of much misunderstanding and misdirected criticism. We describe the limitations of accounting to help you avoid the common error of expecting too much from *accounting reports.* Knowing what has been omitted from such reports is just as important as understanding what has been included.

Although we address the user rather than the preparer of accounting reports, this book also represents an essential first step in the training of a professional accountant. To decode a message and extract its correct meaning, people must understand the process by which the message was originally encoded. For this reason we examine the technology of accounting in considerable detail, not as an end in itself, but as a means of furthering your ability to interpret and utilize accounting reports.

The professional accountant is an information specialist. Therefore, accountants should begin their training with an introduction to the needs of the ultimate consumer—the user of accounting reports. Products of the accounting process are familiar to most of us, but few people are aware of the conventions and choices that enter into the preparation of *accounting numbers.* There is an unfortunate tendency to treat these numbers as revealed truth. In this book we seek to make plain the framework governing the accountant's functions of selection, description, and communication. We look beneath the numbers to the underlying economic events giving rise to these numbers, and we attempt to uncover the decisions that cause these events to occur.

THE ELEMENTS OF ECONOMIC DECISIONS

Accounting is a system for assembling and communicating information that is useful in reaching *economic decisions*. To comprehend fully the meaning of this definition, we must consider both the nature of economic decisions and the procedures involved in arriving at such decisions.

Every *economic decision* entails a choice among alternative means of achieving a given objective. If we want to get around, we must choose between buying a car, renting a car, and using public transportation. When we have money, we must choose between spending it, putting it in a savings account, and investing it. Each alternative involves a *sacrifice*, incurred in expectation of receiving greater *benefits*. Since most benefits and some sacrifices lie in the future, the decision maker must be able to **predict** the future consequences of each course of action, so that the alternatives may be compared, and the choice made, according to some decision rule.

Three aspects of sacrifices and benefits are important in trying to make rational decisions:

1. *Amount*   How large will the expected benefits and sacrifices be? The "rational economic person" prefers more benefits to less, and less sacrifices to more.

2. *Timing*   How soon will the anticipated benefits appear? How soon will the necessary sacrifices have to be made? The rational economic person prefers benefits sooner rather than later, and sacrifices later rather than sooner. In other words, no one likes to postpone gratification.

3. *Uncertainty*   How certain are the amount and timing of the hoped-for benefits and anticipated sacrifices? The rational economic person prefers more certainty to less certainty concerning the amount and timing of both benefits and sacrifices.

For example, if we consider lending $1,000 today (the sacrifice), we want to know how much the borrower promises to return (the potential benefit). If $1,100 is the anticipated benefit, we are **not** indifferent between payment in 1 year and payment 10 years from today. Finally, we certainly want to evaluate the risk that the loan will not be repaid, or will not be repaid when promised. In short, economic theory assumes that a rational person prefers more benefits to less, sooner to later, more certain to less certain. Concerning sacrifices, the rational person prefers less to more, later to sooner, more certain to less certain.

> ### Thought Questions
> Do you think that the assumptions
> about the rational person are realistic?
> Do they accurately describe your own
> decision-making processes? Cite examples.
> Why does the rational person prefer
> more certain to less certain sacrifices?

In summary, economic decision making involves predicting the amount, timing, and uncertainty of sacrifices and benefits resulting from a contemplated action, and comparing them to the amount, timing, and uncertainty of sacrifices and benefits associated with alternative actions. But economic decision making is an ongoing activity. Therefore, an important part of decision making involves monitoring decisions already made, and evaluating these past decisions in order to improve the decision-making process. Thus, we can see that the phrase used earlier, "information useful in reaching economic decisions," refers to all information that helps the decision maker **predict and compare** the **amount, timing, and uncertainty** of the benefits and sacrifices resulting from each alternative designed to achieve a stated objective. Such information specifically includes feedback from decisions already made.

ACCOUNTING UNITS

Economic decisions may be made by *economic units* and by *accounting units.* An *economic unit* is any individual (or group of individuals acting in concert) capable of making economic decisions. An *accounting unit* is any economic unit whose activities are recorded and then reported. These reports are called *accounting reports,* and numbers appearing in such reports are called *accounting numbers.*

Accounting units can be profit-seeking businesses or nonprofit organizations. Such units can be individuals, households, small businesses, giant corporations, charitable foundations, or government agencies. Whether the profit-seeking businesses are proprietorships, partnerships, or corporations, they all engage in the same basic activity. They receive cash from their owners and creditors, and use it to acquire goods and pay for labor services, so that they can provide goods and services to customers in exchange for the receipt of cash.

The cash generated from a business operation can be reinvested either in the operations or in the expansion of the business, so that the cash-generating activities of the business will continue. Alternatively, the cash can be used to repay creditors or to make distributions to owners. But in any event, the basic purpose of all profit-seeking businesses is to generate cash!

With a few inevitable digressions, the accounting unit examined in this book will be the medium- to large-size corporation, although the approach developed here can be adapted readily to the information needs of other accounting units. A corporation is a specific form of business, created by charter in compliance with state law, and made up of investors, directors, officers, and employees. The investors, or stockholders, own the firm and receive all the benefits associated with ownership, they vote on major decisions affecting the company, and elect the directors.

The directors determine the goals and policies under which the firm operates, and appoint officers who are responsible for implementing the policies and managing the activities of the firm as performed by the employees.

ECONOMIC DECISIONS

Economic decisions reached with the help of accounting information can be classified under two headings:

1. *Internal decisions*   Decisions made **by** the accounting unit
2. *External decisions*   Decisions made **about** the accounting unit by some other unit

Decisions of both kinds can be made in connection with each of the accounting units cited above. For instance, a family or individual decides whether or not to buy a car (an internal decision); a bank approves or rejects a loan for this purchase (an external decision). Further examples:

1. A corporation decides whether or not to build a new plant (an internal decision), and the public chooses whether or not to provide the cash needed for the building by purchasing the corporation's stock (an external decision).
2. A hospital considers adding a new wing (an internal decision), and a foundation wonders whether to finance the expansion with a grant (an external decision).
3. A school district contemplates building a new high school (an

internal decision), and voters approve or reject a bond issue to provide funds for the project (an external decision).

For the people weighing such decisions, accounting information helps to predict the amount, timing, and uncertainty of sacrifices and benefits associated with each alternative under consideration.

Information used to reach external decisions is called *financial accounting;* information provided for internal decisions is called *management accounting* or *cost accounting.*

Thought Questions
What important economic decision have you made lately?
What kinds of information did you use,
or would you have liked to have used,
to help you shape your decision?

External decision makers need global, general information about the company as a whole. Internal decision makers need specific, detailed information about a part of the firm. For example, a manager must decide whether to buy a machine for his department. The kind of detail needed for that decision would not interest a potential investor in the firm. But the internal decision maker must also consider the overall financial picture of the firm when weighing specific information requirements. Thus, external decisions are based on general financial information, while internal decisions utilize specific information in a context of general financial information. Since general financial information is needed for all decisions, it makes sense to begin with the needs of external users who require only general information.

There are many users of external financial information, such as government regulatory agencies, tax authorities, and labor unions. **However, we shall emphasize the financial information needs of investors and creditors.** Investors and creditors make a cash sacrifice in the hope of getting greater cash returns in the future. Creditors receive cash directly from the corporation in the form of interest payments and repayments of principal; they also can receive money indirectly by selling the note or bond which they hold as evidence of the obligation. Investors can receive cash directly from the corporation by means of dividends, and indirectly by selling their shares of stock in the marketplace. Investors and creditors selling their securities do not receive cash directly from the corporation, but from others who anticipate future cash receipts of interest and dividends. The amount for which these securities can be sold depends on other people's beliefs about the status and prospects of the corporation, and these beliefs are formed by using financial accounting reports and other sources of information.

Investors or creditors seek information that will enable them to predict the amount, timing, and uncertainty of cash flowing to them from the corporation in the future: directly in the form of dividends and interest, indirectly as a result of selling the security in the marketplace. The firm's capacity to pay dividends and interest is dependent on its ability to generate cash. Therefore, any information helpful in predicting the company's cash flows will help predict cash flows to investors and creditors. This information will also be useful in estimating a future market price for the firm's securities, since this price will be linked to the firm's cash-generating ability. Financial accounting reports should provide information useful for predicting and comparing the amount, timing, and uncertainty of a company's cash flows.

> *Thought Questions*
> How could you predict the market price
> of the common stock of a company
> that is never allowed to make any distributions to owners?
> You play in a poker game with strange rules:
> You may never collect your winnings!
> If you win every hand, have you won anything?

THE ACCOUNTING PROCESS

The process by which financial statements are prepared is a complex one. Accounting is an abstract art! This statement may be greeted with jeers, since it contradicts the popular image of the accountant as a "fussbudget," perched on a high stool, wearing a green eyeshade, and recording trivia ever-so-neatly with an ancient quill pen. But as we shall see, accounting demands a high level of abstraction, and real artistry is required to communicate information so that it is useful in reaching economic decisions.

To aid in predicting future cash flows, **accounting must select, describe, and communicate.** Each of these functions involves abstraction and choice. A modern corporation is involved in a myriad of events every single business day. Not only does the company actively engage in activities such as sales, purchases, hirings, firings, promotions, demotions, manufacturing, advertising, shipping, and research, but numerous external events affect the company as well. For example, prices of raw materials or products may change; customer enthusiasm may wax or wane; new laws may be passed; tax regulations may be altered; new competition may spring up; and so on. Each of these changes in the environment may profoundly affect an accounting unit.

Whether the firm acts or reacts, all these events are potential inputs to the accounting process, since all have an impact on future cash flows. But it is impossible to select all such events. An order or priority must be established, according to which some events will be chosen and become accounting events, while others will be rejected.

Once an event has been selected as an accounting event, its effects must be described. Describing a seemingly simple event, such as a clerk's purchase of paper clips, can represent a substantial challenge. What words should we use: the general term "paper clips," the brand name, or the materials of which the paper clips are made? Once the name has been chosen, what number shall we associate with it: the weight, size, tensile strength, cost or market value? Once we have selected and described an event, we still have to decide **when** and **how** the event shall be communicated: shall it be by press release, by word-of-mouth, or by a formal report? Shall it be reported alone, or in conjunction with other events? When shall we inform the eager multitudes that our clerk purchased a box of paper clips: now, at the end of the month, at the end of the year, or when the paper clips are used?

It should be clear by now that each accounting function does, indeed, demand a high level of abstraction and thoughtful exercise of judgment. Relevant events must be selected, and the essence of their economic effect must be captured by a brief description. This description is communicated at an appropriate time and in a suitable manner so as to facilitate prediction of future cash flows.

Accounting is concerned with utility, not morals or aesthetics. Accounting has only one purpose: to provide information useful in reaching economic decisions. It does not concern itself with questions of right or wrong, beauty or ugliness. Of course this does not mean that accountants condone false or misleading accounting statements. No one seriously suggests that accounting reports should be consciously untruthful. Nevertheless, the commandment, "Go forth and be truthful" offers little guidance to an accountant searching for desirable accounting procedures.

Accounting speaks to many people, each with their own informational needs and their own level of understanding. "Ham," "jambon," and "schinken" all describe the same food, hence all are equally truthful; the word you select depends on your listener's native tongue. Effective communication requires knowledge about your audience and their informational needs.

Accounting descriptions must vary according to the decisions for which they will be used. According to Euclidian geometry, only one line can be drawn through a point, parallel to a given line. But one form of non-Euclidian geometry states that through a point, an infinite number of lines can be drawn parallel to a given line. Which is "true"? Mathematicians found this question to be irrelevant— each type of geometry has its uses. Instead of crusades between warring geometries, it proved more productive to use Euclidian geometry in building bridges, and non-Euclidian geometry for generating nuclear reactions.

We all prefer to deal with a simple, uncomplicated universe in which truth is absolute, singular, and certain. Unfortunately, in our world **truth is probabilistic, multiplistic, and uncertain.** Some people expect accounting reports to reveal the "true value" of objects owned or used by an accounting unit. But this is not a simple matter, as is demonstrated by the following story. A man refused to drive his brand-new car out of the dealer's lot. He had been told that a car loses one-third of its value as soon as it leaves the dealer's lot, and he argued that he had no intention of squandering one-third of the value of his car by driving it home.

Would driving the car away have diminished its value by one-third, as he feared? The answer is both yes and no. If by "value" we mean the **amount** for which he can sell it, then the value of the car has indeed suffered a drastic decline, since he does not have the same skill and comparative economic advantage in selling cars as does the dealer. But, if by "value" we mean its **utility** in delivering his children to school, then it is equally true to say that the car has **no** value until he drives it out of the lot. Thus, depending on his intentions, the act of driving the car out of the dealer's lot can either increase **or** decrease the car's value. What, then, is the "true value" of the car, and how does the act of driving the car away affect that value?

Accountants would answer that such a question is neither relevant nor instructive. In all such situations the question should be: **Which description is most useful in helping users of financial statements to predict, compare, and evaluate the amount, timing, and uncertainty of a company's future cash flows?**

GENERALLY ACCEPTED ACCOUNTING PRINCIPLES

Since the answer to this basic accounting question impacts economic decisions by users of financial statements, and thus is important to the economy as a whole, the need for rules to produce a standardized answer became obvious decades ago. In fact, the stock market crash of 1929 prompted Congress to take an active role in formulating the rules.

Four years after that crash, Congress passed the Securities Act of 1934 establishing the Securities and Exchange Commission (SEC). In addition to its primary responsibility of regulating the securities industry, the SEC was charged with setting accounting principles and standards for publicly traded companies. However, the SEC soon delegated its responsibility to set standards to the accounting profession. Over the years, the accounting profession has fulfilled this obligation in different ways.

In 1939, the American Institute of Certified Public Accountants (AICPA) formed two committees, the Committee on Accounting Procedure and the Committee on Terminology. In 1962, these internal committees of the AICPA were replaced by the Accounting Principles Board (APB) and, in 1973, the Financial Accounting Standards Board (FASB) was organized to succeed the APB. These successive committees and boards researched accounting practices and issued various bulletins, opinions, and statements that established accounting concepts and standard procedures.

In addition to all the opinions and statements issued by the accounting profession, the SEC issues regulations, most importantly Regulation S-X, Financial Reporting Releases, and Staff Accounting Bulletins.

All of these bulletins, opinions, statements, releases, and other interpretations by the profession and academicians are collectively known as *generally accepted accounting principles,* or **GAAP.** With few exceptions, all companies must prepare their financial statements in accordance with GAAP.

USER'S PERSPECTIVE

The objective of financial statements is to provide a historical record of events that is useful for assessing a firm's cash flows. Contrary to popular belief, financial statements do not reveal the value of a firm, nor the value of the individual assets and liabilities of a firm. They also do not provide hot, off-the-press news about a firm because they appear months, and sometimes years, after the events they describe.

Moreover, while *GAAP* provides the accountant with standardized answers to accounting questions, the results are sometimes surprising, as can be seen from this illustration: On the same day that The American Grabule Company hires a new president, a clerk purchases a package of paper clips, on credit, for the president's office. Accounting rules permit only **one** of these two events to be recorded. Which one? In searching for an answer, consider these questions: Which event is more important for the company's future? As a stockholder, which event holds the greater interest for you? Which event is more likely to have a significant impact on future cash flows? Considering the perversity of human nature, you have doubtless guessed correctly that GAAP records the purchase of the paper clips, but not the hiring of the president.

An easy rationalization for recording the purchase of paper clips, and not the hiring of the president, might be that "The president cannot be quantified, but the paper clips can," and, "If I can't quantify it, I can't describe it—so I won't try," but the answer is more complex since we can't quantify the impact on the firm's cash-generating ability from either the paper clips or the president.

Thought Question
What rationale can you think of that would explain the recording of the paper clips, and not the hiring of the president?

Of course, it is folly to think of accounting reports as producing a magical bottom line or a complete record that tells us everything we need to know about a firm. The fact that an event like the hiring of a new president is not revealed in financial statements does not mean that the event did not occur, was not important, and therefore should not be included in evaluating a firm. It merely means that under GAAP, it cannot be recognized as an accounting event.

As this example shows, the rationale underlying *generally accepted accounting principles* is far from obvious, and rules for quantifying and reporting accounting events under GAAP sometimes produce puzzling and counterintuitive results. The rules that comprise GAAP cannot be intuited, but must be learned, and in order to use accounting information wisely in making rational economic decisions, you must understand the limitations as well as the substance of GAAP used in preparing financial statements.

Therefore, an informed user of financial statements must understand GAAP, its limitations and its implications, so that financial statements can be seen for what they are, instead of what some people desire them to be. Whlie GAAP and financial statements have many limitations, and while they do not produce simple answers for complex decisions, we shall see that properly understood and analyzed financial statements do produce much useful information.

PROBLEMS

1. Analyze the decision of whether or not to obtain insurance on your house in terms of the amount, timing, and uncertainty of relevant sacrifices and benefits.

2. Give as many examples as you can to support or refute the assumption that a rational person prefers certainty to uncertainty.

3. Why do you think accounting recognizes the acquisition of paper clips, but does not recognize the hiring of a new company president?

4. How could the acquisition of paper clips be described by the accounting process? How could it be reported?

5. How could the hiring of a company president be described by the accounting process? How could it be reported?

6. What really happened when the car was bought and driven out of the showroom? How should it be described?

7. You have $5,000 in cash and have three alternatives available to you. Analyze and compare the three alternatives in terms of amount, timing, and uncertainty of the relevant sacrifices and benefits. What additional information would you like to have and how would you go about getting it?
   a. Keep the cash under your pillow.
   b. Invest the money in U.S. bonds, which promise you $8,000 in 10 years.
   c. Invest the money in the newly formed The American Grabule Company, which owns a patent on the manufacturing of grabules. The officers of The American Grabule Company, after swearing you to secrecy, show you a grabule and assure you that grabules are sure to sweep the country.

Cash Flows and their Equivalents: Present and Future Values

INTRODUCTION

We have stated that the timing of cash flows is important to decision makers. Just as we prefer more cash to less cash, we prefer to receive cash sooner than later, and are unwilling to trade a dollar now for a dollar in the future. The unwillingness to trade dollars of more distant time periods for dollars of today is due to three factors:

1. If we trade a dollar now for a dollar in the future we must postpone consuming what a dollar would buy now until the future, and human beings do not like to postpone gratification.

2. We know we have a dollar now, but a dollar in the future is a "sometime thing" because the future is uncertain. Perhaps the future dollar will not be forthcoming or perhaps we will not be there to receive it.

3. Even if we assume the future dollar to be certain, it may not buy as much as a present dollar would because of inflation.

These three factors provide persuasive reasons why a dollar in the future cannot be as desirable as a dollar now. A dollar in the future is always worth less than a dollar now, and a dollar now is always worth more than a dollar in the future. (Just because a dollar in the future is **worth less** than a dollar now does not mean that it is **worthless,** of course.) This means that in order to meaningfully evaluate a dollar, we must attach a date or *time dimension* to it. It also means that **only dollars of the same time dimension can be legitimately compared.**

To compare dollars of different time dimensions, you must convert them to dollars of the same time dimension. Dollars of different time dimensions are in effect different currencies, and comparing dollars of different time dimensions requires the same procedure as comparing different units of currencies, such as dollars to francs. To compare a given amount of dollars to a given amount of francs, you must convert them to the same currency (either dollars or francs) by utilizing the appropriate exchange rate between dollars and francs.

The exchange rate for comparing dollars of different *time dimensions* is determined by the **interest rate,** which measures the disadvantage of one dollar one period from now compared to a dollar now. Just as we converted dollars into equivalent francs or the francs into equivalent dollars using the relevant exchange rate, we compare dollars of date X with dollars of date Y, by translating the X-dated dollars into Y-dated dollars, or vice versa, using the relevant interest (exchange) rate.

FUTURE EQUIVALENTS OF PRESENT AMOUNTS, AND PRESENT EQUIVALENTS OF FUTURE AMOUNTS

The interest rate which determines the exchange rate between dollars of different time dimensions is a function of how reluctant we are to postpone gratification for one period (the basic interest rate); the uncertainty of receiving a future dollar (the risk rate); and the possibility of the future dollar being able to purchase less than the present dollar (the expected inflation rate). When we translate a present dollar amount into an equivalent dollar amount of a future time dimension, we call these translated equivalent dollars, *future value* dollars, and when we translate a future amount into an equivalent dollar amount of a present time dimension, we call these translated equivalent dollars, *present value* dollars.

For example, if a bank promises to pay 10 percent interest per year on money deposited in their savings accounts, a $1,000 deposit would accumulate to $1,100 by the end of the first year, the original $1,000 plus 10 percent of $1,000. This sum will accumulate to $1,210 by the end of the second year ($1,100 plus 10 percent of $1,100), and will accumulate to $1,331 by the end of the third year ($1,210 plus 10 percent of $1,210).

The following time line illustrates the progress of the bank's commitment to accumulate money in an account:

← Year 1 →	← Year 2 →	← Year 3 →
(0)	(1)	(2)	(3)
$1,000	$1,100	$1,210	$1,331

If you deposit money, you are agreeing with the bank that $1,000 received today is equal to $1,100 received in 1 year, which is equal to $1,210 received in 2 years, which is equal to $1,331 received in 3 years. In other words, you and the bank are both indifferent between $1,000 now, and $1,100 in 1 year, or $1,210 in 2 years, or $1,331 in 3 years.

Let's look at the time line again. There are many relationships that can be established. While it is correct to say that at 10 percent annually, $1,100 in 1 year, $1,210 in 2 years, and $1,331 in 3 years are all *future values* of $1,000 now, we can also say that $1,210 in 2 years and $1,331 in 3 years are future values of $1,100 in 1 year, and that $1,331 in 3 years is the future value of $1,210 in 2 years. It is also correct to say that $1,210 in 1 year and $1,331 in 2 years are future values of $1,100 now, and that $1,331 in 1 year is the future value of $1,210 now.

It is equally correct to say that at 10 percent annually, $1,000 is the *present value* of $1,100 in 1 year, $1,210 in 2 years, and $1,331 in 3 years; that $1,100 is the present value of $1,210 in 1 year and $1,331 in 2 years; and that $1,210 is the present value of $1,331 in 1 year.

COMPOUND AND SIMPLE INTEREST

In each succeeding year, $100, $110, and $121 of interest would accumulate if no withdrawals were made. The difference between the interest accumulated in the second year and the first year ($10), and that accumulated between the third and second years ($11), represents the interest accumulated on previously earned interest. Interest accumulated on the money originally deposited **and** the interest previously earned is called **compound interest.** Interest accumulated on just the money deposited is called **simple interest.**

THE NUMBER OF PERIODS AND THE PERIODIC INTEREST RATE

An *interest rate* is generally stated as an annual rate. For instance, in the example above, the bank was paying 10 percent annually. Therefore, the **periodic interest rate** was 10 percent. What if the bank paid 10 percent per year, but in two equal semiannual installments? How much would you have accumulated at the end of each of the first 3 years?

During each year you would have two periods, and the periodic interest rate would be 5 percent. So, for 1 year, you would have $n = 2$, $r = 5\%$ instead of $n = 1$, $r = 10\%$, and you would accumulate $1,102.50 instead of $1,100. For 2 years, you would have $n = 4$, $r = 5\%$ instead of $n = 2$, $r = 10\%$, and you would accumulate $1,215.51 instead of $1,210; and for 3 years, $n = 6$, $r = 5\%$ instead of $n = 3$, $r = 10\%$, and you would accumulate $1,340.10 instead of $1,331.

Notice that the product of $n \times r$ for each case remains constant. That is not a coincidence. In adjusting from longer periods to shorter periods (increasing the number of periods), you proportionately decrease the *periodic interest rate*.

FUTURE VALUE AND PRESENT VALUE TABLES

The exchange rate to determine the future value from present dollar amounts is expressed by the following formula: $FV = PA \times (1 + r)^n$ where FV is the future value, PA the present dollar amount, r the periodic interest rate, and n the number of periods between now and the future date. Similarly, the exchange rate to determine present value from future dollar amounts is expressed by the following formula: $PV = FA \div (1 + r)^n$ where PV is the present value, FA the future dollar amount, r the periodic interest rate, and n the number of periods between the future date and now.

To simplify the calculations required to determine the future value of one present dollar, tables have been constructed which give the future value of one present dollar for various periods (n) and at various periodic interest rates (r). These tables (shown on page 24) are called "Future Value of $1.00" tables, but a more descriptive and informative title for these tables would be "Future Equivalent of a Present Dollar."

Returning to the original example, we can see that the results could easily have been determined from the tables. At $n = 1$, $r = 10\%$, the future value of $1.00 is 1.100000. When multiplied by the amount deposited, $1,000, the result is $1,100. At $n = 2$, $r = 10\%$, the future value of $1.00 is 1.210000, and when multiplied by $1,000, the result is $1,210. Finally, at $n = 3$, $r = 10\%$, the future value of $1.00 is 1.331000, and the future value of $1,000 is $1,331.

Similarly, conversion tables have been constructed which give the present value of one future dollar, for various periods (n), and at various periodic interest rates (r). These tables (shown on page 25) are called "Present Value of $1.00" tables. Again, a more meaningful title would be "Present Equivalent of a Future Dollar."

Returning to our example again, we can readily see that at $n = 1$, $r = 10\%$, the present value of $1.00 is 0.909091, and when multiplied by $1,100 (or $1,210, $1,331) the result is $1,000 (or

$1,100, $1,210, respectively). At $n = 2$, $r = 10\%$, the present value of $1.00 is 0.826446, and the present value of $1,210 (or $1,331) is $1,000 (or $1,100). Finally, at $n = 3$, $r = 10\%$, the present value of $1.00 is 0.751315, and the present value of $1,331 is $1,000.

Thought Questions

Can the future value of a present amount be determined
from the Future Value of $1.00 table,
if for a given r, the desired n is not available?
If for a given n, the desired r is not available?

ANNUITIES

We may be interested in the present (or future) equivalent of a series of amounts. Suppose you made annual deposits into the 10 percent savings account (discussed above) at the beginning of each of 4 years.

How much would have accumulated in the account by the beginning of the fourth year? Or, in other words, what is the future value of $1,000 deposited at the beginning of each of 4 years? It is the future value in 3 years of $1,000, **plus** the future value in 2 years of $1,000, **plus** the future value in 1 year of $1,000, **plus** the future value of $1,000 now.

By our previous calculations, we showed the future value of $1,000 in 3 years is $1,331, in 2 years, $1,210, and in 1 year, $1,100. The future value of $1,000 now, is simply $1,000! Taken all together, $4,641 would have accumulated by the beginning of the fourth year.

The following time line illustrates that by the beginning of the fourth year, $4,641 would have accumulated. It also shows that by the beginning of the first, second, and third years, $1,000, $2,100, and $3,310 would have accumulated, respectively.

|← Year 1 →| |← Year 2 →| |← Year 3 →|
(0)	(1)	(2)	(3)
$1,000	$1,100	$1,210	$1,331
	$1,000	$1,100	$1,210
		$1,000	$1,100
			$1,000

When the time period between a series of equal periodic amounts is equal, we call the series of equal amounts an *annuity.* When the amounts occur at the **beginning** of the period, we call it an *annuity in advance* or an *annuity due,* and when the amounts occur at the end of the period, we call it an *annuity in arrears* or an *ordinary annuity.*

Just as tables are provided for future value and present value calculations, tables have been constructed for present value and future value annuities in advance and in arrears, and are shown on pages 26 through 28.

Consider the possibility that instead of depositing your money in the bank each year, you wanted to borrow $2,487 from the bank. Consider further that you and the bank agree that you must repay the loan, with interest at 10 percent, in three equal payments, the first at the end of the first year, the second at the end of the second year, and the third at the end of the third year. How can the amount of each periodic payment be determined? Obviously, the present equivalent of all of the payments must be equal to the amount of money originally borrowed, $2,487, as illustrated by the following time line:

|← Year 1 →| |← Year 2 →| |← Year 3 →|
(0)	(1)	(2)	(3)
$2,487 =	P +	P +	P

In other terms, the present value of the first payment **plus** the present value of the second payment **plus** the present value of the third payment must equal the amount borrowed. Since each payment is of equal amount and equally spaced, this series of amounts is an *annuity*.

From the table of Present Values of an Annuity of $1.00 in Arrears, the present value of $1.00 in 1 year **plus** the present value of $1.00 in 2 years **plus** the present value of $1.00 in 3 years, all at 10 percent ($n = 3$, $r = 10\%$), is equal to $2.49 (rounded). Since $2.49 is the present value of an annuity of $1.00, $2,487 must be the present value of the annuity of three year-end annual $1,000 payments ($2,487 ÷ 2.49 = $1,000).

> ### Thought Question
> Can the future value of an annuity be determined
> from the Future Value of an Annuity of $1.00 table,
> if at a given interest rate r,
> the desired number of periods n is not listed in the table?

USER'S PERSPECTIVE

There are many decisions, and in many areas, that require evaluating dollar amounts of different dates and time dimensions. For instance, when buying a new car, do you accept a cash rebate or the reduced interest rate offered by automobile dealers? When buying a home, how do you choose among the myriad possibilities of mortgage offerings by banks and savings institutions? And how do you decide into which money market account to deposit your money?

In addition, there is the issue of literacy, understanding, and an appreciation for the consequences of historical events. For instance, the proliferation of professional sports leagues in the United States has caused an increased demand for quality athletes, which in turn has caused the average salary to skyrocket. The media reports that college graduates are signing multimillion, multiyear contracts. Two such contracts, signed a few years ago, were each reported as $25 million contracts even though the present equivalent of the two contracts was not the same. Did the media correctly report the facts?

> ### Thought Question
> Is the state's $20 million lottery really a $20 million lottery?

Finally, consider the possibility that if the Indians hadn't sold the island of Manhattan for $24 in 1664, they might have been able to sell it last year for $100,000,000,000,000. Did the Indians make the right decision?

PROBLEMS

1. Compute the future equivalent of the present amount of
   a. $1,000 at 10 percent, for 1 year, compounded annually
   b. $1,000 at 10 percent, for 2 years, compounded annually
   c. $1,000 at 10 percent, for 3 years, compounded annually
   d. $1,000 at 10 percent, for 4 years, compounded annually

2. Compute the future equivalent of the present amount of
   a. $2,000 at 12 percent, for 2 years, compounded annually
   b. $2,000 at 12 percent, for 2 years, compounded semiannually
   c. $2,000 at 12 percent, for 2 years, compounded quarterly
   d. $2,000 at 12 percent, for 2 years, compounded monthly

3. Compute the future equivalent of the present amount of
   a. $3,000 at 6 percent, for 10 years, compounded annually
   b. $4,000 at 6 percent, for 15 years, compounded semiannually
   c. $5,000 at 6 percent, for 5 years, compounded quarterly
   d. $6,000 at 6 percent, for 2 years, compounded monthly

4. Compute the future equivalent of the present amount of
   a. $7,000 at 15 percent, for 33 years, compounded annually
   b. $8,000 at 9 percent, for 17 years, compounded semiannually
   c. $9,000 at 3 percent, for 54 years, compounded semiannually

5. Compute the future equivalent of the present amount of
   a. $12,363 at 12 percent, for 5 years, compounded monthly
   b. $24,770 at 12 percent, for 5 years, compounded monthly
   c. $37,178 at 12 percent, for 5 years, compounded monthly

6. Compute the present equivalent of the future amount of
   a. $1,000 due in 1 year, at 10 percent, compounded annually
   b. $1,000 due in 2 years, at 10 percent, compounded annually
   c. $1,000 due in 3 years, at 10 percent, compounded annually
   d. $1,000 due in 4 years, at 10 percent, compounded annually

7. Compute the present equivalent of the future amount of
   a. $2,000 due in 2 years, at 12 percent, compounded annually
   b. $2,000 due in 2 years, at 12 percent, compounded semiannually
   c. $2,000 due in 2 years, at 12 percent, compounded quarterly
   d. $2,000 due in 2 years, at 12 percent, compounded monthly

8. Compute the present equivalent of the future amount of
   a. $9,000 due in 7 years, at 12 percent, compounded annually
   b. $8,000 due in 10 years, at 12 percent, compounded semiannually
   c. $7,000 due in 8 years, at 12 percent, compounded quarterly
   d. $6,000 due in 3 years, at 12 percent, compounded monthly

9. Compute the present equivalent of the future amount of
   a. $5,000 due in 21 years, at 9 percent, compounded annually
   b. $4,000 due in 44 years, at 6 percent, compounded annually
   c. $3,000 due in 27 years, at 3 percent, compounded semiannually

10. Compute the present equivalent of the future amount of
   a. $22,459 due in 5 years, at 12 percent, compounded monthly
   b. $45,000 due in 5 years, at 12 percent, compounded monthly
   c. $67,541 due in 5 years, at 12 percent, compounded monthly

11. Compute the present equivalent of the future amount of
    a. $48,575 due in 5 years, at 12 percent, compounded semiannually
    b. $45,000 due in 5 years, at 12 percent, compounded semiannually
    c. $41,915 due in 5 years, at 12 percent, compounded semiannually

12. Compute the present equivalent of an *ordinary annuity*, assuming
    a. $1,000 due each year, for 4 years, at 10 percent
    b. $2,500 due each year, for 19 years, at 12 percent
    c. $3,500 due each year, for 10 years, at 5 percent

13. Compute the present equivalent of an ordinary annuity, assuming
    a. $4,500 due each month, for 3 years, at 18 percent
    b. $5,500 due each quarter, for 9 years, at 12 percent
    c. $6,500 due each period, for 26 periods, at 5 percent per period

14. Compute the periodic loan payment under the following conditions:
    a. $100,000 loan, at 10 percent, annual payments made for 10 years
    b. $120,000 loan, at 4 percent, quarterly payments made for 5 years
    c. $150,000 loan, at 18 percent, monthly payments for 30 months

15. The Deem Company purchased a piece of equipment costing $45,000. They borrowed the money from the bank for a period of 5 years, at an interest rate of 12 percent. Compute the periodic loan payments required to pay off the loan if the payments were to be made
    a. Annually
    b. Quarterly
    c. Monthly

16. Compute the present equivalent of an ordinary annuity, assuming
    a. $1,001 due each month, for 5 years, at 12 percent
    b. $726 due each month, for 5 years, at 12 percent
    c. $450 due each month, for 5 years, at 12 percent
    d. $174 due each month, for 5 years, at 12 percent

17. Compute the present equivalent of an ordinary annuity, assuming
    a. $2,429 due semiannually, for 5 years, at 12 percent
    b. $2,700 due semiannually, for 5 years, at 12 percent
    c. $2,934 due semiannually, for 5 years, at 12 percent

18. Compute the present equivalent of an annuity, at 12 percent, assuming
    a. $11,146 payments made at the beginning of each of 5 years
    b. $12,483 payments made at the end of each of 5 years

19. The Jax Company purchased a piece of equipment costing $45,000. The company wanted to determine the optimal financing technique from the following choices. The company assumed a 12 percent interest rate.
    a. Monthly payments, for 5 years, of $1,001
    b. Monthly payments, for 5 years, of $450, and then a $45,000 payment
    c. Semiannual payments of $2,700, for 5 years, and then a $45,000 payment
    d. $11,146 annual payments, made at the beginning of each of 5 years
    e. $12,483 annual payments, made at the end of each of 5 years

20. Compute the future equivalent of an annuity, assuming
    a. $1,000 at 10 percent, each year, for 4 years
    b. $6,500 at 12 percent, each year, for 18 years
    c. $5,500 at 15 percent, each year, for 20 years

21. Compute the future equivalent of an annuity, assuming
    a. $4,500 at 18 percent, for 10 years, compounded semiannually
    b. $3,500 at 12 percent, for 4 years, compounded quarterly
    c. $2,500 at 20 percent, for 6 years, compounded quarterly

22. Compute the periodic deposit required to accumulate $100,000 under the following conditions:
    a. Deposits to be made each year, for 10 years, at 10 percent
    b. Deposits to be made semiannually, for 6 years, at 2 percent
    c. Deposits to be made monthly, for 3 years, at 12 percent

23. Compute the periodic deposit required to accumulate $20,000, in 2 years, assuming a 6 percent interest rate, if deposits are to be made
    a. Annually
    b. Quarterly
    c. Monthly

24. How much would you pay for a promise to receive $1,000 in 3 years, if the appropriate interest rate is 10 percent?

25. How much would you pay for a promise to receive $100 at the end of each of 3 years, **and** $1,000 at the end of the third year, if the appropriate interest rate is
    a. 9 percent
    b. 10 percent
    c. 12 percent

26. Could you have answered Question 25, if all you had was the Present Value of an Annuity of $1.00 in Arrears table?

27. An insurance agent solicited your business, stating that she can sell you insurance that is "cost free." She claimed that a 10-year, $50,000 policy can be purchased by paying a $1,000 premium at the beginning of each year, and can be surrendered at the end of the tenth year for $10,000. Is the salesperson's assertion correct, or should she be charged with fraudulent misrepresentation? Explain your answer.

28. Would your answer to Question 27 be the same if the surrender price was
    a. $11,000
    b. $9,000 Explain your answers.

29. Assume that you want to provide yourself with income for 15 years after you retire. If you expect to receive a $40,000 check on each birthday, beginning on your seventieth birthday, how much will you need to deposit into an account that earns 6 percent interest, if you begin saving on your
    a. Thirtieth birthday
    b. Fiftieth birthday
    c. Seventieth birthday

30. Would your annual deposits be less than, equal to, or greater than that determined in Question 29, if the interest rate was 12 percent, rather than 6 percent, and they began on your
    a. Thirtieth birthday
    b. Seventieth birthday

FUTURE VALUE OF $1

n	½%	1%	1½%	2%	3%	4½%	5%	6%	7%	9%	10%	12%	15%	18%
1	1.005000	1.010000	1.015000	1.020000	1.030000	1.045000	1.050000	1.060000	1.070000	1.090000	1.100000	1.120000	1.150000	1.180000
2	1.010025	1.020100	1.030225	1.040400	1.060900	1.092025	1.102500	1.123600	1.144900	1.188100	1.210000	1.254400	1.322500	1.392400
3	1.015075	1.030301	1.045678	1.061208	1.092727	1.141166	1.157625	1.191016	1.225043	1.295029	1.331000	1.404928	1.520875	1.643032
4	1.020151	1.040604	1.061364	1.082432	1.125509	1.192519	1.215506	1.262477	1.310796	1.411582	1.464100	1.573519	1.749006	1.938778
5	1.025251	1.051010	1.077284	1.104081	1.159274	1.246182	1.276282	1.338226	1.402552	1.538624	1.610510	1.762342	2.011357	2.287758
6	1.030378	1.061520	1.093443	1.126162	1.194052	1.302260	1.340096	1.418519	1.500730	1.677100	1.771561	1.973823	2.313061	2.699554
7	1.035529	1.072135	1.109845	1.148686	1.229874	1.360862	1.407100	1.503630	1.605781	1.828039	1.948717	2.210681	2.660020	3.185474
8	1.040707	1.082857	1.126493	1.171659	1.266770	1.422101	1.477455	1.593848	1.718186	1.992563	2.143589	2.475963	3.059023	3.758859
9	1.045911	1.093685	1.143390	1.195093	1.304773	1.486095	1.551328	1.689479	1.838459	2.171893	2.357948	2.773079	3.517876	4.435454
10	1.051140	1.104622	1.160541	1.218994	1.343916	1.552969	1.628895	1.790848	1.967151	2.367364	2.593742	3.105848	4.045558	5.233836
11	1.056396	1.115668	1.177949	1.243374	1.384234	1.622853	1.710339	1.898299	2.104852	2.580426	2.853117	3.478550	4.652391	6.175926
12	1.061678	1.126825	1.195618	1.268242	1.425761	1.695881	1.795856	2.012196	2.252192	2.812665	3.138428	3.895976	5.350250	7.287593
13	1.066986	1.138093	1.213552	1.293607	1.468534	1.772196	1.885649	2.132928	2.409845	3.065805	3.452271	4.363493	6.152788	8.599359
14	1.072321	1.149474	1.231756	1.319479	1.512590	1.851945	1.979932	2.260904	2.578534	3.341727	3.797498	4.887112	7.075706	10.14724
15	1.077683	1.160969	1.250232	1.345868	1.557967	1.935282	2.078928	2.396558	2.759032	3.642482	4.177248	5.473566	8.137062	11.97375
16	1.083071	1.172579	1.268986	1.372786	1.604706	2.022370	2.182875	2.540352	2.952164	3.970306	4.594973	6.130394	9.357621	14.12902
17	1.088487	1.184304	1.288020	1.400241	1.652848	2.113377	2.292018	2.692773	3.158815	4.327633	5.054470	6.866041	10.76126	16.67225
18	1.093929	1.196147	1.307341	1.428246	1.702433	2.208479	2.406619	2.854339	3.379932	4.717120	5.559917	7.689966	12.37545	19.67325
19	1.099399	1.208109	1.326951	1.456811	1.753506	2.307860	2.526950	3.025600	3.616528	5.141661	6.115909	8.612762	14.23177	23.21444
20	1.104896	1.220190	1.346855	1.485947	1.806111	2.411714	2.653298	3.207135	3.869684	5.604411	6.727500	9.646293	16.36654	27.39303
22	1.115972	1.244716	1.387564	1.545980	1.916103	2.633652	2.925261	3.603537	4.430402	6.658600	8.140275	12.10031	21.64475	38.14206
24	1.127160	1.269735	1.429503	1.608437	2.032794	2.876014	3.225100	4.048935	5.072367	7.911083	9.849733	15.17863	28.62518	53.10901
26	1.138460	1.295256	1.472710	1.673418	2.156591	3.140679	3.555673	4.549383	5.807353	9.399158	11.91818	19.04007	37.85680	73.94898
28	1.149873	1.321291	1.517222	1.741024	2.287928	3.429700	3.920129	5.111687	6.648838	11.16714	14.42099	23.88387	50.06561	102.9666
30	1.161400	1.347849	1.563080	1.811362	2.427262	3.745318	4.321942	5.743491	7.612255	13.26768	17.44940	29.95992	66.21177	143.3706
36	1.196681	1.430769	1.709140	2.039887	2.898278	4.877378	5.791816	8.147252	11.42394	22.25123	30.91268	59.13557	153.1519	387.0368
42	1.233033	1.518790	1.868847	2.297244	3.460696	6.351615	7.761588	11.55703	17.14426	37.31753	54.76370	116.7231	354.2495	1044.827
48	1.270489	1.612226	2.043478	2.587070	4.132252	8.271456	10.40127	16.39387	25.72891	62.58524	97.01723	230.3908	819.4007	2820.567
54	1.309083	1.711410	2.234428	2.913461	4.934125	10.77159	13.93870	23.25502	38.61215	104.9617	171.8719	454.7505	1895.324	7614.272
60	1.348850	1.816697	2.443220	3.281031	5.891603	14.02741	18.67919	32.98769	57.94643	176.0313	304.4816	897.5969	4383.999	20555.14

PRESENT VALUE OF $1

n	½%	1%	1½%	2%	3%	4½%	5%	6%	7%	9%	10%	12%	15%	18%
1	0.995025	0.990099	0.985222	0.980392	0.970874	0.956938	0.952381	0.943396	0.934579	0.917431	0.909091	0.892857	0.869565	0.847458
2	0.990075	0.980296	0.970662	0.961169	0.942596	0.915730	0.907029	0.889996	0.873439	0.841680	0.826446	0.797194	0.756144	0.718184
3	0.985149	0.970590	0.956317	0.942322	0.915142	0.876297	0.863838	0.839619	0.816298	0.772183	0.751315	0.711780	0.657516	0.608631
4	0.980248	0.960980	0.942184	0.923845	0.888487	0.838561	0.822702	0.792094	0.762895	0.708425	0.683013	0.635518	0.571753	0.515789
5	0.975371	0.951466	0.928260	0.905731	0.862609	0.802451	0.783526	0.747258	0.712986	0.649931	0.620921	0.567427	0.497177	0.437109
6	0.970518	0.942045	0.914542	0.887971	0.837484	0.767896	0.746215	0.704961	0.666342	0.596267	0.564474	0.506631	0.432328	0.370432
7	0.965690	0.932718	0.901027	0.870560	0.813092	0.734828	0.710681	0.665057	0.622750	0.547034	0.513158	0.452349	0.375937	0.313925
8	0.960885	0.923483	0.887711	0.853490	0.789409	0.703185	0.676839	0.627412	0.582009	0.501866	0.466507	0.403883	0.326902	0.266038
9	0.956105	0.914340	0.874592	0.836755	0.766417	0.672904	0.644609	0.591898	0.543934	0.460428	0.424098	0.360610	0.284262	0.225456
10	0.951348	0.905287	0.861667	0.820348	0.744094	0.643928	0.613913	0.558395	0.508349	0.422411	0.385543	0.321973	0.247185	0.191064
11	0.946615	0.896324	0.848933	0.804263	0.722421	0.616199	0.584679	0.526788	0.475093	0.387533	0.350494	0.287476	0.214943	0.161919
12	0.941905	0.887449	0.836387	0.788493	0.701380	0.589664	0.556837	0.496969	0.444012	0.355535	0.318631	0.256675	0.186907	0.137220
13	0.937219	0.878663	0.824027	0.773033	0.680951	0.564272	0.530321	0.468839	0.414964	0.326179	0.289664	0.229174	0.162528	0.116288
14	0.932556	0.869963	0.811849	0.757875	0.661118	0.539973	0.505068	0.442301	0.387817	0.299246	0.263331	0.204620	0.141329	0.098549
15	0.927917	0.861349	0.799852	0.743015	0.641862	0.516720	0.481017	0.417265	0.362446	0.274538	0.239392	0.182696	0.122894	0.083516
16	0.923300	0.852821	0.788031	0.728446	0.623167	0.494469	0.458112	0.393646	0.338735	0.251870	0.217629	0.163122	0.106865	0.070776
17	0.918707	0.844377	0.776385	0.714163	0.605016	0.473176	0.436297	0.371364	0.316574	0.231073	0.197845	0.145644	0.092926	0.059980
18	0.914136	0.836017	0.764912	0.700159	0.587395	0.452800	0.415521	0.350344	0.295864	0.211994	0.179859	0.130040	0.080805	0.050830
19	0.909588	0.827740	0.753607	0.686431	0.570286	0.433302	0.395734	0.330513	0.276508	0.194490	0.163508	0.116107	0.070265	0.043077
20	0.905063	0.819544	0.742470	0.672971	0.553676	0.414643	0.376889	0.311805	0.258419	0.178431	0.148644	0.103667	0.061100	0.036506
22	0.896080	0.803396	0.720688	0.646839	0.521893	0.379701	0.341850	0.277505	0.225713	0.150182	0.122846	0.082643	0.046201	0.026218
24	0.887186	0.787566	0.699544	0.621721	0.491934	0.347703	0.310068	0.246979	0.197147	0.126405	0.101526	0.065882	0.034934	0.018829
26	0.878380	0.772048	0.679021	0.597579	0.463695	0.318402	0.281241	0.219810	0.172195	0.106393	0.083905	0.052521	0.026415	0.013523
28	0.869662	0.756836	0.659099	0.574375	0.437077	0.291571	0.255094	0.195630	0.150402	0.089548	0.069343	0.041869	0.019974	0.009712
30	0.861030	0.741923	0.639762	0.552071	0.411987	0.267000	0.231377	0.174110	0.131367	0.075371	0.057309	0.033378	0.015103	0.006975
36	0.835645	0.698925	0.585090	0.490223	0.345032	0.205028	0.172657	0.122741	0.087535	0.044941	0.032349	0.016910	0.006529	0.002584
42	0.811009	0.658419	0.535089	0.435304	0.288959	0.157440	0.128840	0.086527	0.058329	0.026797	0.018260	0.008567	0.002823	0.000957
48	0.787098	0.620260	0.489362	0.386538	0.241999	0.120898	0.096142	0.060998	0.038867	0.015978	0.010307	0.004340	0.001220	0.000355
54	0.763893	0.584313	0.447542	0.343234	0.202670	0.092837	0.071743	0.043001	0.025899	0.009527	0.005818	0.002199	0.000528	0.000131
60	0.741372	0.550450	0.409296	0.304782	0.169733	0.071289	0.053536	0.030314	0.017257	0.005681	0.003284	0.001114	0.000228	0.000049

FUTURE VALUE OF AN ANNUITY OF $1 IN ARREARS

n	½%	1%	1½%	2%	3%	4½%	5%	6%	7%	9%	10%	12%	15%	18%
1	1.000000	1.000000	1.000000	1.000000	1.000000	1.000000	1.000000	1.000000	1.000000	1.000000	1.000000	1.000000	1.000000	1.000000
2	2.005000	2.010000	2.015000	2.020000	2.030000	2.045000	2.050000	2.060000	2.070000	2.090000	2.100000	2.120000	2.150000	2.180000
3	3.015025	3.030100	3.045225	3.060400	3.090900	3.137025	3.152500	3.183600	3.214900	3.278100	3.310000	3.374400	3.472500	3.572400
4	4.030100	4.060401	4.090903	4.121608	4.183627	4.278191	4.310125	4.374616	4.439943	4.573129	4.641000	4.779328	4.993375	5.215432
5	5.050251	5.101005	5.152267	5.204040	5.309136	5.470710	5.525631	5.637093	5.750739	5.984711	6.105100	6.352847	6.742381	7.154210
6	6.075502	6.152015	6.229551	6.308121	6.468410	6.716892	6.801913	6.975319	7.153291	7.523335	7.715610	8.115189	8.753738	9.441968
7	7.105879	7.213535	7.322994	7.434283	7.662462	8.019152	8.142008	8.393838	8.654021	9.200435	9.487171	10.08901	11.06680	12.14152
8	8.141409	8.285671	8.432839	8.582969	8.892336	9.380014	9.549109	9.897468	10.25980	11.02847	11.43589	12.29969	13.72682	15.32700
9	9.182116	9.368527	9.559332	9.754628	10.15911	10.80211	11.02656	11.49132	11.97799	13.02104	13.57948	14.77566	16.78584	19.08585
10	10.22803	10.46221	10.70272	10.94972	11.46388	12.28821	12.57789	13.18079	13.81645	15.19293	15.93742	17.54874	20.30372	23.52131
11	11.27917	11.56683	11.86326	12.16872	12.80780	13.84118	14.20679	14.97164	15.78360	17.56029	18.53117	20.65458	24.34928	28.75514
12	12.33556	12.68250	13.04121	13.41209	14.19203	15.46403	15.91713	16.86994	17.88845	20.14072	21.38428	24.13313	29.00167	34.93107
13	13.39724	13.80933	14.23683	14.68033	15.61779	17.15991	17.71298	18.88214	20.14064	22.95338	24.52271	28.02911	34.35192	42.21866
14	14.46423	14.94742	15.45038	15.97394	17.08632	18.93211	19.59863	21.01507	22.55049	26.01919	27.97498	32.39260	40.50471	50.81802
15	15.53655	16.09690	16.68214	17.29342	18.59891	20.78405	21.57856	23.27597	25.12902	29.36092	31.77248	37.27971	47.58041	60.96527
16	16.61423	17.25786	17.93237	18.63929	20.15688	22.71934	23.65749	25.67253	27.88805	33.00340	35.94973	42.75328	55.71747	72.93901
17	17.69730	18.43044	19.20136	20.01207	21.76159	24.74171	25.84037	28.21288	30.84022	36.97370	40.54470	48.88367	65.07509	87.06804
18	18.78579	19.61475	20.40938	21.41231	23.41444	26.85508	28.13238	30.90565	33.99903	41.30134	45.59917	55.74971	75.83636	103.7403
19	19.87972	20.81090	21.79672	22.84056	25.11687	29.06356	30.53900	33.75999	37.37896	46.01846	51.15909	63.43968	88.21181	123.4135
20	20.97912	22.01900	23.12367	24.29737	26.87037	31.37142	33.06595	36.78559	40.99549	51.16012	57.27500	72.05244	102.4436	146.6280
22	23.19443	24.47159	25.83758	27.29898	30.53678	36.30338	38.50521	43.39229	49.00574	62.87334	71.40275	92.50258	137.6316	206.3448
24	25.43196	26.97346	28.63352	30.42186	34.42647	41.68920	44.50200	50.81558	58.17667	76.78981	88.49733	118.1552	184.1678	289.4945
26	27.69191	29.52563	31.51397	33.67091	38.55304	47.57064	51.11345	59.15638	68.67647	93.32398	109.1818	150.3339	245.7120	405.2721
28	29.97452	32.12910	34.48148	37.05121	42.93092	53.99333	58.40258	68.52811	80.69769	112.9682	134.2099	190.6989	327.1041	566.4809
30	32.28002	34.78489	37.53868	40.56808	47.57542	61.00707	66.43885	79.05819	94.46079	136.3075	164.4940	241.3327	434.7451	790.9480
36	39.33610	43.07688	47.27597	51.99437	63.27594	86.16397	95.83632	119.1209	148.9135	236.1247	299.1268	484.4631	1014.346	2144.649
42	46.60654	51.87899	57.92314	64.86222	82.02320	118.9248	135.2318	175.9505	230.6322	403.5281	537.6370	964.3595	2354.997	5799.038
48	54.09783	61.22261	69.56522	79.35352	104.4084	161.5879	188.0254	256.5645	353.2701	684.2804	960.1723	1911.590	5456.005	15664.26
54	61.81669	71.14105	82.29517	95.67307	131.1375	217.1464	258.7739	370.9170	537.3164	1155.130	1708.719	3781.255	12628.82	42295.96
60	69.77003	81.66967	96.21465	114.0515	163.0534	289.4980	353.5837	533.1282	813.5204	1944.792	3034.816	7471.641	29219.99	114189.7

PRESENT VALUE OF AN ANNUITY OF $1 IN ARREARS

n	½%	1%	1½%	2%	3%	4½%	5%	6%	7%	9%	10%	12%	15%	18%
1	0.995025	0.990099	0.985222	0.980392	0.970874	0.956938	0.952381	0.943396	0.934579	0.917431	0.909091	0.892857	0.869565	0.847458
2	1.985099	1.970395	1.955883	1.941561	1.913470	1.872668	1.859410	1.833393	1.808018	1.759111	1.735537	1.690051	1.625709	1.565642
3	2.970248	2.940985	2.912200	2.883883	2.828611	2.748964	2.723248	2.673012	2.624316	2.531295	2.486852	2.401831	2.283225	2.174273
4	3.950496	3.901966	3.854385	3.807729	3.717098	3.587526	3.545951	3.465106	3.387211	3.239720	3.169865	3.037349	2.854978	2.690062
5	4.925866	4.853431	4.782645	4.713460	4.579707	4.389977	4.329477	4.212364	4.100197	3.889651	3.790787	3.604776	3.352155	3.127171
6	5.896384	5.795476	5.697187	5.601431	5.417191	5.157872	5.075692	4.917324	4.766540	4.485919	4.355261	4.111407	3.784483	3.497603
7	6.862074	6.728195	6.598214	6.471991	6.230283	5.892701	5.786373	5.582381	5.389289	5.032953	4.868419	4.563757	4.160420	3.811528
8	7.822959	7.651678	7.485925	7.325481	7.019692	6.595886	6.463213	6.209794	5.971299	5.534819	5.334926	4.967640	4.487322	4.077566
9	8.779064	8.566018	8.360517	8.162237	7.786109	7.268790	7.107822	6.801692	6.515232	5.995247	5.759024	5.328250	4.771584	4.303022
10	9.730412	9.471305	9.222185	8.982585	8.530203	7.912718	7.721735	7.360087	7.023582	6.417658	6.144567	5.650223	5.018769	4.494086
11	10.67703	10.36763	10.07112	9.786848	9.252624	8.528917	8.306414	7.886875	7.498674	6.805191	6.495061	5.937699	5.233712	4.656005
12	11.61893	11.25508	10.90751	10.57534	9.954004	9.118581	8.863252	8.383844	7.942686	7.160725	6.813692	6.194374	5.420619	4.793225
13	12.55615	12.13374	11.73153	11.34837	10.63496	9.682852	9.393573	8.852683	8.357651	7.486904	7.103356	6.423548	5.583147	4.909513
14	13.48871	13.00370	12.54338	12.10625	11.29607	10.22283	9.898641	9.294984	8.745468	7.786150	7.366687	6.628168	5.724476	5.008062
15	14.41662	13.86505	13.34323	12.84926	11.93794	10.73955	10.37966	9.712249	9.107914	8.060688	7.606080	6.810864	5.847370	5.091578
16	15.33993	14.71787	14.13126	13.57771	12.56110	11.23402	10.83777	10.10590	9.446649	8.312558	7.823709	6.973986	5.954235	5.162354
17	16.25863	15.56225	14.90765	14.29187	13.16612	11.70719	11.27407	10.47726	9.763223	8.543631	8.021553	7.119630	6.047161	5.222334
18	17.17277	16.39827	15.67256	14.99203	13.75351	12.15999	11.68959	10.82760	10.05909	8.755625	8.201412	7.249670	6.127966	5.273164
19	18.08236	17.22601	16.42617	15.67846	14.32380	12.59329	12.08532	11.15812	10.33560	8.950115	8.364920	7.365777	6.198231	5.316241
20	18.98742	18.04555	17.16864	16.35143	14.87747	13.00794	12.46221	11.46992	10.59401	9.128546	8.513564	7.469444	6.259331	5.352746
22	20.78406	19.66038	18.62082	17.65805	15.93692	13.74442	13.16300	12.04158	11.06124	9.442425	8.771540	7.644646	6.358663	5.409901
24	22.56287	21.24339	20.03041	18.91393	16.93554	14.49548	13.79864	12.55036	11.46933	9.706612	8.984744	7.784316	6.433771	5.450949
26	24.32402	22.79520	21.39863	20.12104	17.87684	15.14661	14.37519	13.00317	11.82578	9.928972	9.160945	7.895660	6.490564	5.480429
28	26.06769	24.31644	22.72672	21.28127	18.76411	15.74287	14.89813	13.40616	12.13711	10.11613	9.306567	7.984423	6.533508	5.501601
30	27.79405	25.80771	24.01584	22.39646	19.60044	16.28889	15.37245	13.76483	12.40904	10.27365	9.426914	8.055184	6.565980	5.516806
36	32.87102	30.10751	27.66068	25.48884	21.83225	17.66604	16.54685	14.62099	13.03521	10.61176	9.676508	8.192414	6.623137	5.541201
42	37.79830	34.15811	30.99405	28.23479	23.70136	18.72355	17.42321	15.22454	13.45245	10.81337	9.817397	8.261939	6.647848	5.550238
48	42.58032	37.97396	34.04255	30.67312	25.26671	19.53561	18.07716	15.65003	13.73047	10.93358	9.896926	8.297163	6.658531	5.553586
54	47.22135	41.56866	36.83054	32.83828	26.57766	20.15918	18.56515	15.9498	13.91573	11.00525	9.941817	8.315008	6.663149	5.554826
60	51.72556	44.95504	39.38027	34.76089	27.67556	20.63802	18.92929	16.16143	14.03918	11.04799	9.967157	8.324049	6.665146	5.555285

FUTURE VALUE OF AN ANNUITY OF $1 IN ADVANCE

n	½%	1%	1½%	2%	3%	4½%	5%	6%	7%	9%	10%	12%	15%	18%
1	1.005000	1.010000	1.015000	1.020000	1.030000	1.045000	1.050000	1.060000	1.070000	1.090000	1.100000	1.120000	1.150000	1.180000
2	2.015025	2.030100	2.045225	2.060400	2.090900	2.137025	2.152500	2.183600	2.214900	2.278100	2.310000	2.374400	2.472500	2.572400
3	3.030100	3.060401	3.090903	3.121608	3.183627	3.278191	3.310125	3.374616	3.439943	3.573129	3.641000	3.779328	3.993375	4.215432
4	4.050251	4.101005	4.152267	4.204040	4.309136	4.470710	4.525631	4.637093	4.750739	4.984711	5.105100	5.352847	5.742381	6.154210
5	5.075502	5.152015	5.229551	5.308121	5.468410	5.716892	5.801913	5.975319	6.153291	6.523335	6.715610	7.115189	7.753738	8.441968
6	6.105879	6.213535	6.322994	6.434283	6.662462	7.019152	7.142008	7.393838	7.654021	8.200435	8.487171	9.089012	10.06680	11.14152
7	7.141409	7.285671	7.432539	7.582969	7.892336	8.380014	8.549109	8.897468	9.259803	10.02847	10.43589	11.29969	12.72682	14.32700
8	8.182116	8.368527	8.559332	8.754628	9.159106	9.802114	10.02656	10.49132	10.97799	12.02104	12.57948	13.77566	15.78584	18.08585
9	9.228026	9.462213	9.702722	9.949721	10.46388	11.28821	11.57789	12.18079	12.81645	14.19293	14.93742	16.54874	19.30372	22.52131
10	10.27917	10.56683	10.86326	11.16872	11.80780	12.84118	13.20679	13.97164	14.78360	16.56029	17.53117	19.65458	23.34928	27.75514
11	11.33556	11.68250	12.04121	12.41209	13.19203	14.46403	14.91713	15.86994	16.88845	19.14072	20.38428	23.13313	28.00167	33.93107
12	12.39724	12.80933	13.23683	13.68033	14.61779	16.15991	16.71298	17.88214	19.14064	21.95338	23.52271	27.02911	33.35192	41.21866
13	13.46423	13.94742	14.45038	14.97394	16.08632	17.93211	18.59863	20.01507	21.55049	25.01919	26.97498	31.39260	39.50471	49.81802
14	14.53655	15.09690	15.68214	16.29342	17.59891	19.78405	20.57856	22.27597	24.12902	28.36092	30.77248	36.27971	46.58041	59.96527
15	15.61423	16.25786	16.93237	17.63929	19.15688	21.71934	22.65749	24.67253	26.88805	32.00340	34.94973	41.75328	54.71747	71.93901
16	16.69730	17.43044	18.20136	19.01207	20.76159	23.74171	24.84037	27.21288	29.84022	35.97370	39.54470	47.88367	64.07509	86.06804
17	17.78579	18.61475	19.48938	20.41231	22.41444	25.85508	27.13238	29.90565	32.99903	40.30134	44.59917	54.74971	74.83636	102.7403
18	18.87972	19.81090	20.79672	21.84056	24.11687	28.06356	29.53900	32.75999	36.37896	45.01846	50.15909	62.43968	87.21181	122.4135
19	19.97912	21.01900	22.12367	23.29737	25.87037	30.37142	32.06595	35.78559	39.99549	50.16012	56.27500	71.05244	101.4436	145.6280
20	21.08401	22.23919	23.47052	24.78332	27.67649	32.78314	34.71925	38.99273	43.86518	55.76453	63.00250	80.69874	117.8101	173.0210
22	23.31040	24.71630	26.22514	27.84496	31.45288	37.93703	40.43048	45.99583	52.43614	68.53194	78.54302	103.6029	158.2764	243.4868
24	25.55912	27.24320	29.06302	31.03030	35.45926	43.56521	46.72710	53.86451	62.24904	83.70090	97.34706	132.3339	211.7930	341.6035
26	27.83037	29.82089	31.98668	34.34432	39.70963	49.71132	53.66913	62.70577	73.45382	101.7231	120.0999	168.3740	282.5688	478.2211
28	30.12439	32.45039	34.99870	37.79223	44.21885	56.42303	61.32271	72.63980	86.34653	123.1354	147.6309	213.5828	376.1697	668.4475
30	32.44142	35.13274	38.10176	41.37944	49.00268	63.75239	69.76079	83.80168	101.0730	148.5752	180.9434	270.2926	499.9569	933.3186
36	39.53279	43.50765	47.98511	53.03425	65.17422	90.04134	100.6281	126.2681	159.3374	257.3759	329.0395	542.5987	1166.498	2530.686
42	46.83957	52.39778	58.79199	66.15947	84.48389	124.2764	141.9933	186.5076	246.7765	439.8457	591.4007	1080.083	2708.246	6842.865
48	54.36832	61.83483	70.60870	80.94059	107.5406	168.8594	197.4267	271.9584	377.9990	745.8656	1056.190	2140.981	6274.405	18483.83
54	62.12577	71.85246	83.52960	97.58653	135.0716	226.9180	271.7126	393.1720	574.9286	1259.092	1879.591	4235.005	14523.15	49909.23
60	70.11888	82.48637	97.65787	116.3326	167.9450	302.5254	371.2629	565.1159	870.4668	2119.823	3338.298	8368.238	33602.99	134743.8

CHAPTER 2

Accounting Categories: Assets and Equities

INTRODUCTION

The accountant's job is to describe and communicate only those economic events which qualify under generally accepted accounting principles (GAAP) as *accounting events,* and to show the effects these accounting events have on *accounting assets* and *accounting equities.* In effect, accountants see the world solely in terms of these two categories and ignore all events that do not fit within them.

Because accounting assets and equities are subsets of *economic assets* **and** *equities,* we will begin our discussion with economic assets.

ECONOMIC ASSETS

Economic assets are rights to utilize economic resources. Economic resources are goods or services that, when utilized, are expected to result in incremental benefits. The resources utilized may be human or inanimate. Typical human resources include a factory employee who can provide labor services, an office employee who can provide clerical services, and a lawyer who can provide legal services. Typical inanimate economic resources include such objects as a building that provides shelter and space to carry on various business activities, a machine that can be used to manufacture products, and crops that can be grown on fertile land. Thus, the essential feature of an economic asset is ownership of a **right** to utilize an economic resource, rather than the ownership of an economic resource.

For example, suppose that a company leases a factory building for a year. In signing the lease, the company has obtained an economic asset—the right to use the building for a year. The company owns the right to use the building, even though the building itself belongs to some external party.

This example shows that a company may obtain the rights to utilize resources without necessarily owning the sources of these resources. Conversely, owned objects that are obsolete or irreparably damaged are no longer economic resources since their utilization will not result in incremental benefits. Clearly, ownership of a physical object is neither necessary nor sufficient for the existence of an economic asset.

Economic assets can be acquired by purchasing the resource, by acquiring the right to utilize the resource, or by social contract. When you purchase an economic asset, you have acquired the right to receive **all** the benefits resulting from the utilization of the economic resource. When you acquire the right to utilize an economic asset without purchasing it, you have acquired the right to receive only a portion of the benefits expected from the utilization of the economic resource. A social contract confers on all members of society the right to utilize typical government services, such as police and fire protection, sanitation, and water supply.

Utilization of resources represents the expiration of a right which is expected to result in benefits. It is in anticipation of these benefits that an entity acquires rights to utilize the asset. Nevertheless, the holder of an economic asset has no guarantee that the anticipated benefits will actually occur: the resource may not be available for utilization or utilization of the resource may not bring the anticipated benefit.

For example, a company owns a machine that has been used in the past to manufacture products sold to the public. On the basis of past experience, the machine is classified as an economic asset, since its utilization is expected to result in a product which will be sold to the public. The company may fail to reap the planned benefits if the machine breaks down and is no longer usable, or if the product manufactured by the machine becomes obsolete, and cannot be sold.

The benefits sought by a profit-seeking enterprise are cash flows, and the economic assets of such an enterprise are expected to have a beneficial impact on future cash flows. The benefits anticipated by a corporation from its assets may be an increase in the size of future net cash inflows (by increasing inflows or decreasing outflows), an acceleration of their timing, or a reduction in their uncertainty. **Utilization of an economic asset is expected to cause net future cash flows to be larger, sooner, or more certain.** For example, raw materials may be converted into marketable manufactured products, and these products may be sold. Machinery may be sold or used to transform raw materials into finished products. Buildings may be rented out, lived in, or used as stores, factories, and warehouses. A patent allows its owner to control the use of the patented process. Because each of these examples offers the prospect of direct or indirect increases in future cash flows, each will be an economic asset.

This definition of an economic asset refers to cash benefits, thereby raising three questions: How much cash, when might the cash be available, and how certain is it that the benefit (cash) will result? **In other words, each economic asset has a quantity, a time, and a risk dimension.** How much benefit? When? How sure? These are precisely the same dimensions of cash flows that decision makers need to predict, compare, and evaluate, and assets may vary in terms of any of these dimensions.

Everyone would agree that an asset certain to yield $1,000 tomorrow is different from an asset certain to yield $2,000 tomorrow. These two assets vary only in their quantity dimensions. It is equally clear that assets with the same quantity and risk dimensions, but different time dimensions, are also different. Obtaining $1,000 of benefits now is preferable to obtaining $1,000 of benefits a year from now. You must compare benefits that have the same time dimension.

It is less intuitively obvious that assets with the same time and quantity dimensions, but different risk dimensions, are also different. But ask yourself whether you feel that a promise from the government to pay you $10,000 a year from now is equivalent to a lottery ticket with a payoff to the winner of $10,000 a year from now. Each of these assets has a time dimension of 1 year, and in one sense a quantity dimension of $10,000, since each asset has a potential $10,000 payoff. But the **risk** dimension is very different for these two assets. It is easy to distinguish between a government promise to pay $10,000 a year from now (expected value $10,000), and a lottery ticket with a 1 percent probability of paying $10,000 a year from now (expected value $100).

Even if we use the language of probability, and express the quantity dimension in terms of "expected value," we would still wish to distinguish between a government promise to pay $10,000 a year from now (expected value $10,000), and a lottery ticket with a 1 percent probability of paying $1,000,000 a year from now (expected value also $10,000).

An economic asset is sometimes defined as "something of value." Value is often thought to be absolute and unique, rather than relative. An object is supposed to have one, and only one, "real value."

Thought Questions

You just purchased a car for $10,000.
What is the value of the car to you? To the dealer?
Why does the sale take place?

Actually, an economic asset has many values, depending on the benefit expected and the nature of the recipient of the benefit. This relativity and multiplicity of value makes it impossible to define an asset as "something of value." The expression "right to utilize resources" is less ambiguous, and captures the relationship between user and intended use of this asset.

> *Thought Question*
>
> Under what conditions would it be proper
> to classify a bottle of air as an asset?

ACCOUNTING ASSETS

Economic assets that are recognized by the accounting system are called *accounting assets*. We may picture the situation as follows:

Every accounting asset is necessarily an *economic asset,* but some economic assets are not recognized by the accounting system. For instance, economic assets, or rights to resources, are usually obtained through agreement—essentially, an exchange of promises. When a contract to lease a building is signed, the lessee obtains a legal right to use the building. The lessee has obtained a property right and an economic asset. But agreements alone are not recognized by the accounting process until performance by one of the parties to the agreement has occurred. Thus the contractual right arising from an agreement is often not an accounting asset.

EQUITIES

Equities are the company's responsibilities to provide economic resources to external parties. Provision of economic resources consists of distributing the resources, or permitting the utilization of the economic resources. The question is, how many resources are to be provided, and when will they be provided? Like assets, equities have amount and timing dimensions. But, unlike assets, equities do not have a risk dimension because we never doubt our obligation to perform.

Liabilities are responsibilities to provide resources where the amount and timing of the economic resource to be provided are known and estimable. *Owners' equity* is the company's responsibility to provide economic resources to its owners. In contrast to liabilities, the amount and timing of the responsibilities to be provided to owners is indeterminable.

Not all economic or legal responsibilities to distribute resources are recognized by the accountant. *Accounting equities* recognized by accounting arise from *accounting events*.

ACCOUNTING EVENTS

Most business activity consists of interactions between two accounting units. These interactions generally consist of an *agreement stage* and a *performance stage.* The first stage is an exchange of promises between the parties, and is **never** recognized as an accounting event as we have just seen. The second stage, the performance stage, is the fulfillment of the promises through performance by each of the parties according to the agreement, and is **always** recognized as an accounting event by each of the parties.

Generally, one party promises to provide goods or services to the other while the other party promises to pay cash in exchange. For instance firm A promises to sell goods to firm 1 and firm 1 promises to pay for these goods. Firm 2 promises to pay Ms. B who promises to work for firm 2. Firm 3 agrees to pay insurance premiums to firm C which promises to provide fire insurance protection. None of these exchanges of promises are accounting events. In each of these cases, performance by the "numbered party" consists of the payment of money. When it occurs, the performance is recognized as a cash disbursement for the numbered party and a cash receipt by the "lettered party." Performance by the lettered party consists of providing resources other than money (goods, labor services, and insurance coverage, respectively). When it occurs, the performance is recognized as the provision of goods (or services) by the lettered party, and the acquisition of goods (or services) by the numbered party. Because the receipt of goods, services, and money represents accounting events, the utilization of these goods, services, and money received must also be recognized as accounting events. In short, most accounting events consist of the acquisition, utilization, and provision of cash, goods, and services.

Accounting descriptions consist entirely of names and numbers. **Every accounting event is described in terms of two effects, each measured by the same number.** (Some apparent exceptions to this principle will be explained later.) No pictures, no photographs, no graphs, no sentences, no paragraphs, no ranges, and no probabilities are used—**only two effects and one number.** Since the accountant considers the world to consist solely of assets and equities, each event must produce either two effects on assets; two effects on equities; or one effect on an asset and the other on an equity.

The accountant further assumes that one of the effects of each accounting event will result in a *benefit,* and the other effect will require a *sacrifice.* A benefit is considered an increase in a right or a decrease in a responsibility. A sacrifice represents a decrease in a right or an increase in a responsibility. Thus, given the assumption that each event has two effects, and that one effect represents a benefit and the other effect a sacrifice, four types of accounting events are possible:

Benefit: Right (asset) increases
Sacrifice: Responsibility (equity) increases

Benefit: Right (asset) increases
Sacrifice: Right (asset) decreases

Benefit: Responsibility (equity) decreases
Sacrifice: Right (asset) decreases

Benefit: Responsibility (equity) decreases
Sacrifice: Responsibility (equity) increases

THE CLASSIFICATION OF ACCOUNTING ASSETS

Accounting assets may be classified in the following ways:

1. Discrete or continuous
2. Finite or infinite
3. Current or noncurrent
4. Monetary or nonmonetary
5. Tangible or intangible

Assets are rights to utilize or receive economic resources. That right may be exercisable at a point in time (discrete asset) or over a period of time (continuous asset). Examples of discrete assets, which can only be utilized once, are cash, accounts receivable, and inventory. Examples of continuous assets, which can be used over an extended period of time, are property, plant and equipment, or a patent. The same asset can provide discrete or continuous service, depending on the circumstances: A given machine provides discrete service if it is held for sale, but it provides continuous service if it is held for use.

A discrete or continuous accounting asset may have a finite or infinite life. An infinite asset is an unlimited right to utilize an economic resource that has an unlimited life. In other words, both the right and the economic resource must exist forever. If either the right has a limited duration or the life-span of the economic resource is limited, the asset is finite.

Examples of discrete accounting assets that are infinite are cash that can be spent at any time, or inventory that can be sold at any time. Finite and discrete assets are nonrefundable airplane tickets for a specific date, or the right to receive money only after a certain date. An example of a continuous asset that is infinite is land that is owned, because the right is infinite in duration and the land will always exist as an economic resource. Finally examples of continuous assets that are finite because the rights have limited duration are leases and patents, and those that are limited because the existence of the economic resource is limited are machinery and equipment. A limited life asset providing continuous service over more than one accounting period can be viewed as a collection of assets, each providing the right to utilize the resource for a single accounting period. Thus, a machine that is expected to last for 5 years can be thought of as five separate rights, each good for 1 year's machine services.

A classification based on the time dimension of *assets* is often used in financial statements. We employ the term **current assets** to describe the rights to resources that will be utilized within the next year (or the next operating cycle, if longer than a year). All other assets are classified as **noncurrent assets.**

> ### *Thought Question*
> For which of the classes of assets above,
> is the passage of time always (sometimes) an important event?

We will use the term **monetary assets** when referring to cash or promises by reliable external parties to pay specified cash amounts in the near future. All other assets, such as inventory, land, buildings, equipment, investments, and prepaid services, are called **nonmonetary assets.**

Physical resources owned by the company are called *tangible assets.* All other nonmonetary assets are said to be *intangible assets.* Many intangible assets are legal rights to services, such as contracts, promises, trademarks, franchises, leases, and patents.

ACCOUNTING EVENTS GIVING RISE TO ACCOUNTING ASSETS

A cash receipt will always be reported as an accounting event increasing an asset called Cash. The purchase of *tangible assets* is always an accounting event. If the objects purchased are for resale, the asset is called Inventory. If the objects purchased are for use, the asset is called Property, Plant and Equipment.

A receipt of services, on the other hand, **never** results in an accounting asset, since services cannot be stored and are always utilized as they are received. If such a **right** is not paid for, then no accounting event is recognized and no accounting asset results. However, if a **right** is paid for in advance, an accounting event will be recognized and the asset that will result is called Prepaid Services.

A right to receive cash, which is called a receivable, is recognized when the goods or services for which cash is to be received have already been provided. Until the goods or services are provided, only an agreement (an exchange of promises) exists, so neither an accounting event nor an accounting asset is recognized.

As discussed previously, all accounting events have two effects. The second effect of each of the accounting events giving rise to the assets listed above is either a **decrease** in another asset or an **increase** in the other accounting category—equities.

THE CLASSIFICATION OF EQUITIES: LIABILITIES AND OWNERS' EQUITIES

Nearly all accounting equities can be classified as *liabilities.* Liabilities themselves can be classified in the following ways:

1. Discrete or continuous
2. Current or noncurrent
3. Monetary or nonmonetary
4. Known or estimable

Liabilities are responsibilities to provide resources. The provision of the resource may either occur at a point in time (discrete), or over a period of time (continuous). An example of a discrete liability is accounts payable merchandise, and an example of a continuous liability is a lease obligation.

Current liabilities are liabilities that will be discharged within the current year, or within the next operating cycle if that is longer than a year. All other liabilities are classified as *noncurrent liabilities.* For example, a 90-day promissory note is a current liability, but a 20-year mortgage is a noncurrent liability.

A *monetary liability* is an obligation to pay a fixed amount of money. Most liabilities are *monetary,* such as the obligation to pay suppliers for raw materials purchased on credit. All other liabilities are classified as *nonmonetary liabilities.* A nonmonetary liability is an obligation to provide goods or services. Most *nonmonetary liabilities* arise from transactions with customers: the company receives cash in advance from customers in return for goods or services to be provided in the future.

A *known liability* is a liability that is certain to require the provision of a known amount. An *estimable liability* is a liability that is likely to require the provision of an amount that can be estimated. For example, the obligation to pay suppliers of goods and services is a *known liability* since a known amount of cash must be paid. On the other hand, the liability for warranty repairs is an estimable liability that obligates the company to provide all necessary repairs until the warranty expires. Based on past experience, the amount of the provision can be estimated, but the actual provision depends on future needs for warranty repairs.

Estimable liabilities are classified as such only when there is convincing evidence that a provision will occur, and the amount of the provision can be estimated. Obligations that are less likely to require provisions, or obligations for provisions that cannot be estimated, such as *owners' equities,* are not considered accounting liabilities.

ACCOUNTING EVENTS GIVING RISE TO ACCOUNTING LIABILITIES AND EQUITIES

A company borrows from a bank, promising to repay over the next 2 years. The future cash outflow is certain, and measurable in terms of dollars. The timing and the amount of the cash outflow are both known. The liability is called a Bank Loan.

A company accepts an order for 100 grabules which includes a check for the full price of the grabules. The future outflow is certain, but it is measurable in terms of grabules rather than money. Again, the timing and the amount of the outflow are identifiable. Liabilities of this kind are often called Advances from Customers. However, had the order been accepted without payment having been received, no performance would have taken place, no accounting event would have occurred, and thus no accounting liability would have resulted.

A company purchases raw materials from a supplier, promising to pay some cash at the end of the day and the rest at the end of 30 days. The future outflow is certain, and it is measurable in cash. The timing and the amount of the outflow are known. Liabilities of this kind are called Accounts Payable.

The utilization of services that have not been paid for is recognized as an accounting event, and will result in a liability. Such a liability to pay the supplier of the service is generally called a payable. The specific title of the payable depends on the type of service utilized. For instance, the utilization of labor services is called Wages Payable, and the utilization of borrowed money is called Interest Payable.

> ### Thought Questions
> Could the services utilized above been paid for in advance?
> What would be the consequences of their utilization?

When the board of directors of a company declares a cash dividend, the corporation voluntarily assumes a liability to its stockholders. The outflow is certain, and measurable in terms of dollar amounts. The timing of the outflow is known as are the intended recipients. This liability is known as Dividends Payable.

When a corporation issues stock, an increase in owners' equity is recognized. This portion of equity ownership is called Contributed Capital.

ONE-SIDED EVENTS

We stated that all accounting events are described in terms of two effects. For most events this rule poses no problems, since the two effects are easily determinable. For instance, when we obtain a bank loan, an asset (Cash) increases, and a liability (Bank Loan) increases. Similarly, when we receive payments for an order or buy raw materials on credit, both an asset and a liability increase. When we buy raw materials for cash, the two effects of that event are also easy to ascertain: an asset (Raw Materials) increases, and another asset (Cash) decreases.

Some events, however, appear to be lopsided; they seem to cause only one effect. For instance, assume that a company wins a cash award. An asset (Cash) has increased, but nothing else seems to have changed. No other asset has been affected, and no new responsibility has been created. When a dividend is declared, a responsibility has arisen without a corresponding increase in an asset or a decrease in another liability. These events appear to have only one effect—an increase **or** a decrease in the *residual net-assets* of the firm. (Residual net-assets, also called *residual equity,* is defined as Assets minus Liabilities minus Contributed Capital.)

However, such a state of affairs is not permissible under the accounting rules. Each event must have **two** effects. Therefore, **whenever an event appears to have only one effect, the accountant records another effect to a residual equity account called** *Retained Earnings.* As we will see in the next chapter, **Retained Earnings is a subdivision of Owners' Equity.**

USER'S PERSPECTIVE

Financial statements cannot be effectively analyzed without understanding what accounting assets and equities are. Assets have often erroneously been considered property, rather than property rights. However, it is the **right** to utilize a resource which defines an economic asset's existence. But not all economic rights are accounting assets, and under GAAP, identical rights may or may not be recognized as accounting assets. Many extremely important rights typically arise from contracts where neither side has yet performed. But these contractual rights are not recognized as accounting assets because without performance by either party, no accounting event results and therefore no accounting asset exists.

For example, consider two binding contracts to rent a building for a year. One contract calls for the rent payments to be made at the end of each month, and the other calls for the total yearly payment to be made at the beginning of the year. In the first contract, the economic asset—the right to use the building—is never recognized as an accounting asset. In the second contract, when we make the yearly payment in advance, the right to utilize the building for a year is recognized as an accounting asset when the payment is made. Yet the economic asset, the right to use the building, is identical in both contracts. The difference is not in the rights that are acquired, but in when we perform our part of the agreement. Thus, under GAAP, identical economic rights are sometimes recognized as accounting assets, and sometimes they are not.

As a result of defining accounting assets as rights to utilize economic resources, events that alter the rights are recognized as accounting events, but events that alter the value of those rights rarely are accounting events. If we pay rent in advance for a year and recognize an accounting asset, after 1 month the duration of the right has been reduced and an accounting event results. But this does not mean that the right is necessarily less valuable, especially if the economy is booming. After 1 month has passed, the right to utilize the building for 11 months may be more valuable than the original right to utilize the building for 12 months. The reduction in the duration of the right is always an accounting event since it reduces the right to utilize an economic asset. And since assets are defined in terms of rights rather than value, changes in value are generally not accounting events.

Similar distinctions hold true for equities. Identical obligations may or may not be recognized as accounting liabilities. For example, we enter into two contracts to sell grabules. One contract calls for payment in advance of delivery, and the other for payment upon delivery. Both contracts impose identical legal responsibilities to provide grabules. But, in the first contract, the responsibility to provide those grabules is recognized as an accounting liability when the cash is received, whereas in the second contract, we never recognize an **accounting** obligation to deliver the grabules.

Thus, under GAAP, two firms with identical economic assets may have different accounting assets, and two firms with identical legal obligations may report different liabilities.

PROBLEMS

1. A machine has the capacity to produce two grabules each year for 5 years at no incremental cost. It is known with certainty that **no** grabules can be sold in year 1, two and only two grabules can be sold in years 2 through 5 inclusive, and that no grabules can be sold after year 5. If you produce two grabules in year 1 should these be considered assets? Why? Why not?

2. In the case of a magazine subscription, what happens to the publisher's responsibility as magazines are mailed? How might this be described?

3. In the case of a loan, what happens as time passes? How might that be described?

4. For each of the following events, indicate whether they should be recorded. Explain your answers.
   a. Deposit of money in a bank
   b. Credit sale
   c. Collection of amounts owed you
   d. Purchase of inventory on credit
   e. Entering into a lease for machinery

5. For each of the following items, indicate whether it is an accounting asset, or an economic asset but not an accounting asset. Explain your answers.
   a. Good credit rating based on prompt payment of bills
   b. Well-deserved reputation for public service
   c. New product developed by company research

    d. Famous trademark
    e. Contract providing legal service for the coming year
    f. New machine constructed by the company for its own use
    g. Possible income tax refund still being contested by the government

6. Under what conditions, if any, would each of the following be considered an accounting asset or an accounting liability:
    a. Obligation to provide a tenant with office space for the coming year
    b. Financing charge that will be owed if payment is not made by the end of the month
    c. Class action suit that has been brought against the company
    d. The cost of a disposal facility that will be needed if the Environmental Protection Agency rules that the company may not dispose of its waste by dumping in the nearby river
    e. Obligation to provide repairs under a 2-year guarantee of appliances sold in the past year
    f. Merchandise that was stolen and must be replaced

7. Give examples of assets that are expected to result in
    a. Generating more cash
    b. Accelerating the timing of cash generation
    c. Decreasing the uncertainty of cash generation

8. What accounting assets and accounting liabilities are **necessarily** affected by the passage of time?

9. What direct or indirect cash benefits and sacrifices can be associated with each of the following assets and liabilities:
    a. Receivables from customers
    b. Inventory held for sale
    c. The right to utilize rented space
    d. Machinery
    e. A patent on a broad-spectrum antibiotic
    f. Wages payable
    g. Taxes payable
    h. Advances from customers

10. For each of the following items, determine whether it is a *current asset* (CA), *noncurrent asset* (NCA), *current liability* (CL), or *noncurrent liability* (NCL):
    a. Petty cash
    b. Sixty-day promissory notes held by the company
    c. Oak barrels used by a wine maker
    d. Coal used to heat the factory
    e. Mortgage on a building
    f. Unsold house recently completed by a builder
    g. Lifetime guarantee on an automobile muffler

11. What arguments can be made for recognizing the *agreement stage* between two *accounting units* as an *accounting event*, even though neither party has *performed?* What arguments can be made against?

12. For each of the following, write (E) if it is an *economic asset*, (A) if it is an *accounting asset*, and (N) if it is not an *asset*:
    a. Skillful and well-trained work force
    b. Good name in the community
    c. Patented process purchased from another company

   d. Patented process developed within the company
   e. Insurance coverage for top executives
   f. Famous trademark developed by the company
   g. Backlog of orders for company merchandise
   h. Amounts owed by credit customers
   i. Damaged merchandise
   j. Amount anticipated from another company for patent infringement

13. For each of the following assets estimate, if possible, the quantity, time, and risk dimensions:
    a. Merchandise held for sale (the merchandise is popular, and the current selling price is $25 per unit).
    b. $10,000 owed by credit customers (2 percent of credit sales are usually uncollectible; 90 percent of collections are made within 30 days, and the rest are made within 60 days).
    c. Marketable securities having a current market value of $70,000 (the securities will be sold within the next year; the market price is expected to vary no more than 8 percent during that time).
    d. Office building purchased 3 years ago for $2,500,000 (the same building would cost $3,500,000 today; the cost of living has increased 34 percent in the past 3 years; the company expects to use the building for 7 more years).
    e. As a sales gimmick, United Junk Dealers is offering a $50,000 prize to an entry selected at random from an expected total of 400,000 entries. (This is the twelfth annual contest run by the company.)

14. Classify each of the following as a *monetary* (M) or *nonmonetary* (NM) *asset:*
    a. Machinery
    b. Cash in the bank
    c. Cash owed by credit customers
    d. Bonds bought by the company
    e. Stocks bought by the company
    f. Patented trademarks
    g. Receivables from companies that are being liquidated
    h. Rents owed by tenants (monthly rent is a fixed amount plus a percentage of monthly sales)
    i. Amount of an expected tax refund
    j. Completed ship awaiting delivery (the ship was built under a fixed fee contract)

15. Classify each of the following as a *current liability* (CL), *noncurrent liability* (NCL), *owners' equity* (OE), or not an *equity* (N):
    a. Bonds maturing within the next year
    b. Bonds maturing 2 years from now
    c. Wages owed hourly employees
    d. Possible loss in a lawsuit recently brought against the company
    e. Obligation under a lease to provide space for the next year to tenants who have paid 1 month's rent in advance
    f. Salary to be paid under contract to an executive for the coming year
    g. Magazines to be delivered within the next year to subscribers
    h. Repair services that may be required during the 90-day warranty period on recently sold appliances

CHAPTER **3**

Accounting
Numbers

INTRODUCTION

Every accounting event affects either two assets, or two equities, or one asset and one equity. In describing accounting events, the accountant chooses **names** for the particular assets and/or equities affected by the event, indicates the **direction** of the effects (increase or decrease), and assigns a number to **quantify** the effects. Conventionally, **the same number is used to quantify both effects of an accounting event.** In the previous chapter, we discussed accounting categories. In this chapter, we consider the numbers used to quantify the effects of accounting events.

ACCOUNTING NUMBERS

The *accounting number* used to describe the impact of an accounting event must be a single figure representing the appropriate currency. We cannot describe the effects in terms of pounds, feet, watts, years, or bushels, even though such quantification might be more natural and easier to obtain than dollar amounts. Thus, although it is simpler to say that we acquired 100 pounds of material than to represent that acquisition in dollars, the accounting process uses only the dollar amount. The requirement that the number used must be a single figure also rules out the use of intervals (between $10 and $30), the use of probabilities (40 percent of $5), or the reporting of distributions (mean of $40 with standard deviation of $2) in describing the impact of economic events.

> ### Thought Questions
> What is the advantage of all accounting numbers being in dollars?
> Why do you think accounting numbers must be single values?

This requirement poses severe problems for the accountant since the effects of complex economic events are not easily captured by single dollar amounts. The nature of the events and the limita-

43

tions of the measurement process employed by accounting often make it difficult to generate precise, accurate, and meaningful single value figures.

Accounting numbers present a misleading impression of accuracy. For example, suppose that the accountant wishes to measure raw materials inventory at the end of the month. The inventory consists of materials A and B, each costing $5 per pound. Material A can be placed on a scale, which shows that we have 40 pounds on hand. Although the scale is not renown for its accuracy, we know that it is correct to the nearest ounce, so that any error is unlikely to be significant. Material B lies in an underground storage area, so direct measurement is impossible, and we must rely on a visual estimate by the warehouse manager. The manager reports that we have 60 pounds of material B, but acknowledges that the actual figure might be anything from 50 to 70 pounds. If the accountant reports that we have $500 of raw materials (40 + 60 pounds at $5 per pound), how much reliance can we place on such a figure?

Lack of accuracy in accounting numbers may be due to the quality of the measuring apparatus, or to the nature of the object being measured. Reporting an estimated or average value could be misleading unless some indication is given of probable quantification error.

Furthermore, even if we report only dollar amounts, there are many ways to carry out the calculation. For instance, in describing a piece of machinery owned by the company, should we report:

1. The original dollar cost
2. The present disposal value
3. The current cost of a comparable machine
4. The present value of future cash flows ascribable to the machine

Not surprisingly, the accountant's idea of heaven is an event producing unambiguous dollar effects verifiable through reference to a document displaying the reported figures in bold type. Since reality is seldom so obliging, the reader of accounting reports must be aware of the rules for choosing numbers to quantify the effects of accounting events.

PREFERRED MEASUREMENTS

Every accounting event is described in terms of two effects, both quantified by the same number. Although no authorized pronouncement tells us how to choose this number, the following discussion summarizes existing practice.

To the accountant, a ***preferred measurement*** results when an effect of an event can be satisfactorily, unambiguously, and accurately measured by a single dollar amount, subject to little or no dispersion, and not likely to be corrected in the future. There are two kinds of preferred measurements:

1. *Increases (or decreases) in cash*   The increase (or decrease) in cash represents a *preferred measurement*. The present values of **virtually certain** future increases (or decreases) in cash, of known amount and timing, also represent preferred measurements unless the other effect of the event is an **actual** increase (or decrease) in cash.

2. *A decrease in an existing asset or responsibility*   A decrease in an existing asset or responsibility is also a *preferred measurement*. All existing assets and responsibilities are quantified in terms of a single number. Therefore, a decrease in an asset or responsibility can be satisfactorily, unambiguously, and accurately quantified in terms of the existing quantification.

For instance, if we have an asset quantified at $100, and an event occurs consuming one-half of that asset, few would quarrel that the event produced a $50 reduction in the asset. If all of the asset was consumed, even fewer would argue that a $100 reduction in the asset occurred. Similarly, if we had recognized a responsibility of $100, and discharged one-half of it, a reduction of $50 appears appropriate.

QUANTIFICATION RULES

Given the concept of preferred measurement, we identify the following three quantification rules:

Rule 1   If an event produces only one preferred measurement, quantify both effects of the event in terms of that preferred measurement.

Rule 2   If an event produces two different preferred measurements, treat the event as the combination of two separate events, and use each preferred measurement to quantify the effects of each event.

Rule 3   If an event does not produce a preferred measurement, quantify the effects of the event by estimating the amount of cash that **would** have changed hands in the most likely equivalent cash transaction.

EXAMPLES OF QUANTIFICATION RULES

Examples of Rule 1

1. Two vats of chemicals are purchased for $848 in cash. The cash decrease of $848 quantifies both effects of the event:

Raw Materials and Supplies ↑ increases   848
Cash ↓ decreases   848

2. Six hundred marbles, costing $5,400, are purchased on account. A $3,000 payment is required at the end of the day, and a $2,400 payment is required at the end of 30 days. The amount by which cash will shortly decrease, $5,400, quantifies both effects of the event:

Raw Materials and Supplies ↑ increases   5,400
Accounts Payable ↑ increases   5,400

> **Thought Question**
> Since the present value of the future cash decrease in Example 2 is less than $5,400, shouldn't a number less than $5,400 be used to quantify the purchase of marbles?

3. The firm's raw materials inventory is quantified at $6,248. Then, one-half of the raw materials inventory is placed into production. To apply the quantification rules in such a situation, the accountant first determines what fraction of the item has been altered by the event, and then multiplies that fraction by the item's existing quantification. In this example, one-half of the raw materials have been altered by the event. The existing quantification is $6,248. Therefore, the change in raw materials inventory is quantified at $3,124 ($\frac{1}{2}$ × $6,248) and this number is used to measure both effects of the event:

Work-in-Process ↑ increases   3,124
Raw Materials and Supplies ↓ decreases   3,124

4. A customer orders 100 grabules to be delivered in the future. The order is accompanied by an $8,000 check. The preferred measurement, $8,000, is the amount by which cash increases:

Advances from Customers ↑ increases   8,000
Cash ↑ increases   8,000

5. The company borrows $50,000, promising to repay $9,125 in 1 year and $59,125 in 2 years. Quantify this event at $50,000, the amount by which cash increases, rather than by calculating the

present value of the future cash decreases of $68,250 ($9,125 plus $59,125):

Cash ↑ increases	50,000
Bank Loan ↑ increases	50,000

Thought Questions
What is the relationship between $50,000
and $68,250 in this example?
What does the difference of $18,250 represent?

Example of Rule 2

Events to which this rule generally applies are **sales of goods to customers.** Such sales transactions are treated as a combination of two separate events, a sales inflow and a sales outflow. Thus, the "two effects and one number" convention is preserved.

6. Finished goods with an existing quantification of $1,100 are delivered to the customer who advanced the company $8,000 in cash. Here the cash received is the sales inflow, and the merchandise sold is the sales outflow. The sales inflow is quantified at $8,000, the existing quantification of advances from customers. The sales outflow is quantified at $1,100, the existing quantification of the finished goods.

   The sales inflow has the following effects:

Advances from Customers ↓ decreases	8,000
Retained Earnings ↑ increases	8,000

   The sales outflow has the following effects:

Finished Goods ↓ decreases	1,100
Retained Earnings ↓ decreases	1,100

Example of Rule 3

7. An inventor sells a patent for a specialized process to a corporation in exchange for 2,000 shares of its stock. The patented process suits the needs of this particular corporation, but is useless to anyone else. The corporation's stock is widely traded at $5 per share.

   No market value is available for the patent because of its specialized nature. The corporation could have issued 2,000 shares for $10,000; this transaction would not have affected the stock price, since $5 per share was the prevailing price in an active market.

The accountant reasons that issuing 2,000 shares of stock to the inventor was equivalent to paying him $10,000 in a comparable cash transaction. This number is used to quantify both effects of the event:

Patent ↑ increases	10,000
Common Stock ↑ increases	10,000

Thought Question
What would be an alternative quantification of the event?

THE EFFECT OF THE QUANTIFICATION RULES

The effect of the quantification rules is that all accounting data represent actual cash flows, virtually certain future cash flows, or hypothetical cash flows. To see how this works, let's first consider all events that **do not** decrease existing assets and responsibilities:

1. If such events contain an actual cash flow, then that cash flow quantifies both effects of the event.

2. If such events do not contain an actual cash flow but do involve a virtually certain future cash flow of known amount and timing, then both effects are quantified in terms of that future cash flow.

3. All other events are quantified in terms of a hypothetical cash flow.

Thus it is clear that all events **not** involving a decrease in existing assets or responsibilities are quantified in terms of actual, virtually certain future, or hypothetical cash flows.

If an event **does** decrease an existing asset or responsibility, the effects of the event are quantified in terms of the existing accounting quantification of the asset or responsibility decreased. But that existing accounting quantification originally represented an actual, virtually certain future, or hypothetical cash flow. For example, the advances from customers that are reduced by the delivery of goods were quantified by the cash received, and the raw materials placed into production were quantified by the cash flow associated with the acquisition of those materials.

CASH FLOWS AND THE FUTURE: ACCRUALS AND DEFERRALS

We have seen that all accounting events are quantified in terms of actual, virtually certain future, or hypothetical cash flows. When an event occurs that will require a future cash outflow, a liability will result; when an event occurs that will generate a future cash inflow, an asset will result. For example, if space is leased by a firm for its manufacturing location and the rent payment will be made at the end of each month's utilization, we recognize a liability. This liability, Rent Payable, is called an *accrual.* Examples of assets that are accruals are Accounts Receivable, Interest Receivable, and Dividends Receivable.

On the other hand, when a cash outflow or a cash inflow occurs in anticipation of a future and related event, we recognize an asset or a liability, respectively. In our example above, if the payment had been required prior to each month's utilization of the space, then an asset would have resulted. This asset, Prepaid Services, is called a *deferral.* A common example of a liability that is a deferral is Advances from Customers.

The system of accounting that recognizes only those events that impact cash is called the *cash method* of accounting. The system of accounting that encompasses accruals and deferrals as well as cash events, is called the *accrual method* of accounting.

MEASUREMENT OF ASSETS AND EQUITIES IN TERMS OF CASH FLOWS

We have seen that assets are sources of expected future cash inflows, and equities are responsibilities for future outflows. Unfortunately, measuring these future flows directly in terms of cash is often difficult or impossible. As you can see from the quantification rules, reported accounting measurements are largely based on the cash involved in past or present, rather than future, transactions. The measurement of transactions in terms of past or present cash effects is known as the *historical cost principle.* Let us consider several applications of this principle to the measurements of assets and equities.

Asset Measurement

Cash

The *Cash* account increases when cash is received and decreases when cash is disbursed. Thus, a balance in the account represents coins, paper money, money in the bank, negotiable checks, and money orders available. Increases and decreases to Cash are quantified in terms of past and present cash flows.

Accounts Receivable

The *Accounts Receivable* account increases by providing goods and services on credit, and it decreases when cash is collected from customers. Therefore, a balance in the account indicates the amount owed by credit customers. Increases to Accounts Receivable are quantified in terms of virtually certain future cash flows, and decreases are quantified by current cash collections.

Thought Question
What other event will affect Accounts Receivable?

Prepaid Services

The **Prepaid Services** account increases by prepaying for services, and it decreases by utilizing those services. A balance in the account indicates services paid for and not yet utilized.

Increases to Prepaid Services are quantified in terms of the cash paid in advance of utilization, and decreases are quantified as a percentage of the cash outflows associated with acquiring available prepaid services. The percentage is determined by the ratio of the quantity of services utilized to the quantity of available prepaid services. Other titles for this account are **Prepayments, Prepaid Expenses,** and **Deferred Charges.**

Raw Materials and Supplies

A manufacturing company has three inventory accounts: Raw Materials and Supplies, Work-in-Process, and Finished Goods. The **Raw Materials and Supplies** account increases by acquiring raw materials and supplies, and it decreases by utilizing raw materials and supplies in the manufacturing process. Therefore, a balance in the account represents the cost of raw materials and supplies on hand.

Increases to Raw Materials and Supplies are quantified by the cash flows associated with the acquisition of the raw materials and supplies, and decreases are quantified as a percentage of the cash flows associated with acquiring the raw materials and supplies on hand. This percentage is equal to the ratio of the quantity of raw materials and supplies put into production to the quantity of raw materials and supplies on hand.

Work-in-Process

The **Work-in-Process** account increases by putting raw materials and supplies, machine and space services, and labor services into the manufacturing process, and it decreases when the product is completed. Therefore, a balance in the account represents the cash associated with incomplete products.

Increases to Work-in-Process are quantified by the cash flows associated with the inputs into production. Decreases are quantified as a percentage of the cash flows associated with the inputs to the manufacturing process. This percentage is equal to the ratio of the output from the manufacturing process to the inputs to the manufacturing process.

Finished Goods

The **Finished Goods** account increases when the manufacturing process is complete, and it decreases when the goods are sold. A balance in the account represents the cash associated with completed manufactured products.

Increases to Finished Goods are quantified by the cash flows associated with goods finished, which equals the decrease to the Work-in-Process account, and the decrease is quantified as a percentage of finished goods that are sold. (The methods of determining this percentage are discussed in Chapter 9.)

Property, Plant and Equipment

The **Property, Plant and Equipment** account increases by acquiring physical assets that can be utilized continuously for a period of time, and it decreases by disposing of these assets.

Increases and decreases to Property, Plant and Equipment are quantified by the cash associated with the acquisition of the assets (original cost). A balance in the account represents the original cost of the physical assets on hand. Physical assets, such as buildings and machines, that have limited useful lives are called **depreciable assets.**

Accumulated Depreciation

The **Accumulated Depreciation** account increases as depreciable assets are utilized during a period, and it decreases when a depreciable asset is disposed of. A balance in the account represents the portion of depreciable assets on hand utilized to date.

Increases to Accumulated Depreciation are quantified as a percentage of the original cost of the asset acquired, and decreases are quantified by the cumulative utilization of the disposed asset. (We will discuss the methods used in calculating the utilization of depreciable assets in Chapter 10.)

The **book value** of a *depreciable asset* is defined as the difference between its **original capacity** acquired (original cost of property, plant and equipment) and the **capacity utilized** (*accumulated depreciation*). Thus, *book value* represents the capacity remaining to be utilized.

> ### Thought Question
> What other event will affect Property, Plant and Equipment?

As you can see, most assets in the list above, except for Cash and Accounts Receivable, are quantified in terms of the sacrifice or cost of acquiring the asset (the amount paid or to be paid), and not in terms of the benefit or cash expected from utilizing the asset. Thus, although an asset by definition is a right to utilize a resource expected to result in a future benefit, it is seldom quantified in terms of its expected benefit. The only thing we can say about the benefit is that it is expected to be larger than the accounting quantification of the asset—at least initially when the asset is acquired.

> ### Thought Question
> Why is the expected benefit larger
> than the initial accounting quantification?

Liability Measurement

Accounts Payable

The *Accounts Payable* account increases by purchasing inventory (or raw materials and supplies) on credit, and it decreases when the suppliers of merchandise are paid. A balance in the account indicates the amount to be paid in the future for inventory that was purchased in the past.

Increases to Accounts Payable are quantified by the cash flow associated with purchasing inventory, and decreases are quantified by the cash paid to suppliers of merchandise.

Accounts Payable Services

The *Accounts Payable Services* account increases when services, other than labor, cash, and government, are utilized on credit, and it decreases when the suppliers of the services are paid. A balance in the account indicates the amount to be paid in the future for services utilized in the past.

Advances from Customers

The *Advances from Customers* account increases when cash is received prior to providing goods or services, and it decreases when the goods or services, for which cash had been received, are provided. A balance in the account indicates that cash was received in the past, for which goods and services must be provided in the future.

Increases to Advances from Customers are quantified by the amount of cash received, and decreases are quantified as a percentage of the cash inflows associated with providing the goods or services. The percentage is equal to the ratio of goods or services provided to the total obligation to provide goods or services.

Interest Payable

The *Interest Payable* account increases by the cost (interest) of utilizing borrowed money, and it decreases when the interest is paid.

A balance in the account indicates that borrowed cash was utilized in the past, and the cost of having used the cash must be paid for in the future.

Increases to Interest Payable are usually quantified as a percentage (interest rate) of the amount borrowed, and decreases are quantified by the amount of interest paid.

Wages Payable

The **Wages Payable** account increases as a result of utilizing labor services prior to paying for them, and it decreases when the wages are paid. A balance in the account indicates that labor services utilized in the past, must be paid for in the future.

Increases to Wages Payable are quantified by the cash to be paid for the labor services, and decreases are quantified by the amount of cash paid.

Dividends Payable

The **Dividends Payable** account increases by declaring cash dividends, and it decreases when they are paid. A balance in the account indicates that dividends declared in the past, must be paid for in the future.

Increases to Dividends Payable are quantified by the amount of the cash dividend declared, and decreases are quantified by the amount of dividends paid.

Bank Loan

The **Bank Loan** account increases by borrowing cash, and it decreases as the loan is repaid. A balance in the account indicates that cash borrowed in the past, must be repaid in the future. Increases to Bank Loan are quantified by the amount of cash borrowed, and decreases are quantified by the amount of the loan that is repaid.

Owners' Equity Measurement

Contributed Capital

Contributed Capital represents contributions by stockholders of a corporation in exchange for an ownership interest. There are many types of ownership interests, all of which are explained in Chapter 14. Until then, we will limit our discussion of Contributed Capital to Common Stock.

The **Common Stock** account increases by issuing shares of stock, and it decreases by repurchasing outstanding shares. Since a corporation cannot exist without having issued shares of its common stock, there will always be a balance in the account. Increases to Common Stock are generally quantified by the amount of cash received from the issue, and decreases are generally quantified by the cash paid for the repurchased shares.

Retained Earnings

Retained Earnings represents the *residual equity* of a firm, and equals the cumulative effect of one-sided events (shown on page 38).

> ### Thought Question
> What events will cause a change
> in the balance of Retained Earnings?

THE FUNDAMENTAL ACCOUNTING EQUATION

Recall that **every event has two and only two effects, each measured by the same number,** and the accountant visualizes the world consisting of only **assets and equities.** This system is called *double-entry accounting.*

> ### Thought Question
> Can you think of an example of a single-entry accounting system?

As a result, the only possible combinations of effects from accounting events are

1. Asset ↑ increase and equity ↑ increase
2. Equity ↓ decrease and asset ↓ decrease
3. Asset ↑ increase and asset ↓ decrease
4. Equity ↓ decrease and equity ↑ increase

These events either produce equal changes in assets and equities, as in combinations 1 and 2, or produce a zero change in assets and equities, combinations 3 and 4. Therefore, it must always be true that **assets are equal to equities,** and this relationship is called the *fundamental accounting equation.*

$$\text{Assets} = \text{Equities}$$

Since equities consist of liabilities and owners' equity, and owners' equity consists of contributed capital and retained earnings, we can restate this relationship as

> Assets = Liabilities plus Owners' Equity
> or Assets = Liabilities plus Contributed Capital
>   plus Retained Earnings

or Assets − Liabilities = Contributed Capital
                plus Retained Earnings where
                Assets minus Liabilities
                is called *net-assets*,
or Net-assets − Contributed Capital = Retained Earnings

Net-assets minus Contributed Capital is also called residual net-assets, or residual equity. We think that the concept of *net-assets* and *residual net-assets* is more concrete and easier to understand than owners' equity or retained earnings, respectively. It is clear why a firm wishes to increase its residual net-assets, and why an event which increases residual net-assets is desirable. An increase in residual net-assets occurs when an asset is increased (or a liability is decreased) without a decrease in another asset (or an increase in another liability), and without an increase in contributed capital.

In other words, we have obtained a benefit without having sacrificed. If we consider this event as merely increasing Retained Earnings, it is much less descriptive than saying that residual net-assets increased.

What meaning can be assigned to the quantification of Retained Earnings? If the cash generated by a company's existing assets is used to discharge the company's existing liabilities, the remaining cash will be available for distribution to owners. Since the cash generated (benefit) is expected to be equal to or greater than the accounting quantification of assets, the difference between assets and liabilities is a rough measure of the company's **minimum** ability to make future cash distributions to owners. The dollar amount of Retained Earnings is only an approximation of the minimum potential distributions to owners, in excess of Contributed Capital, because accounting measurements of assets and liabilities are based on past or present events, rather than on predicted future events.

THE COST AND BENEFIT OF AGGREGATION AND PRECISION

Earlier we said that there is no single "correct" answer to most accounting problems. The "best" description of an event depends on the audience to whom the accountant's report is addressed. How broadly or narrowly should the effects of a given event be described? How specific must we be in choosing names for affected assets and equities? At what level of aggregation should accounting categories be defined? Consider, for instance, a bank loan of $50,000, resulting in the receipt of five hundred $100 bills. To achieve maximum generality, we could use the names Assets and Equities, obtaining this description of the event:

Assets ↑ increase	50,000
Equities ↑ increase	50,000

Alternatively, we can use names that describe the incoming assets and the assumed responsibilities more specifically. On the asset side we have the following five choices, in increasing order of specificity or disaggregation:

1. Asset increase

2. Cash increase (this differentiates cash from other assets)

3. Cash on hand increase (this differentiates cash on hand from cash in the bank)

4. Currency on hand increase (this differentiates currency on hand from checks not deposited)

5. One-hundred dollar bills increase (this differentiates $100 bills on hand from other bills on hand)

Which name should be chosen? As is true throughout accounting, there is no one correct choice. The name chosen depends on who is to receive the communication and for what decision the information is to be used. Suppose we opt for the most aggregated description, asset increase: then an acquisition of raw materials would be described identically with the acquisition of cash. Since both raw materials and cash are assets, we would be unable to distinguish between these two events. Had we described the loan in this fashion, we would have no means to describe the subsequent purchase of raw materials for cash, since this event would not alter the only name in this category we have recognized—assets.

If we use the most general description, we are taking the position that the difference between the acquisition of cash or inventory, and the subsequent exchange of cash for goods, is not important enough to be described by the accounting process. We are saying that the difference does not constitute relevant information for decision making. At the other extreme, if we use description 5, we take the position that each event changing the number of $100 bills is important, and that the difference between receiving $100 bills or $10 bills is significant. We would then have to report such earth-shaking events as changing $100 bills into $5 bills. Clearly, description 1 is too general and description 5 is too specific. The choice among the intervening descriptions, however, is not obvious; it depends on the audience to whom we are reporting.

Whenever we use a more general name, whenever we aggregate or lump things together, we lose information. For instance, the statement, "an animal crossed the street," does not tell us whether the animal was a cat, a dog, or a monkey.

The more specific or narrow a name we use, and the more we disaggregate, the more information we provide. Why, then, do we not always use the narrowest, most disaggregated description possible? The answer is that accounting is an economic activity, and like all economic activities, it must be justified by a favorable cost-benefit relationship. We must weigh the benefit of providing more information against the cost of doing so.

There are many costs in using the narrowest and most specific description. Each time a $100 bill is changed, the event would have to be recorded. Recording this minor event is not cost-free. It requires utilization of employees, equipment, and other resources. Another, less obvious cost is also incurred. Since we record all such events, we presumably will communicate these events to the president and stockholders of the firm. If we inundate them with trivial information, we will distract their attention from more important information, thereby decreasing the effectiveness of accounting reports. To repeat, there is no one correct solution to this problem, since accounting attempts to communicate to different audiences with different interests, and therefore different information requirements.

A relatively narrow and specific description is aimed at the supervisor or clerk responsible for minor activities, and a broad general description is given the president who must make global decisions. Supervisors and clerks have narrow spheres of control; they need to be concerned with only a few events, but they need detailed and specific information about these events. The president needs information about the company as a whole, so this greater range of information must be more general and less detailed.

For the purposes of the president, the board of directors, and stockholders, who all make global decisions about the firm, the accountant should provide those details which will aid in estimating the amount, timing, and uncertainty of future cash flows. For example, cash and inventory have different expected cash consequences, and must be distinguished from each other. On the other hand, distinguishing between cash-on-hand and cash-in-the-bank is not worthwhile, since the location of the cash will not likely alter expected future cash flows.

Precision in accounting measurements must also meet a favorable cost-benefit standard. When we acquire merchandise in exchange for a promise to pay $1,000 in 30 days, we may wonder whether to quantify the responsibility as $1,000 or a slightly smaller amount. A smaller amount (about $996 if the monthly interest rate is $\frac{1}{2}$ percent) would be more exact, since an obligation to pay $1,000 right now would be quantified at $1,000. If we show $1,000 in 30 days also as $1,000, we have no way of distinguishing between a responsibility to pay $1,000 now and $1,000 thirty days from now. Nevertheless, we said that we would quantify the 30-day responsibility as $1,000. Why? Because the cost of distinguishing $1,000 now from $1,000 thirty days from now is greater than the additional benefit that would be provided by this information. If we did decide to quantify the 30-day, $1,000 responsibility as $996, we would then have to account for the "growth" of the responsibility from $996 to $1,000 over the 30-day period, a bothersome and costly activity which is not worth the effort.

> ### Thought Question
> Under what conditions would you want to distinguish between
> a responsibility in 30 days, and one due now?

In practice, achieving precision is not cost-free, and the costs must be weighed against the information benefit that precision provides. In statistics, we rarely survey all members of a population. Instead, we use a sample, thereby sacrificing some precision in order to achieve considerable cost-savings. Previously, we rejected as too narrow and specific the use of "$100 bills" as an asset category. This is just one of the reasons there can be no "absolute truth" in accounting: It is not untruthful to combine $100 bills and $10 bills into a category called "cash," nor is it "untruthful" to report both $1,000 due tomorrow and $1,000 due 30 days from now, as $1,000 responsibilities. Accounting is precise and specified only to the extent that precision and specificity are justified by favorable cost-benefit relationships. This underlies the accounting concept of *materiality,* which says that we recognize and quantify events only to the extent the benefit of the information outweighs the cost of acquiring it.

USER'S PERSPECTIVE

In Chapter 2, we saw that identical rights or responsibilities sometimes are, and sometimes are not, recognized as accounting responsibilities. In this chapter, we find that identical rights and responsibilities can be quantified by different amounts, and different rights and responsibilities can be quantified by the same amounts. We quantify the grabules we acquired in terms of the cash we paid or will pay, for example, $3,300. If we had acquired identical grabules from a different vendor at a different price, say $2,300 or $4,300, we would have quantified these grabules by a different amount. Alternatively, for $3,300, we could have acquired 90, 100, or 110 grabules. In this case the $3,300 describes different rights (number of grabules).

If we receive and accept an order to provide 100 grabules with a check for $8,000, we quantify our responsibility to provide grabules at $8,000. Had the same order been accompanied with a check for $4,000, we would have quantified our liability at $4,000, even though in both cases we have an identical legal obligation to provide 100 grabules.

Different responsibilities may be quantified by the same number. For example, a bank lends $1,000 to two firms for 1 year. One is a good credit risk, and the other a poorer credit risk. The obligation for the good credit risk firm will be to pay back $1,000 plus $100 of interest (10 percent), and the obligation for the poorer credit risk firm will be to pay back $1,000 plus $150 of interest (15 percent). Though the poorer credit risk firm will pay more than the good credit risk firm, both loans will be quantified at $1,000.

The fact that identical assets and liabilities may be quantified by different amounts, and different assets and liabilities may be quantified by the same amount, results because one of the effects of an event is always *independently quantified,* while the other effect is *dependently quantified.* When grabules are purchased for cash, the decrease in cash represents an independent quantification because it is quantified only by reference to how much cash was disbursed. It makes no difference whether the cash was spent for grabules, for repaying a loan, or for labor services. When $100 of cash is spent, cash will be decreased by $100.

On the other hand, the increase in grabules cannot be determined by reference to the grabules. If $100 was spent, grabules would increase by $100, but if only $95 was spent, the increase would only be $95, even though we may have acquired the same number of grabules. Thus, the increase in grabules is a dependent quantification; it depends on how much cash was spent. The same circumstance applies to bank loans or advances from customers. The bank loan is quantified not in terms of how much we will pay back, but in terms of the cash we received. The advances from customers are quantified not in terms of our obligation to provide grabules, but again in terms of the cash that we received.

Therefore, it is critically important, when looking at financial statements, to realize which numbers represent *dependent quantifications,* and which numbers represent *independent quantifications,* and to realize that firms with different amounts of assets and liabilities may have the same rights and obligations, while firms with the same net-assets may have different rights and obligations.

PROBLEMS

1. Which names and numbers would you use to describe the following events? For each *asset* or *equity* named, indicate whether the passage of time will necessarily affect it.
   a. A firm pays $1,000 as an incorporation fee and obtains a corporate charter.
   b. A firm buys raw material promising to pay $1,000 in 10 days.
   c. A firm borrows $1,000 at a bank promising to pay $1,050 in 30 days.
   d. A firm buys machinery promising to pay $10,000 in 6 months.
   e. A customer pays the firm $500 he owed.
   f. An officer of the firm embezzles $10,000.

2. In terms of names and numbers, how would you describe each event below?
   a. A firm issues 100 shares of stock for $10,000.
   b. A firm issues 100 shares of stock in exchange for a patent.
   c. A firm buys a machine for $1,000, payable in 10 days.
   d. A firm buys 100 grabules on credit for $1,000.
   e. A firm sells the 100 grabules for $1,150.

3. Given: Retained Earnings = 40% of Contributed Capital
   Stockholders' Equity = $\frac{7}{8}$ of Liabilities
   Assets = $300,000

   then   Liabilities = _____
   Retained Earnings = _____
   Contributed Capital = _____
   Owners' or Stockholders' Equity = _____

4. Given: Liabilities − Retained Earnings = $270,000
   Contributed Capital = $130,000
   Retained Earnings + $1,200,000 = Assets

   then   Assets = _____
   Liabilities = _____
   Retained Earnings = _____
   Owners' or Stockholders' Equity = _____

5. For each of the following independent events, try to decide whether the event would be recorded by the accountant. For those which are accounting events, quantify the effects of the events.
   a. The board of directors declares an ordinary cash dividend of $1.20 per share; 2,000,000 shares are outstanding.
   b. Six weeks after a dividend was declared, a company pays $700,000 in dividends to shareholders.
   c. A new legal counsel is hired for $100,000 per year.
   d. A football club signs a star quarterback to a 3-year contract for annual salaries of $200,000 in the first year, $250,000 in the second year, and $300,000 in the third year; he is also paid a $50,000 bonus for signing with the club.
   e. A construction company repairs the showroom of an automobile dealer; the repairs cost $10,000, and customers are usually charged $15,000 for such repairs. Instead of paying cash for the repairs, the automobile dealer gives the construction company a new car. The car lists for $16,000 and costs the automobile company $12,500.

6. Every accounting event has two effects, both quantified by the same number. Since the effects can only be to increase (↑) or decrease (↓)

assets, liabilities, contributed capital, and retained earnings:
a. Show that there are 16 combinations of accounting events.
b. If you can, provide an example for each event listed in part a.

7. Prepare a chart indicating the effects of the following events on assets, liabilities, contributed capital, retained earnings, and stockholders' equity. Indicate increases with up-arrows (↑), decreases with down-arrows (↓), and no change with (N), and how you would quantify each event.
a. Sale of common stock for cash
b. Payment on account to wholesale suppliers
c. Credit purchase of raw materials
d. Payment in advance of rent for use of a building
e. Exchange of cash plus an old truck for a new truck
f. Collection of cash from credit customers
g. Cash purchase of office furniture
h. Deposit of cash in the bank
i. Utilization of 1 week's services to be paid for at the end of next week
j. Receipt of cash for 12 magazine issues to be delivered monthly next year

8. For each of the following assets and equities, indicate whether they are quantified by past, present, or future cash flows. Identify the cash flow.
a. Accounts Receivable
b. Inventory
c. Property, Plant and Equipment
d. Wages Payable
e. Bank Loan
f. Contributed Capital

9. Under what circumstances would the accounts listed in Question 8 be quantified by the third quantification rule (page 45)?

10. Determine which of the following assets and equities are *independently quantified* and which ones are *dependently quantified*. For those accounts that you determine are dependently quantified, explain on what they are dependent.
a. Dividends Payable
b. Cash
c. Contributed Capital
d. Advances from Customers
e. Property, Plant and Equipment
f. Finished Goods
g. Accumulated Depreciation
h. Interest Payable
i. Taxes Payable

11. Give examples of events that
a. Increase net-assets, but not *residual net-assets*.
b. Decrease net-assets, but not residual net-assets.
c. Increase residual net-assets.
d. Decrease residual net-assets.
e. Do not alter the balance of assets or equities.

CHAPTER 4

The First Day of The American Grabule Company: Debits, Credits, and the Balance Sheet

INTRODUCTION

A corporation's basic events fall into four simple categories:

1. Acquisition of cash, goods, and services
2. Transformation of services (usually by manufacturing operations)
3. Sales
4. Payments

A simplified example will show how some of these basic events are analyzed and recorded by the accountant.

THE AMERICAN GRABULE COMPANY

The genius who founded The American Grabule Company perfected a secret process by which marbles and a chemical solution are combined to produce grabules. The following events, which occurred during the first day of the company's existence, are listed according to the categories above, not in actual order of occurrence.

Acquisition of Assets

The Acquisition of Cash

Event 1 At the beginning of the day, The American Grabule Company, a newly-formed and chartered organization, sold 1,000 shares of common stock for $100 per share.

Event 2   At the end of the day, the company obtained a $50,000, 2-year loan from the bank in exchange for a note promising to pay $9,125 1 year from now, and $59,125 in 2 years.

The Acquisition of Goods and Services

Event 3   At the beginning of the day, the company acquired 600 marbles for conversion into grabules, promising to pay $5,400 in two install-ments—$3,000 at the end of the day, and $2,400 at the end of 30 days.

Event 4   At the beginning of the day, the company acquired two vats of chemical solution, and paid a total of $848 cash for them.

Event 5   The company needed space and machinery in order to manufacture grabules. At the beginning of the day, it leased space and machinery for 1 week (5 days) at a cost of $480. The lessor, not a convinced believer in grabules, demanded and received the entire payment in advance.

Event 6   At the end of the day, the company acquired a truck for delivery of grabules. It paid $26,500 in cash for the truck which was expected to have a useful life of 5 years. At the end of 5 years, it would have an estimated residual value of $500.

Event 7   Two employees were hired. Lomax was hired at the beginning of the day at $10.00 per hour to manufacture the grabules, and she insisted on being paid at the end of each day for that day's work. At the end of the day, Anderson was hired at $12.50 per hour to perform all other essential activities and he agreed to be paid at the end of each week.

Transformation of Services

Event 8   During the first day, 300 marbles were combined with 1 vat of chemicals, 1 day's space and machine services, and 8 hours of labor services.

Event 9   By the end of the day, the transformation process was complete and 300 glorious grabules emerged.

Sales Orders

Event 10   During the first day, the company accepted two orders. One was for 100 grabules and the other for 65 grabules. Both orders were at a price of $80 per grabule, but the order for 100 grabules was accompanied by a check for $8,000, while the order for 65 grabules was payable 3 days after delivery.

Payments

Event 11   At the end of the day, the company paid the $3,000 owed to suppliers of marbles.

Event 12   At the end of the day, the company paid Lomax $80 for her labor services in manufacturing grabules.

These were the explicit events of The American Grabule Company's inaugural day. The next morning, Anderson was asked to memorialize these events in the accounting records. Let us follow his analysis in seeking to account for the first day's activities.

DEBITS AND CREDITS

Event 1   Issue of Common Stock

The corporation's expected future benefits increased by virtue of the cash received. The company, in return, assumed certain responsibilities for providing resources to the owners of these shares. The effects of the stock issue are to increase *Cash* and increase *Common Stock*. The preferred measurement of these effects is $100,000, the amount by which Cash increased. The effects of this event are

Cash ↑ increases	100,000
Common Stock ↑ increases	100,000

At this point let us pause to explore the mystery of **debits** and **credits.** Debits and credits are nothing more than a system of controls that makes it easy to detect errors. We know that each accounting event has two effects and both effects are quantified by the same number, or absolute value. If one effect has a minus sign and the other a plus, then the two effects of the event will sum to zero. Should any sum other than zero emerge for an event, or any combination of events, obviously a mistake must have been made. Periodic checks will tell us whether the effects indeed sum to zero. However, as we can see in our very first event, both effects of an accounting event may represent increases and, psychologically, it is difficult to associate a minus sign with an increase.

To solve this conundrum, someone in antiquity had the bright idea of placing one of the effects of an accounting event on the left and the other effect of the event on the right—instead of assigning pluses and minuses.

Since the two effects of an accounting event are quantified by the same number, the numbers on the left must always equal the numbers on the right. If they are not equal, we know a mistake has been made. This clever practice survives to this day.

All that was needed to perfect this system of controls were rules for determining which effects were to be placed on the left and which effects were to be placed on the right. Two assumptions were sufficient to explain and generate all of the rules. First, **an asset will always increase on the left.** Second, **there must be consistency in placing effects.** That is, if an effect is placed on the left once, then it will always be placed on the left; and an effect placed on the right will always appear there.

There are only four combinations of effects on assets and equities:

An asset increase ↑ and an asset decrease ↓ .

An asset increase ↑ and an equity increase ↑ .

An equity decrease ↓ and an equity increase ↑ .

An equity decrease ↓ and an asset decrease ↓ .

One of the effects of each of these accounting events will always be placed on the left, and one always on the right. Since an asset increase is placed on the left, it logically follows that an asset decrease will be placed on the right, an equity increase will be placed on the right, and an equity decrease will be placed on the left.

One further detail: An effect placed on the left is called a *debit* and an effect placed on the right is called a *credit*. That represents the total significance of the words debits and credits.

People tend to think of debits (lefts) and credits (rights) in terms of value judgments, with debits (lefts) denoting something bad, and credits (rights) denoting something good. This is obviously not the accounting point of view. First, every accounting event has **both** a debit (left) and a credit (right). Since one cannot exist without the other, it doesn't make sense to call one side bad and the other good. Second, we need only look at our first accounting event, where the increase in Cash is a debit (placed on the left) and the increase in Common Stock is a credit (placed on the right). Would anyone maintain that an increase in Cash, although a debit, is something bad or undesirable?

> ### *Thought Questions*
> Can an event have only one debit or only one credit?
> Can an event have more than one debit
> and/or more than one credit?

ANALYSIS OF THE FIRST DAY'S EVENTS

Having solved the mystery of debits and credits, we can record the effects of Event (1) as a debit (Dr.) to the asset Cash for $100,000, and a credit (Cr.) to the equity Common Stock for $100,000. Recording an accounting event by describing the two effects of the event (as well as indicating the date) is called making a *journal entry* or simply an *entry*. (Conventionally, the debit effect is always listed first.)

(1) Dr. Cash	100,000	
Cr. Common Stock		100,000

Event 2 Borrowing from the Bank

The company borrowed $50,000 from the bank. The effects of this event are to increase (Dr.) the asset Cash, and increase (Cr.) *Bank Loan*, the liability to pay the bank back. The preferred measurement of these effects is $50,000, the amount by which cash increased. The *entry* to record this event is

(2) Dr. Cash	50,000	
Cr. Bank Loan		50,000

Event 3 Purchase of Marbles

Our fledgling corporation acquired 600 marbles on credit, promising to pay $5,400 in two installments—$3,000 at the end of the first day, and $2,400 more after 30 days. Since the company expects to produce grabules by combining marbles with the chemical solution, the marbles represent an essential source of future benefits. The effects of this event are to increase (Dr.) the asset *Raw Materials and Supplies*, and increase (Cr.) the liability *Accounts Payable*. The preferred measurement of these effects is $5,400 because the increase in the responsibility represents a virtually certain cash decrease. The entry to record this event is

(3) Dr. Raw Materials and Supplies	5,400	
Cr. Accounts Payable		5,400

Event 4 Purchase of Chemicals

By paying $848, the company acquired two vats of chemicals for use in manufacturing grabules. The analysis here is simple. The effects of this event are to increase (Dr.) the asset Raw Materials and Supplies, and decrease (Cr.) the asset Cash. The preferred measurement of these effects is $848, the amount by which cash decreased. The entry to record this event is

(4) Dr. Raw Materials and Supplies   848
        Cr. Cash   848

Event 5 Renting of Space and Machine

Space and machine services are needed for the manufacture of grabules, so the company rented fully equipped factory space for $480 per week. The right to use these premises clearly represents a right to utilize economic resources because grabules cannot be produced and then sold without utilizing space and machine services. The effects of this event are to increase (Dr.) the asset Space and Machine Services (usually called *Prepaid Services*), and decrease (Cr.) the asset Cash. The preferred measurement of these effects is $480, measured by the amount of cash disbursed for these services. The entry to record this event is

(5) Dr. Prepaid Services   480
        Cr. Cash   480

> ### *Thought Questions*
> If the company had not paid in advance,
> but had rented the same space
> and promised to pay at the end of the week,
> how would the right to use space have been changed?
> How would accounting assets have changed?

Event 6 Purchase of Truck

When the truck was purchased for $26,500 the company acquired 5 years (260 weeks) of truck services as well as an expected salvage value of $500. The effects of the acquisition of the truck are to increase (Dr.) the asset Truck Services (usually referred to as *Property, Plant and Equipment*), and to decrease (Cr.) the asset Cash. The preferred measurement of these effects is $26,500, measured by the amount of cash that changed hands. The entry to record this event is

(6) Dr. Property, Plant and Equipment   26,500
        Cr. Cash   26,500

Event 7 Hiring of Employees

Lomax was hired at the beginning of the first day at $10.00 per hour, to perform the manufacturing operations, and she was to be paid at the end of each day. Anderson was hired at the end of the first day at $12.50 per hour, to perform all other essential activities, and he was to be paid at the end of each week. In hiring these employees, the firm acquired potential benefits, namely, the rights to utilize their services.

Thought Question

How might the acquisition and utilization
of labor services be reported?

Anderson knew that the hiring of employees was not an accounting event and therefore could not be recorded. However, he realized that by the end of the first day, 8 hours of Lomax's labor services had been acquired, utilized, and paid for. Anderson concluded that this represented a transformation of (labor) services into manufactured product, and he would deal with recording it later [see Event (8)]. He would treat the payment for services as a separate event, which he would also record later [see Event (12)].

Event 8 Manufacture of Grabules

In our imaginary firm, 300 marbles were treated with chemicals and transformed into 300 grabules. In this process, 300 marbles, 1 vat of chemicals, 1 day's space and machine services, and 8 hours of labor services were utilized to produce the 300 grabules. Anderson must analyze and record this event in terms of rights and responsibilities.

What was originally represented as the right to utilize an economic resource, became services utilized. Did this utilization result in a right to utilize a new nonmonetary asset? In our example, the answer is clearly **yes,** since the utilization of these services created the right to utilize the resulting grabules.

Thought Question

When will the grabules yield benefits?
How can the expected future benefits of grabules be quantified?

The manufacture of grabules can be separated into four events representing the conversion of specific materials and services.

Event 8a Conversion of Marbles

Three hundred marbles were utilized in the manufacturing process. The effects of this event are to increase (Dr.) the asset *Work-in-*

Process, and decrease (Cr.) the asset Raw Materials and Supplies. The company originally acquired 600 marbles and quantified this purchase at $5,400 [see Event (3)]; since half of these marbles were transformed into grabules, the preferred measurement of these effects is $2,700. The entry to record this event is

(8a) Dr. Work-in-Process   2,700
       Cr. Raw Materials and Supplies   2,700

Event 8b   Conversion of Chemicals

One vat of chemicals was utilized in the manufacturing process. The effects of this event are to increase (Dr.) the asset Work-in-Process, and decrease (Cr.) the asset Raw Materials and Supplies. Since two vats of chemicals, costing a total of $848, were acquired for the manufacture of grabules [see Event (4)], and one vat of chemicals was utilized in the manufacturing process, the preferred measurement of these effects is one-half of $848 (the existing quantification), or $424. The entry to record this event is

(8b) Dr. Work-in-Process   424
       Cr. Raw Materials and Supplies   424

Event 8c   Conversion of Space and Machine Services

One day's space and machine services was utilized in the manufacturing operation [see Event (5)]. The effects of this event are to increase (Dr.) the asset Work-in-Process, and decrease (Cr.) the asset Prepaid Services. Since $480 was prepaid for 5 days of space and machine services, the preferred measurement of these effects is one-fifth of $480 (the existing quantification), or $96. The entry to record this event is

(8c) Dr. Work-in-Process   96
       Cr. Prepaid Services   96

Event 8d   Acquisition and Utilization of Labor Services

The creation of grabules required not only the acquisition and utilization of marbles, chemicals, space and machinery; it also required the acquisition and utilization of labor services. For each of the other conversions in the manufacturing process, we recorded an entry showing an increase in the asset Work-in-Process and a decrease in an existing asset. Clearly, the acquisition and utilization of Lomax's labor services in the manufacturing process must also increase the asset Work-in-Process. But then what other asset could decrease, or what equity could increase? Since Anderson never recorded the hiring of Lomax [see Event (7)], there is no asset to decrease.

When a resource that has **not** been previously recognized as an accounting asset has been utilized, acquisition and utilization occur simultaneously, and an obligation (liability) to pay for the resource has been incurred. Therefore, the effects of this event are to increase (Dr.) the asset Work-in-Process, and increase (Cr.) the liability *Wages Payable*. The preferred measurement of these effects is $80, the cash we will pay Lomax for 1 day's work. The entry to record this event is

(8d) Dr. Work-in-Process   80
       Cr. Wages Payable   80

The **composite** effects of entries a, b, c, and d of entry 8 are

(8) Dr. Work-in-Process   3,300
       Cr. Raw Materials and Supplies   3,124
       Cr. Prepaid Services   96
       Cr. Wages Payable   80

Event 9 Completion of the Manufacturing Process

Since all the grabules that were started at the beginning of the day were completed by the end of the day, Anderson reclassified the completed grabules as Finished Goods. The effects of this event are to increase (Dr.) the asset *Finished Goods,* and decrease (Cr.) the asset Work-in-Process. The preferred measurement of these effects is $3,300, and the entry to record this event is

(9) Dr. Finished Goods   3,300
       Cr. Work-in-Process   3,300

Event 10 Sales Orders

The company accepted two sales orders on the first day. One for 100 grabules was accompanied by an $8,000 check; the other, for 65 grabules, with a promise to pay in full 3 days after delivery. For the order not accompanied by payment, nothing is recorded, since this order merely represents an exchange of promises where neither side has performed. However, the order which was accompanied by payment must be recognized because the customer has performed. The effects of this event are to increase (Dr.) the asset Cash, and to increase (Cr.) the liability *Advances from Customers*. The preferred measurement of these effects is $8,000, the cash received from customers. The entry to record this event is

(10) Dr. Cash	8,000	
Cr. Advances from Customers		8,000

> ### *Thought Questions*
> Is the responsibility to customers $8,000?
> What would the responsibility be if only $4,000 were received?
> How would the responsibility be quantified?

Event 11 Payment to Supplier of Raw Materials and Supplies

The American Grabule Company paid $3,000 to its supplier of raw materials and supplies. The effects of the event are to decrease (Dr.) the liability *Accounts Payable,* and to decrease (Cr.) the asset Cash. The preferred measurement of these effects is $3,000, cash disbursed to pay the supplier. The entry to record this event is

(11) Dr. Accounts Payable	3,000	
Cr. Cash		3,000

Event 12 Payment to Supplier of Labor Services

The company agreed to pay Lomax at the end of each day's work. The effects of paying Lomax are to decrease (Dr.) the liability Wages Payable, and to decrease (Cr.) the asset Cash. The preferred measurement of these effects is $80, the amount of cash disbursed to pay for her services. The entry to record this event is

(12) Dr. Wages Payable	80	
Cr. Cash		80

SUMMARY OF THE FIRST DAY'S EVENTS

Listed below is a summary of the effects of the first day's events:

(1) Issue of Common Stock
        Dr. Cash   100,000
                Cr. Common Stock   100,000

(2) Borrowing from the Bank
        Dr. Cash   50,000
                Cr. Bank Loan   50,000

(3) Purchase of Marbles
        Dr. Raw Materials and Supplies   5,400
                Cr. Accounts Payable   5,400

(4) Purchase of Chemicals
        Dr. Raw Materials and Supplies   848
                Cr. Cash   848

(5) Renting of Space and Machine
        Dr. Prepaid Services   480
                Cr. Cash   480

(6) Purchase of Truck
        Dr. Property, Plant and Equipment   26,500
                Cr. Cash   26,500

(7) Hiring of Employees   No Entries

(8) Manufacture of Grabules
        Dr. Work-in-Process   3.300
                Cr. Raw Materials and Supplies (a)   2,700
                Cr. Raw Materials and Supplies (b)   424
                Cr. Prepaid Services (c)   96
                Cr. Wages Payable (d)   80

(9) Completion of the Manufacturing Process
        Dr. Finished Goods   3,300
                Cr. Work-in-Process   3,300

(10) Sales Orders (Advances from Customers)
        Dr. Cash   8,000
                Cr. Advances from Customers   8,000

(11) Payment to Supplier of Raw Materials and Supplies
        Dr. Accounts Payable   3,000
                Cr. Cash   3,000

(12) Payment to Supplier of Labor Services
        Dr. Wages Payable   80
                Cr. Cash   80

STORAGE DEVICES: T-ACCOUNTS

Journal entries like those that we just developed, suitably dated and listed in chronological order, form the accountant's initial recognition of accounting events. Such a series of journal entries represents a *journal*. A *journal entry* is the accountant's initial recognition that an event has occurred and has affected assets and equities.

A journal entry in actual practice might not consist of a pen and ink recording of the effects of the event. For instance, copies of checks or invoices or vouchers often serve as journal entries. Anything that lists the categories affected, the appropriate quantification, and the date will do.

The accountant wants to report what these effects were, but does not want to communicate these events and their effects instantaneously, or even daily. The accountant, therefore, creates storage devices to collect the effects of recognized events on the categories of assets and equities that are affected. The rules for doing this are quite simple. A clerk or a computer is instructed to create a storage device for each category of asset and equity affected by the accounting events and recorded by a journal entry. Each storage device has a left (debit) side and a right (credit) side. These storage devices are called *accounts* or *ledger accounts* and the sum of all these accounts is called the *general ledger.*

The quantified effects of all recognized events are stored in the appropriate storage device for each category. The clerk or computer is further instructed to store each debit effect on the left side of the storage device, and each credit effect on the right side of the storage device. Since all entries have equal debits and credits, the sum of the numbers stored on the left must equal the sum of the numbers stored on the right, for all *accounts* taken as a whole.

Since there are only four possible types of journal entries:

Dr. Asset (increase)
    Cr. Asset (decrease)

Dr. Asset (increase)
    Cr. Equity (increase)

Dr. Equity (decrease)
    Cr. Equity (increase)

Dr. Equity (decrease)
    Cr. Asset (decrease)

it follows that asset increases and equity decreases are stored on the left (debit) side, and equity increases and asset decreases are stored on the right (credit) side.

While a *ledger account* may be a stack of computer cards or a memory cell in a computer or a page in an ancient ledger, the simplest representation for our purpose is to divide a page in half by drawing a line down the center (effectively separating left from right), and then drawing a horizontal line on top to provide a resting place for the name of the account. This representation is called a **T-account.**

$$
\begin{array}{c|c}
\multicolumn{2}{c}{\text{Title}} \\
\hline
\text{Debit} & \text{Credit}
\end{array}
$$

Now we will integrate *debits* and *credits* with *T-accounts*. An asset T-account will have an asset title on the horizontal line, an up-arrow (↑) indicating an increase on the left side (debit), and a down-arrow (↓) indicating a decrease on the right side (credit).

$$
\begin{array}{c|c}
\uparrow \quad \text{Asset} \quad \downarrow \\
\hline
\text{Debit} & \text{Credit}
\end{array}
$$

An equity T-account will have an equity title on the horizontal line, an up-arrow (↑) indicating an increase on the right side (credit), and a down-arrow (↓) indicating a decrease on the left side (debit).

$$
\begin{array}{c|c}
\downarrow \quad \text{Equity} \quad \uparrow \\
\hline
\text{Debit} & \text{Credit}
\end{array}
$$

At any point in time, the balance of any account can be determined. For assets, the balance in the account is the sum of all increases (debits), less the sum of all decreases (credits) ever made to the account until that point in time. Should the sum of all the decreases (credits) exceed the sum of all the increases (debits) for an asset account, the account would then be listed as an equity account, rather than as an asset account. For example, if Accounts Receivable had a negative balance, then the account would be Accounts Payable, an equity account.

For equities, the balance in the account is the sum of all increases (credits), less the sum of all decreases (debits) ever made to the account until that point in time. Should the sum of decreases (debits) exceed the sum of increases (credits) for an equity account, the account would no longer be listed as an equity account, but rather as an asset account. For example, if Accounts Payable (for services) had a negative balance, then the account would be Prepaid Services, an asset account.

RECORDING THE EFFECTS OF EVENTS

After recording the 12 entries, we obtain the following T-account entries and ending balances (EB):

↑	Cash	↓	↑	Raw Materials and Supplies	↓	↓	Accounts Payable	↑
(1) 100,000		848 (4)	(3) 5,400		2,700 (8a)	(11) 3,000		5,400 (3)
(2) 50,000		480 (5)	(4) 848		424 (8b)			
(10) 8,000		26,500 (6)						
		3,000 (11)						
		80 (12)						
EB 127,092			EB 3,124					2,400 EB

↑	Property, Plant and Equipment	↓	↑	Prepaid Services	↓	↓	Wages Payable	↑
(6) 26,500			(5) 480		96 (8c)	(12) 80		80 (8d)
EB 26,500			EB 384					0 EB

↑	Work-in-Process	↓	↓	Bank Loan	↑
(8a) 2,700		3,300 (9)			50,000 (2)
(8b) 424					
(8c) 96					
(8d) 80					
EB 0					50,000 EB

↑	Finished Goods	↓	↓	Common Stock	↑
(9) 3,300					100,000 (1)
EB 3,300					100,000 EB

↓	Advances from Customers	↑
		8,000 (10)
		8,000 EB

Notice that the balance in an asset account is always on the left (debit balance), while the balance in an equity account is always on the right (credit balance). To see the cumulative effect of the events recorded so far, a clerk or computer can prepare a list of the balances in the accounts, as follows:

Accounts	Debit Balances	Credit Balances
Cash	$127,092	
Prepaid Services	384	
Raw Materials and Supplies	3,124	
Finished Goods	3,300	
Property, Plant and Equipment	26,500	
Accounts Payable		2,400
Advances from Customers		8,000
Bank Loan		50,000
Common Stock		100,000
Total	$160,400	$160,400

Reorder the list so that all assets and all equities are grouped together, add the name of the company, attach the date, and presto! you have a *balance sheet.*

The American Grabule Company
Balance Sheet
End of the First Day

Assets

Cash	$127,092
Prepaid Services	384
Raw Materials and Supplies	3,124
Finished Goods	3,300
Property, Plant and Equipment	26,500
Total Assets	$160,400

Equities

Accounts Payable	$ 2,400
Advances from Customers	8,000
Bank Loan	50,000
Common Stock	100,000
Total Equities	$160,400

What does the *balance sheet* report about cash flows? Every number reported in the balance sheet represents a cash flow that has occurred or will occur. Refer to the balance sheet for The American Grabule Company. The balance in the Cash account represents the cash on hand after all receipts and disbursements. The balance in the Prepaid Services account represents the cash paid for space services to be utilized in the future. The balances in the Raw Materials and Supplies and the Property, Plant and Equipment accounts represent the cash paid for the acquisition of marbles, chemicals, and a truck. The balance in the Finished Goods account represents the cash that was paid for rented space, labor services, and chemicals, and the cash that has been and will be paid for marbles that were input into the process of manufacturing grabules.

The balance in the Accounts Payable account represents the cash payments to suppliers of raw materials, and the balance in the Advances from Customers account represents the cash that has been received from customers, for grabules still to be shipped. The balances in the Bank Loan and the Common Stock accounts represent the cash that has been received from creditors and owners, respectively.

All of the asset balances (excluding Cash) result from direct or indirect cash sacrifices that have been incurred with the expectation that these sacrifices will result in future cash benefits. All of the liability and equity balances result from the direct or indirect cash benefits that have been received and are expected to require future sacrifices.

> ### Thought Question
> In what way does the balance in Accounts Payable represent cash benefits that have been received?

USER'S PERSPECTIVE

The balance sheet reports the cumulative effect of all events recognized by the accountant on the asset and equity categories of the firm, since the firm began. For example, the cash balance of $127,092 reported in the balance sheet says that during the entire history of the firm, events defined by the accountant as increasing cash (cash receipts) exceeded events defined by the accountant as decreasing cash (cash disbursements) by $127,092.

At best, the balance sheet gives only a very imprecise picture. For instance, it tells us nothing about the amount of cash actually available for use. Anyone who has ever done a bank reconciliation realizes that the amount we have available to spend according to the bank may be quite a different number than the balance in our checkbooks. We recognize the receipt of a check as an event increasing cash, but it is available to be spent only after it is deposited and then clears the bank, which sometimes seems to take an eternity. We record the writing of a check as an event decreasing cash. The bank, however, decreases our available balance only when that check is deposited and clears the bank. We won't even mention such other complicating factors as compensating balance requirements. If a primitive category like cash is so hard to pin down, imagine the problem of trying to let the dollar balance in an account project a concrete image of inventory (grabules), or of property, plant and equipment (truck).

As we stated earlier, each balance on the balance sheet should be thought of merely as the difference between events defined as increasing an account and events defined as decreasing an account. For that reason, *comparative balance sheets,* balance sheets for two dates, become so important. The earlier balances are the cumulative effects of all events increasing and decreasing the accounts since the inception of the firm until the earlier date. The later balances are the cumulative effects of all events increasing and decreasing the accounts since the inception of the firm until the later date. **Therefore, the differences between the two balances of all accounts represent the cumulative effects of all events that increased or decreased the accounts during the period between balance sheet dates.**

The American Grabule Company
Comparative Balance Sheets
Beginning and End of the First Day

Assets	Beg. of Day 1	End of Day 1	Account Changes
Cash	$0	$127,092	$127,092
Prepaid Services	0	384	384
Raw Materials and Supplies	0	3,124	3,124
Finished Goods	0	3,300	3,300
Property, Plant and Equipment	0	26,500	26,500
Total Assets	$0	$160,400	
Equities			
Accounts Payable	$0	$ 2,400	$ 2,400
Advances from Customers	0	8,000	8,000
Bank Loan	0	50,000	50,000
Common Stock	0	100,000	100,000
Total Equities	$0	$160,400	

ACTIVITY STATEMENTS

Returning to our example, the $127,092 ending cash balance on the balance sheet says that from the firm's beginning until the end of the first day, cash receipts exceeded cash disbursements by $127,092. The zero cash balance on the beginning balance sheet says that from the moment the firm began until the beginning of the first day (the same moment in time), cash receipts were equal to cash disbursements. Therefore, cash receipts exceeded cash disbursements by $127,092 **during the first day.** This is more relevant and useful information than merely knowing what the excess of cash receipts over cash disbursements was since the beginning of the firm.

As useful as this 1-day total might be, it still does not tell us the specific events (cash receipts and disbursements) that occurred. Was there one cash receipt of $127,092 and no cash disbursements? Were there many cash receipts totaling $1,127,092 and many diverse cash disbursements totaling $1,000,000? Who were the cash receipts from? What did The American Grabule Company have to do to get them? Whom did they pay? Why? An infinite set of events could have created the cash balance of $127,092.

These questions can be answered if, in addition to the comparative balances in the balance sheets, we prepare an *activity statement* that lists all cash events that occurred during the period. If such a statement, called the **statement of cash receipts and disbursements** were prepared for The American Grabule Company, it would appear as follows:

The American Grabule Company
Statement of Cash Receipts and Disbursements
First Day

Cash Receipts

Issue of Common Stock	$100,000
Borrowing from Bank	50,000
Deposits from Customer	8,000
Total Cash Receipts	$158,000

Cash Disbursements

Payment to Supplier of Chemicals	$ 848
Payment of Rent	480
Purchase of Truck	26,500
Payment to Supplier of Marbles	3,000
Payment to Supplier of Labor Services	80
Total Cash Disbursements	$ 30,908
Excess Cash Receipts over Disbursements	$127,092

We would know about the occurrence of each cash event from the *statement of cash receipts and disbursements,* and the cumulative effect of all cash events on assets and equities from the *comparative balance sheets,* if both statements were provided.

If we prepare a statement of cash receipts and disbursements and a balance sheet, we would report two aspects of cash events: the occurrence of the specific cash events during the first day (in the statement of cash receipts and disbursements), and the cumulative effects of all the cash events that occurred during the first day (on the asset and equity accounts in the balance sheet).

Although accounting rules do not call for the presentation of the statement of cash receipts and disbursements, they do require two *activity statements:* the statement of cash flows and the income statement. The statement of cash flows, discussed in Chapter 6, presents cash receipts and disbursements classified in terms of operating, financing, and investing events. The income statement, which is the topic of the next chapter, presents the events affecting residual net-assets—revenues and expenses.

PROBLEMS

1. What information can you deduce from each of the following bits of information?
   a. Cash increased from $10,000 to $32,000.
   b. Accounts Receivable increased from $50,000 to $75,000.
   c. Inventory decreased from $40,000 to $35,000.
   d. Prepaid Services increased from $6,000 to $8,000.
   e. Accounts Payable Merchandise increased from $10,000 to $14,000.
   f. Bank Loan increased from $0 to $20,000.
   g. Common Stock increased from $80,000 to $85,000.
   h. Retained Earnings increased from $16,000 to $31,000.

2. Provide accounting descriptions (two names and one number) for the following unrelated events:
   a. Raw materials costing $15,000 are purchased on account.
   b. An office machine is purchased for $6,000; $1,200 is paid in cash, and the balance is payable in 24 equal monthly payments.
   c. A $16,000 check is issued for 2 years' insurance on the sales showroom.
   d. $5,000 is paid on account to suppliers of merchandise.

3. Describe the effects of each of the following events, using names, numbers, and direction (debit or credit):
   a. Company A sells 100,000 shares of its common stock for $10 per share.
   b. Company B buys a 3-year insurance policy for $150.
   c. Company C buys a machine in exchange for 100 shares of its common stock that trade at $2,000 per share.
   d. Company D
      i. Buys 100 grabules on credit for $1,000.
      ii. Collects $500 from customers.

4. Given the following accounts, what events are most probably described by each pair of letters? Note that every letter is used twice to show the **two** effects of each event.

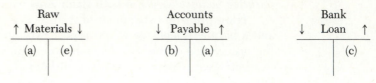

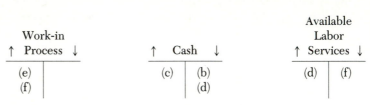

5. List the events described by each of the pair of letters and identify the three accounts that are not titled. One event is described incorrectly. Which one? How do you know it is wrong?

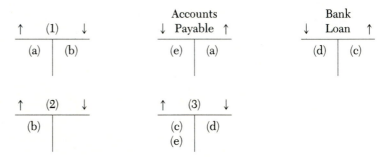

6. Make journal entries for the following events:
   a. Payments for credit purchases of raw materials in the amount of $200,000
   b. Purchases of inventory for cash in the amount of $150,000
   c. Borrowing $400,000 from a bank
   d. Labor services of $150,000 utilized in the manufacturing process
   e. Payments to suppliers of factory labor services for $135,000
   f. Property, plant and equipment acquired for $80,000 in cash
   g. Raw materials of $325,000 utilized in the manufacturing process
   h. Credit purchases of raw materials for $175,000
   i. Issue of common stock for $100,000 in cash

7. As a result of the events in Question 6, what was the change in
   a. Cash
   b. Assets
   c. Net-assets
   d. Residual net-assets

8. From the following events, determine
   a. Purchases of raw material
   b. Raw materials utilized in the manufacturing process
   c. The difference between the beginning and ending balances in the Accounts Payable Raw Materials account
   (1) Labor utilized in the manufacturing process was $100,000.
   (2) The utilization of all manufacturing services, other than labor and material, was $90,000.
   (3) The balance in the Work-in-Process account decreased by $10,000.
   (4) Goods completed in the manufacturing process were $360,000.
   (5) The balance in the Raw Materials account increased by $15,000.
   (6) Payments to suppliers of raw materials were $200,000.

9. If the ending balance of Raw Materials was $50,000 **greater than** its beginning balance, and the ending balance in Accounts Payable Raw Materials was $10,000 **less than** its beginning balance, then RAW MATERIALS INPUT INTO THE MANUFACTURING PROCESS was greater than or less than PAYMENTS TO SUPPLIERS OF RAW MATERIALS by $_____, or they were equal.

10. If PAYMENTS TO SUPPLIERS OF MERCHANDISE were $100,000, and the ending balance in Accounts Payable Merchandise was **greater than** its beginning balance by $50,000, then PURCHASES OF INVENTORY were $_____.

11. If PAYMENTS TO SUPPLIERS OF RAW MATERIALS were **less than** RAW MATERIALS INPUT INTO THE MANUFACTURING PROCESS, then either the beginning balance of the _____ account must be greater than, less than, or equal to its ending balance, or the beginning balance of the _____ account is greater than, less than, or equal to its ending balance.

12. If during a period, PURCHASES OF INVENTORY were $250,000, and the balance in Accounts Payable Merchandise decreased by $25,000, can you determine what PAYMENTS TO SUPPLIERS OF MERCHANDISE were without knowing cash purchases?

CHAPTER 5

The Second Day of The American Grabule Company: The Income Statement

INTRODUCTION

Accounting utilizes two forms of reports. One is the balance sheet, which describes the cumulative effect of all events on the assets and equities of the firm. The other form of report is the event statement, which reports the occurrence of certain events considered critically important. Two such event statements are required: the income statement and the statement of cash flows. The *income statement,* which is the topic of this chapter, reports all operating events that affect the *residual net-assets* of the firm. The *statement of cash flows,* discussed in Chapter 6, reports cash receipts and disbursements classified in terms of operating, financing, and investing events.

EVENTS THAT OCCURRED DURING THE SECOND DAY

The gods continued to smile on The American Grabule Company during its second day of operations. The following events occurred:

Event 13   During the second day, the company bought an additional 1,400 marbles for $12,600. Because of their prompt payment the first day, the company was able to obtain credit for the purchase of marbles, and the payment is due at the end of the month.

Event 14   Six additional vats of chemicals costing $2,544 were acquired and paid for in cash.

Event 15   In a replay of the first day's manufacturing process, 300 marbles, 1 vat of chemicals, 1 day's space and machine services, and 8 hours of Lomax's labor services were combined to produce 300 grabules.

Event 16   By the end of the second day, 300 grabules emerged.

Event 17   Lomax was paid $80 at the end of the second day.

Event 18   At the beginning of the second day, the company acquired additional space for office and store use, paying a week's rent of $375 in advance.

Event 19   During the day, the company filled the two sales orders it had
and   received the first day and also sold 400 grabules for cash. The selling
Event 20   price for each grabule sold was $80.

Event 21   At the end of the second day, Anderson recorded the utilization of 1 day's rented space for selling and administrative services.

Event 22   At the end of the second day, Anderson recorded the company's utilization of his administrative services during the second day.

Event 23   At the end of the second day, Anderson recorded the utilization of the truck during the second day.

Event 24   At the end of the second day, Anderson recorded the utilization of borrowed cash (the loan) during the second day.

Event 25   At the end of the second day, the company acquired a patent in exchange for 100 shares of its common stock.

Event 26   The American Grabule Company declared a cash dividend at the end of the second day.

RECORDING THE EFFECTS OF THE EVENTS OF THE SECOND DAY

Recording the purchase of additional marbles and chemicals, the manufacture of grabules, the payment of wages, and the prepayment of rent did not present a problem for Anderson, since they represented repetitions of previously recorded events. He recorded them just as he did on the first day (see page 73), as follows:

(13) Purchase of Marbles
        Dr. Raw Materials and Supplies   12,600
            Cr. Accounts Payable   12,600

(14) Purchase of Chemicals
        Dr. Raw Materials and Supplies   2,544
            Cr. Cash   2,544

(15) Manufacture of Grabules

Dr. Work-in-Process	3,300	
Cr. Raw Materials and Supplies		3,124
Cr. Prepaid Services		96
Cr. Wages Payable		80

(16) Completion of the Manufacturing Process

Dr. Finished Goods	3,300	
Cr. Work-in-Process		3,300

(17) Payment to Supplier of Labor Services

Dr. Wages Payable	80	
Cr. Cash		80

(18) Renting of Space

Dr. Prepaid Services	375	
Cr. Cash		375

Event 19 Sales Inflow
and
Event 20 Sales Outflow

Recording the sales events, however, presented some difficulty to Anderson. During the second day the company filled three orders, the two orders received the previous day and a third order received during that day, paid for in cash. Let us look at the cash sale first. Four hundred grabules were sold for $80 each. What happened? Cash increased and finished goods decreased—but by how much? Cash increased by $32,000 (400 × $80). Since the 600 grabules produced during the first 2 days of operations (300 units the first day and 300 units the second day) are quantified at $6,600, each grabule produced has an accounting quantification of $11. The sale of 400 grabules must, therefore, decrease finished goods by $4,400 (400 × $11).

This result seems to violate the rule that every accounting event affects two accounts by the same dollar amount. However, this is an event which produces **two** equally preferred measurements. One is a cash flow and the other represents a decrease in an existing accounting asset. According to our quantification rules, as well as common sense, **both** preferred measurements must be utilized in describing the impact of the event. The cash flow is used to quantify the cash received, and the previously recorded quantification of grabules is used to quantify the decrease in grabules.

Clearly, it would not be useful to quantify the cash increase in terms of the decrease in grabules or vice versa. But, whenever two independent or equally preferred measurements are used to describe the two effects of an event, a change in the residual net-

assets (Assets minus Liabilities minus Contributed Capital) is likely
to result.

Thus, Anderson might describe the cash sale event by a three-
part entry, increasing cash by $32,000, decreasing finished goods
by $4,400, and—to maintain equality between assets and equities—
also increasing the residual equity (or Retained Earnings) by
$27,600.

> ### Thought Question
> If only one independent measurement is used to describe both
> effects of an event, can residual net-assets change?

In practice, this same result is accomplished by a different
method of recording. Events changing the residual net-assets of a
firm, and therefore the residual equity, are considered so important
that the accountant generally gives these events special treatment
in two respects:

1. Repetitive events which are part of the principal activities of the
   firm, are called **operating events.** Operating events consist of the
   provision of goods and services to customers, and the utilization
   of goods and services associated with such provisions. *Operating
   events* increasing residual net-assets are called **operating revenues,** or simply **revenues,** and represent the provision of goods
   and services. Operating events decreasing residual net-assets are
   called **operating expenses,** or simply **expenses,** and represent the
   utilization of resources necessary in providing those goods or
   services. When an operating event, such as the sales event, produces both an independently quantifiable increase **and** decrease
   in the residual net-assets, it is recorded as two separate events:
   one a revenue and the other an expense.

2. Not only are two events recorded for events such as sales, but
   different aspects of each of these events are reported in two
   separate accounting reports. The **effect** of the event on the assets
   or equities (other than Retained Earnings) is reported in the
   balance sheet. The **occurrence** of the event is reported in an
   activity or event statement called the *income statement.*

The cash sale in this instance is thought of as the sum of two
events: a **sales inflow** (sales revenue) event with two effects, an
increase in cash and an increase in the residual equity by $32,000;
and a **sales outflow** (cost of goods sold) event with two effects, a
decrease in finished goods and a decrease in the residual equity by
$4,400. Since accounting requires reporting the occurrence of this

event, as well as reporting the effect of the event on the assets and equities, the entry used is one which facilitates this dual reporting. One part of this accounting entry records the effect of the event in an **effect account** (an asset or equity account). The other part of the entry records the occurrence of the activity in an **event account.** Thus, for the cash sale, Anderson first disaggregates the sales event into two separate events: a sales inflow and a sales outflow. He then records the effect of these events on the assets or equities (other than Retained Earnings), and the occurrence of the event. The sales inflow event produced an increase in cash of $32,000, and the entry to record this event is

(19a) Dr. Cash (*effect account*)   32,000
          Cr. Sales Inflow (*event account*)   32,000

Thought Question
Why is the sales inflow a credit entry?

The sales event also produced a decrease in finished goods of $4,400. The entry to record this event is

(20a) Dr. *Sales Outflow* (event account)   4,400
          Cr. Finished Goods (effect account)   4,400

Thought Question
Why is the sales outflow a debit entry?

This system of entries has several advantages. Most importantly, it allows a comparison and analysis of SALES INFLOWS with SALES OUTFLOWS, and with other outflows or utilizations necessary to produce the sales, such as the utilization of the delivery truck, Anderson's services, and the store space. It also allows the accountant to record SALES INFLOWS and related SALES OUTFLOWS at different times, should that be considered useful.

Thought Question
When might it be useful to record *sales inflows* and *sales outflows* at different times?

You will notice that the entry that was just made does not record the effect of the event on the residual equity (Retained Earnings). The effects of these events on residual equity are not recorded until financial statements are prepared, as you will see on pages 99–102.

The accountant treats the other sales events, those not made for cash, in a similar fashion. One of the two orders filled during the day was for 100 grabules for which payment in full had been received in advance. How will Anderson record this sale event? When the company received $8,000 in advance, he recorded the event as increasing cash by $8,000 and creating a responsibility or liability to customers called Advances from Customers in the amount of $8,000. Now, when the goods are provided, what has happened? Obviously the company has discharged its responsibility in full and has decreased its finished goods by 100 grabules. Both of these effects represent decreases in existing accounting quantifications and so we have two equally preferred measurements—an $8,000 decrease in the responsibility, and a $1,100 (100 × $11) decrease in finished goods. As he did before, the accountant splits this event into a SALES INFLOW and a SALES OUTFLOW, and for each, records the effect on residual net-assets as well as the occurrence of the activity which caused that effect. The entry to record this event is

(19b) Dr. Advances from Customers (effect account)   8,000
       Cr. Sales Inflow (event account)   8,000

> ### Thought Question
> In what respect is Event (19b) a sales inflow?

(20b) Dr. Sales Outflow (event account)   1,100
       Cr. Finished Goods (effect account)   1,100

Finally, the company filled the order received on the first day for 65 grabules, with payment promised 3 days after the delivery of the grabules. When this order was filled, there also were two preferred measurements—the known cash flow which the company expects to receive, and to which it is entitled, and the reduction of grabules. Following the examples of the last two cases, the event is recorded as the sum of a SALES INFLOW and a SALES OUTFLOW as follows:

(19c) Dr. Accounts Receivable (effect account)   5,200
       Cr. Sales Inflow (event account)   5,200

(20c) Dr. Sales Outflow (event account)   715
       Cr. Finished Goods (effect account)   715

Notice that entries in accounts like Sales Inflow and Sales Outflow are quite different from entries to accounts like *Accounts Receivable* and Finished Goods. Events occur that increase or decrease *Finished Goods* and Accounts Receivable and the balances in those accounts will go up and down over time as different events occur. But, the Sales Inflow and Sales Outflow accounts are not representations of assets (or equities), but rather describe activities that have occurred. Once a SALES INFLOW has occurred and has been recorded, no subsequent event can decrease the balance in the Sales Inflow account, nor can a subsequent event decrease the balance in the Sales Outflow account. ("The moving finger writes and having writ/Moves on. . . .") Event accounts will contain only debits **or** credits, **not both,** and the balance in these accounts will continue to accumulate until the accounts are terminated, or *closed* (or unless a mistake is rectified).

Each of the sales inflow entries is similar in that each records the seller's provision of goods and the resulting increase in the residual net-assets of the firm. The assets received—Cash or Accounts Receivable—increase the residual net-assets of the firm because no further responsibility to the buyer exists. The three events [(19a), (19b), and (19c)] differ, however, as to when the customer has performed or will perform its part of the agreement. In the case of the cash sale, the customer performs (pays) when the sale takes place. In the sale where an advance was received, the customer performed prior to the sales event; and in the case of the credit sale, the customer will perform (hopefully) subsequent to the sale. The three sales outflow entries describe the goods that were utilized (delivered to the customer) as a result of the seller's provision.

TERMINAL UTILIZATION

When resources are utilized, an accounting event is always recognized. We have seen that when goods or services are utilized in manufacturing and a salable product results, the utilization is described as converting the goods or services into an accounting asset called Work-in-Process. Such utilizations are called *intermediate utilizations,* since the utilization results in an asset which in turn will be utilized at a future date. Under existing accounting rules, utilization of goods and services can be described as resulting in an accounting asset only if these utilizations are part of the manufacturing process and a physical salable product emerges.

Event 21   Utilization of Rented Space

However, goods and services are often utilized in activities other than the manufacturing process. How are such utilizations recorded? For example, how should the utilization of the space used by The American Grabule Company for selling and administrative activities be described?

When this space was acquired and paid for on the morning of the second day, the right to utilize this space was recognized as an asset (Prepaid Rent) and quantified at $375, the amount by which cash decreased. On the morning of the second day, the company had the right to utilize this space for 5 days. At the end of the day, they had a right to utilize the space for the 4 remaining days. The right to 1 day's space was utilized as a result of the passage of time. Since the right to use space was decreased by one-fifth, we decrease the Prepaid Rent account by $75 ($\frac{1}{5} \times$ $375).

What other effects did the passage of time and the resulting utilization of space have? We might argue that the space utilization created goodwill among those prospective customers who visited the company's attractive showroom—and stayed comfortable and dry, having found refuge from the rain outside. But, clearly, the utilization of this space was not part of the manufacturing process and did not produce a physical salable product, so accounting does not permit us to show an asset emerging. It is also evident that the space utilization did not have the effect of discharging any previously existing responsibilities. Thus, the utilization of the space for selling and administrative services appears to be a one-sided event decreasing residual net-assets. A utilization where no other accounting asset results is a *terminal utilization,* and is also called an **expense.** The two effects of a terminal utilization are a decrease in the residual net-assets of the firm and a decrease in the residual equity (Retained Earnings). The entry for events of this type records (1) the effect of the event on the residual net-assets, and (2) the activity which produced that effect. The entry to record the utilization of selling and administrative services is

(21) Dr. Operating Expenses (event account)   75
      Cr. Prepaid Services (effect account)   75

Event 22   Utilization of Labor Services

Several other *terminal utilizations* needed to be recorded. One day of Anderson's services was utilized in selling and administrative activities. Since the right to utilize his services was never recognized as an asset (no prepayment had been made), the utilization cannot be viewed as a reduction of an asset, as in Event (21). Instead, this utilization of services results in a recognition of a responsibility to pay Anderson and represents an increase in Wages Payable. No other asset or responsibility (except the residual equity) was affected. Therefore, a change in residual net-assets occurred.

Since the company agreed to pay him $100 per day, the entry to record this event is

(22) Dr. Operating Expenses (event account)   100
        Cr. Wages Payable (effect account)   100

Event 23   **Utilization of Truck Services**

In addition to the utilizations above, two other utilizations took place. The company acquired a truck for delivery services and we borrowed money. The truck was expected to last for 5 years, or 260 weeks, or 1,300 working days. This truck has now been used for 1 day to deliver grabules, and the utilization of the right to 1 day's truck services must be recorded. As a result of the passage of 1 day, the company now has the right to beneficially utilize the truck only 1,299 (its remaining capacity) rather than 1,300 days, and a reduction in the rights to truck services is in order. We could record this utilization by decreasing the asset, Property, Plant and Equipment, directly. By doing it this way, we would lose information about the original capacity of the asset that we acquired, and the portion of that capacity utilized to date. Therefore, all that we would have is a record of the remaining capacity of the asset.

Since it is useful to maintain the record of both the original capacity acquired, and the portion of that capacity utilized to date, accounting records this utilization in a novel and rather clever fashion. Instead of having one account to describe the truck asset, accounting sets up two accounts: an asset account, to record the original capacity of property, plant and equipment acquired, and a *contra-asset* account, to record the portion of original capacity utilized to date, as a result of the passage of time. The difference in the balances between the asset account and the related contra-asset account reflects the remaining capacity of the asset.

In other words, a contra-asset account is a credit (Cr.) balance account that is not an equity account; its balance is always subtracted from the balance of its related asset account, to reflect the remaining right to utilize an economic resource.

When the truck was purchased for $26,500, an entry was made increasing (debiting) Property, Plant and Equipment by $26,500. This $26,500 quantifies the right to use the truck for its estimated useful life as an economic resource ($26,000), plus the $500 which is expected to result when the truck is discarded. The account which describes this original capacity does not change until and unless the asset is disposed of or is augmented.

How is the utilization of the original capacity of the asset recorded? At the end of the day, 1 day's capacity has been utilized and the utilization is quantified at $20 ($26,000 ÷ 1,300).

The utilization of property, plant and equipment is called *depreciation expense* (or more generally, OPERATING EXPENSE), and the *contra-asset* account used to record the effect of the utilization of property, plant and equipment is called *Accumulated Depreciation*. The entry for this event is

(23) Dr. Operating Expenses (event account)   20
         Cr. Accumulated Depreciation (effect account)   20

After this event is recorded, the accounting description of the truck would look as follows:

Property, Plant and Equipment	$26,500
Less: Accumulated Depreciation	(20)
Book value (or remaining capacity)	$26,480

The balances in Property, Plant and Equipment and Accumulated Depreciation are actual balances in accounts. However, the $26,480 book value, which describes the remaining capacity of Property, Plant and Equipment, is **not** a balance in any account. It is the difference between the balance in the Property, Plant and Equipment account and the Accumulated Depreciation account.

Event 24   Utilization of Borrowed Cash

Finally, the utilization of borrowed cash must be recorded. The company borrowed $50,000 (which was to be repaid in 2 years), and promised to pay an additional $9,125 per year, for 2 years, for the use of this money. Thus, they promised to pay $25 per day for the use of the money ($9,125 ÷ 365). At the end of the first day, the company utilized borrowed money for 1 day. This utilization does not represent a reduction of an accounting asset, so it is recorded by recognizing an obligation to pay $25 to the bank for the use of their money. Since the utilization does not create a new asset, nor does it decrease a liability or contributed capital, it results in a decrease in the residual net-assets of the firm. However, this utilization is not considered to be an operating expense because it is a result of borrowing, which is a financing event. The entry for this event is

(24) Dr. *Interest Expense* (event account)   25
         Cr. Interest Payable (effect account)   25

Event 25   Acquisition of Patent

The acquisition of the *patent* in exchange for 100 shares of stock is in some respects a troublesome event to record. No preferred measurement exists for this event, since the event produces neither a cash flow nor a decrease in an existing asset or liability. Therefore, the event must be quantified in terms of the cash impact that **would have been produced** by an analogous event. Anderson must choose between the cash increase that would have occurred had the stock been sold for cash, and the cash decrease that would have resulted had the patent been acquired in a cash transaction. He felt more comfortable quantifying the event in terms of the cash that would have been received had stock been sold for cash, since the firm had indeed sold common stock for $100 a share just yesterday, and since he was not aware of a market for grabule patents. Thus, Anderson made the following entry for the event:

(25) Dr. *Patent* (effect account)	10,000	
Cr. Common Stock (effect account)		10,000

SUMMARY OF SECOND DAY'S EVENTS

Listed below is a summary of the effects of the second day's events:

(13) Purchase of Marbles		
Dr. Raw Materials and Supplies	12,600	
Cr. Accounts Payable		12,600
(14) Purchase of Chemicals		
Dr. Raw Materials and Supplies	2,544	
Cr. Cash		2,544
(15) Manufacture of Grabules		
Dr. Work-in-Process	3,300	
Cr. Raw Materials and Supplies		3,124
Cr. Prepaid Services		96
Cr. Wages Payable		80
(16) Completion of the Manufacturing Process		
Dr. Finished Goods	3,300	
Cr. Work-in-Process		3,300
(17) Payment to Supplier of Labor Services		
Dr. Wages Payable	80	
Cr. Cash		80
(18) Renting of Space		
Dr. Prepaid Services	375	
Cr. Cash		375
(19) Sales Inflow		
Dr. Cash (a)	32,000	
Dr. Advances from Customers (b)	8,000	
Dr. Accounts Receivable (c)	5,200	
Cr. Sales Inflow		45,200

(20) Sales Outflow
    Dr. Sales Outflow   6,215
        Cr. Finished Goods   6,215

(21) Utilization of Rented Space
    Dr. Operating Expenses   75
        Cr. Prepaid Services   75

(22) Utilization of Labor Services
    Dr. Operating Expenses   100
        Cr. Wages Payable   100

(23) Utilization of Truck Services
    Dr. Operating Expenses   20
        Cr. Accumulated Depreciation   20

(24) Utilization of Borrowed Cash
    Dr. Interest Expense   25
        Cr. Interest Payable   25

(25) Acquisition of Patent
    Dr. Patent   10,000
        Cr. Common Stock   10,000

RECORDING THE EFFECTS OF EVENTS

Anderson now had to record, or **post,** these entries to the appropriate accounts. To do this, he had to set up four additional effect (or balance sheet) accounts—Patents, Interest Payable, Accumulated Depreciation, and Accounts Receivable. He also had to set up four event (or income statement) accounts—Sales Inflow (or Sales Revenue), Sales Outflow (or Cost of Goods Sold), Operating Expenses, and Interest Expense. After setting these accounts up and posting the entries to the account, he calculated the balances as follows:

Cash
↑ Cash ↓

BB 127,092			
(19a) 32,000	2,544	(14)	
	80	(17)	
	375	(18)	
EB 156,093			

Raw Materials and Supplies
↑ Raw Materials and Supplies ↓

BB 3,124			
(13) 12,600	3,124	(15)	
(14) 2,544			
EB 15,144			

Accounts Payable
↓ Accounts Payable ↑

	2,400	BB
	12,600	(13)
	15,000	EB

Property, Plant and Equipment
↑ Property, Plant and Equipment ↓

BB 26,500	
EB 26,500	

Prepaid Services
↑ Prepaid Services ↓

BB 384			
(18) 375	96	(15)	
	75	(21)	
EB 588			

Wages Payable
↓ Wages Payable ↑

	0	BB
(17) 80	80	(15)
	100	(22)
	100	EB

Accumulated Depreciation
↓ Accumulated Depreciation ↑

	0	BB
	20	(23)
	20	EB

Work-in-Process
↑ Work-in-Process ↓

BB 0			
(15) 3,300	3,300	(16)	
EB 0			

Bank Loan
↓ Bank Loan ↑

	50,000	BB
	50,000	EB

Patent
↑ Patent ↓

BB 0	
(25) 10,000	
EB 10,000	

Finished Goods
↑ Finished Goods ↓

BB 3,300			
(16) 3,300	6,215	(20)	
EB 385			

Common Stock
↓ Common Stock ↑

	100,000	BB
	10,000	(25)
	110,000	EB

Accounts Receivable
↑ Accounts Receivable ↓

BB 0	
(19c) 5,200	
EB 5,200	

Advances from Customers
↓ Advances from Customers ↑

	8,000	BB
(19b) 8,000		
	0	EB

Sales Inflow
Sales Inflow

	0	BB
	32,000	(19a)
	8,000	(19b)
	5,200	(19c)
	45,200	EB

Interest Payable
↓ Interest Payable ↑

	0	BB
	25	(24)
	25	EB

Sales Outflow
Sales Outflow

BB 0	
(20a) 4,400	
(20b) 1,100	
(20c) 715	
EB 6,215	

Operating Expenses
Operating Expenses

BB 0	
(21) 75	
(22) 100	
(23) 20	
EB 195	

Interest Expense
Interest Expense

BB 0	
(24) 25	
EB 25	

THE INCOME STATEMENT

Anderson then reported the balances in the event accounts in an
event statement called the *income statement*. He listed the credit
balances in the event accounts as *revenues,* the debit balances in
the event accounts as *expenses,* and the difference between the
credit and debit balances as **net income,** in the following manner:

The American Grabule Company
Income Statement
The First Two Days

Revenues		
Sales Inflow (Sales Revenue)		$45,200
Total Revenues		$45,200
Expenses		
Sales Outflow (Cost of Goods Sold)	$6,215	
Operating Expenses	195	
Interest Expense	25	
Total Expenses	$6,435	(6,435)
Net Income		$38,765

What does the income statement report in terms of cash flows?
Looking at the revenue section of the income statement, we see
that revenues report the provision of goods and services for which
cash has been or will be received, without the need for additional
direct or indirect cash sacrifices. Expenses, on the other hand, represent the utilization of goods and services for which cash has been
or will be paid that will not result in future benefits.

Combining the cash implications reported in the income statement and in the balance sheet clarifies the relationship between
the two accounting reports and cash flows. An accounting event
such as the UTILIZATION OF RENTED SPACE, that has required or will
require a cash outflow and is **not** expected to result in a future
benefit, is an expense and is reported in the income statement. An
accounting event such as the PURCHASE OF INVENTORY, that has required or will require a cash outflow and is expected to result in a
future benefit, increases an asset and affects the balance sheet.

An accounting event such as the PROVISION OF GOODS AND SERVICES, that has generated or will generate a cash inflow and is **not** expected to require a future cash sacrifice, is a revenue and is reported in the income statement. Finally, an accounting event such as BORROWING FROM THE BANK, that has generated a cash inflow and is expected to require a future cash sacrifice, increases a liability and affects the balance sheet.

> ### Thought Question
> Can an accounting event that will generate a future cash inflow, and is expected to require a future cash sacrifice, increase a liability?

RECORDING THE EFFECT OF REVENUES AND EXPENSES ON RETAINED EARNINGS

After presenting the income statement to the board of directors of The American Grabule Company, Anderson tried to construct a balance sheet in the same way that he did on the first day (see page 77), by listing the nonzero balances in the asset and equity accounts. However, when he tried to do that, he had a rude awakening, because the balance sheet did not balance. The balances in the asset accounts looked as follows:

Assets

Cash	$156,093
Accounts Receivable	5,200
Prepaid Services	588
Raw Materials and Supplies	15,144
Finished Goods	385
Property, Plant and Equipment	26,500
Accumulated Depreciation	(20)
Patent	10,000
Total Assets	$213,890

Liabilities and Owners' Equities

Accounts Payable	$15,000
Interest Payable	25
Wages Payable	100
Bank Loan	50,000
Common Stock	110,000
Total Liabilities and Owners' Equities	$175,125

The asset total of $213,890 was $38,765 larger than the equity total. Anderson realized that a Retained Earnings balance of $38,765 was necessary in order to balance the totals of assets and equities. When the light dawned that this difference matched the amount of income reported in the income statement, Anderson realized what had happened. Balance sheets balance because each event is assumed to have two effects. But for the events affecting the residual net-assets of the firm—the events reported in the income statement—Anderson had recorded only one effect—the effect on the specific asset or equity. Instead of recording a second effect on the residual equity for one-sided events, he had recorded the occurrence of the event in an event account, so that he could prepare the income statement. Now that the income statement had been prepared and the event accounts had served their purpose, Anderson could record the effect of these events by closing them to Retained Earnings. The *closing process* is done by debiting the credit balance event accounts (those increasing residual net-assets), and crediting the debit balance event accounts (those decreasing residual net-assets). After closing these event accounts their ending balances are zero. The difference between the credit and debit balances in the event accounts is credited to Retained Earnings. The entry for this is

Dr. Sales Inflow	45,200	
Cr. Sales Outflow		6,215
Cr. Operating Expenses		195
Cr. Interest Expense		25
Cr. Retained Earnings		38,765

<table>
<tr><td colspan="2" align="center">Sales Inflow</td><td colspan="2" align="center">Sales Outflow</td></tr>
<tr><td></td><td>0 BB</td><td>BB</td><td>0</td></tr>
<tr><td>45,200</td><td>32,000 (19a)</td><td>(20a) 4,400</td><td>6,215</td></tr>
<tr><td></td><td>8,000 (19b)</td><td>(20b) 1,100</td><td></td></tr>
<tr><td></td><td>5,200 (19c)</td><td>(20c) 715</td><td></td></tr>
<tr><td></td><td>0 EB</td><td>EB 0</td><td></td></tr>
</table>

<table>
<tr><td colspan="2" align="center">Operating Expenses</td><td colspan="2" align="center">Interest Expense</td></tr>
<tr><td>BB</td><td>0</td><td>BB</td><td>0</td></tr>
<tr><td>(21)</td><td>75</td><td>(24) 25</td><td>25</td></tr>
<tr><td>(22)</td><td>100</td><td></td><td></td></tr>
<tr><td>(23)</td><td>20</td><td></td><td></td></tr>
<tr><td>EB</td><td>0</td><td>EB 0</td><td></td></tr>
<tr><td>195</td><td></td><td></td><td></td></tr>
</table>

↓ Retained Earnings ↑

	0 BB
38,765	
38,765	EB

Event 26   Declaration of Cash Dividend

The board of directors was so pleased by the results of operations for the first 2 days, as reported in the income statement, that they declared a cash dividend of $2 per share of common stock, payable on the twentieth day of the following month to all stockholders on the fifteenth day of that month.

The dividend declaration results in a specific liability to distribute $2,200 to known stockholders at a known date. This liability must be recorded. There is no other effect on any other liability or any other asset and thus a change in residual net-assets has taken place. The two effects of the event are to decrease (Dr.) the residual equity (Retained Earnings) by $2,200, and to increase (Cr.) a current liability called *Dividends Payable* by $2,200, the amount of the impending cash decrease. The dividend declaration represents an exception to the practice we have used until now of recording events which impact residual net-assets. For the DECLARATION OF DIVIDENDS, no event account is set up. Instead the entry records the effect on residual net-assets and the effect on the residual equity as follows:

(26) Dr. Retained Earnings (effect account)	2,200	
Cr. Dividends Payable (effect account)		2,200

↓ Retained Earnings ↑		↓ Dividends Payable ↑	
	0 BB		0 BB
(26) 2,200	38,765		2,200 (26)
	36,565 EB		2,200 EB

COMPARATIVE BALANCE SHEETS FOR THE SECOND DAY

Anderson was able to prepare the comparative balance sheets for the second day after balancing all of the assets and equities.

The American Grabule Company
Comparative Balance Sheets
Beginning and End of the Second Day

Assets	Beg. of Day 2	End of Day 2
Cash	$127,092	$156,093
Accounts Receivable	0	5,200
Prepaid Services	384	588
Raw Materials and Supplies	3,124	15,144
Finished Goods	3,300	385
Property, Plant and Equipment	26,500	26,500
Accumulated Depreciation	0	(20)
Patent	0	10,000
Total Assets	$160,400	$213,890

Liabilities and Owners' Equities		
Accounts Payable	$ 2,400	$ 15,000
Advances from Customers	8,000	0
Interest Payable	0	25
Wages Payable	0	100
Dividends Payable	0	2,200
Bank Loan	50,000	50,000
Common Stock	100,000	110,000
Retained Earnings	0	36,565
Total Liabilities and Owners' Equities	$160,400	$213,890

USER'S PERSPECTIVE

Revenues and expenses are activities reported in the income statement. Cash receipts (or collections) and cash disbursements (payments or expenditures), are activities reported in the statement of cash receipts and disbursements.

Revenues are events that increase residual net-assets while cash receipts increase cash. Expenses decrease residual net-assets while cash disbursements decrease cash.

Revenues represent the provision of goods and services in a given period for which cash has been, is, or will be received. However, the receipt of the cash (which is **always** associated with the revenues) need not occur during the same period. Similarly, expenses represent the terminal utilization of goods and services in a given period for which cash has been, is, or will be disbursed. However, the disbursement of the cash (which is **always** associated with the expenses) need not occur during the same period.

In other words, receipts represent **all** the cash received during a given period, whether as a result of a revenue or other event, and disbursements represent **all** the cash disbursed during a given period, whether as a result of an expense or other event.

It has often been said that "dividends are paid out of earnings," but who wants to receive "earnings"? Dividends are **paid** in **cash.** This quote reflects the fact that in most states, dividends may not be paid by an amount that exceeds the balance in Retained Earnings. The declaration of the cash dividend is recorded as follows:

Declaration of Cash Dividends
    Dr. Retained Earnings
        Cr. Dividends Payable

These dividends cannot be paid until there is enough cash to pay them. When they are paid, the entry to record the payment will be

Payment of Cash Dividends
    Dr. Dividends Payable
        Cr. Cash

Many people believe that Retained Earnings represents a cash reserve, and therefore a firm with ample Retained Earnings needs no other cash. But consider the following situation: Two lawyers incorporate their business on a Friday afternoon, each contributing $5,000 for half of the shares. On Monday, they consult with clients and bill them a total of $20,000. At the end of the day, they prepare comparative balance sheets for Monday, as follows:

Assets	Beg. of Day 1	End of Day 2
Cash	$10,000	$10,000
Accounts Receivable	0	20,000
Total Assets	$10,000	$30,000
Owners' Equities		
Common Stock	$10,000	$10,000
Retained Earnings	0	20,000
Total Equities	$10,000	$30,000

At this point, the lawyers want to declare a $15,000 cash dividend. It is clear that the balance in the Retained Earnings account is sufficient to cover the declaration—but it is equally clear that the balance in the Cash account is not sufficient.

When the lawyers analyze the events that occurred during the first 2 days, they realize that Retained Earnings increased because of the revenue that they had earned. As a result, residual net-assets increased by the increase in Accounts Receivable, not in Cash. In fact, the balance in the Cash account represents only the initial capital contributions by each of the lawyers.

This example demonstrates the clear distinction that must always be made between cash receipts and revenues, and between the accounts Cash and Retained Earnings. Similar examples relating to cash disbursements and expenses would reveal their differences as well.

Transactional Analysis: The Events Approach to Accounting

INTRODUCTION

In this appendix, we will demonstrate the technique of **transactional analysis.** The purpose of this kind of exercise is to determine what events occurred during the period of time covered by a set of financial statements.

DETERMINING COLLECTIONS FROM CREDIT CUSTOMERS FROM CREDIT SALES REVENUES AND ACCOUNTS RECEIVABLE

Consider a firm that reports $45,200 in Sales Revenue in its income statement. If the beginning and ending balances in Accounts Receivable were $0 and $5,200, respectively, and if all of the sales were on credit, then COLLECTIONS FROM CREDIT CUSTOMERS would be $40,000, determined as follows:

↑		Accounts Receivable		↓
BB	0			
		Credit	Collections	
		Sales	from Credit	
		Inflow	Customers	
EB	5,200			

Since CREDIT SALES were greater than COLLECTIONS FROM CREDIT CUSTOMERS by $5,200 (the change in the account), and CREDIT SALES were $45,200, then

↑		Accounts Receivable		↓
BB	0			
	45,200	Credit	Collections	
		Sales	from Credit	**40,000**
		Inflow	Customers	
EB	5,200			

COLLECTIONS FROM CREDIT CUSTOMERS are $40,000.

DETERMINING COLLECTIONS FROM CUSTOMERS
FROM SALES REVENUES AND ACCOUNTS RECEIVABLE

Instead, if half of the $45,200 sales were for cash, and the other half on credit, then COLLECTIONS FROM CUSTOMERS (cash and credit) would be determined by summing the cash sales to COLLECTIONS FROM CREDIT CUSTOMERS. COLLECTIONS FROM CREDIT CUSTOMERS would be

↑	Accounts Receivable		↓
BB 0			
	Credit	Collections	
22,600	Sales	from Credit	**17,400**
	Inflow	Customers	
EB 5,200			

Thus, COLLECTIONS FROM CUSTOMERS equals CASH SALES of $22,600 plus COLLECTIONS FROM CREDIT CUSTOMERS of $17,400, or $40,000.

> ### *Thought Question*
> What is the minimum that CREDIT SALES could have been?

Consider further that CASH SALES were $30,000 and CREDIT SALES were $15,200. Then, COLLECTIONS FROM CUSTOMERS would have been $40,000, determined as follows: CASH SALES of $30,000 plus COLLECTIONS FROM CREDIT CUSTOMERS of $10,000 ($15,200 minus $5,200). Notice, that irrespective of how much of the $45,200 SALES REVENUE was for cash and how much was for credit, COLLECTIONS FROM CUSTOMERS was always $40,000.

> ### *Thought Question*
> Is it important to differentiate between COLLECTIONS FROM CASH CUSTOMERS and COLLECTIONS FROM CREDIT CUSTOMERS?

DETERMINING COLLECTIONS FROM CUSTOMERS FROM
SALES REVENUES, ACCOUNTS RECEIVABLE, AND ADVANCES
FROM CUSTOMERS

Consider, finally, the financial statements of The American Grabule Company. SALES REVENUE as reported in the income statement was $45,200, and the beginning and ending balances in Accounts Receivable were $0 and $5,200, respectively, and the beginning and ending balances in Advances from Customers were $0 and $0, respectively. If we were to assume that three-quarters of the sales were on credit, and that the remaining quarter were prepaid sales — sales for which advances have been received — then COLLECTIONS FROM CUSTOMERS would be determined as follows:

↑	Accounts Receivable		↓
BB	0		
		Credit	Collections	
	33,900	Sales	from Credit	**28,700**
		Inflow	Customers	
EB	5,200		

↓	Advances from Customers		↑
			0 BB
		Prepaid	Advances	
	11,300	Sales	from	**11,300**
		Inflow	Customers	
			0 EB

Thus COLLECTIONS FROM CUSTOMERS, both in advance and on credit, is $40,000, $28,700 from credit customers and $11,300 from advances from customers.

You can readily see that you can make any assumption you want about how much of sales were for cash, on credit, or prepaid, as long as

1. The total of all SALES equals $45,200.

2. CREDIT SALES were at least $5,200.

Irrespective of how you disaggregate sales, TOTAL SALES (cash, credit, and prepaid) will always be $45,200, and total COLLECTIONS FROM CUSTOMERS (cash, credit, and advances) will always be $40,000.

THE DOUBLE T-ACCOUNT

The events approach to accounting stresses the determination of accounting events from financial statements. The events that occurred during the period had the effect of producing the changes in each of the balance sheet accounts. Therefore, as a first step, it is necessary to know the changes in the balance sheet accounts in order to deduce events.

> *Thought Question*
> In determining events, do you need to know the amount of the beginning and ending balances, or just their difference?

The **double T-account** nets the beginning and ending balance of the *T-account*. The double T-accounts for Accounts Receivable and Advances from Customers would appear as follows:

↑	Accounts Receivable		↓
5,200			
	Credit	Collections	
33,900	Sales	from Credit	28,700
	Inflow	Customers	

↓	Advances from Customers		↑
	=		
	Prepaid	Advances	
11,300	Sales	from	11,300
	Inflow	Customers	

THE PROBLEM

Having introduced the essence of the solution approach, let's apply it to the financial statements relating to The American Grabule Company, a manufacturing concern. From the following comparative balance sheets, income statement, and statement of cash receipts and disbursements, determine the events that occurred during the first 2 days of its operations.

The American Grabule Company
Comparative Balance Sheets
Beginning of the First Day and the End of the Second Day

Assets	Beg. of Day 1	End of Day 2
Cash	$0	$156,093
Accounts Receivable	0	5,200
Prepaid Services	0	588
Raw Materials and Supplies	0	15,144
Finished Goods	0	385
Property, Plant and Equipment	0	26,500
Accumulated Depreciation	0	(20)
Patent	0	10,000
Total Assets	$0	$213,890

Liabilities and Owners' Equities

	Beg. of Day 1	End of Day 2
Accounts Payable	$0	$ 15,000
Interest Payable	0	25
Wages Payable	0	100
Dividends Payable	0	2,200
Bank Loan	0	50,000
Common Stock	0	110,000
Retained Earnings	0	36,565
Total Liabilities and Owners' Equities	$0	$213,890

The American Grabule Company
Income Statement
The First Two Days

Revenues

Sales Revenue (Sales Inflow)		$45,200
Total Revenues		$45,200

Expenses

Cost of Goods Sold (Sales Outflow)	$6,215	
Operating Expenses	195	
Interest Expense	25	
Total Expenses	$6,435	(6,435)
Net Income		$38,765

The American Grabule Company
Statement of Cash Receipts and Disbursements
The First Two Days

Cash Receipts

Issue of Common Stock	$100,000
Borrowing from Bank	50,000
Collections from Customers	40,000
Total Cash Receipts	$190,000

Cash Disbursements

Payment to Supplier of Raw Materials and Supplies	$ 6,392
Payment to Suppliers of Labor Services	160
Prepayment of Rent	855
Purchase of Truck	26,500
Total Cash Disbursements	$ 33,907
Excess Cash Receipts over Disbursements	$156,093

RECORDING THE GIVEN EVENTS

From the comparative balance sheets, we determine the changes in the accounts. From the income statement, we record the effects of revenues and expenses, as represented by journal entries 1 through 5, below. These events are marked with (I/S) indicating that they are reported in the income statement. From the statement of cash receipts and disbursements, we record the effects of receipts and disbursements, as represented by journal entries 6 through 12.

(1) Sales Revenue (Sales Inflow)
      Dr. Accounts Receivable   45,200
           Cr. Sales Revenue (I/S)   45,200

(2) Cost of Goods Sold (Sales Outflow)
      Dr. Cost of Goods Sold (I/S)   6,215
           Cr. Finished Goods   6,215

(3) Utilization of Services
      Dr. Operating Expenses (I/S)   195
           Cr. Prepaid Services   195

(4) Utilization of Borrowed Cash
      Dr. Interest Expense (I/S)   25
           Cr. Interest Payable   25

(5) Closing Net Income to Retained Earnings
      Dr. Income Summary   38,765
           Cr. Retained Earnings   38,765

(6) Issue of Common Stock
      Dr. Cash   100,000
           Cr. Common Stock   100,000

(7) Borrowing from the Bank
      Dr. Cash   50,000
           Cr. Bank Loan   50,000

(8) Collections from Customers
      Dr. Cash   40,000
           Cr. Accounts Receivable   40,000

(9) Payment to Supplier of Raw Materials
    and Supplies
      Dr. Accounts Payable   6,392
           Cr. Cash   6,392

(10) Payment to Suppliers of Labor Services
      Dr. Wages Payable   160
           Cr. Cash   160

(11) Renting of Space and Machine
      Dr. Prepaid Services   855
           Cr. Cash   855

(12) Purchase of Truck
      Dr. Property, Plant and Equipment   26,500
           Cr. Cash   26,500

↑			Cash		↓
	156,093				
(6)	100,000	Receipts	Disbursements	6,392	(9)
(7)	50,000	(Given)	(Given)	160	(10)
(8)	40,000			855	(11)
				26,500	(12)

↓			Accounts Payable		↑
				15,000	
(9)	6,392	Payments to Supplier of Raw Materials and Supplies (Given)	Credit Purchase of Raw Materials and Supplies (To Be Deduced)		

↑			Accounts Receivable		↓
	5,200				
(1)	45,200	Sales Revenue (Given)	Collections from Credit Customers (Given)	40,000	(8)

↓			Interest Payable		↑
				25	
	0	Payment of Interest (Given)	Interest Expense (Given)	25	(4)

↑			Prepaid Services		↓
	588				
(31)	855	Prepayment of Services (Given)	Utilization of Prepaid Services (Given and To Be Deduced)	195	(3)

↓			Wages Payable		↑
				100	
(10)	160	Payment to Supplier of Labor Services (Given)	Utilization of Labor Services (To Be Deduced)		

↑			Raw Materials and Supplies		↓
	15,144				
		Purchase of Raw Materials and Supplies (To Be Deduced)	Transfer to Work-in-Process (To Be Deduced)		

↓			Dividends Payable		↑
				2,200	
	0	Payment of Cash Dividend (Given)	Declaration of Cash Dividends (To Be Deduced)		

↑			Work-in-Process		↓
		Inputs into Production (To Be Deduced)	Transfer to Finished Goods (To Be Deduced)		

↓			Bank Loan		↑
				50,000	
	0	Repayment of Bank Loan (Given)	Borrowing from the Bank (Given)	50,000	(7)

↑			Finished Goods		↓
	385				
		Transfer from Work-in-Process (To Be Deduced)	Cost of Goods Sold (Given)	6,215	(2)

↓			Common Stock		↑
				110,000	
	0	Repurchase of Common Stock (Given)	Issue of Common Stock (Given and To Be Deduced)	300,000	(6)

↑			Property, Plant and Equipment		↓
	26,500				
(12)	26,500	Acquisition of Property, Plant and Equipment (Given)	Disposal of Property, Plant and Equipment (Given)	0	

↓			Retained Earnings		↑
				36,565	
		Declaration of Dividends (To Be Deduced)	Net Income (Given)	38,765	(5)

↓			Accumulated Depreciation		↑
				20	
	0	Accumulated Depreciation Associated with Disposal (Given)	Depreciation Charge (To Be Deduced)		

↑			Patent		↓
	10,000				
		Acquisition of Patent (To Be Deduced)	Amortization of Patent (Given)	0	

DEDUCING AND RECORDING DEDUCED EVENTS

After having recorded the given information (journal entries 1 through 12), we notice that the events explain the changes in Cash, Accounts Receivable, Property, Plant and Equipment, Interest Payable, and Bank Loan and, therefore, no other events affecting these accounts could have occurred. In addition, we also know that there WAS no AMORTIZATION OR SALE OF PATENTS, PAYMENT OF DIVIDENDS, or REPURCHASE OF COMMON STOCK.

The known events do not explain the changes in the other accounts, and therefore we must deduce the additional events that must have occurred to produce the changes in the balance sheet accounts.

The derivation of Events A through D pose no problems.

(A) Purchase of Raw Materials and Supplies
Dr. Raw Materials and Supplies   21,392
    Cr. Accounts Payable   21,392

(B) Input of Raw Materials and Supplies into Production
Dr. Work-in-Process   6,248
    Cr. Raw Materials and Supplies   6,248

(C) Completion of the Manufacturing Process
Dr. Finished Goods   6,600
    Cr. Work-in-Process   6,600

(D) Declaration of Cash Dividend
Dr. Retained Earnings   2,200
    Cr. Dividends Payable   2,200

Recording the UTILIZATION OF PROPERTY, PLANT AND EQUIPMENT could be treated either as an OPERATING EXPENSE, or as an input to the manufacturing process. When we recorded the effect of OPERATING EXPENSES (entry 3), by crediting the total amount to Prepaid Services, we assumed that no DEPRECIATION EXPENSE was included in OPERATING EXPENSE. Therefore, DEPRECIATION EXPENSE must be a manufacturing input.

(E) Utilization of Property, Plant and Equipment
Dr. Work-in-Process   20
    Cr. Accumulated Depreciation   20

In order to reconcile the change in Prepaid Services, a credit (Cr.) entry of $72 is required. Since this cannot be an OPERATING EXPENSE, it must be a manufacturing input.

(F) Input of Services into Production
Dr. Work-in-Process   72
    Cr. Prepaid Services   72

We know that $260 of labor services were utilized. Since this event is also not an OPERATING EXPENSE, it must be a manufacturing input.

(G) Input of Labor Services into Production
Dr. Work-in-Process	260	
Cr. Wages Payable		260

> **Thought Question**
> Why can't either the UTILIZATION OF PREPAID SERVICES
> or the UTILIZATION OF LABOR SERVICES
> be treated as OPERATING EXPENSES?

The only two accounts whose changes have not been reconciled are Patent and Common Stock. The Common Stock account, which increased by $110,000, already has an entry of $100,000 made to it for the ISSUE OF COMMON STOCK. In addition, from the statement of cash receipts and disbursements, there was no REPURCHASE OF COMMON STOCK. Therefore, $10,000 of common stock must have been issued for something other than cash.

Again, the statement of cash receipts and disbursements shows neither a cash acquisition nor a sale of a patent for cash, and the income statement shows no expense for the AMORTIZATION OF THE PATENT, so a patent must have been acquired for $10,000.

Finally, since these are the only two remaining accounts, it seems reasonable to assume that the ACQUISITION OF THE PATENT was done with the ISSUE OF COMMON STOCK.

(H) Acquisition of Patent
Dr. Patent	10,000	
Cr. Common Stock		10,000

This reconstruction explains all of the events that actually occurred, except for the composition of SALES REVENUE, OPERATING EXPENSES, and INPUTS TO WORK-IN-PROCESS. In the beginning of this appendix, we demonstrated that the relationship between SALES REVENUE and COLLECTIONS FROM CUSTOMERS is unaffected by this composition.

We assumed that OPERATING EXPENSES decreased Prepaid Services, and as a result we described the INPUTS TO THE MANUFACTURING PROCESS differently than the way in which they actually occurred. We assumed that OPERATING EXPENSES of $195 represented the UTILIZATION OF PREPAID SERVICES, when actually they represented the utilization of $75 of prepaid services, $100 utilization of labor services, and $20 of depreciation. As a result, we described the inputs to Work-in-Process as consisting of $6,248 of

↑		Cash		↓
	156,093			
(6)	100,000	Receipts	Disbursements	6,392 (9)
(7)	50,000	(Given)	(Given)	160 (10)
(8)	40,000			855 (11)
				26,500 (12)

↓		Accounts Payable		↑
				15,000
(9)	6,392	Payments to Supplier of Raw Materials and Supplies (Given)	Credit Purchase of Raw Materials and Supplies (Deduced)	21,392 (A)

↑		Accounts Receivable		↓
	5,200			
(1)	45,200	Sales Revenue (Given)	Collections from Credit Customers (Given)	40,000 (8)

↓		Interest Payable		↑
				25
	0	Payment of Interest (Given)	Interest Expense (Given)	25 (4)

↑		Prepaid Services		↓
	588			
(11)	855	Prepayment of Services (Given)	Utilization of Prepaid Services (Given and Deduced)	195 (3)
				72 (F)

↓		Wages Payable		↑
				100
(10)	160	Payment to Supplier of Labor Services (Given)	Utilization of Labor Services (Deduced)	260 (G)

↑		Raw Materials and Supplies		↓
	15,144			
(A)	21,392	Purchase of Raw Materials and Supplies (Deduced)	Transfer to Work-in-Process (Deduced)	6,248 (B)

↓		Dividends Payable		↑
				2,200
	0	Payment of Cash Dividend (Given)	Declaration of Cash Dividends (Deduced)	2,200 (D)

↑		Work-in-Process		↓
(B)	6,248	Inputs	Transfer	
(E)	20	into	to	6,600 (C)
(F)	72	Production	Finished Goods	
(G)	260	(Deduced)	(Deduced)	

↓		Bank Loan		↑
				50,000
	0	Repayment of Bank Loan (Given)	Borrowing from the Bank (Given)	50,000 (7)

↑		Finished Goods		↓
	385			
(C)	6,600	Transfer from Work-in-Process (Deduced)	Cost of Goods Sold (Given)	6,215 (2)

↓		Common Stock		↑
				110,000
	0	Repurchase of Common Stock (Given)	Issue of Common Stock (Given and Deduced)	100,000 (6)
				10,000 (H)

↑		Property, Plant and Equipment		↓
	26,500			
(12)	26,500	Acquisition of Property, Plant and Equipment (Given)	Disposal of Property, Plant and Equipment (Given)	0

↓		Retained Earnings		↑
				36,565
(D)	2,200	Declaration of Dividends (Deduced)	Net Income (Given)	38,765 (5)

↓		Accumulated Depreciation		↑
				20
	0	Accumulated Depreciation Associated with Disposal (Given)	Depreciation Charge (Deduced)	20 (E)

↑		Patent		↓
	10,000			
(H)	10,000	Acquisition of Patent (Deduced)	Amortization of Patent (Given)	0

raw materials and supplies, $72 of prepaid services, $260 of labor services, and $20 of depreciation, whereas the inputs were actually $6,248 for raw materials and supplies, $192 for prepaid services, and $160 of labor services. In both cases, the inputs to the manufacturing process were $6,600, only the composition was described differently.

PROBLEMS

1.

Balance Sheet
April 1, 19X0

Assets	4/1/X0
Cash	$ 50,000
Accounts Receivable	270,000
Raw Materials	30,000
Work-in-Process	50,000
Finished Goods	80,000
Property, Plant and Equipment	520,000
Accumulated Depreciation	(100,000)
Total Assets	$900,000

Liabilities and Owners' Equities	
Accounts Payable	$ 25,000
Rent Payable	10,000
Wages Payable	20,000
Taxes Payable	75,000
Dividends Payable	100,000
Long-Term Debt	200,000
Common Stock	260,000
Retained Earnings	210,000
Total Liabilities and Owners' Equities	$900,000

Describe events which might cause the following changes:

(1) Property, Plant and Equipment increased $50,000; Long-Term Debt increased $50,000.
(2) Dividends Payable decreased $30,000; Cash decreased $30,000.
(3) Accounts Receivable decreased $42,000; Cash increased $42,000.
(4) Raw Materials decreased $12,000; Work-in-Process increased $12,000.
(5) Rent Payable increased $5,000; Retained Earnings decreased $5,000.
(6) Cash increased $27,000; Common Stock increased $27,000.

(7) Raw Materials increased $8,000; Accounts Payable increased $8,000.

(8) Work-in-Process decreased $14,000; Finished Goods increased $14,000.

(9) Wages Payable increased $1,200; Work-in-Process increased $1,200.

(10) Dividends Payable increased $16,000; Retained Earnings decreased $16,000.

Required:

Before these events took place, the company had the following equation:

$$A \ (900,000) \ = \ L \ (430,000) \ + \ CC \ (260,000) \ + \ RE \ (210,000)$$

where *A* stands for Assets, *L* for Liabilities, *CC* for Contributed Capital, and *RE* for Retained Earnings. Rewrite the equation above after each of the given events, and prepare a new balance sheet after the last event.

2. Dollar Bill Retailers was organized on May 1, 19X0. During the first month of its existence, the following events occurred:

(1) The corporation issued 20,000 shares of common stock for $100,000.

(2) The company borrowed $20,000 from a bank on May 15, agreeing to repay the entire loan amount, with interest, in 2 years. The annual interest rate is 12 percent.

(3) Merchandise costing $30,000 was purchased on account from the Odd Lot Trading Company, with the payment due in 30 days.

(4) On May 1, the corporation signed a 3-year lease for an office and showroom. The monthly rental was $2,000, and 4 months' rent was paid in advance.

(5) Two salespeople were hired. Each was paid $1,000 on May 15 and May 30.

(6) During the month, Dollar Bill Retailers made credit sales for $27,000. The cost of the merchandise sold was $18,000.

(7) Credit customers paid $22,000 on account.

(8) Dollar Bill Retailers paid Odd Lot Trading Company $30,000 on account, on May 29.

(9) The board of directors met on May 31, and declared a cash dividend of $20 per share, to be paid on June 15.

Required:

a. Prepare accounting descriptions for each event that occurred.

b. Prepare a balance sheet as of the end of May.

3. Complete the chart below by indicating in which statement you would find each of the following events. If you have marked "Neither Statement," then explain how you could derive the event. The first two events have been done for you.

	Cash Statement	Income Statement	Neither Statement
Payments to suppliers of merchandise	x		
Cost of goods sold		x	
Credit purchases of inventory	————	————	————
Advances from customers	————	————	————
Collections from credit customers	————	————	————
Cash sales revenue	————	————	————
Credit sales revenue	————	————	————
Sales revenue from advances	————	————	————
Payment of interest	————	————	————
Interest expense	————	————	————
Payment of taxes	————	————	————
Tax expense	————	————	————
Payment of cash dividend	————	————	————
Declaration of cash dividend	————	————	————
Payment to suppliers of services	————	————	————
Operating expenses	————	————	————
Purchase of property, plant and equipment	————	————	————
Depreciation expense	————	————	————
Long-term borrowing	————	————	————
Reclassification of long-term debt	————	————	————
Repayment of debt	————	————	————
Issue of common stock	————	————	————
Repurchase of common stock	————	————	————

4.

The Dover Company
Comparative Balance Sheets
Years Ending December 31, 19X0 and December 31, 19X1

Assets	12/31/X0	12/31/X1
Cash	$ 5,000	$ 3,000
Accounts Receivable	25,000	28,000
Inventory	10,000	15,000
Prepaid Rent	3,000	2,000
Total Assets	$43,000	$48,000

Liabilities and Owners' Equities		
Accounts Payable Merchandise	$10,000	$ 5,000
Accounts Payable Services	1,000	2,000
Bank Loan	9,000	11,000
Common Stock	12,000	15,000
Retained Earnings	11,000	15,000
Total Liabilities and Owners' Equities	$43,000	$48,000

Some of the events that occurred during 19X1:

(1) The company signed a promissory note for a $2,000 bank loan.
(2) Sales inflow was $50,000, all on credit.
(3) Purchases of merchandise were $25,000, all on credit.
(4) Rent payments to the landlord were $10,000.
(5) Various services, costing $5,000, were utilized on credit.

Required:
a. Prepare journal entries for all the events that occurred during 19X1.
b. Prepare a statement of cash receipts and disbursements for 19X1.
c. Prepare an income statement for 19X1.

5.

The Queen McPea Company
Balance Sheet
February 1, 19X0

Assets	2/1/X0
Cash	$ 70,000
Accounts Receivable	200,000
Inventory	500,000
Supplies	25,000
Property, Plant and Equipment	900,000
Accumulated Depreciation	(225,000)
Total Assets	$1,470,000

Liabilities and Owners' Equities	
Accounts Payable Merchandise	$ 300,000
Wages Payable	10,000
Interest Payable	16,000
Bank Loan	400,000
Common Stock	300,000
Retained Earnings	444,000
Total Liabilities and Owners' Equities	$1,470,000

Events of February 19X0:

(1) Common stock was issued for $200,000.
(2) The company borrowed $300,000 from the bank.
(3) Merchandise was sold for $60,000 cash.
(4) Credit sales were $400,000.
(5) $300,000 was collected from credit customers.
(6) Office supplies were purchased for $12,000 cash.
(7) Merchandise costing $650,000 was purchased on credit.
(8) $280,000 was paid on account to suppliers of merchandise.
(9) $2,000 of supplies had been consumed (used) during the month.
(10) Labor services costing $23,000 were utilized during the month.
(11) Interest on the loan is paid every June and December, at the rate of $16,000 per month.
(12) Buildings and machinery depreciated at a rate of $9,000 per month.
(13) Net income for February was $160,000.
(14) Wages of $18,000 were paid.

Required:
From the beginning balance sheet and the list of events relating to The Queen McPea Company, above, prepare
a. A balance sheet as of the end of February 19X0
b. An income statement for February 19X0
c. A statement of cash receipts and disbursements for February 19X0

6. The letters [(a) to (f)] in the T-accounts below describe entries for events. One entry is incomplete, and one entry is wrong.

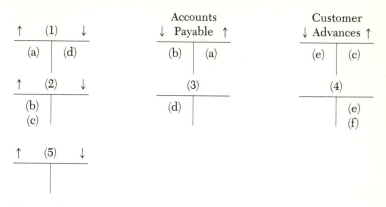

Required:
a. Identify the five accounts [(1) to (5)].
b. Identify the six events [(a) to (f)].
c. Which entry is incomplete?
d. Which entry is wrong? Why?

7. If the beginning balance of Prepaid Services was $25,000 **less than** its ending balance, the beginning balance of Accounts Payable Services $25,000 **greater than** its ending balance, and there was no Property, Plant and Equipment, what is the relationship between PAYMENTS TO SUPPLIERS OF SERVICES and OPERATING EXPENSES during the period?

8. During July, PAYMENTS TO SUPPLIERS OF SERVICES were $100,000, and OPERATING EXPENSES (excluding Depreciation) were $175,000. If the decrease in Prepaid Services was twice the increase in Accounts Payable Services, by how much did each account change?

9. If NET INCOME during a period was **greater than** the PAYMENT OF A CASH DIVIDEND, then either account:
   _____ increased, decreased, or remained the same; or
   _____ increased, decreased, or remained the same.

10. If SALES OUTFLOW (Cost of Goods Sold) during January was **less than** PAYMENTS TO SUPPLIERS OF MERCHANDISE, then either account:
   _____ increased, decreased, or remained the same; or
   _____ increased, decreased, or remained the same.

11. A firm inputs only labor and raw materials into its manufacturing process, completing all it begins every day. If the sum of PURCHASES OF RAW MATERIALS and PAYMENTS FOR LABOR SERVICES was **greater than** SALES OUTFLOW during the month, then either account:
   _____ increased, decreased, or remained the same; or
   _____ increased, decreased, or remained the same; or
   _____ increased, decreased, or remained the same.

12.

The Alpha Company
Comparative Balance Sheets
December 31, 19X0 and January 31, 19X1

Assets	12/31/X0	1/31/X1
Cash	$ 10,000	$ 32,000
Accounts Receivable	50,000	75,000
Inventory	40,000	35,000
Prepaid Services	6,000	8,000
Total Assets	$106,000	$150,000

Liabilities and Owners' Equities

	12/31/X0	1/31/X1
Accounts Payable Merchandise	$ 10,000	$ 14,000
Bank Loan	0	20,000
Common Stock	80,000	85,000
Retained Earnings	16,000	31,000
Total Liabilities and Owners' Equities	$106,000	$150,000

Statement of Cash Receipts and Disbursements
January 19X1

Cash Receipts

From Customers	$ 60,000
From Bank Loan	20,000
From Issue of Common Stock	5,000
Total Cash Receipts	$ 85,000

Cash Disbursements

Payments to Suppliers of Merchandise	$ 40,000
Payments to Employees	23,000
Total Cash Disbursements	$ 63,000
Excess Cash Receipts over Cash Disbursements	$ 22,000

Required:
List all the events that occurred during the month of January 19X1.

13a.

The Beta Company (A)
Comparative Balance Sheets
February 28, 19X0 and March 31, 19X0

Assets	2/28/X0	3/31/X0
Cash	$ 15,000	$ 13,000
Accounts Receivable	135,000	129,000
Inventory	100,000	140,000
Total Assets	$250,000	$282,000

Liabilities and Owners' Equities

	2/28/X0	3/31/X0
Accounts Payable Merchandise	$ 55,000	$ 50,000
Accounts Payable Services	30,000	40,000
Dividends Payable	5,000	1,000
Common Stock	110,000	129,000
Retained Earnings	50,000	62,000
Total Liabilities and Owners' Equities	$250,000	$282,000

Income Statement
March 19X0

Revenues

Sales Revenue		$200,000
Total Revenues		$200,000

Expenses

Cost of Goods Sold	$120,000	
Operating Expenses	30,000	
Total Expenses	$150,000	(150,000)
Net Income		$ 50,000

Required:
a. List all the events that occurred during the month of March.
b. Prepare a statement of cash receipts and disbursements for March 19X0.

13b.

The Beta Company (B)
Comparative Balance Sheets
February 28, 19X0 and March 31, 19X0

Assets	2/28/X0	3/31/X0
Cash	$?	$ 13,000
Accounts Receivable	135,000	?
Inventory	100,000	140,000
Total Assets	$?	$282,000

Liabilities and Owners' Equities		
Accounts Payable Merchandise	$?	$?
Accounts Payable Services	30,000	40,000
Dividends Payable	5,000	1,000
Common Stock	110,000	129,000
Retained Earnings	50,000	62,000
Total Liabilities and Owners' Equities	$250,000	$?

Income Statement
March 19X0

Revenues		
Sales Revenue		$200,000
Total Revenues		$200,000

Expenses		
Cost of Goods Sold	$?	
Operating Expenses	30,000	
Total Expenses	$?	(?)
Net Income		$ 50,000

Required:
a. Fill in all the question (?) marks.
b. List all the events that occurred during the month of March.
c. Prepare a statement of cash receipts and disbursements for March 19X0.

13c.

The Beta Company (C)
Comparative Balance Sheets
February 28, 19X0 and March 31, 19X0

Assets	2/28/X0	3/31/X0
Cash	$ 15,000	$ 13,000
Accounts Receivable	135,000	129,000
Inventory	100,000	140,000
Total Assets	$250,000	$282,000

Liabilities and Owners' Equities		
Accounts Payable Merchandise	$ 55,000	$ 50,000
Accounts Payable Services	30,000	40,000
Dividends Payable	5,000	1,000
Common Stock	110,000	129,000
Retained Earnings	50,000	62,000
Total Liabilities and Owners' Equities	$250,000	$282,000

Statement of Cash Receipts and Disbursements
March 19X0

Cash Receipts

From Credit Customers	$206,000
From Issue of Common Stock	19,000
Total Cash Receipts	$225,000

Cash Disbursements

Payment to Suppliers of Merchandise	$165,000
Payment to Suppliers of Services	20,000
Payment of Dividends	42,000
Total Cash Disbursements	$227,000
Excess Cash Disbursements over Cash Receipts	$ 2,000

Required:
a. List all the events that occurred during the month of March.
b. Prepare an income statement for March 19X0.

13d.

The Beta Company (D)
Comparative Balance Sheets
February 28, 19X0 and March 31, 19X0

Assets	2/28/X0	3/31/X0
Cash	$ 15,000	$ 13,000
Accounts Receivable	135,000	?
Inventory	?	140,000
Total Assets	$250,000	$282,000

Liabilities and Owners' Equities

	2/28/X0	3/31/X0
Accounts Payable Merchandise	$ 55,000	$ 50,000
Accounts Payable Services	?	40,000
Dividends Payable	5,000	?
Common Stock	110,000	129,000
Retained Earnings	50,000	62,000
Total Liabilities and Owners' Equities	$?	$?

Statement of Cash Receipts and Disbursements
March 19X0

Cash Receipts

From Credit Customers	$?
From Issue of Common Stock	19,000
Total Cash Receipts	$225,000

Cash Disbursements

Payment to Suppliers of Merchandise	$165,000
Payment to Suppliers of Services	?
Payment of Dividends	42,000
Total Cash Disbursements	$?
Excess Cash Disbursements over Cash Receipts	$?

Required:
a. Fill in all the question (?) marks.
b. List all the events that occurred during the month of March.
c. Prepare an income statement for March 19X0.

13e.

During the month of March 19X0 the following events occurred at The Beta Company:

(1) Sales inflows were $200,000.
(2) Dividends declared were $38,000.
(3) Payments to suppliers of services were $20,000.
(4) Purchase of inventory on credit was $160,000.
(5) Issue of common stock for cash was $19,000.
(6) Payment of cash dividends was $42,000.
(7) Collections from credit customers were $206,000.
(8) Sales outflows were $120,000.
(9) Payment to suppliers of merchandise was $165,000.
(10) Operating expenses were $30,000.
(11) Net income for the month was $50,000.

Required:
From the events listed above, prepare
a. A statement of cash receipts and disbursements for March 19X0
b. An income statement for March 19X0
c. A schedule of balance sheet changes for March 19X0

13f.

The Beta Company (F)
Comparative Balance Sheets
February 28, 19X0 and March 31, 19X0

Assets	2/28/X0	3/31/X0
Cash	$?	$ 13,000
Accounts Receivable	?	129,000
Inventory	?	140,000
Total Assets	$?	$282,000

Liabilities and Owners' Equities		
Accounts Payable Merchandise	$?	$ 50,000
Accounts Payable Services	?	40,000
Dividends Payable	?	?
Common Stock	?	129,000
Retained Earnings	?	62,000
Total Liabilities and Owners' Equities	$?	$282,000

Required:

From the incomplete comparative balance sheets above, and the events listed in The Beta Company (E) problem (Question 13e):

a. Fill in all the question (?) marks.

b. List all the events that occurred during the month of March.

c. Prepare a statement of cash receipts and disbursements for March 19X0.

d. Prepare an income statement for March 19X0.

CHAPTER 6

The First Two Days of The American Grabule Company: The Statement of Cash Flows

INTRODUCTION

At the end of the first day of The American Grabule Company, we prepared a balance sheet from the events of the first day. We saw that the balance sheet reported the cumulative effect of the firm's accounting events **at a point in time.**

At the end of the second day of The American Grabule Company, we prepared another balance sheet, as well as an income statement, from the events of the second day. We saw that the income statement reported all the accounting events (except dividends declared) that increased or decreased retained earnings **during a period of time** (between the balance sheet dates).

From the comparative balance sheets and income statement, we can deduce the cash impact of revenues (gains) and expenses (losses). What cannot be determined from these two statements are the actual *operating, financing,* and *investing cash flow* events that have occurred. Therefore, in addition to the *comparative balance sheets* and the *income statement,* a third statement, the *statement of cash flows,* is required.

A BRIEF HISTORY OF THE STATEMENT OF CASH FLOWS

As analysis of financial statement information developed through the years, the importance attributed to different aspects of economic events presented in the various accounting reports has shifted. At the beginning of the century, analysts focused on the impact of accounting events on assets and equities as reported in the balance sheet. During the first half of the twentieth century, the income statement, which reports the operating events affecting the residual net-assets, became increasingly important. After World War II, the technology underlying business operations substantially changed. Manufacturing, and later even service activities, became increasingly complex as machines augmented and replaced manual operations in a process called automation. Companies, as a result, became larger and more diversified. This created a need for more information about investment activities—the acquisition of long-lived assets, and the manner in which these acquisitions were financed.

In 1969, the Accounting Principles Board (APB) mandated that profit-oriented entities must prepare a statement of changes in financial position (sometimes called the funds statement) whenever they prepare an income statement. The APB's objectives were to "summarize the financing and investing activities of the entity, including the extent to which the enterprise has generated FUNDS FROM OPERATIONS during the period. . . ."

The APB allowed the reporting entities to define **funds** themselves. The definition of funds, which could vary from cash to **working capital** (*current assets* minus *current liabilities*) would be the basis upon which operating, financing, and investing flows would be reported. Since many firms used working capital as their definition of funds, the statement was often thought of as a statement of events increasing and decreasing working capital, even though that was not the intent of the statement.

During the late 1970s, financial analysts recognized the central role that cash-generating ability played in the success and survival of businesses. Users of financial statements increasingly called for more information about the actual cash events of a firm.

In 1987, the Financial Accounting Standards Board (FASB) replaced the statement of changes in financial position with the *statement of cash flows*. The statement of cash flows presents the *operating, financing*, and *investing cash flows* occurring **during a period of time** (between the balance shèet dates). Thus, the new statement still reports the operating, financing, and investing flows, but it does so only on a cash basis.

OPERATING, FINANCING, AND INVESTING CASH FLOWS

To understand operating, financing, and investing cash flows, we must first distinguish between *cash assets, operating assets,* and *nonoperating assets,* and between *operating* and *nonoperating equities.*

Cash assets consist of cash and securities that are readily salable for cash without **any** risk of loss. *Operating assets* are assets that result from income-producing activities (for example, Accounts Receivable), or current assets that will be utilized in income-producing activities (Inventory, Prepaid Services). *Nonoperating assets* are all other assets, such as Property, Plant and Equipment, that will be utilized in income-producing activities over an extended period, or investments that will not be utilized in income-producing activities.

Operating equities are liabilities that will be discharged as a result of the income-producing activities of a firm (Advances from Customers) or that result from the income-producing activities of a firm (Accounts Payable Services). *Nonoperating equities* are all other equities.

Operating cash flows are revenues and expenses that directly impact cash (cash sales and cash expenses), as well as cash flows that impact operating assets and liabilities and thus are associated with revenues and expenses; operating assets and liabilities are also impacted by revenues and expenses.

Revenues are events that increase the residual net-assets of a firm, while cash receipts increase cash. Except for the rare barter transaction, revenues—the provision of goods and services—are expected to result in a cash receipt. That cash receipt may not occur in the same period that the revenue occurred. Instead, the cash receipt may occur in a prior period or a subsequent period. COLLECTIONS FROM CREDIT CUSTOMERS are an example of cash receipts that occur subsequent to the revenue recognition, and ADVANCES FROM CUSTOMERS are cash receipts that occur prior to the revenue recognition.

> ### Thought Question
> Will COLLECTIONS FROM CREDIT CUSTOMERS always occur
> in a period subsequent to the period
> in which the related SALES REVENUE was recognized?

Similarly, *expenses*—the terminal utilization of rights to economic resources—require a cash disbursement in order to obtain the rights to the resource (except for barter transactions). The cash disbursement may occur in a prior or subsequent period to the recognition of the expense. PREPAYMENT FOR SERVICES is an example of a cash disbursement that occurs prior to its related expense, while PAYMENTS FOR LABOR SERVICES already utilized is an example of a cash disbursement that occurs subsequent to the recognition of its related expense.

Thus, operating cash flows of a period are always directly or indirectly associated with revenues and expenses, even when those revenues and expenses occur in a different period. Examples of operating cash (in)flows are CASH SALES, COLLECTIONS FROM CREDIT CUSTOMERS, and ADVANCES FROM CUSTOMERS. Examples of operating cash (out)flows are PAYMENTS TO SUPPLIERS OF MERCHANDISE,

PAYMENTS TO SUPPLIERS OF SERVICES, PREPAYMENTS, PAYMENT OF INTEREST, and PAYMENT OF TAXES.

When payments precede revenues or expenses, the payer debits accounts sometimes called **Deferred Expense** or *Deferred Charges*, although titling these accounts as **Deposits** or *Prepayments* would be preferable. The recipient of the money credits accounts called **Deferred Revenue** or **Unearned Revenue,** although calling these accounts liabilities (or other responsibilities to provide services) would be preferable. Collectively, as defined on page 49, these are *Deferrals*.

When revenues and expenses precede payments, the user records an accrued expense or liability (possibly both), and the provider records an accrued revenue or receivable (possibly both). Collectively, these are *accruals* (see page 49).

The operating cash flows of a firm, as defined by the FASB, include **all** cash flows related to income, whether or not these flows result from operating activities. Thus interest payments and interest receipts, which are related to interest expense and interest revenue, respectively, are included in *cash flows from operations*, even though they do not result from operating events as we defined them in Chapter 5. The FASB, in mandating the statement of cash flows, realized that interest expense and interest revenue result from financing and investing events, respectively. But in an attempt to simplify the concept of operating events, the Board decided to treat **all** events affecting *net income* as if they were operating events. This decision presupposes that the income statement reports only operating events. Though some of the events reported in the income statement are operating events, not all of them are. Therefore, the authors of this book strongly disagree with the Board's decision. But, since FASB pronouncements are GAAP, we will adopt the Board's classification of cash flows.

> ### Thought Question
> Can you give instances where each of the cash receipts
> and cash disbursements mentioned above
> occur in a different period
> than its related revenue or expense?

Financing cash flows are events between the firm and its owners and creditors that increase (or decrease) cash assets and increase (or decrease) nonoperating equities. Examples of such events are the ISSUE AND REPURCHASE OF STOCK, the PAYMENT OF DIVIDENDS, and the BORROWING AND REPAYMENT OF DEBT (short-term and long-term).

Investing cash flows are events that increase (or decrease) cash assets and decrease (or increase) nonoperating assets. Examples of such events are the ACQUISITION AND DISPOSAL OF PROPERTY, PLANT AND EQUIPMENT, and INVESTMENT AND SALE OF SECURITIES.

THE STATEMENT OF CASH FLOWS OF THE AMERICAN GRABULE COMPANY

In order to prepare the required statement of cash flows for The American Grabule Company, we must identify all the events that directly impacted cash during the period. Then we will classify these events as operating, financing, or investing cash flows.

A summary of all the events that occurred **during** the first 2 days follows. Events marked with an asterisk are events affecting cash.

*Issue of Common Stock (Event 1)

Dr. Cash	100,000	
Cr. Common Stock		100,000

*Borrowing from the Bank (Event 2)

Dr. Cash	50,000	
Cr. Bank Loan		50,000

Purchases of Marbles (Events 3 and 13)

Dr. Raw Materials and Supplies	18,000	
Cr. Accounts Payable		18,000

*Purchases of Chemicals (Events 4 and 14)

Dr. Raw Materials and Supplies	3,392	
Cr. Cash		3,392

*Renting of Space and Machine (Events 5 and 18)

Dr. Prepaid Services	855	
Cr. Cash		855

*Purchase of Truck (Event 6)

Dr. Property, Plant and Equipment	26,500	
Cr. Cash		26,500

Manufacture of Grabules (Events 8 and 15)

Dr. Work-in-Process	6,600	
Cr. Raw Materials and Supplies		6,248
Cr. Prepaid Services		192
Cr. Wages Payable		160

Completion of the Manufacturing Process (Events 9 and 16)

Dr. Finished Goods	6,600	
Cr. Work-in-Process		6,600

*Sales Orders (Event 10)
  Dr. Cash   8,000
    Cr. Advances from Customers   8,000

*Payments to Supplier of Raw Materials
(Event 11)
  Dr. Accounts Payable   3,000
    Cr. Cash   3,000

*Payments to Supplier of Labor Services
(Events 12 and 17)
  Dr. Wages Payable   160
    Cr. Cash   160

**Sales Inflow (Event 19)
  Dr. Cash (a)   32,000
  Dr. Advances from Customers (b) 8,000
  Dr. Accounts Receivable (c)   5,200
    Cr. Sales Inflow (I/S)   45,200

Sales Outflow (Event 20)
  Dr. Sales Outflow (I/S)   6,215
    Cr. Finished Goods   6,215

Utilization of Rented Space (Event 21)
  Dr. Operating Expenses (I/S)   75
    Cr. Prepaid Services   75

Utilization of Labor Services (Event 22)
  Dr. Operating Expenses (I/S)   100
    Cr. Wages Payable   100

Utilization of Truck Services (Event 23)
  Dr. Operating Expenses (I/S)   20
    Cr. Accumulated Depreciation   20

Utilization of Cash Services (Event 24)
  Dr. Interest Expense (I/S)   25
    Cr. Interest Payable   25

Acquisition of Patent (Event 25)
  Dr. Patent   10,000
    Cr. Common Stock   10,000

   Recall that at the end of Chapter 4 (page 80), we introduced an activity statement that reported all the events that affected cash on the first day, called the statement of cash receipts and disbursements. If we prepare a statement of cash receipts and disbursements for the first 2 days of The American Grabule Company, it would include all the events that affected cash during the first 2 days, marked by asterisks above. [*Note:* The event SALES INFLOW is double-asterisked (**) because the Cash account was only increased by $32,000, the amount of CASH SALES.] The activity report would look as follows:

Cash Receipts	
Issue of Common Stock	$100,000
Borrowing from the Bank	50,000
⁺Advances from Customers	8,000
⁺Cash Sales	32,000
Total Cash Receipts	$190,000
Cash Disbursements	
⁺Payments to Supplier of Chemicals	$3,392
⁺Payments for Rent of Space and Machine	855
Purchase of Truck	26,500
⁺Payment to Supplier of Marbles	3,000
⁺Payments to Supplier of Labor Services	160
Total Cash Disbursements	$ 33,907
Excess Cash Receipts over Disbursements	$156,093

Notice all of the events in the schedule above marked by a plus (⁺) sign. These events are all related to the revenues and expenses of the firm, and are necessarily interdependent. That is, we could not have cash receipts from customers (ADVANCES FROM CUSTOMERS and CASH SALES) for the provision of goods and services (revenues) without cash disbursements (PAYMENTS TO SUPPLIER OF CHEMICALS, PAYMENT FOR RENT OF SPACE AND MACHINE, PAYMENT TO SUPPLIER OF MARBLES, and PAYMENTS TO SUPPLIER OF LABOR SERVICES) for those goods and services utilized on behalf of customers (expenses).

These interdependent cash operating events determine CASH FLOWS FROM OPERATIONS. Listing CASH FLOWS FROM OPERATIONS separately from *financing cash flows* and from *investing cash flows* results in a statement of cash flows, as follows:

The American Grabule Company
Statement of Cash Flows
The First Two Days

Cash Flows from Operations

Cash Receipts

Advances from Customers	$ 8,000	
Cash Sales	32,000	
Total Cash Receipts	$ 40,000	$ 40,000

Cash Disbursements

Payments to Supplier of Chemicals	$ 3,392	
Payments for Rent of Space and Machine	855	
Payment to Supplier of Marbles	3,000	
Payments to Supplier of Labor Services	160	
Total Cash Disbursements	$ 7,407	(7,407)
Total Cash Flows from Operations		$ 32,593

Cash Flows from Financing Events

From the Issue of Common Stock	$100,000	
From Bank Borrowing	50,000	
Total Cash Flows from Financing Events	$150,000	150,000

Cash Flows from Investing Events

Purchase of Truck	$ 26,500	
Total Cash Flows from Investing Events	$ 26,500	(26,500)
Increase in Cash		$156,093

THE INDIRECT METHOD OF REPORTING CASH FROM OPERATIONS ·

The format for reporting *operating cash flows* presented above is called the **direct method** of reporting cash from operations. This method simply lists each of this period's operating cash events. Alternatively, the FASB permits a firm to report operating cash flows by the **indirect method.** The indirect method appears clearly less informative and more cumbersome than the direct method, but since most firms use this method, financial statement preparers and users must understand the indirect method as well.

The indirect method determines CASH FLOWS FROM OPERATIONS by making adjustments to the reported NET INCOME of the period. These adjustments are for (a) revenues and expenses that are not associated with operating cash flows of any period, and (b) cash flows of this period that are associated with revenues and expenses of a different period, and revenues and expenses of this period that are associated with cash flows of a different period.

The American Grabule Company has one example of the first type of adjustment—DEPRECIATION EXPENSE. DEPRECIATION EXPENSE represents the utilization of property, plant and equipment. The cash flows associated with property, plant and equipment are the cash paid in acquiring it, and the cash received when it is sold. The ACQUISITION AND SALE OF PROPERTY, PLANT AND EQUIPMENT are investing events. Thus, DEPRECIATION EXPENSE is **not** associated with, and does not affect, the operating cash flows of any period. The first adjustment, then, is to add expenses like depreciation to NET INCOME.

The second type of adjustment needed is to adjust NET INCOME for those revenues and expenses that are associated with cash flows of a prior or a subsequent period, and for those cash flows of this period that are associated with revenues and expenses of a prior or subsequent period.

Returning to our example, The American Grabule Company reported CREDIT SALES as part of TOTAL SALES REVENUES. This credit sale is expected to result in a future cash inflow, but since it has not yet been collected, it has not increased cash this period. Therefore, the amount of sales revenue that has not been collected must be subtracted from NET INCOME to determine CASH FLOWS FROM OPERATIONS.

The American Grabule Company also had a cash outflow for prepaid services, services to be utilized in subsequent periods. This prepayment is a cash disbursement, which must be subtracted in determining CASH FLOWS FROM OPERATIONS even though it was not an expense, and did not reduce NET INCOME. Therefore, the amount prepaid for services not yet utilized must be subtracted from NET INCOME to determine CASH FLOWS FROM OPERATIONS.

On the other hand, The American Grabule Company utilized labor services in this period which are to be paid for in a subsequent period. The utilization represents an expense which decreased NET INCOME, but did **not** decrease cash or CASH FLOWS FROM OPERATIONS. Therefore, labor services utilized but not paid for must be added to NET INCOME to determine CASH FLOWS FROM OPERATIONS.

The second type of adjustment discussed above is accomplished by adjusting NET INCOME for the changes in the operating assets and liabilities. For example, consider the change in Accounts Receivable. Accounts Receivable is determined from SALES REVENUE:

(a) Credit Sales Inflow
     Dr. Accounts Receivable
         Cr. Credit Sales Inflow (I/S)

and from the related event, COLLECTIONS FROM CREDIT CUSTOMERS, that would be recorded as follows:

(b) Collections from Credit Customers
     Dr. Cash
         Cr. Accounts Receivable

CREDIT SALES INFLOW is an event that increases NET INCOME **but not** cash (or CASH FLOWS FROM OPERATIONS). On the other hand, the event COLLECTIONS FROM CREDIT CUSTOMERS increases cash (and CASH FLOWS FROM OPERATIONS) in the current period, **but not** NET INCOME.

> ### *Thought Question*
> What is the relationship between CREDIT SALES INFLOW and COLLECTIONS FROM CREDIT CUSTOMERS?

If you record these events in the T-accounts, they would appear as follows:

Sales Revenue		↑	Cash	↓
	Credit (a)	(b) Collections		
	Sales	from		
	Inflow	Credit		
		Customers		

↑	Accounts Receivable	↓
(a) Credit	Collections (b)	
Sales	from	
Inflow	Credit	
	Customers	

You can readily see that CREDIT SALES INFLOW (part of NET INCOME) is the debit (Dr.) entry to Accounts Receivable, and that COLLECTIONS FROM CREDIT CUSTOMERS (part of CASH FLOWS FROM OPERATIONS) is the credit (Cr.) entry in the same account, Accounts Receivable. Therefore, in adjusting NET INCOME to CASH FLOWS FROM OPERATIONS, COLLECTIONS FROM CREDIT CUSTOMERS must be substituted for CREDIT SALES INFLOW. This is done by **subtracting** CREDIT SALES INFLOW from NET INCOME and **adding** COLLECTIONS FROM CREDIT CUSTOMERS to NET INCOME.

But the difference between CREDIT SALES INFLOW (the amount to be subtracted) and COLLECTIONS FROM CREDIT CUSTOMERS (the amount to be added) is nothing more than the change in Accounts Receivable. A debit (Dr.) change in Accounts Receivable means that CREDIT SALES INFLOW is larger than COLLECTIONS FROM CREDIT CUSTOMERS by the amount of the change; therefore, this debit (Dr.) change must be subtracted from NET INCOME in determining CASH FLOWS FROM OPERATIONS. Similarly, a credit (Cr.) change in Accounts Receivable means that COLLECTIONS FROM CREDIT CUSTOMERS is larger than CREDIT SALES INFLOW. The credit (Cr.) change must be added to NET INCOME in determining CASH FLOWS FROM OPERATIONS.

In general, noncash revenues such as CREDIT SALES INFLOW **do not increase cash,** but they do affect operating accounts such as Accounts Receivable, and are recorded as debits (Dr.) to these accounts. Noncash revenues must be subtracted from NET INCOME in determining CASH FLOWS FROM OPERATIONS.

Correspondingly, operating cash inflows that **are not revenues** of the current period are not included in net income. These operating cash flows, such as COLLECTIONS FROM CREDIT CUSTOMERS, are recorded as debits (Dr.) to Cash and credits (Cr.) to operating accounts (Accounts Receivable). The cash inflows must be added to NET INCOME in determining CASH FLOWS FROM OPERATIONS.

Noncash expenses, such as ACCRUED INTEREST EXPENSE, are deducted in determining NET INCOME, but should not be deducted in determining CASH FLOWS FROM OPERATIONS because they **do not decrease cash.** These noncash expenses affect operating accounts such as Interest Payable, and are recorded as credits (Cr.) to these accounts. Therefore, noncash expenses must be **added** to NET INCOME in determining CASH FLOWS FROM OPERATIONS.

Operating cash outflows such as PAYMENT OF INTEREST that **are not expenses** of the current period are recorded as debits (Dr.) to the operating account Interest Payable, and as credits (Cr.) to Cash. Because they decrease cash, but not net income, they must be subtracted from NET INCOME in determining CASH FLOWS FROM OPERATIONS.

Taken all together, then, debits (Dr.) to operating accounts arise either from operating cash outflows that are not expenses, or from noncash revenues, and must be **subtracted** from NET INCOME in determining CASH FLOWS FROM OPERATIONS. Credits (Cr.) to operating accounts represent either noncash expenses or operating cash inflows that are not revenues, and must be **added** to NET INCOME in determining CASH FLOWS FROM OPERATIONS.

Thus, debit changes in operating assets and liabilities are caused by revenues exceeding operating cash inflows, or by pay-

ments exceeding related expenses, and must be subtracted from
NET INCOME in determining CASH FLOWS FROM OPERATIONS. Credit
changes in operating assets and liabilities arise from operating cash
inflows exceeding revenues, or by expenses exceeding related payments, and must be added to NET INCOME in determining CASH
FLOWS FROM OPERATIONS.

In general, if the debit entry in an operating account is greater
than the credit entry (a debit change), merely subtract the debit
change. If the credit entry in an operating account is greater than
the debit entry (a credit change), add the change in order to adjust
NET INCOME to CASH FLOWS FROM OPERATIONS.

Using the *indirect method* to determine CASH FLOWS FROM
OPERATIONS requires reference to the comparative balance sheets
and income statement. For The American Grabule Company, these
statements are reproduced below.

The American Grabule Company
Comparative Balance Sheets
Beginning of the First Day and the End of the Second Day

Assets	Beg. of Day 1	End of Day 2	Account Increases
Cash	$0	$156,093	$156,093
Accounts Receivable	0	5,200	5,200
Prepaid Services	0	588	588
Raw Materials and Supplies	0	15,144	15,144
Finished Goods	0	385	385
Property, Plant and Equipment	0	26,500	26,500
Accumulated Depreciation	0	(20)	20
Patent	0	10,000	10,000
Total Assets	$0	$213,890	
Equities			
Accounts Payable	$0	$ 15,000	15,000
Interest Payable	0	25	25
Wages Payable	0	100	100
Dividends Payable	0	2,200	2,200
Bank Loan	0	50,000	50,000
Common Stock	0	110,000	110,000
Retained Earnings	0	36,565	36,565
Total Equities	$0	$213,890	

The American Grabule Company
Income Statement
The First Two Days

Revenues

Sales Inflow (Sales Revenue)	$45,200
Total Revenues	$45,200

Expenses

Sales Outflow (Cost of Goods Sold)	$6,215	
Operating Expenses*	195	
Interest Expense	25	
Total Expenses	$6,435	(6,435)
Net Income		$38,765

*Includes Depreciation Expense of $20.

An examination of the income statement reveals that NET INCOME is $38,765, and that the only revenue or expense not associated with CASH FLOWS FROM OPERATIONS is DEPRECIATION EXPENSE of $20. Thus, the first adjustment is to **add** $20 to NET INCOME. An examination of the comparative balance sheets indicates the following changes in operating assets and liabilities:

The American Grabule Company
Schedule of Changes in the Operating Accounts
The First Two Days

Account	Debit Change	Credit Change
Accounts Receivable	$ 5,200	
Prepaid Services	588	
Raw Materials and Supplies	15,144	
Finished Goods	385	
Accounts Payable		$15,000
Interest Payable		25
Wages Payable		100
Total Changes	$21,317	$15,125
Net Debit Change	$6,192	

Thus, the second type of adjustment requires us to **subtract** the net debit change of $6,192 from NET INCOME. CASH FLOWS FROM OPERATIONS is therefore $32,593 ($38,765 + $20 − $6,192). Surprise! This is the same result that we got earlier in the chapter by using the *direct method*.

THE STATEMENT OF CASH FLOWS PRESENTED USING THE INDIRECT METHOD

The presentation for the statement of cash flows using the indirect method is as follows:

The American Grabule Company
Statement of Cash Flows
The First Two Days

Net Income		$ 38,765
Adjustment for Depreciation Expense	$ 20	
Adjustment for Changes in Operating Accounts:		
Accounts Receivable	(5,200)	
Prepaid Services	(588)	
Raw Materials and Supplies	(15,144)	
Finished Goods	(385)	
Accounts Payable	15,000	
Interest Payable	25	
Wages Payable	100	
Total Adjustments	(6,172)	(6,172)
Cash Flows from Operations		$ 32,593
Cash Flows from Financing Events		
From the Issue of Common Stock	$100,000	
From Bank Borrowing	50,000	
Total Cash Flows from Financing Events	$150,000	150,000
Cash Flows from Investing Events		
Purchase of Truck	$ 26,500	
Total Cash Flows from Investing Events	$ 26,500	(26,500)
Increase in Cash		$156,093

SCHEDULE OF SIGNIFICANT NONCASH FINANCING AND INVESTING EVENTS

In addition to the new statement of cash flows, GAAP requires a schedule of those events that do not affect cash, but are financing events, such as CONVERSION OF BONDS TO COMMON STOCK; or investing events, such as the EXCHANGE OF INVESTMENT ASSETS; or a combined financing event and an investing event, such as an issue of common stock for the acquisition of a patent.

The American Grabule Company had such an event, Event 25, when they acquired the patent by issuing shares of their common stock. The journal entry for this event was

Acquisition of Patent [Event (25)]
    Dr. Patent   10,000
        Cr. Common Stock   10,000

This event will be presented in the schedule of noncash financing and investing events, as follows:

The American Grabule Company
Significant Noncash Financing and Investing Events
The First Two Days

Issue of Common Stock for Acquisition of Patent $10,000

USER'S PERSPECTIVE

The emphasis on cash flows, and the emergence of the statement of cash flows as an important financial report, does not mean that operating cash flows are a substitute for, or are more important than, net income. In order to analyze financial statements correctly, we need to consider **both** operating cash flows and net income.

Many people misunderstand the meaning of CASH FLOWS FROM OPERATIONS and of NET INCOME, as was graphically illustrated during the controversy leading up to the 1985 baseball players' strike. One crucial issue that separated the owners from the players was the players' claim that the owners had enough cash to meet their demands, and the owners' counterclaim that their teams were unprofitable, and therefore they were unable to increase basic salaries.

The truth lay between the two parties: The owners did not have as much cash available for salaries as the players thought, and a portion of the losses reported by the owners, determined in accordance with GAAP, was not related to past, present, or future cash flows necessary for the operations of their baseball teams. Thus, these losses were not relevant in determining their ability to pay the players' salaries.

On the other hand, the players' claim that the owners had enough operating cash flows to meet their demands disregarded future commitments that the owners had made to the players in the form of deferred compensation plans. Many players had signed long-term contracts calling for payments to be made over a period of time that exceeded the related playing time.

Take, for example, a player we'll call Dave Losefield. Losefield played for a period of 5 years, but was to be paid over a period of 20 years. His contract called for him to be paid in the year 2000 for services rendered in 1985. Obviously, the cash outflows for his team during 1985 would not reflect any of the payments for his deferred compensation. But did this mean that the club was profitable? Not necessarily! Unless the revenues generated as a result of Losefield's (and his teammates') services in 1985 were sufficient to cover all of the expenses for 1985 plus the present value of the deferred compensation for Losefield (and any of his teammates), then the team would not be profitable.

In effect, Losefield, in negotiating a deferred compensation contract, was loaning his club a portion of his 1985 salary until the year 2000. If the revenues in 1985 were not sufficient to cover Losefield's salary in 2000, then either the players playing in 2000 would finance his 1985 salary, or Losefield would not get paid in the year 2000 for his 1985 services. In short, the cash inflows during 1985 had to cover both the 1985 cash outflows and any future cash obligations that resulted from the 1985 season.

This example demonstrates that neither cash flows from operations, nor net income, are by themselves sufficient to guide us to reasonable conclusions about financial controversies. Both CASH FLOWS FROM OPERATIONS **and** NET INCOME must play a role.

PROBLEMS

1. From the following events relating to The Nast Company, a merchandising concern, prepare
   a. A statement of balance sheet changes
   b. An income statement
   c. A statement of cash flows
   No events not described or derivable from the information below, occurred.
   (1) Common Stock issued by the company was $50,000. No stock was repurchased.
   (2) The Dividends Payable account decreased by $10,000.
   (3) Operating expenses **excluding** depreciation were $100,000.
   (4) The Inventory account increased by $10,000.
   (5) Collections from credit customers were $670,000.
   (6) The Retained Earnings account increased by $50,000.
   (7) The Prepaid Services account decreased by $5,000.
   (8) The Accounts Payable Merchandise account increased by $5,000.
   (9) Taxes paid during the year were $100,000.
   (10) Depreciation expense for the year was $50,000.
   (11) Cash dividends declared during the year were $80,000.
   (12) The Taxes Payable account decreased by $5,000.
   (13) The Accounts Receivable account decreased by $10,000.
   (14) The Accounts Payable Services account increased by $5,000.
   (15) Property, plant and equipment, with an original cost of $20,000 and accumulated depreciation associated with it of $15,000, was sold for $5,000. No other property, plant and equipment was disposed of during the year.
   (16) There **was** cost of goods sold during the year.
   (17) Property, plant and equipment was acquired for $30,000 cash.

For Problems 2 through 4, fill in the account title in the blank space, and circle "increased," "decreased," or "remained the same" for the account changes, and "greater than," "less than," or "equal to" in comparing NET INCOME to CASH FLOWS FROM OPERATIONS. Assume no other differences between NET INCOME and CASH FLOWS FROM OPERATIONS.

2. If PAYMENTS TO SUPPLIERS OF MERCHANDISE are **greater than** COST OF GOODS SOLD, and COST OF GOODS SOLD is **greater than** PURCHASES OF INVENTORY, then account:
   _____ increased, decreased, or remained the same; and
   _____ increased, decreased, or remained the same; and
   NET INCOME is greater than, less than, or equal to CASH FLOWS FROM OPERATIONS.

3. If PAYMENTS TO SUPPLIERS OF MERCHANDISE are **less than** PURCHASES OF INVENTORY, and PURCHASES OF INVENTORY are **greater than** COST OF GOODS SOLD, then account:
   _____ increased, decreased, or remained the same; and
   _____ increased, decreased, or remained the same; and
   NET INCOME is greater than, less than, or equal to CASH FLOWS FROM OPERATIONS.

4. If PAYMENTS TO SUPPLIERS OF MERCHANDISE are **less than** COST OF GOODS SOLD, and COST OF GOODS SOLD is **less than** PURCHASES OF INVENTORY, then account:
   _____ increased, decreased, or remained the same; and
   _____ increased, decreased, or remained the same; and
   NET INCOME is greater than, less than, or equal to CASH FLOWS FROM OPERATIONS.

5. From the following information, determine NET INCOME and CASH FLOWS FROM OPERATIONS.
   (1) The balance in the Property, Plant and Equipment account increased by $100,000.
   (2) The balance in the Common Stock account increased by $60,000.
   (3) The balance in the Bank Loan account increased by $15,000.
   (4) No property, plant and equipment was retired or sold.
   (5) The balance in the Accumulated Depreciation account increased by $20,000.
   (6) Except for Retained Earnings, no other account balances changed.

6. From the following information, determine NET INCOME and CASH FLOWS FROM OPERATIONS:
   (1) The balance in Accounts Receivable increased by $15,000.
   (2) The balance in Inventory decreased by $18,000.
   (3) The balance in the Cash account changed.
   (4) The balance in Accounts Payable decreased by $8,000.
   (5) The balance in Dividends Payable increased by $1,000.
   (6) The payment of dividends was $16,000.
   (7) No other account balances changed.

7.

<hr>

The Monsor Company
Comparative Balance Sheets
Years Ending December 31, 19X0 and December 31, 19X1

Assets	12/31/X0	12/31/X1
Cash	$200,000	$222,000
Accounts Receivable	500,000	?
Inventory	300,000	335,000
Property, Plant and Equipment	400,000	900,000
Accumulated Depreciation	(100,000)	(?)
Total Assets	$?	$?

Liabilities and Owners' Equities		
Accounts Payable Merchandise	$ 85,000	$100,000
Accounts Payable Services	40,000	35,000
Taxes Payable	30,000	40,000
Interest Payable	0	5,000
Dividends Payable	30,000	25,000
Bank Loan	0	90,000
Common Stock	200,000	375,000
Retained Earnings	?	?
Total Liabilities and Owners' Equities	$?	$?

Notes
(1) Purchases of inventory during the year were $285,000.
(2) Purchases of property, plant and equipment during the year were $550,000, paid for in cash.
(3) Only fully depreciated equipment (original cost equals accumulated depreciation) was disposed of during the year. There were no proceeds from the disposition of this equipment.
(4) Payments to suppliers of miscellaneous services were $160,000.
(5) No bank loan was repaid during the year.
(6) No common stock was repurchased during the year.
(7) The Retained Earnings account increased by $87,000.

The Monsor Company
Income Statement
19X1

Revenues

Sales Revenue	$690,000
Total Revenues	$690,000

Expenses

Cost of Goods Sold	$?	
Operating Expenses	?	
Depreciation Expense	50,000	
Interest Expense	8,000	
Tax Expense	75,000	
Total Expenses	$?	(?)
Net Income		$?

Required:
a. Determine all the events that occurred during 19X1.
b. Fill in the question (?) marks.
c. Prepare a statement of cash flows for 19X1.

8.

The Da-aD Company
Comparative Balance Sheets
Years Ending December 31, 19X0 and December 31, 19X1

Assets	12/31/X0	12/31/X1
Cash	$?	$?
Accounts Receivable	250,000	150,000
Interest Receivable	5,000	4,000
Prepaid Services	11,000	15,000
Inventory	100,000	?
Investment in Debentures	150,000	110,000
Total Assets	$?	$?

Liabilities and Owners' Equities		
Accounts Payable Merchandise	$ 95,000	$105,000
Accounts Payable Services	55,000	50,000
Dividends Payable	16,000	20,000
Common Stock	200,000	250,000
Retained Earnings	150,000	370,000
Total Liabilities and Owners' Equities:	$516,000	$795,000

The Da-aD Company
Income Statement
19X1

Revenues

Sales Revenue	$800,000	
Interest Revenue	?	
Total Revenues	$?	

Expenses

Cost of Goods Sold	$400,000	
Operating Expenses	100,000	
Total Expenses	$500,000	(500,000)
Net Income		$?

Statement of Cash Flows for 19X1

Cash Flows from Operating Events $ 0

Cash Flows from Financing Events

Payment of Cash Dividend	$(?)	
Issue of Common Stock	?	
Total Financing Events	$ (35,000)	(35,000)

Cash Flows from Investing Events

Sale of Debentures	$?	
Total Investing Events	$?	?
Increase in Cash		$456,000

Required:
a. Determine all the events that occurred during 19X1.
b. Fill in the question (?) marks.

9.

Shog Ltd.
Comparative Balance Sheets
Years Ending December 31, 19X0 and December 31, 19X1

Assets	12/31/X0	12/31/X1
Cash	$ 600,000	$ 504,000
Accounts Receivable	550,000	850,000
Interest Receivable	1,000	2,000
Prepaid Services	4,000	3,000
Inventory	300,000	350,000
Investment in Government Bonds	80,000	80,000
Property, Plant and Equipment	800,000	900,000
Accumulated Depreciation	(100,000)	(140,000)
Total Assets	$?	$?

Liabilities and Owners' Equities		
Accounts Payable Merchandise	$ 60,000	$ 55,000
Accounts Payable Services	35,000	40,000
Common Stock	400,000	450,000
Retained Earnings	?	?
Total Liabilities and Owners' Equities	$?	$?

Shog Ltd.
Income Statement
19X1

Revenues

Sales Revenue	$900,000
Interest Revenue	5,000
Total Revenues	$905,000

Expenses

Cost of Goods Sold	$ 240,000	
Operating Expenses	?	
Total Expenses	$?	(?)
Net Income		$?

Statement of Cash Flows for 19X1

Cash Flows from Operating Events		$199,000

Cash Flows from Financing Events

Payment of Cash Dividend	$(245,000)	
Issue of Common Stock	?	
Total Financing Events	$?	?

Cash Flows from Investing Events

Purchase of Property, Plant and Equipment	$?	
Total Investing Events	$?	(?)
(Decrease) in Cash		$ (96,000)

Required:
a. Determine all the events that occurred during 19X1.
b. Fill in the question (?) marks.

10.

The Gamma Company
Comparative Post-Closing Trial Balance Sheets
December 31, 19X0 and January 31, 19X1

Debit Balance Accounts	12/31/X0	1/31/X1
Cash	$100,000	$160,000
Accounts Receivable	192,000	221,000
Raw Materials	50,000	40,000
Finished Goods	150,000	170,000
Total Debit Balance Accounts	$?	$?

Credit Balance Accounts		
Accounts Payable Raw Materials	$10,000	$ 8,000
Wages Payable	40,000	45,000
Dividends Payable	5,000	17,000
Common Stock	300,000	350,000
Retained Earnings	137,000	171,000
Total Credit Balance Accounts	$492,000	$591,000

Notes

(1) Purchases of raw materials in January were $130,000.
(2) Inputs to Manufacturing Process consisted solely of labor services and raw materials.

The Gamma Company
Income Statement
January

Revenues

Sales Revenue		$?
Total Revenues		$?

Expenses

Cost of Goods Sold	$300,000	
Operating Expenses	100,000	
Total Expenses	$400,000	(400,000)
Net Income		$?

Statement of Cash Flows for January

Cash Flows from Operating Events		$?

Cash Flows from Financing Events

Payment of Cash Dividend	$ (54,000)	
Issue of Common Stock	?	
Total Financing Events	$?	?
Increase in Cash		$?

Required:
a. Fill in the question (?) marks.
b. Determine all the events that occurred during January.

CHAPTER 7

Recognizing and Quantifying, Recording and Reporting Accounting Events

INTRODUCTION

The purpose of this chapter is to abstract and synthesize the preceding six chapters into a unified accounting model. So far, we have described the general rules that govern how accounting events are recognized and quantified, recorded and reported. In this chapter, we present specific criteria for recognizing and quantifying accounting events; we describe how these events are classified and recorded as operating, financing, and investing events; and we show how they are reported in the financial statements. Then, in the rest of this book, we will examine in greater detail how operating, financing, and investing events are accounted for and analyzed by users of financial statements.

We saw in Chapter 2 that the accounting process recognizes only certain economic events as accounting events. These accounting events are then quantified and recorded in the accounts by means of journal entries, and reported in the financial statements. The authoritative accounting literature does not list explicit criteria for recognizing or quantifying accounting events, but the seven criteria that we present here are implicit in, and consistent with, current accounting practice. According to these criteria:

1. All cash receipts and disbursements are accounting events.

2. The acquisition of an economic resource is an accounting event.

3. The provision of an economic resource is an accounting event.

4. The utilization of an economic resource is an accounting event.

5. The impairment of assets is an accounting event.

6. Any event, other than an exchange of promises, resulting in a virtually certain and measurable increase or decrease of cash is an accounting event.

7. A descriptive change is an accounting event.

CRITERIA FOR RECOGNIZING ACCOUNTING EVENTS

Accounting events are actions that have monetary consequences, or events that alter previously recorded monetary consequences. Usually, the actions are recorded as part of a three-stage exchange transaction.

The first stage is an *agreement* between two parties that results in each party's receiving a right to receive cash, goods, or services, in exchange for assuming an obligation to provide cash, goods, or services. The second and third stages of an exchange transaction consist of the *performance* by each party pursuant to such agreements. Accounting's recognition criteria exclude the agreement stage of an exchange transaction, but performance by either party is always recognized as an accounting event by both parties.

The first three criteria of the seven listed above assure that performance pursuant to an agreement by either party to the agreement is recognized as an accounting event by both parties to the agreement. The remaining four criteria specify events that alter previously recorded monetary consequences.

Criterion 1

All cash receipts and disbursements are accounting events. Cash receipts or cash disbursements usually represent actions by one party or another pursuant to an agreement. In some cases, donations and similar events represent unilateral actions by the accounting unit or some other unit. Since the main objective of financial statements is to facilitate the assessment of cash flows, a rule requiring the recognition of cash events is self-explanatory.

Current cash flows are quantified by the cash that changes hands. Cash flows can be classified into three groups: operating, financing, and investing. The following journal entries illustrate a cash receipt from each group:

Advances for Rent (operating)
    Dr. Cash
        Cr. Advances for Rent

Borrowing from the Bank (financing)
    Dr. Cash
        Cr. Bank Loan

Sale of Investments (investing)
>Dr. Cash
>>Cr. Investments

and the following journal entries represent examples of a cash disbursement from each group:

Prepayments to Suppliers of Services (operating)
>Dr. Prepaid Services
>>Cr. Cash

Repurchase of Common Stock (financing)
>Dr. Common Stock
>>Cr. Cash

Acquisition of Property, Plant and Equipment (investing)
>Dr. Property, Plant and Equipment
>>Cr. Cash

Criterion 2

The acquisition of an economic resource is an accounting event. An economic resource is acquired when an entity obtains all or substantially all of the ownership rights to it from another entity. Under this criterion, the purchase of goods or other assets is recognized as an accounting event. Usually, when an economic resource is acquired, the selling party to an agreement has performed, and under this criterion, the seller's performance is recognized as an accounting event by the buyer. This criterion also covers the receipt of an economic resource, which represents unilateral performance, as in the receipt of a gift.

The acquisition of an economic resource is quantified by the cash outflow associated with the acquisition of the resource. The cash outflow associated with an acquisition is the cash paid for the resource, the present value of the cash required to be paid in the future, or in the case of a barter transaction or a gift, the cash would have been paid in an analogous transaction to acquire the resource.

If an economic resource is acquired for cash, as in the purchase of merchandise, it is recorded by the following journal entry:

Purchase of Inventory
>Dr. Inventory
>>Cr. Cash

If the merchandise is acquired on credit, the journal entry would be

Credit Purchase of Inventory
>Dr. Inventory
>>Cr. Accounts Payable Merchandise

Criterion 3

The provision of an economic resource is an accounting event. An economic resource is provided when the reporting entity transfers all or substantially all of the ownership rights to another entity, or when another entity's right to utilize resources owned by the reporting entity expires. For example, when a product is sold, an entity transfers all of the ownership rights to another entity.

For services, another entity acquires the right to utilize the reporting entity's resources for a specified period of time as a result of a formal or informal agreement. The provision of the services occurs as time passes, and the right expires. For example, the provision of rented space occurs as time passes, and the tenant's right expires.

The provision of an economic resource is quantified by the cash inflow associated with the provision. The cash inflow associated with the provision of the resource is the cash that has been received, the present value of the cash expected to be received, or, as in a barter transaction, the cash that would have been received in an analogous cash transaction for the provision of the resource.

The regular and recurring provision of economic resources, when the financial consequences resulting from such provision are known or estimable with virtual certainty, is called **revenue.** The entry for revenue depends on whether cash has been received prior to the provision of the service or not. If cash has been received first, as in the case of rent collected in advance, the revenue is recorded by the following journal entry:

Rent Revenue
    Dr. Advances of Rent
        Cr. Rent Revenue (I/S)

But if the cash will be collected after the provision, the entry is

Rent Revenue
    Dr. Rent Receivable
        Cr. Rent Revenue (I/S)

When an agreement specifies the amount of cash to be received in exchange for the provision of the resource, and only part of the resource is provided, then only the partial provision will be recognized. For example, if an agreement calls for the provision of 50 grabules at a price of $4,000, and only 20 have been shipped, then only $1,600 will be recognized [(20 ÷ 50) × $4,000].

Criterion 4

The utilization of an economic resource is an accounting event. Utilization occurs when the right to utilize the economic resource expires. Rights can expire because the quantity of resources to which rights exist is reduced, because the duration that the resources will exist is reduced, or because the duration of the right is reduced. A reduction in the quantity of resources occurs when raw materials are converted into manufactured product, or inventory is sold. DEPRECIATION represents a reduction in the duration that a resource exists, whereas the UTILIZATION OF RENTED SPACE represents a reduction in the duration of a right. All three of these events represent the utilization of economic resources and therefore must be recognized as accounting events. Utilizations are recorded as accounting events whether or not a right has previously been recognized as an accounting asset. The recognition of COST OF GOODS SOLD clearly represents a decrease in an accounting asset. Similarly, if a prepayment to obtain the right to a service has been made, and a prepaid asset recognized, the decrease in the duration of that right as time passes represents a reduction in that asset. On the other hand, if the right to utilize a service is acquired without a prepayment, no accounting asset has been recognized. But when that right expires, an accounting event results and is recorded as an increase in a liability.

For example, the utilization of rented space is recognized whether or not prepaid rent has been recognized previously as an asset. Analogously, the utilization of labor services, government services, or legal services also is recognized as an accounting event, whether or not an accounting asset had been previously recognized. The regular and recurring utilization of economic resources, except in manufacturing, is called an **expense.**

The utilization of an economic resource is quantified by the cash outflow that was, will be, or would have been required to obtain the expired right. The *terminal utilization* of an economic resource, such as Prepaid Services, that was an accounting asset is recorded by the following journal entry:

Operating Expenses
    Dr. Operating Expenses (I/S)
        Cr. Prepaid Services

and the *intermediate utilization* of an accounting asset is recorded by the following journal entry:

Input Services into Production
    Dr. Work-in-Process
        Cr. Prepaid Services

If the economic resource utilized was not a previously recorded accounting asset, the terminal utilization would be recorded by the following journal entry:

Operating Expenses
    Dr. Operating Expenses (I/S)
        Cr. Accounts Payable Services

and the intermediate utilization of the economic resource not previously recorded as an accounting asset would be recorded by the following journal entry:

Input Services into Production
    Dr. Work-in-Process
        Cr. Accounts Payable Services

Criterion 5

The impairment of assets is an accounting event. An asset is said to be impaired if the direct or indirect cash benefit expected from utilizing the asset is less than the accounting quantification of the asset. For assets held for sale rather than use, such as inventory and marketable securities, a decline in the market price below the accounting quantification indicates that impairment has occurred and must be recognized. For assets held for use rather than sale, the expected cash benefit is not measured by the market price of the asset, and thus a decline in market value does not necessarily indicate impairment. These assets are considered impaired only if the nondiscounted cash benefit expected from utilizing the asset is less than the accounting quantification.

An asset impairment is quantified by the difference between the accounting description of the asset, and the direct or indirect cash benefit (not discounted) expected from utilizing the asset. For example, the IMPAIRMENT OF INVENTORY would be recorded by the following journal entry:

Decline in Market Value of Inventory
    Dr. Loss from Decline in Market Value of Inventory (I/S)
        Cr. Inventory

Criterion 6

Any event, other than an exchange of promises, resulting in a virtually certain and measurable increase or decrease of cash is an accounting event. The most common example of the application of this rule is the DECLARATION OF A CASH DIVIDEND. When the board of directors declares a cash dividend, a cash outflow becomes virtually certain and measurable. The dividend declaration is not an exchange of promises, so the DECLARATION OF A CASH DIVIDEND qualifies as an accounting event.

Any event, other than an exchange of promises, resulting in a virtually certain and measurable increase or decrease in cash is quantified in terms of the present value of that increase or decrease. For our example above, the DECLARATION OF A CASH DIVIDEND will be recorded by the following journal entry:

Declaration of Cash Dividends
    Dr. Retained Earnings
        Cr. Dividends Payable

Criterion 7

A descriptive change is an accounting event. A descriptive change does not reflect a change in the amount, timing, or uncertainty of the entity's future cash flow, but it does represent a change from a less preferred to a more preferred accounting description. For example, a descriptive change may be a reclassification of Work-in-Process to Finished Goods when the manufacturing process is completed.

Another example of a reclassification would be the closing entry, where the balances in the event accounts are reduced to zero and their effect on Retained Earnings is recorded. Obviously, nothing has changed in the world. But, since an income statement has been prepared, *event accounts* no longer serve a purpose, and it is now more useful to reflect the impact of revenues and expenses on Retained Earnings.

Other accounting events that are recognized under this criterion include error corrections and changes in accounting principles. When the state of the world is incorrectly described, an error correction remedies the flawed description; when accounting principles change, the way in which accountants describe the world has changed.

Some descriptive changes are mandatory, including error corrections and mandated changes in accounting principles. Some are customarily made, including the reclassification of Work-in-Process as Finished Goods, and some are optional, such as nonmandated changes in accounting principles. Optional changes must be justified by demonstrating that the new description is more accurate, more reliable, or more useful than the original description.

Reclassifications are quantified in terms of existing accounting quantification; error corrections are quantified by the amount of the error; and changes in accounting principles are quantified as required by the FASB.

Because error corrections and changes in accounting principles apply to all accounting events, we will not give examples of the appropriate journal entries. However, reclassifications apply to a limited number of cases, some of which are described by the following journal entries:

Completion of the Manufacturing Process
Dr. Finished Goods
 Cr. Work-in-Process

Reclassification of Long-Term Debt
Dr. Long-Term Debt
 Cr. Current Portion of Debt

Reclassification of Investment in Securities
Dr. Noncurrent Securities
 Cr. Current Securities

RECORDING ACCOUNTING EVENTS

In our examples, we have assumed that events are discrete and readily identifiable. In reality, however, economic activity is continuous and any attempt to subdivide this continuum into separate events is necessarily arbitrary. Even when dealing with seemingly simple, familiar, and repetitive events, we may find it difficult to determine the precise time that the event occurred. We may find it even more difficult to decide upon an appropriate time to record the event.

Consider, for instance, a CREDIT SALE. Clearly it is an accounting event—but when should the sale be recognized by the accountant? When the consumer prepares a shopping list, enters the store, selects the goods, charges the purchase on account? Or, when the store ships the goods, bills the customer, or collects the money? In a sense, all of these moments are part of a continuous sales event, but which one is chosen as **the** occasion to recognize the sale? In general, the moment at which to recognize this event is when the seller has performed, by providing the goods. Performance is usually said to occur at the time the right to the goods passes to the buyer, commonly marked by the cashier's ringing-up of the sale.

There are some events that have many stages, like sales, and there are others that have only one stage, like cash receipts and disbursements. However, all events must have a *recording signal.* A recording signal is anything that causes the accountant to record the occurrence of an accounting event with a journal entry. Most recording signals appear close in time to the event's recognition, and provide convenient evidence for quantifying the event. In some cases the recording signal is the preparation or receipt of a document. In others, it is inferred from the ocurrence of another event. And in others, it is merely the end of the accounting period.

RECORDING EVENTS RECOGNIZED BY DOCUMENTATION

Voluntary interactions between two independent accounting units are called market transactions. Market transactions are easily verifiable and quantifiable because they generate ample documentary evidence that they occurred and other data that serves as the basis for quantifying the event. Market transactions include purchases and payments, sales and collections, loans and repayments, stock issues and repurchases.

The preparation or receipt of a document is often used as a *recording signal*. For instance, a CREDIT SALE is recorded when a sales invoice is prepared, and a CREDIT PURCHASE is recorded when the bill is received. Observe that in each case, the event is recognizable before it is recorded. The CREDIT SALE is often consummated before the invoice is prepared, and well before the cash is collected from the customer. Similarly, the CREDIT PURCHASE is complete when the goods have been constructively received (control or legal title has passed), often before receipt of the vendor's invoice and before paying for the goods.

A cash disbursement is usually recorded when a check is drawn, even though the check is prepared before the actual cash outflow, and a cash receipt is recorded when a check is received, even though the check is received before the actual cash inflow.

RECORDING EVENTS RECOGNIZED BY INFERENCE

Event (B) may be a *recording signal* for event (A), if event (A) necessarily preceded event (B). The act of filling an automobile's gasoline tank illustrates such a relationship. Suppose that you begin a cross-country trip in the morning with a full tank of gasoline. When you stop for the night and find that you must buy 15 gallons of gasoline to refill the tank, you infer that 15 gallons of gasoline must have been consumed during the day.

It is important to understand the difference between the occurrence of an event and the recording of that event. Suppose that the tank is only half-empty, and that you choose to wait until it is nearly empty before refilling it. Since replenishment is the recording signal for both the replenishment (acquisition) and the consumption (utilization) of the gasoline, failure to replenish means failure to record the consumption of the half tank of gasoline. Does that mean that no gasoline was consumed? Of course not. Similarly, the fact that the accountant has not recorded an event does not mean that an important event has not occurred.

Thought Question
Can you think of other events
that might be recorded by inference?

RECORDING EVENTS BECAUSE AN ACCOUNTING PERIOD HAS ENDED: ADJUSTING ENTRIES

During an accounting period, a firm utilizes services from its suppliers and provides services to its customers. Some of these services will be recorded when they are evidenced by documents, or are inferred from other events. Yet there are other recognizable and recordable accounting events of the period whose only *recording signal* is the end of the accounting period.

For example, when a firm borrows money, it acquires the right to **utilize** the money for a finite period of time. As time passes, that right to utilize the money diminishes, and the utilization is recognized as an accounting event, INTEREST EXPENSE. Correspondingly, the lender **provides** the borrower the use of the money for a finite period of time. As time passes, the provision is recognized as INTEREST REVENUE.

These are continuous rather than discrete events, and their utilization (provision) is a function of the passage of time. These events are generally recorded at the end of the accounting period. Such entries are called *adjusting entries.* There are various kinds of adjusting entries, some of which are described here.

Utilization of Prepaid Services

If a firm prepays $1,000 for a 1-year insurance policy on July 1, then on December 31, the end of their accounting period, the amount of prepaid services utilized is recognized by the following adjusting entry:

Operating Expenses
    Dr. Operating Expenses (I/S)   500
        Cr. Prepaid Services   500

Utilization of Equipment

A company purchases equipment, expected to last for 5 years, for $5,000 on January 2. The following adjusting entry would be recorded at the end of the year:

Depreciation Expense
    Dr. Depreciation Expense (I/S)   1,000
        Cr. Accumulated Depreciation   1,000

Company Provides Prepaid Services

On October 1, a landlord receives $3,000 in advance for 1 year's rent. On December 31, the end of the accounting period, the landlord would record the provision of space services by the following adjusting entry:

Rent Revenue

    Dr. Prepaid Rent Revenue   750

        Cr. Rent Revenue (I/S)   750

Company Provides Services in Advance of Payment

On July 2, a company lends $10,000 to another company, repayable in 5 years, with semiannual interest payments of $600, payable on January 2 and July 2 of each year. On December 31, the end of the accounting period, the following adjusting entry would be made:

Interest Revenue

    Dr. Interest Receivable   600

        Cr. Interest Revenue (I/S)   600

Corrections and Revisions

Various corrections and revisions are recorded by adjusting entries at the end of the accounting period. If a recording signal has sounded, but a recognizable event has not occurred by the end of the accounting period, an adjusting entry must be made. For example, if the preparation of checks is the recording signal for cash disbursements, and $3,000 of checks have been prepared but not mailed, cash disbursements have been recorded even though cash has not been disbursed. The following adjusting entry would be made:

Correction

    Dr. Cash   3,000

        Cr. Accounts Payable   3,000

If a normal recording signal has not sounded, but a recognizable event has occurred, an adjusting entry must also be made. For example, consider a company that pays $5,000 every 2 weeks to its employees. If the end of the accounting period occurs 1 week after the last payroll, and the normal recording signal for the UTILIZATION OF LABOR SERVICES is the preparation of the payroll, an adjusting entry is recorded for labor services utilized since the last payroll, and the following adjusting entry would be recorded:

Labor Expense

    Dr. Operating Expenses (I/S)   2,500

        Cr. Wages Payable   2,500

OPERATING, FINANCING, AND INVESTING EVENTS

Operating events represent the events related to the regular and recurring provision of goods and services to customers. For example, operating events include SALES REVENUE and the related COLLECTIONS FROM CUSTOMERS, COST OF GOODS SOLD and OPERATING EXPENSES and their related cash payments, PAYMENTS TO SUPPLIERS OF MERCHANDISE, and PAYMENTS TO SUPPLIERS OF SERVICES.

Investing events represent the acquisition and sale of all assets, other than current operating assets, for cash. For example, firms invest in and dispose of property, plant and equipment, patents, and securities of other firms. Financing events represent the receipt of cash from creditors and owners, and the payment of cash to creditors and owners (except suppliers of inventory and services). For example, firms borrow and repay loans, and issue and repurchase (or retire) common stock.

All other investments in, or sales of, assets, other than current operating assets, financed by borrowing or issuing common stock (repaying or repurchasing common stock) are **joint** investing **and** financing events. For example, the ACQUISITION OF A PATENT BY THE ISSUANCE OF COMMON STOCK, or the ACQUISITION OF PROPERTY, PLANT AND EQUIPMENT BY THE ISSUANCE OF A MORTGAGE.

All investing events and all financing events are reported in the statement of cash flows under their appropriate headings. Events that are **joint** investing **and** financing events are reported in a schedule of significant noncash financing and investing events.

Operating, financing, and *investing events* that affect the *residual net-assets* of the firm are reported in the income statement as revenues and expenses, or **gains and losses.** Gains are similar to revenues and losses are similar to expenses in the sense that gains increase the residual net-assets (Retained Earnings) while losses decrease the residual net-assets (Retained Earnings). For nonroutine events that occur infrequently, inflows and outflows are combined and are reported as gains if the inflow exceeds .the outflow, and as losses if the outflow exceeds the inflow.

For example, a parcel of land is sold for $110,000. Its original cost was $100,000. To record this sale (or disposal), the asset, quantified at its original cost of $100,000, must be removed from the firm's books. The $100,000 outflow of the asset from the books (book value) in conjunction with the $110,000 cash inflow (market value) results in an increase in residual net-assets, represented by a $10,000 increase in Retained Earnings. Instead of recording a credit to Retained Earnings, we record a credit to the event account GAIN ON DISPOSAL. This gain will be reported in the income statement.

Sale of Land (for more than book value)

Dr. Cash	110,000	
Cr. Property, Plant and Equipment		100,000
Cr. Gain on Disposal (I/S)		10,000

Thought Questions

Suppose that the asset that originally cost $100,000 was destroyed. If the market value of the asset at the time it was destroyed was $110,000, and it was insured for $105,000, would the company recognize a gain? Did the company really have a gain?

If the proceeds (cash received) were $90,000, rather than $110,000, we would record a $10,000 LOSS ON DISPOSAL instead of the gain.

Sale of Land (for less than book value)

Dr. Loss on Disposal (I/S)	10,000	
Dr. Cash	90,000	
Cr. Property, Plant and Equipment		100,000

Finally, if this property was declared uninhabitable because it had once been a toxic waste dump, and the firm had failed to insure themselves for such a loss, the loss would be recorded as follows:

Loss from Condemnation of Land

Dr. Loss on Condemnation (I/S)	100,000	
Cr. Property, Plant and Equipment		100,000

The next three sections summarize where specific operating, financing, and investing events are reported in the income statement, the statement of cash flows, or the footnotes and schedules.

REPORTING OPERATING EVENTS

1. The regular and recurring provision of goods and services is reported in the income statement as REVENUE, if the cash consequence is virtually certain.

2. The utilization of resources, other than in the manufacturing process, necessary and beneficial for the provision of goods and services that qualify as revenues, is reported in the income statement as EXPENSES.

3. Cash receipts resulting from the provision of goods and services are reported directly, or indirectly, in the statement of cash flows as part of CASH FLOWS FROM OPERATIONS.

4. Cash disbursements required in utilizing goods and services are reported directly, or indirectly, in the statement of cash flows as part of CASH FLOWS FROM OPERATIONS.

REPORTING FINANCING EVENTS

1. Cash receipts from the issue of debt or stock are reported in the statement of cash flows as part of cash flows from financing events.

2. Cash disbursements for the retirement of debt or the repurchase of stock, or for the payment of cash dividends, are reported in the statement of cash flows as part of cash flows from financing events.

3. Cash disbursed as a result of utilizing borrowed money (interest payments) is reported in the statement of cash flows as part of CASH FLOWS FROM OPERATIONS.

4. The noncash acquisition or retirement of debt, or repurchase of stock, is reported in the financial statements as a footnote or in the schedule of significant noncash financing and investing events.

5. The cost of utilizing borrowed money is reported in the income statement as INTEREST EXPENSE.

6. The excess (deficiency) between the cash disbursed for the retirement of debt and the accounting quantification of the debt (book value) is reported in the income statement as a LOSS (GAIN).

REPORTING INVESTING EVENTS

1. Cash disbursed for the acquisition of investments is reported in the statement of cash flows as part of cash flows from investing events.

2. Cash receipts from disposing of investments are reported in the statement of cash flows as part of cash flows from investing events.

3. Cash received as dividends and interest on investments is reported in the statement of cash flows as part of CASH FLOWS FROM OPERATIONS.

4. The noncash acquisition of investments is reported in the financial statements as a footnote or in the schedule of significant noncash financing and investing events.

5. The income earned (dividends and interest) as a result of owning investments is reported in the income statement as REVENUE.

6. The excess (deficiency) between the proceeds received from the disposal of the investment, and the accounting quantification of the investment, is reported in the income statement as a GAIN (LOSS).

7. Impairments of assets are reported as LOSSES in the income statement.

SUMMARY REVIEW OF EVENTS AND ACCOUNTS

In this section, we will summarize the relationship between accounting events (represented by journal entries), the accounts they affect (represented by T-accounts), and the resultant financial statements. This summary is limited to the events and accounts that we have encountered in discussing The American Grabule Company.

All the following accounting events are represented by journal entries which are listed on the pages that follow. We have referenced each accounting event by a three-digit number, ordered in terms of income (revenues and expenses), cash (receipts and disbursements), or neither income nor cash events.

Revenues	(101–102)	
Expenses	(201–205)	
Closing Net Income	(–399)	
Cash Receipts	(401–402)	Operating Events
	(421–)	Debt Financing Events
	(431–)	Equity Financing Events
	(441–)	Investing Events
Cash Disbursements	(501–506)	Operating Events
	(521–)	Debt Financing Events
	(531–532)	Equity Financing Events
	(541–)	Investing Events
Neither Income nor Cash	(601–607)	Operating Events
	(621–)	Debt Financing Events
	(631–)	Equity Financing Events
	(651–)	Financing **and** Investing Events

The effects of these events can be traced through the accompanying T-accounts, and the results can be seen in the accompanying related financial statements: the balance sheet, income statement, and statement of cash flows. Reordering of the events in terms of operating, financing, and investing events, with the same referencing numbers, results in

Operating Events	(101–102)	Revenues
	(201–205)	Expenses
	(401–402)	Cash Receipts
	(501–506)	Cash Disbursements
	(601–607)	Neither Income **nor** Cash
Closing Net Income	(–399)	
Debt Financing Events	(421–)	Cash Receipts
	(521–)	Cash Disbursements
	(621–)	Neither Income **nor** Cash
Equity Financing Events	(431–)	Cash Receipts
	(531–)	Cash Disbursements
	(631–)	Neither Income **nor** Cash
Investing Events	(441–)	Cash Receipts
	(541–)	Cash Disbursements
Financing and Investing Events	(651–)	Neither Income **nor** Cash

HOW TO USE THIS SUMMARY OF EVENTS AND ACCOUNTS

Suppose you were given comparative balance sheets and a statement of cash receipts and disbursements, and were required to determine COST OF GOODS SOLD for the period. All you would have to know is that COST OF GOODS SOLD is an expense, and from the list of journal entries for expenses, you would find journal entry (201):

Cost of Goods Sold
    Dr. Cost of Goods Sold (I/S)
        Cr. Inventory

Thus, the account that needs to be examined is Inventory. By tracing the effect of the event to the Inventory account, you would see that the credit (Cr.) entry to the Inventory account is for the COST OF GOODS SOLD, and the debit (Dr.) entry is for the CREDIT PURCHASES OF INVENTORY (601). Tracing journal entry (601):

Credit Purchases of Inventory
    Dr. Inventory
        Cr. Accounts Payable Merchandise

to Accounts Payable Merchandise reveals that the credit (Cr.) entry to the account is for the CREDIT PURCHASES OF INVENTORY, and the debit (Dr.) entry is for PAYMENTS TO SUPPLIERS OF MERCHANDISE (501). Since the event PAYMENTS TO SUPPLIERS OF MERCHANDISE is reported in the statement of cash receipts and disbursements, COST OF GOODS SOLD can easily be determined.

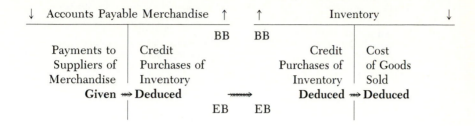

Beginning with the PAYMENTS TO SUPPLIERS OF MERCHANDISE [the debit (Dr.) entry to Accounts Payable Merchandise], and the beginning and ending balances in Accounts Payable Merchandise (as provided in the comparative balance sheets), you can deduce CREDIT PURCHASES OF INVENTORY [the credit (Cr.) entry to Accounts Payable Merchandise]. From CREDIT PURCHASES OF INVENTORY [the debit (Dr.) entry to Inventory], and the beginning and ending balances in the Inventory account, you can deduce COST OF GOODS SOLD [the credit (Cr.) entry to Inventory].

Conversely, if comparative balance sheets and an income statement were presented, you would be required to deduce PAYMENTS TO SUPPLIERS OF MERCHANDISE from COST OF GOODS SOLD.

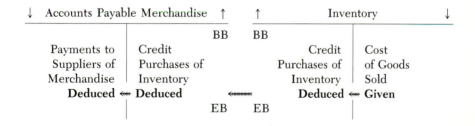

Journal entries for revenues:

(101) Sales Revenue
    Dr. Accounts Receivable
    Dr. Advances from Customers
        Cr. Sales Revenue (I/S)

(102) Interest Revenue
    Dr. Interest Receivable
        Cr. Interest Revenue (I/S)

Journal entries for expenses:

(201) Cost of Goods Sold
    Dr. Cost of Goods Sold (I/S)
        Cr. Inventory (Finished Goods)

(202) Operating Expenses
    Dr. Operating Expenses (I/S)
        Cr. Prepaid Services
        Cr. Accounts Payable Services

(203) Depreciation Expense
    Dr. Depreciation Expense (I/S)
        Cr. Accumulated Depreciation

(204) Interest Expense
    Dr. Interest Expense (I/S)
        Cr. Interest Payable

(205) Tax Expense
    Dr. Tax Expense (I/S)
        Cr. Taxes Payable

(206) Amortization of Patent
    Dr. Amortization of Patent (I/S)
        Cr. Patent

Journal entry to close net income to Retained Earnings:

(399) Closing Net Income to Retained Earnings
    Dr. Income Summary
        Cr. Retained Earnings

Journal entries for cash receipts:

(401) Collections from Customers
    Dr. Cash
        Cr. Accounts Receivable
        Cr. Advances from Customers

(402) Collection of Interest
    Dr. Cash
        Cr. Interest Receivable

(421) Borrowing from the Bank (long-term)
    Dr. Cash
        Cr. Long-Term Debt

(431) Issue of Common Stock
    Dr. Cash
        Cr. Common Stock

(441) Sale of Property, Plant and Equipment
    Dr. Cash
    Dr. Accumulated Depreciation
        Cr. Property, Plant and Equipment

Journal entries for cash disbursements:

(501) Payments to Suppliers of Merchandise
    Dr. Accounts Payable Merchandise
        Cr. Cash

(502) Payments to Suppliers of Services
    Dr. Prepaid Services
    Dr. Accounts Payable Services
        Cr. Cash

(503) Payments to Suppliers of Raw Materials
    Dr. Accounts Payable Raw Materials
        Cr. Cash

(504) Payments to Suppliers of Labor Services
    Dr. Wages Payable
        Cr. Cash

(505) Payment of Interest
    Dr. Interest Payable
        Cr. Cash

(506) Payment of Taxes
    Dr. Taxes Payable
        Cr. Cash

(521) Repayment of Debt
    Dr. Current Portion of Long-Term Debt
        Cr. Cash

(531) Payment of Cash Dividends
    Dr. Dividends Payable
        Cr. Cash

(532) Repurchase of Common Stock
    Dr. Common Stock
        Cr. Cash

(541) Purchase of Property, Plant and Equipment
    Dr. Property, Plant and Equipment
        Cr. Cash

Events affecting *neither* income nor cash:

(601) Credit Purchases of Inventory
    Dr. Inventory
        Cr. Accounts Payable Merchandise

(602) Credit Purchases of Raw Materials
    Dr. Raw Materials
        Cr. Accounts Payable Raw Materials

(603) Input Raw Materials into Production
    Dr. Work-in-Process
        Cr. Raw Materials

(604) Input Labor Services into Production
    Dr. Work-in-Process
        Cr. Wages Payable

(605) Input Services into Production
    Dr. Work-in-Process
        Cr. Accounts Payable Services

(606) Input Equipment into Production
    Dr. Work-in-Process
        Cr. Accumulated Depreciation

(607) Transfer Finished Goods out of Work-in-Process
    Dr. Finished Goods
        Cr. Work-in-Process

(621) Reclassification of Long-Term Debt
    Dr. Net Long-Term Debt
        Cr. Current Portion of Long-Term Debt

(631) Declaration of Cash Dividends
    Dr. Retained Earnings
        Cr. Dividends Payable

(651) Acquisition of Patent for Common Stock
    Dr. Patent
        Cr. Common Stock

↑	Cash		↓
Cash Receipts from		Cash Disbursements for	
(401)	Customers	Suppliers of	(501)
		Merchandise	
(402)	Interest	Suppliers of	(502)
		Services	
		Suppliers of	(503)
		Raw Materials	
		Suppliers of	(504)
		Labor Services	
		Interest	(505)
		Taxes	(506)
	Operations		
(421)	Borrowing from	Repayment of Debt	(521)
	the Bank		
(431)	Issue of	Payment of Cash	(531)
	Common Stock	Dividends	
		Repurchase of	(532)
		Common Stock	
(441)	Sale of	Purchase of	(541)
	Property, Plant	Property, Plant	
	and Equipment	and Equipment	

	Income Summary		
(201)	Cost of Goods Sold	Sales Revenue	(101)
(202)	Operating	Interest Revenue	(102)
	Expenses		
(203)	Depreciation		
	Expense		
(204)	Interest Expense		
(205)	Tax Expense		
(206)	Amortization		
	Expense		
(399)	Net Income		

Statement of Cash Flows

Cash Flows from Operating Events

(401) Collections from Customers
(402) Collection of Interest

Total Operating Cash Inflows

(501) Payments to Suppliers of Merchandise
(502) Payments to Suppliers of Services
(503) Payments to Suppliers of Raw Materials
(504) Payments to Suppliers of Labor Services
(505) Payment of Interest
(506) Payment of Taxes

Total Operating Cash Outflows

Total Cash Flows from Operating Events

Cash Flows from Financing Events

(421) Borrowing from the Bank
(431) Issue of Common Stock
(521) Repayment of Debt
(531) Payment of Cash Dividends
(532) Repurchase of Common Stock

Total Cash Flows from Financing Events

Cash Flows from Investing Events

(441) Sale of Property, Plant and Equipment
(541) Purchase of Property, Plant and Equipment

Total Cash Flows from Investing Events

Increase (Decrease) in Cash

Significant Noncash Financing and Investing Events

(651) Acquisition of Patent for Common Stock

Income Statement

Revenues

(101) Sales Revenue
(102) Interest Revenue

Total Revenues

Expenses

(201) Cost of Goods Sold
(202) Operating Expenses
(203) Depreciation Expense
(204) Interest Expense
(205) Tax Expense
(206) Amortization of Patent

Total Expenses

(399) **Net Income**

↑	Interest Receivable	↓
(102) Interest Revenue	Collection of Interest	(402)

↑	Accounts Receivable	↓
(101) Credit Sales Revenue	Collections from Credit Customers	(401)

↑	Property, Plant and Equipment	↓
(541) Purchase of Property, Plant and Equipment	Sale of Property, Plant and Equipment (original cost)	(441)

↑	Prepaid Services	↓
(502) Prepayment for Services	Operating Expense	(202)

↓	Accumulated Depreciation	↑
(441) Accumulated Depreciation associated with disposed Property, Plant and Equipment	Depreciation Expense (203) Depreciation Charge (606)	

↑	Inventory	↓
(601) Credit Purchases of Inventory	Cost of Goods Sold	(201)

↑	Patent	↓
(651) Acquisition of Patent	Amortization of Patent	(206)

Balance Sheet

Assets

Cash
Accounts Receivable
Inventory
Raw Materials
Work-in-Process
Finished Goods
Prepaid Services
Interest Receivable
Property, Plant and Equipment
  Less: Accumulated Depreciation
Patent

Total Assets

Liabilities and Owners' Equities

Advances from Customers
Accounts Payable Merchandise
Accounts Payable Services
Accounts Payable Raw Materials
Wages Payable
Interest Payable
Taxes Payable
Current Portion of Debt
Dividends Payable
Long-Term Debt
Common Stock
Retained Earnings

Total Liabilities and Owners' Equities

All account titles in **bold letters** are operating accounts.

↑	Raw Materials	↓
(602) Credit Purchases of Raw Materials	Transfer Raw Materials into Production	(603)

↑	Work-in-Process	↓
(603) Input Raw Materials	Transfer Finished Goods out of Work-in-Process	(607)
(604) Input Labor Services		
(605) Input Services		
(606) Input Equipment		

↑	Finished Goods	↓
(607) Transfer from Work-in-Process	Cost of Goods Sold	(201)

↓	Advances from Customers	↑
(101)	Deferred Sales Revenue	Advances from Customers (401)

↓	Accounts Payable Services	↑
(502)	Payments to Suppliers of Services	Operating Expenses (202) Services in Production (605)

↓	Accounts Payable Merchandise	↑
(501)	Payments to Suppliers of Merchandise	Credit Purchases of Inventory (601)

↓	Accounts Payable Raw Materials	↑
(503)	Payments to Suppliers of Raw Materials	Credit Purchases of Raw Materials (602)

↓	Wages Payable	↑
(504)	Payments to Suppliers of Labor Services	Utilization of Labor Services in Production (604)

↓	Interest Payable	↑
(505)	Payment of Interest	Currently Payable (204) Interest Expense

↓	Taxes Payable	↑
(506)	Payment of Taxes	Currently Payable (205) Tax Expense

↓	Dividends Payable	↑
(531)	Payment of Cash Dividends	Declaration of Cash Dividends (631)

↓	Retained Earnings	↑
(631)	Declaration of Cash Dividends	Net Income (399)

↓	Common Stock	↑
(532)	Repurchase of Common Stock	Issue of Common Stock (431) Acquisition of Patent (651)

↓	Long-Term Debt	↑
(621)	Reclassification of Long-Term Debt	Borrowing (421)

↓	Current Portion of Long-Term Debt	↑
(521)	Repayment of Debt	Reclassification of Long-Term Debt (621)

PROBLEMS

1. From the following information relating to The Bildell Company, a merchandising company, prepare
   a. A statement of balance sheet account changes
   b. An income statement
   c. A statement of cash receipts and disbursements
   d. A statement of cash flows
   No events not described or derivable from the information below occurred.

   (1) The Common Stock account increased by $300,000.
   (2) The Accumulated Depreciation account increased by $50,000.
   (3) Payments to suppliers of services were $200,000.
   (4) Cost of goods sold was $500,000.
   (5) Sales revenue was $1,000,000.
   (6) Tax expense was $100,000.
   (7) The Cash account increased by $350,000.
   (8) The Property, Plant and Equipment account increased by $50,000. (Property, plant and equipment acquired during the year was acquired for cash.)
   (9) The Interest Payable account decreased by $10,000.
   (10) The company paid taxes during the year.
   (11) Property, plant and equipment with original cost of $70,000, and accumulated depreciation of $50,000, was sold for $15,000. No other property, plant and equipment was retired or disposed of during the year.
   (12) Collections from customers were $1,100,000.
   (13) Interest expense for the year was $35,000.
   (14) The Accounts Payable Services account decreased by $10,000.
   (15) Operating expenses, exclusive of depreciation expense, were $195,000.
   (16) Dividends **paid** were $20,000.
   (17) No common stock was repurchased.
   (18) Acquisitions of merchandise inventory were $500,000.
   (19) The Retained Earnings account increased by $50,000.
   (20) The Accounts Payable Merchandise increased by $20,000.

2. From the following information, some concerning events that occurred during 19X1, and some concerning changes in account balances from December 31, 19X0 to December 31, 19X1, for The Hamo Company, a merchandising company, prepare
   a. A statement of balance sheet account increases or decreases from December 31, 19X0, to December 31, 19X1
   b. An income statement for 19X1
   c. A statement of cash receipts and disbursements for 19X1
   d. A statement of cash flows for 19X1
   No events not described or derivable from the information below occurred.

   (1) Interest paid during the year was $10,000.
   (2) The Retained Earnings account increased by $150,000.
   (3) The Accounts Payable Merchandise account increased by $7,000.
   (4) The Property, Plant and Equipment account increased by $50,000.

(5) No property, plant and equipment was disposed of during the year, and any property, plant and equipment acquired was acquired for cash.
(6) Sales revenue was $1,100,000.
(7) The Cash account increased by $301,000.
(8) Net income for the year was $200,000.
(9) The Interest Payable account increased by $2,000.
(10) Tax expense for the year was $180,000.
(11) Selling and administrative expense for the year, excluding depreciation expense, was $150,000.
(12) There was depreciation expense, and none of it is included in cost of goods sold or selling and administrative expense.
(13) Purchases of inventory for the year were $140,000.
(14) The Accounts Payable Selling and Administrative Services account decreased by $10,000.
(15) Cost of goods sold was $500,000.
(16) The Dividends Payable account increased by $8,000.
(17) Collections from credit customers were $896,000.
(18) Some taxes were paid during the year.

3. During the period, the only balances that changed were Prepaid Services, which decreased by $50,000, Accounts Payable Services, which increased by $125,000, and Cash. If no property, plant and equipment was disposed of or sold, then PAYMENTS TO SUPPLIERS OF SERVICES were greater than or less than OPERATING EXPENSES by: $_____, or were equal to OPERATING EXPENSES.

4. If CASH FLOWS FROM OPERATIONS was **greater than** NET INCOME by $20,000, and there was no change in the balances of the *operating accounts*, then what event must have occurred?

5. If a firm's balance sheet shows changes in just three accounts, Accounts Payable, Accounts Receivable, and Retained Earnings, and has **no** depreciable assets, then for each of the following cases, determine if the firm had NET INCOME or a NET LOSS, and if the NET INCOME (LOSS) was greater than, less than, or equal to CASH FLOWS FROM OPERATIONS:
   a. The increase in Accounts Payable **equalled** the increase in Accounts Receivable.
   b. The increase in Accounts Payable was **greater than** the increase in Accounts Receivable.
   c. The increase in Accounts Payable was **greater than** the decrease in Accounts Receivable.
   d. The increase in Accounts Payable was **less than** the increase in Accounts Receivable.
   e. The increase in Accounts Payable was **less than** the decrease in Accounts Receivable.

6.

The Soothsayer Merchandising Company
(Contributed by John Bildersee)
Comparative Post-Closing Trial Balance Sheets
Years Ending December 31, 19X0 and December 31, 19X1

Debit Balance Accounts	12/31/X0	12/31/X1
Cash	$?	$?
Accounts Receivable	354,000	?
Inventory	101,000	115,000
Investment in Bonds (at cost)	100,000	?
Prepayments	11,000	20,000
Property, Plant and Equipment	150,000	220,000
Total Debit Balance Accounts	$?	$?

Credit Balance Accounts		
Accumulated Depreciation	$ 11,000	$ 25,000
Accounts Payable Merchandise	150,000	145,000
Accounts Payable Services	70,000	100,000
Common Stock	500,000	?
Retained Earnings	?	?
Total Credit Balance Accounts	$1,166,000	$1,170,000

Notes
(1) The company collected $10,000 in interest.
(2) Acquisitions and disposals of property, plant and equipment occurred at the end of the year. The disposals brought $2,000 in cash.
(3) Depreciation expense was $15,000.
(4) Payments to suppliers of merchandise were $519,000.
(5) No bonds were bought for the Investment account. Market value for the bonds increased from $100,000 to $104,000. Half were sold at year-end.
(6) Common stock of $10,000 was retired. There were no other stock transactions during the year.
(7) The Cash account decreased by $39,000.

The Soothsayer Merchandising Company
Income Statement
19X1

Revenues

Sales Revenue	$1,000,000
Interest Revenue	?
Sale of Investments	?
Total Revenues	$?

Expenses

Cost of Goods Sold	$?	
Operating Expenses	200,000	
Depreciation Expense	?	
Loss on Disposal of Equipment	1,000	
Total Expenses	$?	(?)
Net Income		$?

Required:
a. Prepare a statement of cash receipts and disbursements for 19X1.
b. Prepare a statement of cash flows for 19X1.
c. Fill in all the question (?) marks.

7.

The Dadson Company
Comparative Balance Sheets
Years Ending December 31, 19X0 and December 31, 19X1

Assets	12/31/X0	12/31/X1
Cash	$168,000	$?
Accounts Receivable	190,000	200,000
Interest Receivable	?	4,000
Prepaid Services	11,000	15,000
Inventory	100,000	80,000
Investment in Debentures	150,000	?
Property, Plant and Equipment	400,000	600,000
Accumulated Depreciation	(?)	(300,000)
Total Assets	$?	$984,000

Liabilities and Owners' Equities		
Accounts Payable Merchandise	$100,000	$110,000
Accounts Payable Services	125,000	?
Dividends Payable	22,000	20,000
Common Stock	375,000	425,000
Retained Earnings	200,000	420,000
Total Liabilities and Owners' Equities	$822,000	$?

The Dadson Company
Income Statement
19X1

Revenues

Sales Revenue	$?
Interest Revenue	11,000
Total Revenues	$?

Expenses

Cost of Goods Sold	$400,000	
Operating Expenses	100,000	
Depreciation Expense	100,000	
Total Expenses	$600,000	(600,000)
Net Income		$?

Statement of Cash Flows for 19X1

Cash Flows from Operating Events		$?

Cash Flows from Financing Events

Payment of Dividend	$(103,000)	
Issue of Common Stock	?	
Total Financing Events	$(?)	(?)

Cash Flows from Investing Events

Acquisition of Property, Plant and Equipment	$(?)	
Sale of Debentures	30,000	
Total Investing Events	$?	(?)
Increase in Cash		$?

Required:
a. Determine all the events that occurred during 19X1.
b. Fill in all the question (?) marks.

8. From the following incomplete T-accounts, determine
   a. Events (a) through (n) [Note: Event (m) has four effects.],
   b. Accounts (1) through (13).

Income Accounts

Sales Revenue

| | (a) |
| | (b) |

Balance Sheet Accounts

(1)

| (a) | (c) |

(2)

| (b) | (d) |

(3)

| (e) | |

(4)

(c)	(g)
(d)	(h)
(m)	(j)
	(l)

(5)

| (f) | (e) |

(6)

| (i) | |
| (k) | |

(7)

| (h) | (i) |

(8)

| (g) | (f) |

(9)

| (n) | |

(10)

| (j) | (k) |

(11)

| (l) | (m) |

(12)

| | (m) |

(13)

| (m) | (n) |

PART TWO

Operating Events

In Part One, we described the basic accounting model in terms of which events are recognized and recorded, and how they are quantified and reported in financial statements. In the rest of this book, we will take a more detailed look at the events of a business entity, explore the alternative accounting methods that are used to describe these events, and show how the resulting financial statements can be analyzed to gain information useful for understanding and evaluating these events, their effects, and their impact on cash flows.

The events of a business entity are most usefully classified as operating, financing, and investing events. Operating events consist of the events related to the provision of goods and services to customers, and the acquisition, utilization, and payment for economic resources that are required for those provisions. These events are the subject matter of Part Two of this book.

Financing events, the topic of Part Three of this book, represent the incurring and repayment of debt, the issue and retirement of securities, and the related events associated with these events. Investing events, the subject matter of Part Four of this book, consist of the acquisition and disposition of investment assets, and the related events associated with these acquisitions.

CHAPTER 8

Revenues and Operating Expenses

INTRODUCTION

All operating events are related to the revenue and the cash generated by the provision of goods and services. The provision of goods and services requires the utilization of economic resources. The terminal utilization of economic resources necessary and beneficial in providing goods and services, are COST OF GOODS SOLD AND OPERATING EXPENSES.

The operating cycle begins with the acquisition of operating goods and services and payment for them, continues with the utilization of these goods and services, as well as of property, plant and equipment, and ends with the sale of goods and services to customers and clients, and the collection of cash from them.

The first chapter of Part Two discusses the recognition and quantification of revenues and operating expenses impacting Accounts Receivable, Accounts Payable Merchandise, and Accounts Payable Services. Chapter 9 covers COST OF GOODS SOLD and its impact on Inventory, and Chapter 10 describes accounting for DEPRECIATION and its impact on Work-in-Process and Accumulated Depreciation. Chapter 11 discusses TAX EXPENSE, Taxes Payable, and Deferred Taxes. In addition to describing the effects of these events on financial statements, we will show how the cash flow implications of these events can be determined.

Notice that in the discussion above, we have not included INTEREST EXPENSE, because we consider INTEREST EXPENSE as a financing event rather than an operating event.

REVENUE

The provision of goods and services during a period, with known or knowable cash consequences, is defined as *revenue*. The following conditions must be satisfied in order for revenue to be **recognized:**

1. Goods or services must have been provided.
2. The cash inflow associated with the provision must either have occurred or the amount to be received must be knowable with virtual certainty.
3. The cash outflow associated with the resources utilized in providing the goods or services must either have occurred, or be knowable with virtual certainty.

We believe that revenues should be quantified by the cash inflows resulting from the provision of goods and services minus estimated future cash outflows associated with such provisions. The expected cash inflows associated with these provisions are quantified by the amount of sales billed to customers less an estimate for returns, discounts, and uncollectibility.

The expected future cash outflows associated with these provisions consist of cash that must be paid for repairs, warranties, or other commitments agreed upon at the time of the sale. Therefore, NET SALES REVENUE is equal to GROSS SALES REVENUE less RETURNS, DISCOUNTS, UNCOLLECTIBILITY, REPAIRS, WARRANTIES, and perhaps other commitments.

The provision of goods and services often occurs in stages even though only the dollar amount for the total provision is known. Long-term construction projects and lease agreements are examples of goods and services provided over a number of accounting periods. Therefore, in order to quantify revenue, we must

1. Estimate the amount of future cash inflows from such provisions
2. Estimate the amount of future cash outflows required for these provisions
3. Quantify the different stages of provision of goods and services when such goods and services are provided over time

ESTIMATING THE TOTAL CASH INFLOW

Customers generally have the right to return goods purchased for a full or partial refund, and some of them will exercise that right. Sales returns, therefore, must be deducted from gross revenues. Since these are usually relatively small amounts, most companies deduct the actual returns for the period. The more theoretically correct method is to deduct the estimated returns from gross revenues.

When sales are made for credit, discounts are often offered to customers for prompt payment or for other reasons. If these discounts are expected to be taken, as they usually are, they should be subtracted from the amounts billed. Only the amount of billings after discounts, which is the amount expected to be received, should be recognized as revenue and as a receivable.

In addition to returns and discounts, the amount billed for credit sales must be adjusted for uncollectibility in order to properly reflect the cash to be received. Whenever credit sales are made, some of those sales will never be collected. For the financial cash consequences of the provision of the goods and services to be knowable, and for revenue to be recognized, the amount of collections resulting from credit sales must be estimable. This does not mean that we must know how much will be collected from **each** customer, but it does require knowing how much will be collected from customers as a whole.

Sales that are billed but never collected turn out to be gifts rather than sales. Should we estimate and recognize these gifts when the sales are made, or should we postpone recognition until we finally determine who is not going to pay, and how much will not be collected? Since credit sales and the final determination of uncollectibility usually occur in different periods, this is an important timing problem. However, if we recognize revenue during a period, we must recognize uncollectibility in the period in which the sale was made because

1. We know that credit sales will result in credit losses. In fact, the absence of credit losses usually indicates that a company's credit policy is too strict.

2. We can make an accurate estimate of uncollectibility based on the seller's past experience and the experience of other firms in the same industry.

3. Gifts—goods provided for which no payment will be received—occur when the goods are provided, rather than when collection attempts are finally abandoned.

4. According to our criteria, the proper measure of CREDIT SALES INFLOW is the cash that will be received, rather than the amounts billed to customers.

Suppose that a jeweler "sells" gold watches on a downtown street by offering them to passersby together with a request to "send me a check sometime." Suppose these "sales" occurred on December 31. By treating the full invoice price of the watches as sales revenue, and postponing recognition of uncollectibility to a subsequent period, the jeweler's reported income will be unrealistically high. We should not claim sales inflow when we know that nothing will flow in, nor should we list a receivable as an asset when we expect that nothing will be received. Deferring recognition of uncollectible sales to another period distorts both the balance sheet and the income statement.

Just as we do not postpone recognition of sales until cash has been collected, so we should not defer recognition of uncollectible sales and receivables until individual nonpayers have been identified. **Therefore, uncollectibility must be recognized in the period when the goods are provided if an accurate estimate of uncollectibles is available. If no such estimate is available, then the cash consequences of the provision are not known, and no revenue may be recognized.**

> ### Thought Question
> Suppose we bill customers $100,000 for goods or services,
> expecting to collect only $96,000.
> How should we record this event?

The net effects of sales billed at $100,000, when we expect to collect $96,000, are an increase in Receivables of $96,000 and an equal increase in Retained Earnings because of SALES INFLOW. We **might** consider recording the event by the following entry:

Sales Revenue
      Dr. Accounts Receivable   96,000
            Cr. Sales Revenue (I/S)   96,000

This description has several deficiencies:

1. By recording only net sales (gross billings less estimated uncollectibility adjustment) we cannot differentiate between billings of $100,000 of which only $4,000 will be uncollectible, and billings of $196,000 of which $100,000 will be uncollectible.

2. The amounts billed to customers (gross billings) are precisely quantified through sales invoices and similar documents which provide objective certification for our quantification, whereas uncollectibles must be quantified by an estimation process. It is undesirable to combine numbers resulting from dissimilar measuring processes.

3. This description does not give explicit recognition to estimated uncollectibles, thereby preventing a comparison between actual and estimated amounts.

To avoid these problems, we record GROSS BILLINGS and the ESTIMATED UNCOLLECTIBILITY ADJUSTMENT as separate events:

To record gross billings
      Dr. Accounts Receivable   100,000
            Cr. Sales Revenue (I/S)   100,000

To record the estimate of uncollectibility
      Dr. Uncollectibility Adjustment (I/S)   4,000
            Cr. Estimated Uncollectibles   4,000

The balances in Accounts Receivable represent the total potential cash collections from credit sales. The balances in Estimated Uncollectibles represent the best estimate of outstanding accounts that will not result in cash collections. Therefore, the net of Accounts Receivable and Estimated Uncollectibles, Net Accounts Receivable, represents the net amount of past credit sales that are expected to result in cash collections.

The UNCOLLECTIBILITY ADJUSTMENT, usually called BAD DEBT EXPENSE, is generally treated as an expense in the income statement. We believe that the UNCOLLECTIBILITY ADJUSTMENT should be treated as a contra-revenue account and subtracted from SALES REVENUE in the income statement to measure the actual inflow expected to result from the provision of goods or services.

While the two treatments above result in identical income figures, there are two objections to the traditional method. The first is that BAD DEBT EXPENSE is treated as if it were a utilization, whereas it really represents a reduction in an expected inflow. The utilization of resources directly related to sales events is measured solely by cost of goods sold, which includes the cost of the goods that are "given" away. The net income figure is correct because the incorrect addition of expenses is offset by an equal overstatement of expected sales inflow.

The second objection is that the term "BAD DEBT EXPENSE," with its negative connotation, conveys the misleading impression that such "expenses" should be eliminated. On the contrary. We extend credit in order to enlarge our customer base. The profit realized from sales to those additional credit customers who will pay, greatly exceeds the amount we may lose in bestowing "gifts" on ingrates who fail to pay. Eliminating all CREDIT SALES, and only selling for cash, would reduce BAD DEBT EXPENSE to zero, but most firms have found that they gain far more than they lose by extending credit.

When it is determined that a specific invoice will not be collected, the customer's account is ***written-off.*** The WRITEOFF of an account represents the transformation of what was previously an estimate into an actuality, and is recorded by decreasing Accounts Receivable, and decreasing Estimated Uncollectibles by the following entry:

Writeoffs
> Dr. Estimated Uncollectibles
>> Cr. Accounts Receivable

This entry affects only balance sheet accounts. It does not indicate a change in Retained Earnings, net income, or the amount expected to be collected.

> ### Thought Questions
> If the Estimated Uncollectibles account has a balance at year-end,
> does this indicate that
> the UNCOLLECTIBILITY ADJUSTMENT was overstated?
> Suppose that a customer that declared bankruptcy
> vowed to pay all of his debts in full,
> and you had reason to believe him.
> Would you record a journal entry, and if so, what would it be?

SUMMARY OF EVENTS AND ACCOUNTS REFLECTING UNCOLLECTIBILITY

The preceding discussion can be summarized as follows:

Event 1 The journal entry for GROSS BILLINGS (potential cash inflow) is

> Dr. Accounts Receivable
>> Cr. Sales Revenue (I/S)

Event 2 The journal entry for the ESTIMATE OF UNCOLLECTIBILITY is

> Dr. Uncollectibility Adjustment (I/S)
>> Cr. Estimated Uncollectibles

Event 3 The journal entry for COLLECTIONS FROM CREDIT CUSTOMERS is

> Dr. Cash
>> Cr. Accounts Receivable

Event 4 The journal entry for WRITEOFFS is

> Dr. Estimated Uncollectibles
>> Cr. Accounts Receivable

Balance Sheet Accounts			**Income Statement Accounts**		
↑ Accounts Receivable		↓	Sales Revenue		
(1) Gross Billings	Collections	(3)		Gross Billings	(1)
	Writeoffs	(4)			

↓ Estimated Uncollectibles		↑	Uncollectibility Adjustment		
(4) Writeoffs	Estimate of Uncollectibility	(2)	(2) Estimate of Uncollectibility		

↑ Cash	↓
(3) Collections	

If we cannot determine the amount of cash collections from sales at the time of sale because of inadequate knowledge about the creditworthiness of customers, or other reasons, we cannot recognize revenue when the sale is made. When this occurs, the ***installment method*** of recognizing income is used. The installment method recognizes income only as cash is received. For example, goods costing $600,000 are sold for $900,000, with payment to be made in equal annual installments over 3 years. No estimate of uncollectibility is available, so the installment method is used. At the time of the sale, the following entry is made:

Installment Sales
Dr. Installment Receivable   900,000
  Cr. Inventory   600,000
  Cr. Unrealized Profit on Installment Sales 300,000

The Unrealized Profit account is a contra-asset account, whose balance is subtracted from Installment Receivable in the balance sheet. (Often, this account is incorrectly reported as a liability.) Subsequently, for each dollar collected, one-third will be recognized as profit. Thus, if $300,000 is collected in the first year, the following entry will be made:

Installment Collection
Dr. Cash   300,000
  Cr. Installment Receivable   300,000

Profit from Installment Sales
Dr. Unrealized Profit   100,000
  Cr. Profit from Installment Sales (I/S)   100,000

Notice that when the *installment method* is used, we do not report SALES REVENUES and COST OF GOODS SOLD separately, but only record the net of the two as profit (SALES minus COST OF GOODS SOLD) from Installment Sales when cash is collected.

If collections from customers cannot even be estimated, but are also unlikely to occur, then the even more conservative *cost recovery method* of recognizing income is used. When this method is used, no profit is recognized until the cash collections equal the cost of the product that was sold. For example, as in the previous case, goods costing $600,000 were sold for $900,000 to a foreign country. A day after the sale, a revolution occurred and collection was assumed to be dubious, at best. In such situations, the *cost recovery method* is used. At the time of the sale, the entry to record the sale was

Sales Revenue
Dr. Accounts Receivable   900,000
    Cr. Sales Revenue (I/S)   900,000

Cost of Goods Sold
Dr. Cost of Goods Sold (I/S)   600,000
    Cr. Inventory   600,000

Since the firm is unsure that it will collect, it would reverse the entries above, and in their place, record the following entry:

Unrealized Profit
Dr. Accounts Receivable   900,000
    Cr. Inventory   600,000
    Cr. Unrealized Profit   300,000

In effect, what was accomplished by the combination of the reversing entries and the new entry was to reverse the recognition of SALES REVENUE and COST OF GOODS SOLD, and aggregate them into a balance sheet account called Unrealized Profit. Under this method, when the first $600,000 is collected, no profit is recognized, and the only entry that is made is

Collection from Credit Customer
Dr. Cash   600,000
    Cr. Accounts Receivable   600,000

For each dollar subsequently collected, a dollar of profit is recognized. If the total remaining $300,000 is collected, the following entry is made:

Collection from Credit Customer
Dr. Cash   300,000
    Cr. Accounts Receivable   300,000

Realization of Profit
    Dr. Unrealized Profit   300,000
        Cr. Profit (I/S)   300,000

FUTURE OUTFLOWS

Many sales are made that require future outflows. For instance, automobiles are sold with warranties for parts and repairs. Warranties obligate the company to provide goods and services, free of additional charge, for a specified period of time. The cost of providing these goods and services must be estimated, and this estimate, in turn, must be subtracted from the sales price when recognizing revenue.

Suppose that a car is sold for $15,000 with a 3-year warranty, and it is estimated that the average cost of repairs to be made for this car will be $1,000. Then, at the time of sale, the company would record the sale of the automobile by one of the following entries:

Sales Revenue
    Dr. Accounts Receivable (or Cash)   15,000
        Cr. Sales Revenue (I/S)   14,000
        Cr. Warranty Liability   1,000

or

Sales Revenue
    Dr. Accounts Receivable (or Cash)   15,000
         Cr. Sales Revenue (I/S)   15,000

and

Warranty Liability
    Dr. Provision for Warranties (I/S)   1,000
        Cr. Warranty Liability   1,000

The PROVISION FOR WARRANTIES can be treated either as an expense or as a contra-revenue in the income statement. We believe that it should be treated as a contra-revenue because in essence, two sales have really occurred. The car was sold for $14,000, and a service contract was sold for $1,000. But at the time of the sale, only $14,000 qualified for revenue recognition since the warranty services had not yet been provided. When the expected $1,000 is spent on repairs, the following entry is made:

Provision of Warranty Repair
    Dr. Warranty Liability   1,000
        Cr. Cash   1,000

Thought Questions
Notice that when using this method,
no profit is attributable to the repairs.
Is this reasonable?
How could profit become recognizable on repair activities?
Suppose that the warranty period expires,
and no repairs had to be made.
What entries would be made?

PARTIAL PROVISION

Often, an agreement to provide goods is fulfilled in several stages. For example, an agreement may call for the provision of 100 gra-bules in exchange for a specified amount of money, with the first shipment consisting of 20 units. The provision of services also is usually accomplished in stages. Thus, an agreement may call for providing space (rent), legal services, or the use of money for a year. As time passes, these services are provided and revenue is recognized. But the agreement often specifies the amount of cash to be received for the total provision, such as an annual rent of $24,000 or an annual retainer fee for legal services of $50,000. In these cases, the following formula is used to quantify the revenue recognized:

$$\text{Revenue recognized to date} = \frac{\text{provision to date}}{\text{total provision}} \times \text{cash inflows for the provision}$$

A special case of partial provision occurs when large projects, such as roads, bridges, and buildings, are built to order on a contract basis for an established fee. In these cases, when costs can be reasonably estimated, revenues are recognized as construction proceeds. This method is called the *percentage-of-completion method.* The formula for calculating revenue under the *percentage-of-completion method* is similar to that for partial contracts:

$$\text{Revenue recognized to date} = \frac{\text{cost incurred to date}}{\text{total costs}} \times \text{cash inflows for the construction}$$

The cost ratio above is generally used to measure the stage of completion of the project, and the percentage of completion to date.

When costs cannot be reasonably estimated, the method used to account for the project is called the *completed-contract method.* Under this method, all revenues and expenses are recognized when the project is complete.

FINANCIAL STATEMENT PRESENTATION OF REVENUES

SALES REVENUE and the UNCOLLECTIBILITY ADJUSTMENT affect net income and are reported in the income statement. Most firms report gross billings as SALES REVENUES and include the UNCOLLECTIBILITY ADJUSTMENT as part of OPERATING EXPENSES.

Most firms, like The New York Times Company, simply report the beginning and ending balances in Net Accounts Receivable, and parenthetically disclose the beginning and ending balances of Estimated Uncollectibles in the comparative balance sheets as illustrated in Example 1.

EXAMPLE 1

The New York Times Company Consolidated Balance Sheets		
	December 31	
Assets (Dollars in thousands)	1987	1986
Current Assets		
Cash (including short-term investments at cost which approximates market: 1987, $72,002,000; 1986, $18,675,000)	$ 75,887	$ 25,945
Accounts Receivable (net of allowances: 1987, $26,949,000; 1986, $29,448,000)	153,485	153,783
Inventories	35,738	31,800
Other	53,827	21,895
Total Current Assets	$318,937	$233,423

Some firms, like GE, merely report Net Accounts Receivable (Accounts Receivable minus Estimated Uncollectibles) in the balance sheet and provide more detailed information about Accounts Receivable, UNCOLLECTIBILITY ADJUSTMENT, and Estimated Uncollectibles in the footnotes to the financial statements as illustrated in Example 2.

A few firms present both the balance in Accounts Receivable and in Estimated Uncollectibles (Allowance for Doubtful Accounts) in the balance sheet, and SALES REVENUE and the UNCOLLECTIBILITY ADJUSTMENT (BAD DEBT EXPENSE) in the income statement.

The cash impact of sales revenue and uncollectibility is reported as part of CASH FLOWS FROM OPERATIONS in the statement of cash flows. If the direct method of reporting CASH FLOWS FROM OPERATIONS is used, then COLLECTIONS FROM CUSTOMERS is reported. If the indirect method is used, then COLLECTIONS FROM CUSTOMERS is indirectly determined. The credit (debit) changes in Accounts Receivable, Estimated Uncollectibles, and Advances from Cus-

EXAMPLE 2

General Electric Company		
At December 31 (in millions)	**1987**	**1986**
Assets		
Cash	$ 1,834	$ 1,698
Marketable Securities	858	221
Current Receivables	6,782	7,208
Inventories	6,265	5,161
Current Assets	15,739	14,288
Property, Plant and Equipment—net	9,255	9,841
Funds Held for Business Development	81	397
Other Investments	5,621	3,914
Intangible Assets	4,430	3,581
Other Assets	3,794	2,570
Total Assets	$38,920	$34,591

[10]**Current Receivables**

December 31 (in millions)	**1987**	**1986**
Receivable from:		
Customers	$5,463	$5,748
Associated companies	155	178
Nonconsolidated affiliates	100	13
Others	1,274	1,425
	6,992	7,364
Less allowance for losses	(210)	(156)
	$6,782	$7,208

tomers are added to (or subtracted from) NET INCOME (which includes SALES REVENUE and the UNCOLLECTIBILITY ADJUSTMENT) to determine CASH FLOWS FROM OPERATIONS (which includes COLLECTIONS FROM CUSTOMERS).

EXPENSES

Expenses are the regular and recurring expiration of rights to utilize resources, except for those utilized in the manufacturing process. Expense events fall into two main classes. The first type of expense—cost of goods sold—has a direct causal relationship to the generation of revenue, since goods cannot be provided without being utilized—you can't sell your cake and have it too! The second type of expense event is called a *period expense,* and is indirectly related to the generation of revenue, as we shall see. Every expense event, whether cost of goods sold or a period expense, represents a terminal utilization because resources are utilized without resulting in a new *nonmonetary asset.*

THE TIMING OF EXPENSE RECOGNITION

The timing of expense recognition is governed by the "matching principle." The purpose of the matching principle is to associate or match the reporting of benefits (revenues) with the reporting of sacrifices (expenses) that were necessary to generate the benefits. To that end, the costs of resources utilized in manufacturing a salable product are allocated to each unit of product produced; thus they become part of the accounting quantification of the manufactured product. These costs are recognized as expenses—costs of goods sold—when the product is sold to the customer. However, the matching principle is imperfectly implemented because of the accountant's treatment of "period expenses."

PERIOD EXPENSES

Period expenses represent all utilizations of goods or services that are neither sales outflow nor manufacturing transformations. Period expenses include the utilization of sales and management personnel, the nonmanufacturing labor force, as well as of services provided by external parties, such as advertising agencies, consulting firms, insurance companies, law firms, and others. These utilizations will be classified as operating expenses even if a future benefit is likely to result. For example, the utilization of resources in a firm's research and development activities are recorded as expenses, even if a patented process results from these activities. Clearly, no firm would undertake research and development activities unless it expected to derive benefits from them and unless it expected them to result in economic assets. Under present rules, however, no accounting asset can be recognized since these utilizations are not part of manufacturing and therefore must be reported as expenses this period, even though the benefits resulting from their utilization will occur in a subsequent period. Other activities that are undertaken with the expectation of future benefits, but that must be expensed, are advertising, employee training, new client development, etc. Since these activities are expensed, no accounting asset results even though economic benefits are expected. Thus, these activities give rise to nonaccounting assets.

> *Thought Questions*
> How will the income of a firm
> growing in the amount of nonaccounting assets
> compare with the income of a firm
> having comparable growth in accounting assets?
> How will you expect the relationship between the market value
> and book value of these firms to differ?

FINANCIAL STATEMENT PRESENTATION OF OPERATING EXPENSES

The expenses that comprise OPERATING EXPENSES can be classified and reported in various ways. The two most common ways are called the natural and functional classifications. The natural classification of expenses is made in terms of the nature of the resource utilized. For example, LABOR EXPENSE, INSURANCE EXPENSE, and LEGAL EXPENSE represent labor, insurance, and legal resources utilized in the generation of revenues.

The functional classification of expenses is made in terms of the purpose for which the resource was utilized. For example, the utilization of labor, insurance, and legal services might have been in connection with selling efforts, administrative duties, or research and development. Therefore, the expenses would have been classified as SELLING EXPENSES, ADMINISTRATIVE EXPENSES, and RESEARCH AND DEVELOPMENT EXPENSES. Most companies, like The New York Times Company, classify their expenses on a functional basis as illustrated in Example 3.

Irrespective of which method is used, INTEREST EXPENSE must be listed separately in the income statement because, though it represents the utilization of a resource, its utilization is **not** directly associated with the generation of revenues.

EXAMPLE 3

The New York Times Company
Consolidated Statements of Income*

	Year Ended December 31		
	1987	1986	1985
Revenues	$1,689,598	$1,564,663	$1,393,772
Costs and Expenses			
Raw materials cost	312,649	285,843	287,046
Operating costs	602,711	572,278	521,313
Selling, general and administrative expenses	482,910	434,926	372,288
Total	1,398,270	1,293,047	1,180,647
Operating profit	291,328	271,616	213,125
Interest expense, net of interest income	22,911	35,535	19,653
Income before income taxes and equity in earnings of associated companies	268,417	236,081	193,472
Income taxes	126,074	123,414	98,541
Income before equity in earnings of associated companies	142,343	112,667	94,931
Equity in earnings of associated companies	17,990	19,560	21,387
Net Income	$ 160,333	$ 132,227	$ 116,318

*Dollars in thousands

USER'S PERSPECTIVE

So far in this chapter, we have described how revenues and period expenses and the related receivable and payable accounts are quantified. But this tells only half the story. We are interested not only in how much cash will be collected or paid as a result of the revenues, expenses, receivables, and payables, but how soon receivables and revenues will result in cash inflows, and how long before expenses and payables will require cash outflows. In other words, we are vitally concerned not only with the quantity dimension, but also the timing dimension. The time before receivables will result in cash inflows and payables will require cash outflows is defined as the *duration period*. The duration period can be approximated from information in financial statements.

The Duration Dimension of Accounts Receivable

The approximate time before Accounts Receivable will be collected is called the *collection period*, and is determined by the following ratio:

Average Accounts Receivable

Average daily sales

From the income statement of the most recent period, preferably the last month or last quarter, we know the amount of SALES REVENUE. By dividing SALES REVENUE by the number of business days in the period, we determine AVERAGE DAILY SALES. Dividing the amount of average Accounts Receivable, determinable from the comparative balance sheets, by DAILY SALES, we determine the collection period.

> **Thought Question**
> Why is a month or quarter preferable to annual statements
> in calculating this ratio?

For example, if a firm had sales of $210,000 last month, a month consisting of 21 business days, a beginning balance in Accounts Receivable of $90,000, and an ending balance of $110,000, the average *collection period* is 10 days. Average DAILY SALES were $10,000 ($210,000 ÷ 21), and the average Accounts Receivable was $100,000 [($90,000 + $110,000) ÷ 2]. The average balance in Accounts Receivable contains 10 days of sales. In other words, the last 10 days of sales have not been collected.

What happened to the sales made 11 days ago? Since the sale from 11 days ago is not part of Accounts Receivable, it was presumably collected. Thus, assuming that DAILY SALES were stable during the last month, the time between sale and collection was approximately 10 days. If the proper figures are available from financial statements, Net Accounts Receivable (Accounts Receivable minus Estimated Uncollectibles) should be used in calculating the numerator, and NET DAILY SALES (DAILY SALES minus RETURNS, DISCOUNTS, and UNCOLLECTIBILITY ADJUSTMENT) should be used in calculating the denominator.

> **Thought Questions**
> Why do we use average Net Accounts Receivable
> and average NET DAILY SALES instead of
> average Accounts Receivable and average DAILY SALES
> in calculating the collection period?
> Consider a firm that has $100,000 in sales,
> and expects to collect $96,000.
> What is the expected collection period
> for the $100,000 of gross sales?
> Can it be calculated?

The reason why we must consider the duration dimension of receivables as well as the quantity dimension is dramatically shown by the following example. Consider two identical firms, each with NET SALES of $520,000 per year, except that firm A experiences a collection period of 1 week, and firm B a collection period of 2 weeks. During the first week, neither firm will collect any money. During the second week, firm A will collect $10,000, and firm B will collect nothing. But from the third week onward, the Accounts Receivable balances will consistently be $10,000 for firm A, and $20,000 for firm B. This imbalance will continue, even though each firm collects $10,000 per week thereafter. Firm B has twice the receivables of firm A, and if the receivables are liquidated, firm B will collect $20,000 and firm A $10,000. But, unless their receivables decrease, both firms will have the same cash-generating ability!

The Duration Dimension of Accounts Payable Services

To approximate the time between the acquisition and utilization of operating services, and the payment for these services, we use the following ratio:

$$\frac{\text{Average Accounts Payable Services}}{\text{Average daily acquisition and utilization of services}}$$

For merchandising firms, the average ACQUISITION AND UTILIZATION OF SERVICES is provided by the OPERATING EXPENSE figure in the income statement, and the average balance in Accounts Payable Services is provided by the comparative balance sheets. Again we use the financial statements of the most recent period, preferably a month or quarter.

For example, consider a firm that reports $105,000 in OPERATING EXPENSES in a period of 21 business days, and a beginning and an ending balance in Accounts Payable Services of $18,000 and $22,000, respectively. The average Accounts Payable Services balance is $20,000 [($18,000 + $22,000) ÷ 2], the average DAILY ACQUISITION AND UTILIZATION OF SERVICES is $5,000 ($105,000 ÷ 21), and therefore the average payment period is 4 days ($20,000 ÷ $5,000).

> ### Thought Questions
> Why will this method not work in calculating the duration dimension of Accounts Payable Services for manufacturing firms? What adjustments would have to be made?

Is a firm that is identical to another firm in all respects except that it has more Accounts Payable Services than the other, necessarily worse off? No! Consider the following example: Suppose that two firms incur wage expense of $520,000 each year, but firm A pays its employees once every 4 weeks, and firm B pays weekly. The average Wages Payable for the first firm will be $20,000 (2 weeks of wages), and for the second firm, $5,000 (one-half week of wages). The amount of wages payable of firm A is 4 times the amount of wages payable of firm B, but since the duration dimension of Wages Payable for firm A is also 4 times greater than that for firm B, the required monthly wage payments for the two firms are the same—$40,000.

Indeed, as long as the firms continue operations at the same level, and the employees continue to get paid at the same intervals, the firm with the larger Wages Payable account will have a cash advantage over the other firm. While both firms will pay $40,000 every 4 weeks to their employees, the first firm will have to pay $10,000 each week, whereas the second firm will have to pay $40,000 at the end of each 4-week period. Therefore, the firm with the larger Wages Payable account has more time to accumulate the cash to pay its employees than the firm with the smaller Wages Payable account, and can start each 4-week period with less cash to meet its obligations.

The current ratio (current assets ÷ current liabilities) is often calculated and used to assess the adequacy of current assets in relation to current liabilities. Conventional "wisdom" often considers a current ratio of 2:1 to be minimally acceptable. Assume that for firms A and B, the only current asset is Accounts Receivable and the only current liability is Wages Payable. Since firm A's average Accounts Receivable is $10,000 and average Wages Payable $20,000, its current ratio is 1:2. Similarly, firm B's average Accounts Receivable is $20,000 and average Wages Payable $5,000, and its current ratio is 4:1. Since both firms have identical operating cash flows, this clearly indicates the deficiency of using the current ratio blindly. The current ratio compares only amounts, and not duration.

Thus, even for receivables and payables that are quantified in terms of prospective cash flows, it is necessary to know both the amount of the cash flows represented by those receivables and payables, and the timing or duration of the cash flows, in order to properly evaluate the potential benefit provided by the asset, and the potential sacrifice required by the liability.

Calculating the Uncollectibility Adjustment

INTRODUCTION

There are two methods used to calculate the UNCOLLECTIBILITY ADJUSTMENT, a direct method and an indirect one. The direct method is called the *pecentage-of-sales,* or the income statement, approach; and the indirect method is called the *aging-of-receivables,* or the balance sheet, approach.

THE INCOME STATEMENT APPROACH: PERCENTAGE-OF-SALES

Using the income statement approach, the UNCOLLECTIBILITY ADJUSTMENT is estimated (calulated) as a percentage of SALES REVENUE for the period.

	Estimated ↓ Uncollectibles ↑	
(*a*) Beginning Balance (given)		(*a*) BB
(*b*) Writeoffs (given)	(*b*)	
(*c*) Uncollectibility Adjustment (calculated)		(*c*)
(*d*) Ending Balance (end result)		(*d*) EB

For example, if SALES REVENUE during the period was $100,000, and the estimated percentage of uncollectibility was 4 percent, then the UNCOLLECTIBILITY ADJUSTMENT (*c*) would be $4,000. Furthermore, if the beginning balance of the Estimated Uncollectibles account (*a*) was $2,000, and WRITEOFFS during the period (*b*) were $1,000, then the ending balance in the Estimated Uncollectibles account would be $5,000.

THE BALANCE SHEET APPROACH: AGING-OF-RECEIVABLES

Alternatively, instead of calculating the UNCOLLECTIBILITY ADJUSTMENT, the ending balance of the Estimated Uncollectibles account is estimated (calculated), by using the balance sheet approach.

	Estimated
	↓ Uncollectibles ↑
(a) Beginning Balance (given)	(a) BB
(b) Writeoffs (given)	(b)
(c) Uncollectibility Adjustment (end result)	(c)
(d) Ending Balance (calculated)	(d) EB

From the chart below, you can see that the ending balance in Accounts Receivable (in our example, $50,000), is stratified into four layers: $30,000, $10,000, $8,000, and $2,000; each layer uncollected for a period of 1 to 30, 31 to 60, 61 to 90, and greater than 90 days, respectively. Of the $30,000 of CREDIT SALES that remain uncollected from the most recent period (1 to 30 days), 2 percent (or $600) are estimated never to be collected; as are 9 percent (or $900) of the next $10,000; 30 percent (or $2,400) of the next $8,000; and 55 percent (or $1,100) of the last $2,000. The total estimate of uncollectibility of the ending balance in Accounts Receivable is $5,000.

	Age of Accounts (in days)			
	1–30	31–60	61–90	Over 90
Estimated Uncollectible Percentage	2	9	30	55
Accounts Receivable	$30,000	$10,000	$8,000	$2,000
Estimate of Uncollectibility	$ 600	$ 900	$2,400	$1,100

So, if the beginning balance (a) of the Estimated Uncollectibles account was $2,000, WRITEOFFS during the period (b) were $1,000, and the ending balance in the Estimated Uncollectibles account [(d), as calculated above] was $5,000, the UNCOLLECTIBILITY ADJUSTMENT (c) required would be $4,000.

Which method should be used? The answer is both. The UNCOLLECTIBILITY ADJUSTMENT is originally calculated as a *percentage-of-sales*, and the validity of the balance in the Estimated Uncollectibles account is verified by *aging-of-receivables*.

PROBLEMS

1. Luman Company began operations on January 1, 19X1. The following information is available for the year ended December 31, 19X1:

Total merchandise purchases	$700,000
Merchandise Inventory at December 31, 19X1	140,000
Collections from customers	400,000

All merchandise is marked to sell at 40 percent above cost. Assume that all sales were on credit and all receivables are collectible. The balance in Accounts Receivable at December 31, 19X1, should be
a. $160,000
b. $244,000
c. $300,000
d. $384,000

2. Baof Company's account balances at December 31, 19X1, for Accounts Receivable and the related Allowance for Doubtful Accounts (Estimated Uncollectibles) were $1,200,000 and $60,000, respectively. An aging of accounts receivable indicated that $106,000 of the December 31, 19X1, receivables may be uncollectible. The net realizable value of Accounts Receivable was
a. $1,034,000
b. $1,094,000
c. $1,140,000
d. $1,154,000

3. The Froh company is preparing its cash budget for the month of May. The following information is available concerning its receivables:

Estimated credit sales for May	$200,000
Actual credit sales for April	$150,000
Estimated collections in May for credit sales in May	20%
Estimated collections in May for credit sales in April	70%
Estimated collections in May for credit sales prior to April	$ 12,000
Estimated writeoffs in May for uncollectible credit sales	$ 8,000
Estimated provision for bad debts in May for credit sales in May	$ 7,000

What are the estimated cash receipts from receivables in May?
a. $142,000
b. $149,000
c. $150,000
d. $157,000

4. Thure Company, which began business on January 1, 19X1, appropriately uses the installment sales method of accounting. The following data are available for 19X1:

Installment Accounts Receivable, December 31, 19X1	$200,000
Deferred gross profit, December 31, 19X1 (before recognition of realized gross profit)	$140,000
Gross profit on sales	40%

The cash collections and the realized gross profit on installment sales for the year ended December 31, 19X1, should be

	Cash Collections	Realized Gross Profit
a.	$100,000	$80,000
b.	$100,000	$60,000
c.	$150,000	$80,000
d.	$150,000	$60,000

5. Ennui Corporation owns an office building and leases the offices under a variety of rental agreements involving rent paid monthly in advance and rent paid annually in advance. Not all tenants make timely payments of their rent. Ennui's balance sheets contained the following information:

	19X1	19X0
Rentals receivable	$3,100	$2,400
Unearned rentals	6,000	8,000

During 19X1, Ennui received $20,000 cash from tenants. How much rental revenue should Ennui record for 19X1?
a. $17,300
b. $18,700
c. $21,300
d. $22,700

6. Danny Company prepared an aging of its receivables at December 31, 19X1, and determined that the net realizable value of the receivables at that date is $100,000. Additional information is available as follows:

Accounts Receivable, January 1, 19X1	$ 96,000
Accounts Receivable, December 31, 19X1	108,000
Allowance for Doubtful Accounts, December 31, 19X1—credit balance	12,000
Accounts written off as uncollectible during 19X1	10,000

Danny's bad debt expense for the year ended December 31, 19X1, is
a. $ 6,000
b. $ 8,000
c. $10,000
d. $14,000

7. When the allowance method of recognizing bad debt expense is used, the entries at the time of collection of a small account previously written off would
   a. Increase net income
   b. Have **no** effect on total current assets
   c. Decrease net receivables
   d. Decrease total current liabilities

8. A method of estimating bad debts that focuses on the income statement rather than the balance sheet is the allowance method based on
   a. Direct writeoff
   b. Aging the receivable accounts
   c. Credit sales
   d. The balance in the receivable accounts

9. (*AICPA adapted*) From inception of operations to December 31, 19X1, Henshaw Corporation provided for uncollectible receivables under the allowance method: provisions were made monthly at 2 percent of credit sales; bad debts written-off were charged to the allowance account; recoveries of bad debts previously written-off were credited to the allowance account; and, no year-end adjustments to the allowance account were made. Henshaw's usual credit terms are net 30 days.
   The balance in the Allowance for Doubtful Accounts was $130,000 at January 1, 19X1. During 19X1 credit sales totaled $9,000,000, interim provisions for doubtful accounts were made at 2 percent of credit sales, $90,000 of bad debts were written-off, and recoveries of accounts previously written off amounted to $15,000. Henshaw installed a computer facility in November 19X1 and an aging-of-receivables was prepared for the first time as of December 31, 19X1. A summary of the aging is as follows:

Classification by Month of Sale	Balance in Each Category	Estimated Percent Uncollectible
Nov.–Dec. 19X1	$1,140,000	2
July–Oct.	600,000	10
Jan.–June	400,000	25
Prior to Jan. 1, 19X1	130,000	75
	$2,270,000	

Based on the review of collectibility of the account balances in the "prior to January 1, 19X1" aging category, additional receivables totaling $60,000 were written-off as of December 31, 19X1. Effective with the year ended December 31, 19X1, Henshaw adopted a new accounting method for estimating the Allowance for Doubtful Accounts at the amount indicated by the year-end aging analysis of Accounts Receivable.

Required:
a. Prepare a schedule analyzing the changes in the Allowance for Doubtful Accounts for the year ended December 31, 19X1.
b. Prepare the journal entry for the year-end adjustment to the Allowance for Doubtful Accounts balance as of December 31, 19X1.

10. (*AICPA adapted*) When a company has a policy of making sales for which credit is extended, it is reasonable to expect a portion of those sales to be uncollectible. As a result of this, a company must recognize BAD DEBT EXPENSE. There are basically two methods of recognizing BAD DEBT EXPENSE: (1) direct writeoff method, and (2) allowance method.

    Required:
    a. Describe fully both the direct writeoff method and the allowance method of recognizing bad debt expense.
    b. Discuss the reasons why one of the above methods is preferable to the other and the reasons why the other method is not usually in accordance with generally accepted accounting principles.

11. When the allowance method of recognizing bad debt expense is used, the typical writeoff of a specific customer's account
    a. Has **no** effect on net income
    b. Decreases net income
    c. Decreases current assets
    d. Decreases net receivables

12. During 19X1 Widan Company introduced a new line of machines that carry a 2-year warranty against manufacturer's defects. Based on industry experience, the estimated warranty costs related to dollar sales are as follows:

Year of sale	4%
Year after sale	6%

    Sales and actual warranty expenditures for the years ended December 31, 19X0 and 19X1 were as follows:

	19X0	19X1
Sales	$500,000	$700,000
Actual warranty expenditure	15,000	47,000

    What amount should Widan report as its Estimated Warranty Liability at December 31, 19X1?
    a. $0
    b. $16,000
    c. $42,000
    d. $58,000

13. The calculation of the income recognized in the first year of a 4-year construction contract accounted for by using the percentage-of-completion method is generally based on the ratio of
    a. Total estimated costs to estimated costs to complete
    b. Total estimated costs to actual costs incurred to date
    c. Actual costs incurred to date to total estimated costs
    d. Estimated costs to complete to total estimated costs

14. Some costs cannot be directly related to particular revenues but are incurred to obtain benefits in the period in which the costs are in-

curred. An example of such a cost is
a. Electricity used to light offices
b. Transportation to customers
c. Cost of merchandise sold
d. Sales commissions

15. The completed-contract method of accounting for long-term construction-type contracts is preferable when
    a. A contractor is involved in numerous projects.
    b. The contracts are of a relatively long duration.
    c. Estimates of costs to complete and extent of progress toward completion are reasonably dependable.
    d. Lack of dependable estimates or inherent hazards cause forecasts to be doubtful.

16. The premium on a 3-year insurance policy which expires in 19X4 was paid in advance in 19X0. What is the effect of this transaction on the 19X0 financial statements for each of the following?

Prepaid Assets	**Expenses**
a. Increase	No effect
b. Increase	Increase
c. No effect	Increase
d. No effect	No effect

17. If the duration dimension of Accounts Payable Services is 30 days (assume 300 days per year), and PAYMENT TO SUPPLIERS OF SERVICES for the year were $120,000, and the account balance increased during the year by $30,000, then the beginning balance of Accounts Payable Services was _____.

18. If SALES REVENUE plus WRITEOFFS were greater than COLLECTIONS FROM CREDIT CUSTOMERS plus the UNCOLLECTIBILITY ADJUSTMENT, then either

    Account _____ must have increased/decreased
    or Account _____ must have increased/decreased
    or Account _____ must have increased/decreased

19.

↑ Accounts Receivable ↓		↓ Estimated Uncollectibles ↑		Sales Revenue
160,000			900	
?	? ?	?	?	1,200,000

If the company estimated that 1 percent of credit sales were uncollectible, then
a. Writeoffs were _____.
b. Collections from credit customers were _____.

20.

The Tertia Company
Comparative Balance Sheets
Months Ending December 31, 19X1 and January 31, 19X2

Assets	12/31/X1	1/31/X2
Cash	$ 25,000	$ 16,000
Accounts Receivable	46,000	62,000
Estimated Uncollectibles	(5,000)	(7,000)
Prepaid Services	12,000	11,000
Inventory	50,000	65,000
Property, Plant and Equipment	45,000	75,000
Accumulated Depreciation	(16,000)	(18,000)
Total Assets	$157,000	$204,000

Liabilities and Owner's Equities		
Accounts Payable Services	$ 17,000	$ 22,000
Accounts Payable Merchandise	36,000	44,000
Interest Payable	2,000	3,000
Mortgage Payable	25,000	40,000
Common Stock	40,000	50,000
Retained Earnings	37,000	45,000
Total Liabilities and Owner's Equities	$157,000	$204,000

Notes
(1) Depreciation expense for the year, included in operating expenses, was $4,000.
(2) Payments to suppliers of merchandise were $53,000.
(3) A fire destroyed a building whose original cost was $4,000. The insurance proceeds were $3,000.

The Tertia Company
Income Statement
January 19X2

Revenues and Gains

Sales Revenue		$?
Uncollectibility Adjustment		(3,000)
Net Sales Revenue		$?
Gain Recognized from Insurance Proceeds (note 3)		?
Total Revenues and Gains		$104,000

Expenses

Cost of Goods Sold	$?	
Operating Expenses (note 1)	34,000	
Interest Expense	?	
Total Expenses	?	(?)
Net Income		$ 22,000

Required:
From the comparative balance sheets, incomplete income statement, and related notes of The Tertia Company, prepare a statement of cash flows for January 19X2.

21.

The Prima Company
Comparative Post-Closing Trial Balance Sheets
Years Ending December 31, 19X0 and 19X1

Debit Balance Accounts	12/31/X0	12/31/X1
Cash	$ 87,000	$?
Accounts Receivable	41,000	46,700
Prepaid Services	4,000	5,200
Inventory	56,000	49,500
Total Debit Balance Accounts	$188,000	$?

Credit Balance Accounts		
Estimated Uncollectibles	$ 5,000	$ 6,000
Accounts Payable Services	27,000	17,500
Accounts Payable Merchandise	44,000	53,000
Property Tax Payable	1,000	1,500
Common Stock	35,000	40,000
Retained Earnings	76,000	?
Total Credit Balance Accounts	$188,000	$?

Statement of Cash Receipts and Disbursements
19X1

Cash Receipts

Collections from Credit Customers	$145,000
Cash Sales	63,000
Issue of Common Stock	5,000
Total Cash Receipts	$213,000

Cash Disbursements

Payments to Suppliers of Services	$ 58,000	
Payments to Suppliers of Merchandise	119,000	
Payment of Property Tax	1,200	
Payment of Dividends	2,000	
Total Cash Disbursements	$180,200	(180,200)
Excess Cash Receipts over Cash Disbursements		$ 32,800

Note: Writeoffs of Accounts Receivable were $700 during the year.

Required:
Prepare an income statement for 19X1.

22. Fill in the question (?) marks in the accounts below assuming that the profit margin (SALES minus COST OF GOODS SOLD) on INSTALLMENT SALES is 50 percent.

↓	Unrealized Profit on Installment Sales	↑		↑	Installment Receivables		↓
					100,000		
		250,000			?		?

23. (1) Total sales revenue for the period was $1,225,000.
    (2) The company received $49,000 in advances from customers.
    (3) Five percent of credit sales are estimated to be uncollectible.
    (4) The balance in the Advances from Customers account increased by $24,000.
    (5) Credit sales are three times greater than cash sales.
    (6) Collections from customers were $1,100,000.
    (7) The balance in the Accounts Receivable account increased by $100,000.

    Required:
    From the information above, determine the following:
    a. Credit sales
    b. Writeoffs
    c. The uncollectibility adjustment
    d. The change in the Estimated Uncollectibles account

24. From the following information relating to The MoMa Company a merchandising concern, prepare
    a. A statement of balance sheet changes
    b. An income statement
    c. A statement of cash flows
    No events not described or derivable from the information below occurred.
    (1) Common stock was issued for $300,000 in cash.
    (2) The company had depreciation expense.
    (3) Payments to suppliers of services were $500,000.
    (4) The balance in the Inventory account increased by $60,000.
    (5) The balance in the Accounts Receivable account increased by $300,000.
    (6) Taxes paid were $150,000.
    (7) The balance in the Cash account increased by $40,000.
    (8) The balance in the Property, Plant and Equipment account did not change.
    (9) The balance in the Interest Payable account decreased by $15,000.
    (10) The balance in the Taxes Payable account increased by $10,000.
    (11) Property, plant and equipment, with accumulated depreciation of $50,000, was scrapped. No proceeds were realized but a loss of $7,000 was recognized.
    (12) Collections from customers were $1,100,000.
    (13) Interest paid was $65,000.

(14) The balance in the Estimated Uncollectibles account increased by $10,000.

(15) The balance in the Accounts Payable Merchandise account increased by $20,000.

(16) The balance in the Retained Earnings account increased by $50,000.

(17) The balance in the Dividends Payable account increased by $10,000.

(18) Writeoffs were $51,000.

(19) The balance in the Advances from Customers account increased by $5,000.

(20) Dividends were paid during the year.

(21) The balance in the Estimated Warranty account decreased by $5,000.

(22) The balance in the Prepaid Services account increased by $5,000.

(23) Selling, administrative, and other expenses, exclusive of depreciation, warranty, and bad debts, was $475,000.

(24) Purchases of inventory were $500,000.

CHAPTER 9

Consumption of Inventory: Cost of Goods Sold

INTRODUCTION

This chapter deals with events related to the consumption of inventory. The cash flow associated with the consumption of inventory is the cash paid to the suppliers of merchandise (in the case of a merchandsing concern), and to suppliers of raw materials, labor services, and other manufacturing services (in the case of a manufacturing concern).

The accountant's job is to allocate these cash flows to goods that have been sold—COST OF GOODS SOLD—and to goods that remain in inventory—ending inventory. Several alternative accounting procedures may be used for this allocation. The use of one, rather than another, of these allocation procedures will have different effects on both the income statement and the balance sheet, but obviously will have no impact on the cash paid to suppliers, and therefore no impact on the statement of cash flows. The only cash impact of the allocation methods is indirect: the extent to which their use determines the amount of taxes a company pays.

COST OF INVENTORY

When the rights and responsibilities associated with merchandise are transferred from the seller to the buyer, a merchandising firm debits the Inventory account for the cash outflow necessary to acquire the merchandise, which consists of the invoice price less any discounts, plus all other costs incurred in attaining the right to utilize those goods, such as freight, handling, insurance, and storage.

For a manufacturing firm, the Finished Goods account is quantified by the cost of the inputs to the manufacturing process. These inputs include raw materials, labor services, utilities, rent, and depreciation, as well as freight, handling, insurance, and storage.

COST FLOW ASSUMPTIONS

The COST OF GOODS AVAILABLE FOR SALE for a merchandising firm during the period equals the sum of beginning inventory and PURCHASES OF INVENTORY during the period. This represents the cash outflows associated with the acquisition of inventory in this or a prior period. Of this total, some will be sold, some will be lost, and some will remain in the inventory. If we ignore inventory losses, then these relationships can be summarized for merchandising companies by the *basic inventory equation*:

$$\text{Beginning inventory} + \text{purchases} = \text{ending inventory} + \text{cost of goods sold}$$

The total of the left side of this equation (goods available for sale) is a known accounting quantification. The beginning balance of inventory is known because it represents the ending balance of the previous period, and PURCHASES OF INVENTORY for the period are quantified by their acquisition cost. The accounting problem is to allocate the portion of goods available for sale that represents COST OF GOODS SOLD, and the portion that represents the cost of ending inventory. How is this allocation accomplished when inventory is acquired at varying costs?

There are many possible allocation methods, but we will only discuss four of them. The first assumes that the cost of the first items purchased will be the cost of the first items sold, or simply *first-in, first-out* (**FIFO**). The second method assumes that the cost of the last items purchased will be the cost of the first items sold, or *last-in, first-out* (**LIFO**). The third method quantifies the unit cost of items sold in terms of the *average cost* of the units available for sale (average cost). Under the fourth method, the cost of each item sold is the actual purchase price of the specific item sold (specific identification).

Suppose a firm buys 100 grabules at $1.00 per grabule, and later buys another 100 grabules at $1.50 per grabule. (As is all too often true in contemporary society, prices have risen between purchase dates.) The firm then sells 100 grabules. How should COST OF GOODS SOLD be quantified, and what number is used to measure the ending inventory?

FIFO and LIFO are procedures for quantifying COST OF GOODS SOLD. **FISH** (*first-in, still-here*) and **LISH** (*last-in, still-here*) are names coined by one of the authors to describe the corresponding quantification of ending inventory. The method usually described as FIFO is really *FIFO-LISH*, and the method usually described as LIFO is really *LIFO-FISH*.

Some of the possibilities are given below.

	Unit Cost of Goods Sold	Unit Cost of Ending Inventory
Average	$1.25	$1.25
FIFO-LISH	1.00	1.50
LIFO-FISH	1.50	1.00
FIFO-FISH	1.00	1.00
LIFO-LISH	1.50	1.50

Accountants are not permitted by GAAP to employ FIFO-FISH or LIFO-LISH. At first, the prohibition against the use of FIFO-FISH and LIFO-LISH may appear eminently reasonable. After all, how can the same units be sold and yet remain in inventory? Obviously this is impossible in the physical sense, but all methods, except specific identification, are unrealistic in the physical sense. Does it make economic sense to describe a unit sold differently from a unit retained, when the two units are identical in all relevant economic attributes? True, two identical grabules may have been obtained at different prices, but that difference ceases to have economic relevance once they have been purchased by the firm. If some number provides the best description of the units sold, why not describe the remainng units by the same number? Using different numbers to quantify units sold and units retained will result in the association of different costs with sales of economically indistinguishable units.

However, the accounting prohibition against use of FIFO-FISH and LIFO-LISH probably reflects the fact that adoption of either method would invalidate the *basic inventory equation*, since ending inventory plus COST OF GOODS SOLD would no longer equal COST OF GOODS AVAILABLE FOR SALE.

Neither FIFO nor LIFO provides a completely current description of inventory costs. FIFO-LISH provides a more current description of ending inventory (LISH) on the balance sheet, but as a consequence the FIFO measure of COST OF GOODS SOLD on the income statement is relatively out of date. The reverse is true for LIFO-FISH, which provides a current measure (LIFO) of sales outflow in return for a noncurrent quantification (FISH) of ending inventory.

The simplest approach to calculate COST OF GOODS SOLD is the *average cost*, calculated as follows:

$$\text{Average cost per unit} = \frac{\text{total cost of units available for sale}}{\text{number of units available for sale}}$$

The last method, as the name specific identification implies, requires that detailed records be maintained listing the cost of each inventory item; it requires, too, that we physically trace which unit is sold and which remains. Unless inventory consists of a few readily distinguishable items, specific identification is not practical, and this method is rarely used.

> ### *Thought Question*
> The specific identification method gives the most opportunity for managing income. Why?

The physical flow of inventory does not depend on the flow assumption chosen by the accountant. Therefore, we might ask, should the accountant's cost flow assumption be determined by the physical flow of goods? To visualize the situation, suppose the inventory is kept in a bin, with each newly purchased layer placed on top of the older layers.

| Layer 3 |
| Layer 2 |
| Layer 1 |

If the physical flow dictated the accounting method, then we would use LIFO whenever inventory was removed from the top by a crane or shovel, and we would use FIFO whenever inventory was removed from the bottom by a chute or trap door.

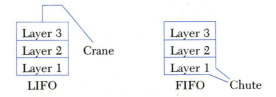

The use of a crane or chute obviously has no economic significance and should have no bearing on the choice of accounting method. Whichever method is most useful in reaching economic decisions should be chosen.

PERIODIC AND PERPETUAL INVENTORY METHODS

Regardless of which method is used to allocate COST OF GOODS AVAILABLE FOR SALE to COST OF GOODS SOLD and ending inventory, a firm has two choices about when to make this allocation. One method, called the *perpetual inventory method,* makes such an allocation as sales are made. The other, the *periodic inventory method,* only makes this allocation at periodic intervals, usually when the annual financial statements are prepared.

The perpetual method assigns a portion of COST OF GOODS AVAILABLE FOR SALE to COST OF GOODS SOLD by employing the FIFO, LIFO, or average cost assumption, each time a sale is made, with the remainder then quantifying the ending inventory. This method can be represented as follows:

$$\text{Cost of goods available for sale} - \text{cost of goods sold} = \text{ending inventory}$$

In the periodic method, the cost of ending inventory is directly quantified by physically counting inventory (taking inventory) at periodic intervals, and assigning a portion of the COST OF GOODS AVAILABLE FOR SALE to the ending inventory by utilizing the LISH, FISH, or average cost assumption. The remainder then quantifies the COST OF GOODS SOLD. This method can be represented as follows:

$$\text{Cost of goods available for sale} - \text{cost of ending inventory} = \text{cost of goods sold}$$

Both of the methods use the same variables, but under the perpetual method the directly quantified variables are COST OF GOODS AVAILABLE FOR SALE and COST OF GOODS SOLD, while the cost of the ending inventory is the derived quantification. Using the periodic method, the directly quantified variables are COST OF GOODS AVAILABLE FOR SALE and cost of ending inventory, while the COST OF GOODS SOLD is the derived quantification.

The *perpetual inventory method* has several advantages over the *periodic inventory method.* First, at all times (perpetually) management has information about both the ending inventory and COST OF GOODS SOLD to date, while under the periodic system, this information is available only when inventory is counted (periodically). Perhaps more importantly, by using the perpetual inventory method, the derived quantification of the cost of ending inventory can be independently verified by counting the inventory and estimating its costs. Therefore, a discrepancy between the inventory on hand (physical count) and what should be on hand (perpetual inventory balance), can be identified, and remedial action can be taken. If the periodic method is used, the derived quantification is COST OF GOODS SOLD, and this quantification cannot be independently verified. Thus discrepancies between what is, and what should be, are not readily identifiable. The main disadvantage of the perpetual method over the periodic method is that it costs more to measure COST OF GOODS SOLD at the point of every sale.

The three principal quantification methods (average, FIFO, LIFO) may be combined with the two inventory systems (periodic, perpetual) to produce six ways of measuring COST OF GOODS SOLD and ending inventory. Only **five** sets of figures result, since **FIFO-periodic for a given period will always yield the same figures as FIFO-perpetual for the same period.** (Most firms using LIFO combine it with the periodic inventory method of measuring COST OF GOODS SOLD and ending inventory.)

> *Thought Questions*
> Why will periodic FIFO always be the same
> as perpetual FIFO for the same period?
> Why do firms using LIFO
> prefer LIFO-periodic to LIFO-perpetual?

THE EFFECT OF LIFO AND FIFO ON THE FINANCIAL STATEMENTS

How does the choice of inventory flow assumption affect published accounting reports? In seeking to answer this question we present three exhibits showing LIFO and FIFO firms in periods of changing prices and varying inventory levels.

In the exhibits, sales are unaffected by the inventory method used. (Would you be willing to pay more for grabules because the selling firm used LIFO?) Cash outflows to suppliers of merchandise are also unaffected by the choice of inventory method. TAX EXPENSE and TAX PAYMENT, however, are affected because the tax laws state that if LIFO is used for tax purposes, **LIFO must** be used for financial statements also.

Exhibit 1 shows that in years 1 and 2, periods of rising costs, the FIFO firm has less COST OF GOODS SOLD and therefore reports more INCOME BEFORE TAXES. Because it has more INCOME BEFORE TAXES, it incurs a greater TAX EXPENSE and pays more in taxes. As a result, the FIFO firm will have more NET INCOME and a higher ending inventory but **less** cash! The statement of cash flows shows why the FIFO firm has less CASH FLOWS FROM OPERATIONS. The COLLECTIONS FROM CUSTOMERS, and PAYMENTS TO SUPPLIERS OF MERCHANDISE are identical for the two firms, but the tax payments for

EXHIBIT 1

The Differences between FIFO and LIFO
at Times of Increasing and then Stable Costs

	Year 1		Year 2		Years 3–10	
	FIFO	**LIFO**	**FIFO**	**LIFO**	**FIFO**	**LIFO**
Initial Inventory:						
Batch 0: 10 units @ $1.00	$10.00	$10.00				
Purchases of Inventory:						
Batch 1: 10 units @ $1.50	15.00	15.00				
Batch 2: 10 units @ $2.00			$20.00	$20.00		
Batch 3–10: 10 units @ $2.00					$20.00	$20.00
Sales: 10 units						
Unit Price: $3.00	$30.00	$30.00	$30.00	$30.00	$30.00	$30.00
Cost of Goods Sold:						
Batch 0	(10.00)					
Batch 1		(15.00)	(15.00)			
Batch 2				(20.00)		
Batch 2–9					(20.00)	
Batch 3–10						(20.00)
Income Before Taxes	$20.00	$15.00	$15.00	$10.00	$10.00	$10.00
Taxes (40%)	(8.00)	(6.00)	(6.00)	(4.00)	(4.00)	(4.00)
Net Income	$12.00	$ 9.00	$ 9.00	$ 6.00	$ 6.00	$ 6.00
Ending Inventory:						
Batch 0		$10.00		$10.00		$10.00
Batch 1	$15.00					
Batch 2			$20.00			
Batch 3–10					$20.00	
*Collections from Customers	$30.00	$30.00	$30.00	$30.00	$30.00	$30.00
*Payments to Suppliers of Merchandise	(15.00)	(15.00)	(20.00)	(20.00)	(20.00)	(20.00)
*Payment of Taxes	(8.00)	(6.00)	(6.00)	(4.00)	(4.00)	(4.00)
Cash Flows from Operations	$ 7.00	$ 9.00	$ 4.00	$ 6.00	$ 6.00	$ 6.00

*Assuming zero balances in all Payables or Receivables.

the FIFO firm are greater than that of the LIFO firm. The net result for the two firms in years 1 and 2, as described in Exhibit 1, is that the FIFO firm reports $3.00 more NET INCOME, but $2.00 less CASH FLOWS FROM OPERATIONS. In years 3–10, there are no additional differences.

The FIFO firm also has $2.00 less cash (the difference in cash flows is due solely to the difference in taxes, since all other cash flows were identical). The FIFO firm, however, reports $5.00 more of ending inventory.

The adoption of LIFO will also produce differences in reported income for the same firm in different time periods if costs change, or inventory is liquidated. For instance, compare the income of the LIFO firm in year 2 (Exhibit 1) and in year 11 as shown in Exhibit 2. Note that the LIFO firm has more income in year 11 when it liquidates inventory or when costs decline, but will have less CASH FLOWS FROM OPERATIONS because it will pay more taxes.

> ### Thought Questions
> Do you think that management and stockholders
> are ecstatic about this difference in earnings? Why?

Exhibit 3 summarizes the annual and cumulative differences between FIFO and LIFO. In periods of rising costs, LIFO firms report higher COST OF GOODS SOLD and less income than FIFO firms, but they pay less taxes and generate more cash than their FIFO counterparts.

The LIFO firm will also show a lesser ending inventory by an amount equal to the cumulative difference in COST OF GOODS SOLD. These differences will be reversed only if the firms reduce their inventory balances or if inventory costs decline. If a firm does not liquidate **all** its inventory, or if costs do not return to their original level, the LIFO firm will have obtained an absolute cash flow advantage, because it will have paid less taxes over its life. In order to obtain this tax savings, the LIFO firm has to report less book income.

If inventory is liquidated or costs decline following a period of rising costs, LIFO firms will pay less taxes early on, and more taxes later, thus obtaining a *present value* advantage over FIFO firms. The disadvantage is that less income is reported in the earlier years. Thus, LIFO produces an advantage in the amount or timing of cash flows at the expense of a permanent or temporary reduction in reported income. The LIFO firm can be viewed as selling book income to the government in exchange for less taxes and the resulting greater cash.

Should a firm prefer more cash or more profits? The answer depends on the perceived value of book income, especially as a determinant of stock values. Expert opinion is divided on this issue. Some believe that reported income has no impact on stock prices, while others believe income to be a major determinant of stock prices.

Business firms seem to behave as if the truth lies somewhere between these extremes. For a long time, most firms reported COST OF GOODS SOLD on a FIFO basis, showing that they were willing to

EXHIBIT 2

The Effects of
Inventory Liquidation and Declining Costs on
FIFO and LIFO

	Year 11 Inventory Liquidation		Year 11 Declining Prices	
	FIFO	**LIFO**	**FIFO**	**LIFO**
Initial Inventory:				
Batch 0: 10 units @ $1.00		$10.00		$10.00
Batch 10: 10 units @ $2.00	$20.00		$20.00	
Purchases of Inventory:				
Batch 11: 10 units @ $1.00	None	None	10.00	10.00
Sales: 10 units				
Unit Price: $3.00	$30.00	$30.00	$30.00	$30.00
Cost of Goods Sold:				
Batch 0		(10.00)		
Batch 10	(20.00)		(20.00)	
Batch 11				(10.00)
Income Before Taxes	$10.00	$20.00	$10.00	$20.00
Taxes (40%)	(4.00)	(8.00)	(4.00)	(8.00)
Net Income	$ 6.00	$12.00	$ 6.00	$12.00
Ending Inventory:				
Batch 0	None	None		$10.00
Batch 11	None	None	$10.00	
*Collections from Customers	$30.00	$30.00	$30.00	$30.00
*Payments to Suppliers of Merchandise	0	0	(10.00)	(10.00)
*Payment of Taxes	(4.00)	(8.00)	(4.00)	(8.00)
Cash Flows from Operations	$26.00	$22.00	$16.00	$12.00

*Assuming zero balances in all Payables or Receivables.

EXHIBIT 3

The Differences between FIFO and LIFO (FIFO minus LIFO)

	Year 1	Year 2	Years 3–10	Cumulative 1–10	Year 11	Cumulative 1–11
Sales	0	0	0	0	0	0
Cost of Goods Sold	(5.00)	(5.00)	0	(10.00)	10.00	0
Income Before Taxes	5.00	5.00	0	10.00	(10.00)	0
Taxes	2.00	2.00	0	4.00	(4.00)	0
Income After Taxes	3.00	3.00	0	6.00	(6.00)	0
Ending Inventory	5.00	10.00	10.00	10.00	0	0
Cash Flows from Operations	(2.00)	(2.00)	0	(4.00)	4.00	0

sacrifice tax savings in order to report higher income. In the mid-1970s, many of these companies switched to LIFO; the severe inflation of the period magnified the tax advantages of LIFO, and company managers were no longer willing to sacrifice these advantages in order to report higher income.

In summary then, factors which favor the choice of LIFO are

1. Increases in cost of inventory

2. High inventory levels

3. High interest rates

4. High tax rates

5. A long period of time before inventory levels or costs are expected to decline

6. An expectation that tax rates will fall before inventory or costs decline

> ### *Thought Question*
> Why do each of the factors mentioned above favor choosing LIFO?

LOWER-OF-COST-OR-MARKET

An existing quantification for inventory may be altered to reflect inventory impairment. The *"lower-of-cost-or-market"* (**LCM**) rule states that inventory shall be quantified at the lower of "cost" (the existing quantification) or "market." Three numbers must be calculated, and the middle one is defined to be "market." The three numbers are

1. Net realizable value (current selling price less disposal costs)

2. Net realizable value less normal profit

3. Replacement cost (current cost of obtaining that item)

If market is less than original cost, an *adjusting entry* is required.

Dr. Reduction of Inventory to Market (I/S)
   Cr. Inventory

where the debit (Dr.), REDUCTION OF INVENTORY TO MARKET, is reported in the income statement as a loss.

The LCM rule may be applied separately to each unit in inventory, to groups of similar items, or to the inventory as a whole. Each approach will lead to a different quantification of the inventory.

> ### *Thought Question*
> Which approach will lead to the highest valuation of inventory, and which will lead to the lowest valuation?

Again it is important to emphasize that the application of the lower-of-cost-or-market rule does not affect the cash flows related to inventory. The LCM rule merely affects how much of these cash flows are allocated to the current period as a loss or expense, rather than to future periods as goods available for sale.

LIFO may not be used in conjunction with the LCM rule. In a period of rising costs and stable or increasing levels of inventory, a firm using LIFO would report higher COST OF GOODS SOLD, and therefore lower taxable income, than would be reported using FIFO (see Exhibit 1). In a period of declining costs and stable or declining levels of inventory, the reverse is true. If firms were allowed to combine LIFO with LCM, they would reap a tax benefit when costs rise, and lose nothing (by comparison with FIFO) when costs decline. This is so because the market quantification of ending inventory will approximate the FIFO quantification of ending inventory, and therefore the LIFO COST OF GOODS SOLD plus the REDUCTION OF INVENTORY TO MARKET will equal FIFO COST OF GOODS SOLD. The IRS rule against combining LIFO and LCM is designed to prevent firms from being able to reduce taxes when costs rise without the risk of paying higher taxes when costs decline.

COST OF GOODS OF A MANUFACTURING FIRM

For manufacturing companies, the inventory equation is as follows:

> Beginning inventory + purchases of raw materials
> + services utilized in manufacturing
> = cost of goods sold + ending inventory

The inventories of manufacturing companies consist of Raw Materials and Supplies, Work-in-Process, and Finished Goods. The inputs to the manufacturing process consist of the raw materials or supplies utilized directly or indirectly, labor services utilized directly or indirectly, and other resources utilized such as machines, utilities, and insurance. All materials and services utilized in manufacturing are viewed as contributing to the cost of inventory produced, and therefore are allocated to the accounting quantifications of Work-in-Process, Finished Goods, and COST OF GOODS SOLD. Assuming a given level of sales, the COST OF GOODS SOLD for a manufacturing firm may vary with the level of production.

Consider the following simplified example: In order to produce grabules, a company utilizes marbles, labor, and a grabule-making machine. Each marble costs $1.00. The employee manufacturing grabules is paid $10.00 per grabule produced. Thus, the total cost of material and labor per grabule varies directly with the number of grabules manufactured. A total cost that varies directly with the number of units produced is called a *variable cost.* On the other hand, the machine is rented at a cost of $1,000 per month. The machine has the capacity to turn out 100 grabules per month. Thus, whether 1 or 100 grabules are produced during the month, the cost of utilizing the machine is $1,000. Such a cost, a cost that in total does not vary in relation to units produced, is called a *fixed cost.*

Now, suppose that the company produced and sold 50 grabules. The total inputs to the manufacturing process were $1,550: $500 in labor services, $50 in raw materials, and $1,000 for machine services. Assuming there was no beginning inventory, and since all that was manufactured was sold, COST OF GOODS SOLD equals the total INPUTS TO THE MANUFACTURING PROCESS, which were $1,550.

Now assume that the same company manufactured 100 units instead of 50. The manufacturing inputs would be $2,100: $1,000 for labor services, $100 for materials, and $1,000 for machine costs. Since half of the units produced were sold, then COST OF GOODS SOLD for these 50 units was $1,050.

Thus, when the company manufactured more units than it sold, it reported less COST OF GOODS SOLD. Therefore, the COST OF GOODS SOLD for a manufacturing company is a function of the quantity produced, if there are fixed costs of manufacturing. To the extent that there are *fixed costs,* COST OF GOODS SOLD will be less if a company manufactures more than it sells, and greater if its sells more than it manufactures, than if the company had manufactured the exact quantity it sold.

While the COST OF GOODS SOLD would be less, and the net income greater if a company produces more than it sells, in our example the operating cash outflow of the company that produced and sold 50 grabules would be $1,550, but will be $2,100 for the company that manufactured 100 units and sold 50. Therefore, the firm that manufactures 100 units will report $500 more in net income but will have $550 less in cash.

FINANCIAL STATEMENT PRESENTATION

The method used in determining COST OF GOODS SOLD and ending inventory, FIFO, LIFO, or average cost must be disclosed in the notes to the financial statements. Most firms, like The New York Times Company, disclose the method in the summary of accounting policies as shown in Example 1.

EXAMPLE 1

The New York Times Company
Notes to Consolidated Financial Statements

1. **Summary of Significant Accounting Policies**
   Inventories. Inventories are stated at the lower of cost or current market value. Inventory cost generally is based on the last in, first out ("LIFO") method for newsprint and magazine paper and the first-in, first-out, ("FIFO") method for other inventories.

For those firms that use LIFO, the current cost or the FIFO (LISH) cost of inventory must be disclosed. This disclosure is usually provided in a footnote as illustrated in Example 2.

EXAMPLE 2

The New York Times Company
Notes to Consolidated Financial Statements

5. **Inventories**
Dollars in thousands

December 31	1987	1986
Newsprint and magazine paper	$31,073	$27,844
Work-in-process, etc.	4,665	3,956
Total	$35,738	$31,800

Utilization of the LIFO method reduced inventories as calculated on the FIFO method by approximately $5,900,000 and $4,700,000 at December 31, 1987 and 1986, respectively.

This disclosure permits a user to convert COST OF GOODS SOLD on a LIFO basis to COST OF GOODS SOLD on a FIFO basis, as follows: From the comparative balance sheets, we know the change in the Inventory account. That change, when added to COST OF GOODS SOLD as reported in the income statement, will determine PURCHASES OF INVENTORY for the period. Since the current cost of inventory approximates the balances in Inventory for a FIFO (LISH) firm, the change in the Inventory account using the current cost amount as balances, when subtracted from PURCHASES OF INVENTORY, yields COST OF GOODS SOLD on a FIFO basis.

If the indirect method of determining CASH FLOWS FROM OPERATIONS is used, the credit (debit) changes in the Inventory and Accounts Payable Merchandise accounts are added to (or subtracted from) NET INCOME in the statement of cash flows in order to adjust NET INCOME to CASH FLOWS FROM OPERATIONS.

USER'S PERSPECTIVE

Inventory and Accounts Payable Merchandise also have duration dimensions as did Accounts Receivable and Accounts Payable Services. In determining the time that inventory is held in a merchandising firm, that is, the time between acquisition and sale, we utilize a variant of a ratio often called the *inventory turnover ratio,* or the *inventory holding period.* We calculate this ratio as follows:

$$\frac{\text{Average inventory}}{\text{Average daily purchases of inventory}}$$

Financial statements do not report the amount of PURCHASES OF INVENTORY, but PURCHASES OF INVENTORY can readily be derived from the statements. From the most recent income statement (preferably from the last month or quarter) we get COST OF GOODS SOLD. Adding the increase (or subtracting the decrease) in Inventory to COST OF GOODS SOLD gives us PURCHASES OF INVENTORY. Dividing PURCHASES OF INVENTORY by the number of business days in the period gives us the average DAILY PURCHASES OF INVENTORY. If our firm had COST OF GOODS SOLD of $95,000, 21 business days, and the beginning and ending balances in Inventory were $100,000 and $152,000, respectively, then PURCHASES OF INVENTORY were $147,000 [$95,000 + ($152,000 − $100,000)], and average DAILY PURCHASES OF INVENTORY were $7,000 ($147,000 ÷ 21). Average Inventory was $126,000 [($100,000 + $152,000) ÷ 2], and therefore the inventory holding period was 18 days ($126,000 ÷ $7,000).

On the average, inventory consisted of PURCHASES OF INVENTORY for the 18 previous days. Since the PURCHASES OF INVENTORY made 19 or more days ago were no longer in inventory, they were presumably sold. Therefore, on the average, the time between purchase and sale was 18 days.

In calculating this ratio, the inventory balances should be quantified by the current cost of inventory or by the FIFO inventory balances. Conventionally, this ratio is often calculated by using sales, or cost of sales, rather than PURCHASES OF INVENTORY. However, the use of sales distorts the ratio because sales are quantified by the unit sale price, whereas inventory is quantified by unit cost. The use of COST OF GOODS SOLD also is inadvisable, because the amount of COST OF GOODS SOLD is affected by the choice between FIFO and LIFO, whereas PURCHASES OF INVENTORY are not.

For manufacturing companies, only the Finished Goods duration can be calculated. The duration for Finished Goods is determined by dividing average Finished Goods by the average COST OF GOODS FINISHED DAILY. This latter amount is derived by adding the increase (or subtracting the decrease) in Finished Goods to COST OF GOODS SOLD and dividing by the number of days in the period. The duration dimension of Work-in-Process, which is dependent upon the length of the manufacturing cycle, and the duration dimension of Raw Materials and Supplies can only be calculated by utilizing information generally not available from financial statements.

The Duration Dimension of Accounts Payable Merchandise

The following ratio is used to calculate the duration dimension for Accounts Payable Merchandise, the time between the purchase and payment for merchandise:

$$\frac{\text{Average Accounts Payable Merchandise}}{\text{Average daily purchases of inventory}}$$

We previously calculated that our sample firm had average DAILY PURCHASES OF INVENTORY of $7,000. If the beginning and ending balances of Accounts Payable Merchandise are $38,000 and $46,000, respectively, then the average balance is $42,000 [($38,000 + $46,000) ÷ 2], and the duration dimension of Accounts Payable Merchandise is 6 days ($42,000 ÷ $7,000).

Calculating the Length of the Operating Cash Cycle for a Merchandising Firm

The operating cash cycle of a merchandising firm is the time between the payment for goods and the receipt of cash from customers. It can be determined by combining the duration dimensions of Accounts Receivable, Inventory, and Accounts Payable Merchandise. The time between the PURCHASE AND SALE OF GOODS represents the *inventory holding period*, which in our example was 18 days. The additional time between Sale and subsequent collection was 10 days, therefore the time between the purchase of goods and the collection from the sale of those goods is 28 days (18 + 10). But since the goods were not paid for at the time they were purchased, we subtract the time between purchase and payment for the goods, which in our example was 6 days, to find the operating cash cycle to be 22 days (28 − 6).

The operating cash cycle is equal to the duration dimension of Accounts Receivable, plus the duration dimension of Inventory, minus the duration dimension of Accounts Payable Merchandise.

In assessing the significance of the cash generated by operations, it is important to know not only how much cash was generated, but how long the period was between related cash outflows and cash inflows.

PROBLEMS

1. The following costs were among those incurred by Wotan Corporation during 19X1:

Merchandise purchased for resale	$500,000
Salesmen's commissions	40,000
Interest on notes payable to vendors	5,000

How much should be charged to the cost of the merchandise purchases?
a. $500,000
b. $505,000
c. $540,000
d. $545,000

2. Shure Company's inventory records for product Y provide the following data for 19X1:

	Units	Unit Cost
Inventory, Jan. 1, 19X1	12,000	$ 9.00
Purchases:		
Apr. 8	20,000	9.50
Oct. 25	8,000	10.00

A physical inventory on December 31, 19X1, shows 10,000 units on hand. Under the FIFO cost flow method, the December 31, 19X1, inventory should be
a. $100,000
b. $ 99,000
c. $ 95,000
d. $ 90,000

3. During 19X3 Ohlig Company discovered that the ending inventories reported on its financial statements were understated as follows:

Year	Understatement
19X0	$50,000
19X1	60,000
19X2	0

Ohlig ascertains year-end quantities on a periodic inventory system. These quantities are converted to dollar amounts using the FIFO cost flow method. Assuming no other accounting errors, Ohlig's Retained Earnings at December 31, 19X2, will be
a. Correct
b. $60,000 understated
c. $60,000 overstated
d. $110,000 understated

4. In a periodic inventory system which uses the weighted average cost flow method, the beginning inventory is the
   a. Net purchases minus the cost of goods sold
   b. Net purchases minus the ending inventory
   c. Total goods available for sale minus the net purchases
   d. Total goods available for sale minus the cost of goods sold

5. In a period of rising prices, the use of which of the following inventory cost flow methods would result in the highest cost of goods sold?
   a. FIFO
   b. LIFO
   c. Weighted average cost
   d. Moving average cost

6. In a periodic inventory system which uses the FIFO cost flow method, the cost of goods available for sale is net purchases
   a. Plus the ending inventory
   b. Plus the beginning inventory
   c. Minus the ending inventory
   d. Minus the beginning inventory

7. In a periodic inventory system which uses the LIFO inventory cost flow method, the cost of goods sold is the total cost of goods available for sale
   a. Plus the ending inventory
   b. Minus the ending inventory
   c. Plus the beginning inventory
   d. Minus the beginning inventory

8. Juniper Company is preparing its cash budget for the month of August 19X1. Projections for the month include the following:

Sales	$400,000
Gross profit (Sales − Cost of Goods Sold)	25%
Increase in inventories	$30,000
Decrease in trade accounts payable	$12,000

   What are the estimated cash disbursements for inventories in August 19X1?
   a. $142,000
   b. $312,000
   c. $318,000
   d. $342,000

9. Barry Distribution Company has valued its December 31, 19X1, inventory on a FIFO basis at $100,000. Information pertaining to that inventory is as follows:

Estimated selling price	$102,000
Estimated cost of disposal	5,000
Normal profit margin	15,000
Current replacement cost of inventory	90,000

Barry records a loss for any decline in inventory which is to be written down to a lower-of-cost-or-market basis. At December 31, 19X1, the loss which Barry should recognize is

a. $10,000
b. $7,000
c. $3,000
d. $0

10. The following pertains to an inventory item held by Mono Wholesalers, Inc., at the end of the year:

Cost	$60
Estimated selling price	68
Estimated cost of disposal	1
Normal profit margin	11
Replacement cost	51

By the lower-of-cost-or-market rule, this inventory item should be valued at

a. $51
b. $56
c. $60
d. $67

11. The original cost of an inventory item is above the replacement cost. The replacement cost is above the net realizable value. Under the lower-of-cost-or-market method, the inventory item should be priced at its

a. Replacement cost
b. Original cost
c. Net realizable value
d. Net realizable value less the normal profit margin

12. (*AICPA adapted*) Selected information from the accounting records of the Code Company is as follows:

Cost of goods sold for 19X1	$1,200,000
Inventories at December 31, 19X0	350,000
Inventories at December 31, 19X1	310,000

Required:
a. Assuming a business year consisting of 300 days, what was the number of days' sales in average inventories for 19X1?
   (1) 36.5
   (2) 77.5
   (3) 82.5
   (4) 87.5
b. What was the number of days purchases in average inventory?
c. What accounts for the difference?

13. (*AICPA adapted*) The Iftan Company was formed on December 1, 19X0. The following information is available from Iftan's inventory records for product Ply:

	Units	Unit Cost
Jan. 1, 19X1 (beginning inventory)	800	$ 9.00
Purchases:		
Jan. 5, 19X1	1,500	10.00
Jan. 25, 19X1	1,200	10.50
Feb. 16, 19X1	600	11.00
Mar. 26, 19X1	900	11.50

A physical inventory on March 31, 19X1, shows 1,600 units on hand.

Required:
Prepare schedules to compute the ending inventory at March 31, 19X1, under each of the following inventory methods:
a. LIFO
b. FIFO
c. Weighted average

14. From the following information, answer the questions below.
    (1) The only cash receipts and disbursements for the year consisted of COLLECTIONS FROM CUSTOMERS and PAYMENTS TO SUPPLIERS OF MERCHANDISE. The balance in the Cash account increased by $10,000.
    (2) Sixty percent of sales are collected during the month in which the sale is made, 35 percent in the following month, and 5 percent are estimated to be uncollectible. SALES were $1,500,000 last month and $1,700,000 this month.
    (3) The balances in the Accounts Receivable, Accounts Payable Merchandise, and Inventory accounts increased by $105,000, $50,000, and $75,000, respectively.
    a. Purchases of inventory during the month were _____.
    b. Cost of goods sold for the month were _____.
    c. Writeoffs during the month were _____.
    d. The change in the Estimated Uncollectibles account was _____.

15.

LISH and FISH Companies
Comparative Post-Closing Trial Balance Sheets
Years Ending December 31, 19X0 and December 31, 19X1

	LISH Company		FISH Company	
Debit Balance Accounts	**12/31/X0**	**12/31/X1**	**12/31/X0**	**12/31/X1**
Cash	$150,000	$250,000	$150,000	$266,000
Accounts Receivable	200,000	300,000	200,000	300,000
Inventory	100,000	?	100,000	?
Property, Plant and Equipment	300,000	400,000	300,000	400,000
Total Debit Balance Accounts	$750,000	$?	$750,000	$?
Credit Balance Accounts				
Estimated Uncollectibles	$ 20,000	$ 30,000	$ 20,000	$ 30,000
Accumulated Depreciation	20,000	50,000	20,000	50,000
Accounts Payable Merchandise	40,000	60,000	40,000	60,000
Accounts Payable Services	10,000	40,000	10,000	40,000
Common Stock	400,000	550,000	400,000	550,000
Retained Earnings	260,000	?	260,000	?
Total Credit Balance Accounts	$750,000	$?	$750,000	?

Notes

(1) No Property, Plant and Equipment was retired during the year for either firm.
(2) The inventory, as of December 31, 19X0, consisted of 50,000 units. In June 19X1, 50,000 units of inventory were purchased at $2.50 per unit, and in July 19X1 an additional 30,000 units were purchased at $3.00 per unit.
(3) Sales for the year were 60,000 units.
(4) Assume a tax rate of 40 percent.

LISH and FISH Companies
Income Statements
19X1

	LISH Company	FISH Company
Revenues		
Sales Revenue	$600,000	$600,000
Uncollectibility Adjustment	(15,000)	(15,000)
Total Revenues	$585,000	$585,000
Expenses		
Cost of Goods Sold	$?	$?
Operating Expenses	200,000	200,000
Tax Expense	?	?
Total Expenses	$? (?)	$? (?)
Net Income	$?	$?

Required:
Fill in the question (?) marks and prepare a statement of cash flows
for each firm, assuming that the LISH Company uses **FIFO**, and the
FISH Company uses **LIFO**.

16.

The Lambda Company
Comparative Balance Sheets
Months Ending December 31, 19X1 and January 31, 19X2

Assets	12/31/X1	1/31/X2
Cash	$ 100,000	$ 120,000
Accounts Receivable	190,000	250,000
Raw Materials	400,000	380,000
Work-in-Process	200,000	230,000
Finished Goods	520,000	510,000
Property, Plant and Equipment	700,000	740,000
Accumulated Depreciation	(200,000)	(280,000)
Total Assets	$1,910,000	$1,950,000

Liabilities and Owners' Equities

	12/31/X1	1/31/X2
Accounts Payable Services	$ 100,000	$ 20,000
Accounts Payable Raw Materials	50,000	50,000
Wages Payable	40,000	60,000
Common Stock	900,000	900,000
Retained Earnings	820,000	920,000
Total Liabilities and Owners' Equities	$1,910,000	$1,950,000

Notes
(1) All wages represent direct labor. Each month's wages are always paid on the second day of the following month.
(2) No property, plant and equipment was retired during January. All property, plant and equipment was utilized in the manufacturing process.
(3) Payments to suppliers of manufacturing services were $150,000.
(4) Work-in-Process is charged (debited) with **actual** indirect manufacturing costs.
(5) No common stock was retired.

The Lambda Company
Income Statement
January 19X2

Revenues

Sales Revenue		$900,000
Total Revenues		$900,000

Expenses

Cost of Goods Sold	$600,000	
Total Expenses	600,000	(600,000)
Net Income		$300,000

Required:
From the comparative balance sheets, income statement, and related notes of The Lambda Company, prepare a statement of cash flows for January 19X2.

17. There once were two companies identical in all respects except that one company used FIFO and the other LIFO.

In year 1, both companies purchased more units than they sold, and it was a year of increasing prices.

In year 2, both companies purchased the same number of units that they sold, and it was a year of increasing prices.

In year 3, both companies purchased fewer units than they sold, and it was a year of decreasing prices.

Sales, in both quantity and price, were the same in all 3 years for both companies.

Required:
Fill in the blank spaces in each of the following questions with "smaller," "equal," or "greater."
a. The COST OF GOODS SOLD of the FIFO company in year 1 was _____ than the COST OF GOODS SOLD of the LIFO company in year 2.
b. NET INCOME of the LIFO company in year 2 was _____ than NET INCOME of the FIFO company in year 1.
c. The difference in NET INCOME in part b above is _____ than the difference in COST OF GOODS SOLD in part a above.
d. The ending balance in the Inventory account of the LIFO company in year 2 is _____ than the ending balance in the Inventory account of the FIFO company in year 1.
e. The difference in ending Inventory in part d above is _____ than the difference in COST OF GOODS SOLD in part a above.

18. You are the president of The BerLu Company and are responsible for choosing accounting methods. You have a bonus plan which pays you 10 percent of the difference between net income and 15 percent of total assets at the beginning of the period. In other words, your bonus is equal to $[0.10(\text{net income} - 0.15 \times \text{total assets})]$. Assume that prices will increase over the next 2 years and then remain stable, and that you can invest all of your assets at 12 percent.

Required:
a. If you want to maximize your bonus in year 1, will you choose FIFO or LIFO?
b. If you want to maximize your bonus over 5 years, will you choose FIFO or LIFO?

19. Assume that two firms, both in business for 6 years, are identical in all respects except that one uses FIFO and the other LIFO, that the cost of inventory over the 6-year period has been steadily increasing, and that the number of units purchased each year exceeds the number of units sold.

Required:
Fill in the blank spaces in each of the following questions with "smaller," "equal," or "greater."
a. For the current year, COST OF GOODS SOLD of the FIFO firm is _____ than COST OF GOODS SOLD of the LIFO firm.

b. The ending balance in the Inventory account of the FIFO firm will be _____ the ending balance in the Inventory account of the LIFO firm, and the difference in their ending balances will be _____ the difference in their COST OF GOODS SOLD.

c. In the first year, the difference between CASH FLOWS FROM OPERATIONS for the two firms will be _____ than the difference in NET INCOME.

d. The ratio of NET INCOME to total assets of the LIFO firm will be _____ than the ratio of NET INCOME to total assets for the FIFO firm.

20. Refer to the note to the financial statements of The New York Times Company (page 227). Assume that the entire difference between FIFO and LIFO was associated with raw materials, and that the tax rate was 40 percent.

Required:
a. What were the FIFO raw material costs during the year?
b. What were the tax savings during the year having used LIFO rather than FIFO?
c. What were the cumulative tax savings having used LIFO rather than FIFO?

21. The Voda Company expects to begin operations on December 31, 19X1. During each **half** year, beginning with 19X2 through and including 19X5, they expect to purchase 1,000 units, and in 19X6 purchase no units at all. In addition, they expect to sell 1,000 units each year, beginning in 19X2 through and including 19X5 and 4,000 units in 19X6.

	19X2	19X3	19X4	19X5	19X6
Purchases:					
First 6 months	$ 2,000	$ 4,000	$ 6,000	$ 8,000	0
Second 6 months	4,000	6,000	6,000	10,000	0
Total	$ 6,000	$10,000	$12,000	$18,000	0
Sales	$10,000	$10,000	$10,000	$10,000	$40,000

If the tax rate is 40 percent, and taxes are payable on December 31 of each year, what is the anticipated present value as of December 31, 19X1, of the tax advantage of using LIFO-periodic rather than FIFO-periodic for the entire 5-year period if the appropriate interest rate is 6 percent?

CHAPTER 10

Amortization of
Long-Lived Assets

INTRODUCTION

This chapter deals with the utilization of long-lived assets. The utilization of a long-lived asset is an operating event that is quantified in terms of its related investment event—the cash outflow necessary to acquire the asset. In acquiring an asset, a firm purchases the right to utilize the asset beneficially over an extended period of time. This right is quantified by the cash necessary to acquire the asset, and is then allocated to the periods in which the asset can be productively utilized.

Thus, the accounting problem associated with the utilization of long-lived assets is to allocate the investment cash outflow necessary to acquire the asset to the time periods in which the asset is utilized. The process by which this is done is called the amortization of long-lived assets.

To accountants, **amortization** means the systematic reduction of an accounting quantification over time. Though the generic name given to allocating these costs is amortization, for property, plant and equipment it is called **depreciation,** for natural resources like oil, gas, and lumber, it is called **depletion,** and for intangible assets such as patents, copyrights, and franchises, it remains *amortization*.

In the previous chapter, we found that the choice of LIFO for tax purposes dictated the use of LIFO for financial reporting, and therefore had cash consequences. However, the choice of an amortization method used for tax purposes does not dictate the method used for financial reporting purposes, and will have no cash consequences whatsoever! The choice of amortization methods for book purposes will impact the balance sheet and income statement.

DEPRECIATION METHODS

Depreciation methods fall into two categories: equal charge and unequal charge. While there is only one equal charge method, the **straight-line method** (SL), there are many unequal charge methods. However, we will discuss and illustrate only two of them: *sum-of-*

the-years'-digits *method* (SYD) and *double-declining balance method* (DDB). All three methods make use of three numbers:

1. Acquisition cost
2. Useful life to the firm
3. Residual value, also called salvage value, scrap value, or disposal value

The useful life to the firm is the number of periods in which the firm expects to utilize the assets productively. The useful life can be expressed in terms of units of activity or units of time. For example, an automobile can have a useful life of 100,000 miles (activity) or 5 years (time). Both methods have advantages and disadvantages, but most firms measure the useful life of assets in units of time.

> ### Thought Questions
> Why do you think most firms measure useful life
> in terms of units of time?
> What are some of the advantages and disadvantages
> of each method?

The residual value of the asset is its expected market value less expected disposal costs at the time of disposal. The acquisition cost of the asset is derived from the actual transaction, in contrast to the useful life and residual value, which are **estimates** based on predictions of future events. Total depreciation charges over the useful life of the asset are equal to the acquisition cost minus the residual value (also called the depreciable base). In the year that an asset is acquired, depreciation may be calculated for the actual time the asset was in use during the year, or a half year of depreciation may be recorded arbitrarily, regardless of when the asset was acquired during the year.

STRAIGHT-LINE METHOD OF DEPRECIATION

In *straight-line depreciation,* the annual depreciation charge is

$$\frac{\text{Original cost} - \text{residual value}}{\text{Useful life}} =$$

$$(\text{original cost} - \text{residual value}) \times \frac{1}{\text{useful life}}$$

For example, an asset costing \$17,000 is acquired by the firm. The asset is expected to have a useful life of 5 years and a residual value (at the end of 5 years) of $2,000. In other words, the firm purchased 5 years of service quantified at $15,000 and a residual value of $2,000, for a total of $17,000. The annual depreciation charge, using the straight-line method of depreciation, would be calculated as follows:

$$\frac{\$17,000 - \$2,000}{5} = \$3,000$$

or 20% × 15,000. (20% is called the depreciation rate.)

SUM-OF-THE-YEARS'-DIGITS METHOD OF DEPRECIATION

In determining depreciation using the *sum-of-the-years'-digits* method, the annual charge is also a fraction of the depreciation base, but the fractions decline from year to year. All the fractions have the same denominator, which is the sum-of-the-years'-digit, or more precisely, the sum of the integers from 1 to n, where n = the useful life. The sum-of-the-years'-digit is determined by SYD = $1 + 2 + \cdots + (n - 1) + n$. The mathematical expression for the summation of consecutive digits is $n(n + 1) \div 2$.

If $n = 3$, then $\quad$ SYD $= 6 = \dfrac{3 \times 4}{2} = 1 + 2 + 3$

If $n = 4$, then $\quad$ SYD $= 10 = \dfrac{4 \times 5}{2} = 1 + 2 + 3 + 4$

If $n = 5$, then $\quad$ SYD $= 15 = \dfrac{5 \times 6}{2} = 1 + 2 + 3 + 4 + 5$

The numerator of the fraction is always the remaining duration at the beginning of the year. Returning to our previous example, if the original cost of an asset acquired is $17,000, the residual value $2,000, and the expected useful life 5 years, then the sum-of-the-years'-digits is 15, and the annual depreciation charges, using the sum-of-the-years'-digits method, are as follows:

Year	Fraction		Depreciation Base		Annual Depreciation Charge
1	$\frac{5}{15}$	×	$15,000 ($17,000 − $2,000)	=	$ 5,000
2	$\frac{4}{15}$	×	15,000	=	4,000
3	$\frac{3}{15}$	×	15,000	=	3,000
4	$\frac{2}{15}$	×	15,000	=	2,000
5	$\frac{1}{15}$	×	15,000	=	1,000
Total					$15,000

The successive numerators of the fractions are simply the years' integers: n, $n - 1$, . . ., 2, 1, in descending order.

DOUBLE-DECLINING BALANCE METHOD OF DEPRECIATION

In determining depreciation using the *double-declining balance* method, no explicit use is made of the residual value. Instead, the annual depreciation charge equals $(2 \div n)$ times the asset's book value at the beginning of each period, where n is the asset's estimated useful life.

Since the depreciation rate under straight-line depreciation is $1 \div n$, and the depreciation rate under double-declining balance depreciation is $2 \div n$, DDB is sometimes called "twice straight-line." However, the name "twice straight-line" is misleading, since the total charge under double-declining balance is **not** twice the charge under straight-line. The depreciation rate is double that of straight-line, but the depreciation rate is applied to a declining book value, rather than to a stable basis, original cost minus salvage value.

Consider our example of an asset acquired at a cost of $17,000, with an estimated residual value of $2,000 and an estimated useful life of 5 years. Using the double-declining method, the annual depreciation charge would be as follows:

Year	Fraction	Depreciation Base		Annual Depreciation Charge
1	$\frac{2}{5}$	$\times$	$17,000 ($17,000 − $0) =	$ 6,800
2	$\frac{2}{5}$	$\times$	10,200 ($17,000 − $6,800) =	4,080
3	$\frac{2}{5}$	$\times$	6,120 ($10,200 − $4,080) =	2,448
4	$\frac{2}{5}$	$\times$	3,672 ($6,120 − $2,448) =	1,469
5		Remainder =		203
Total				$15,000

Since accounting rules require that the total depreciation charges for an asset must be equal to the asset's depreciable base (original cost minus residual value), the depreciation charge in the last year is limited to $203, instead of $881 ($\frac{2}{5} \times$ $2,203). Otherwise, the total depreciation charged would have exceeded the depreciable base of $15,000.

Thought Question

Which depreciation method necessarily gives the greatest amount of depreciation expense in the first year of the useful life of the asset?

Suppose that the asset illustrated above had a residual value of zero. Then, the depreciation expense for the fifth year would be $2,203, the remainder of the depreciable base. Thus, the depreciation schedule would appear as follows:

Year	Fraction	Depreciation Base		Annual Depreciation Charge
1	$\frac{2}{5}$	× $17,000 ($17,000 − $0)	=	$ 6,800
2	$\frac{2}{5}$	× 10,200 ($17,000 − $6,800)	=	4,080
3	$\frac{2}{5}$	× 6,120 ($10,200 − $4,080)	=	2,448
4	$\frac{2}{5}$	× 3,672 ($6,120 − $2,448)	=	1,469
5		Remainder	=	2,203
Total				$17,000

Notice that the depreciation charge in the fifth year is greater than that in the fourth year. That is because the total depreciation must equal the depreciable base. A firm can anticipate these results, and switch from DDB to SL at some point in the asset's useful life. When that is done, the annual charge for the remaining duration equals

$$\frac{\text{Book value } - \text{ estimated residual value}}{\text{Remaining duration}}$$

Suppose that the firm decides to switch from DDB to SL. When should the firm switch? From the following chart, it is clear that for this asset, the firm should switch after the third year.

Year	Beginning Book Value	Annual DDB Depreciation Charge	SL Depreciation Charge If Switch Occurs at the End of Year:			
			1	2	3	4
2	$10,200	$4,080	$2,550			
3	6,120	2,448	2,550	$2,040		
4	3,672	1,469	2,550	2,040	$1,836	
5	2,203	2,203	2,550	2,040	1,836	$2,203

Firms using DDB are expected to switch over to SL at some stage, usually when half the useful life has expired. Firms using any other depreciation method for existing assets are not allowed to adopt a new method of depreciation for these assets.

GROUP METHOD OF DEPRECIATION

Assets may be depreciated on an individual basis (***unit depreciation***) or in homogeneous groups (***group depreciation***). The unit method of depreciation assumes that the estimate of useful life and of residual value is relevant for **each** depreciable asset. Any difference between the estimated and actual life, and/or residual value of each individual asset, is assumed to have significance and must be accounted for.

Under the *group method* of depreciation, the estimate of useful life and residual value is an average for a group of assets, and this average has meaning only for the group of assets being depreciated. Therefore, if the actual life and/or residual value of an individual asset differs from the estimated average group life and residual value, the difference is not considered significant. The consequences of these different assumptions mainly impact accounting for the retirement of depreciable assets; they are illustrated and discussed in Chapter 15.

ILLUSTRATION OF DIFFERENT DEPRECIATION METHODS: SINGLE-ASSET FIRM

Suppose that a firm has one asset, with an original cost of $17,000, an estimated useful life of 5 years, and a salvage value of $2,000. The depreciation charge under each of the methods would be as follows:

Year	SL	SYD	DDB
1	$ 3,000	$ 5,000	$ 6,800
2	3,000	4,000	4,080
3	3,000	3,000	2,448
4	3,000	2,000	1,469
5	3,000	1,000	203
Total	$15,000	$15,000	$15,000

ILLUSTRATIONS OF DIFFERENT DEPRECIATION METHODS: MULTIPLE-ASSET FIRM

A firm acquires its first asset, costing $17,000, with an estimated useful life of 5 years and a salvage value of $2,000, and continues to acquire an identical new asset each year. During the first 5 years, the number of assets increases from one to five. In year 6, the newly acquired asset, asset number six, will replace asset number one

EXHIBIT 1

Depreciation for Multiple-Asset Firms Growing and Then Stabilizing*
Using Straight-Line, Sum-of-the-Years'-Digits, and Double-Declining Methods

Straight-Line

Year Asset Number	1	2	3	4	5	6
1	$3,000	3,000	3,000	3,000	3,000	0
2		3,000	3,000	3,000	3,000	3,000
3			3,000	3,000	3,000	3,000
4				3,000	3,000	3,000
5					3,000	3,000
6						3,000
Total	$3,000	$6,000	$9,000	$12,000	$15,000	$15,000

Sum-of-the-Years'-Digits

Year Asset Number	1	2	3	4	5	6
1	$5,000	4,000	3,000	2,000	1,000	0
2		5,000	4,000	3,000	2,000	1,000
3			5,000	4,000	3,000	2,000
4				5,000	4,000	3,000
5					5,000	4,000
6						5,000
Total	$5,000	$9,000	$12,000	$14,000	$15,000	$15,000

Double-Declining

Year Asset Number	1	2	3	4	5	6
1	$6,800	4,080	2,448	1,469	203	0
2		6,800	4,080	2,448	1,469	203
3			6,800	4,080	2,448	1,469
4				6,800	4,080	2,448
5					6,800	4,080
6						6,800
Total	$6,800	$10,880	$13,328	$14,797	$15,000	$15,000

*The firm acquires one asset each year until it reaches five assets. Then, the firm retires and acquires one asset each year. Each asset has an original cost of $17,000, a salvage value of $2,000, and an expected life of 5 years.

Depreciation for Growing Multiple-Asset Firms*
Using Straight-Line Method

Year Asset Number	1	2	3	4	5	6	7	8	9	10	11	12
1	$3,000	3,000	3,000	3,000	3,000	0	0	0	0	0	0	0
2		3,000	3,000	3,000	3,000	3,000	0	0	0	0	0	0
3			3,000	3,000	3,000	3,000	3,000	0	0	0	0	0
4				3,000	3,000	3,000	3,000	3,000	0	0	0	0
5					3,000	3,000	3,000	3,000	3,000	0	0	0
6						3,000	3,000	3,000	3,000	3,000	0	0
7						3,000	3,000	3,000	3,000	3,000	0	0
8							3,000	3,000	3,000	3,000	3,000	0
9							3,000	3,000	3,000	3,000	3,000	0
10								3,000	3,000	3,000	3,000	3,000
11								3,000	3,000	3,000	3,000	3,000
12									3,000	3,000	3,000	3,000
13									3,000	3,000	3,000	3,000
14										3,000	3,000	3,000
15										3,000	3,000	3,000
16											3,000	3,000
17											3,000	3,000
18											3,000	3,000
19												3,000
20												3,000
21												3,000
Total	$3,000	$6,000	$9,000	$12,000	$15,000	$18,000	$21,000	$24,000	$27,000	$30,000	$33,000	$36,000

*The firm acquires one more asset than it retires each year. Each asset has an original cost of $17,000, a salvage value of $2,000, and an expected life of 5 years.

Depreciation for Growing Multiple-Asset Firms*
Using Double-Declining Balance Method

Asset Number	Year 1	2	3	4	5	6	7	8	9	10	11	12
1	$6,800	4,080	2,448	1,469	203	0	0	0	0	0	0	0
2		6,800	4,080	2,448	1,469	203	0	0	0	0	0	0
3			6,800	4,080	2,448	1,469	203	0	0	0	0	0
4				6,800	4,080	2,448	1,469	203	0	0	0	0
5					6,800	4,080	2,448	1,469	203	0	0	0
6						6,800	4,080	2,448	1,469	203	0	0
7						6,800	4,080	2,448	1,469	203	0	0
8							6,800	4,080	2,448	1,469	203	0
9							6,800	4,080	2,448	1,469	203	0
10								6,800	4,080	2,448	1,469	203
11								6,800	4,080	2,448	1,469	203
12									6,800	4,080	2,448	1,469
13									6,800	4,080	2,448	1,469
14										6,800	4,080	2,448
15										6,800	4,080	2,448
16											6,800	4,080
17											6,800	4,080
18											6,800	4,080
19												6,800
20												6,800
21												6,800
Total	$6,800	$10,880	$13,328	$14,797	$15,000	$21,800	$25,880	$28,328	$29,747	$30,000	$36,800	$40,880

*The firm acquires one more asset than it retires each year. Each asset has an original cost of $17,000, a salvage value of $2,000, and an expected life of 5 years.

EXHIBIT 3A

Depreciation for Growing and Stable Firms with Increasing Costs*
Using Straight-Line Method

Asset Number	Year 1	2	3	4	5	6	7	8	9	10	11	12
1	$3,000	3,000	3,000	3,000	3,000	0	0	0	0	0	0	0
2		3,000	3,000	3,000	3,000	3,000	0	0	0	0	0	0
3			3,000	3,000	3,000	3,000	3,000	0	0	0	0	0
4				3,000	3,000	3,000	3,000	3,000	0	0	0	0
5					3,000	3,000	3,000	3,000	3,000	0	0	0
6						3,300	3,300	3,300	3,300	3,300	0	0
7							3,630	3,630	3,630	3,630	3,630	0
8								3,993	3,630	3,993	3,993	3,993
9									4,392	3,993	3,993	4,392
10										4,392	4,392	4,392
11										4,832	4,832	4,832
12											5,315	5,315
												5,846
Total	$3,000	$6,000	$9,000	$12,000	$15,000	$15,300	$15,930	$16,923	$18,315	$20,147	$22,162	$24,378

*The cost of each asset acquired during the first 5 years is $17,000 with a salvage value of $2,000. The cost of assets acquired subsequently increases by 10 percent per year as does the salvage value. For example, the cost of asset number six is $18,700, and its salvage value is $2,200.

Depreciation for Growing and Stable Firms with Increasing Costs*
Using Double-Declining Balance Method

Year	1	2	3	4	5	6	7	8	9	10	11	12
Asset Number												
1	$6,800	4,080	2,448	1,469	203	0	0	0	0	0	0	0
2		6,800	4,080	2,448	1,469	203	0	0	0	0	0	0
3			6,800	4,080	2,448	1,469	203	0	0	0	0	0
4				6,800	4,080	2,448	1,469	203	0	0	0	0
5					6,800	4,080	2,448	1,469	203	0	0	0
6						7,480	4,488	2,693	1,616	223	0	0
7							8,228	4,937	2,962	1,777	246	0
8								9,051	5,430	3,258	1,955	270
9									9,956	5,974	3,584	2,151
10										10,951	6,571	3,943
11											12,047	7,228
12												13,251
Total	$6,800	$10,880	$13,328	$14,797	$15,000	$15,680	$16,836	$18,353	$20,167	$22,183	$24,403	$26,843

*The cost of each asset acquired during the first 5 years is $17,000 with a salvage value of $2,000. The cost of assets acquired subsequently increases by 10 percent per year as does the salvage value. For example, the cost of asset number six is $18,700, and its salvage value is $2,200.

acquired in year 1. In year 7, the newly acquired asset, asset number seven, will replace the one acquired in year 2, and so on. Therefore, from year 6 on, each newly acquired asset replaces an older one, and the firm always has just five assets. Such a firm is called a growing and then stable firm.

Depreciation charges reported each year under each of the methods is illustrated in Exhibit 1. Exhibit 1 shows that a multiple-asset firm during its growth period has an increasing amount of depreciation each year, and then maintains the same amount during its stable period. The firm that chooses an accelerated method of depreciation, rather than straight-line, will have an even higher depreciation charge during a growth period, and the same depreciation once the firm stops growing and becomes stable.

Consider a firm that acquires one more asset than it retires each year, and that the cost of each new asset acquired is $17,000, with an estimated useful life of 5 years and a salvage value of $2,000. During the first 5 years, the number of assets increases from one to five. In years 6 through 10, the firm acquires two new assets each year: one to replace the asset retired, and one for growth. In years eleven through fifteen, the firm acquires three new assets each year: two to replace the two retired ones, and one for growth. Such a firm is called a growing firm.

Exhibit 2 shows that multiple-asset firms that continue to grow will have an ever increasing amount of depreciation expense, and that growth firms using an accelerated method of depreciation will always have more depreciation than straight-line firms.

Consider a stable firm that replaces its assets at a cost 10 percent higher each year. A firm using straight-line depreciation will have an increasing amount of depreciation expense, and an accelerated depreciation firm will always have more depreciation than the straight-line firm, as Exhibit 3 illustrates.

As you would expect, growing firms during times of increasing prices will have an ever increasing depreciation charge, and an even greater one if they adopt an accelerated method rather than the straight-line method of depreciation.

Growth in the dollar amount of depreciable assets is likely to occur for most firms because (1) surviving firms generally grow; (2) changes in technology, particularly increasing automation, tend to make the quantity of depreciable assets grow, even if a firm does not grow in other respects; and (3) inflation causes the dollar amount of depreciable assets to increase even if the quantity of depreciable assets does not. Therefore, we can expect multiple-asset firms utilizing accelerated depreciation to have greater depreciation than straight-line firms.

REPAIRS

Estimates of an asset's useful life presuppose certain periodic expenditures to keep the asset in good working order. Such routine costs are called ordinary repairs and maintenance, and they are reported as period expenses or manufacturing costs.

A nonfunctioning machine is not an economic resource. By repairing a nonfunctioning machine, we restore the right to utilize an economic resource. Why then isn't the repair event described by a debit to the asset account? The explanation is that repairing the asset signals the recording of **two** events.

The repair itself can be described by the entry

Dr. Asset
    Cr. Cash

but the repair also implies that an asset impairment, not previously recognized by the accountant, must have occurred in the past.

This impairment could have been described by the entry

Dr. Expense (I/S)
    Cr. Asset

Just as filling the gas tank of a car measures the amount of gasoline consumed since the last fill-up, so the cost of the repairs measures the amount of prior impairment. Since both entries are quantified by the same number, they are combined into one entry for ordinary repairs:

Dr. Repairs Expense (I/S)
    Cr. Cash

Users of accounting reports must realize that an ordinary repair is a restoration, serving to recognize impairment that has already taken place. Although accounting recognition of impairment can be postponed, the impairment itself cannot be avoided by refusing to acknowledge that it occurred. Once this is clearly understood by all, a foreman will have no incentive to temporarily enhance his performance report by postponing needed repairs. A condition revealed and cured by an operation is not **caused** by the operation. In the same way, the repair signals recognition of prior impairment, but the repair did not **cause** that impairment to occur.

Extraordinary (or major) repairs is the name given substantial nonrecurring expenditures designed to increase the capacity or useful life of the asset. These expenditures are recorded as debits to the asset being repaired. Similar treatment is accorded expenditures for replacements, betterments, improvements, additions, rearrangements, and such. Some accountants prefer to debit the asset account when utility (productive capacity) has been increased, but debit Accumulated Depreciation to reflect an increase in the useful life of the asset. (Whether such a distinction can actually be drawn is doubtful.) As a practical matter, this distinction is unimportant, since it will not affect the asset's book value.

Consider a firm that acquired a machine costing $17,000. At the time, the estimated useful life was 5 years, and the salvage value $2,000. The firm employed straight-line depreciation in accounting for this machine. After 3 years, the firm spent $4,000 on extraordinary repairs to the machine, thereby extending its remaining duration an additional 2 years. Before the repairs, the balances in the accounts relating to this equipment were as follows:

Balance Sheet Presentation

Property, Plant and Equipment	$15,000
Accumulated Depreciation	(9,000)
Net Property, Plant and Equipment	$ 6,000

The journal entry to record the extraordinary repairs would be either

Extraordinary Repairs		
Dr. Property, Plant and Equipment	4,000	
Cr. Cash		4,000

or

Extraordinary Repairs		
Dr. Accumulated Depreciation	4,000	
Cr. Cash		4,000

Either way, the book value of the repaired machine becomes $10,000. Therefore, the annual depreciation expense entry for the remaining 4 years will be

Dr. Depreciation Expense (I/S)	2,500	
Cr. Accumulated Depreciation		2,500

CHANGES IN ESTIMATES

Useful life and residual value are estimates used in quantifying depreciation. The firm should review these estimates periodically, and revise them when appropriate. A change in estimated residual value will alter the remaining depreciation base—book value less residual value. A change in estimated useful life will alter the remaining depreciation duration. When estimates are changed, we do not alter previously recorded depreciation. Instead, the new depreciation base must be allocated to the revised estimate of remaining duration.

For a familiar example, an asset costing $17,000 is acquired by the firm. Its estimated residual value is $2,000, and its estimated useful life is 5 years. The firm uses straight-line depreciation. Depreciation charges for the first 3 years would be as follows:

Year	Fraction	Depreciation Base		Annual Depreciation Charge
1	$\frac{1}{5}$ ×	$15,000 ($17,000 − $2,000)	=	$3,000
2	$\frac{1}{5}$ ×	15,000	=	3,000
3	$\frac{1}{5}$ ×	15,000	=	3,000
Total				$9,000

At the end of the third year, the firm revises its original estimates of residual value and useful life. The new estimates are that the useful life will be a total of 7 years (an additional 2 years), but at that point, the residual value would be zero. After the change in estimates, the book value of the asset was $8,000 ($17,000 − $9,000), and the remaining depreciable base was $8,000 ($8,000 − $0), and the remaining duration was 4 years. Therefore, the annual depreciation charge for the remaining 4 years would be $2,000 ($8,000 ÷ 4) a year.

AMORTIZING INTANGIBLE ASSETS

Intangible assets are amortized over the number of periods in which the firm expects to utilize the assets productively. For some of these assets, patents and copyrights, the maximum productive life is limited by statute. The rights granted by a patent or a copyright expire after a given number of years. Thus, for these assets, the amortization period cannot exceed the statutory life because at the end of the asset's statutory life, the rights represented by the asset cease to exist. That is, the patent holder no longer has the exclusive right to use the process. Regardless of the expected productive life, all intangible assets must be amortized over a period not to exceed 40 years.

For example, suppose that a cable company has a franchise for 50 years. However, the expected productive life of that franchise is 25 years. Then, if it cost $100,000 to acquire the franchise, the amortization period will be 25 years, and the yearly amortization charge will be $4,000. However, if the productive life is expected to be 50 years, the franchise must be amortized over 40 years, with an annual amortization charge of $2,500.

DEPLETION OF NATURAL ASSETS

The cost of natural assets, such as oil, gas, and timber, must be allocated to the units sold. This is done by dividing the cost of the asset by the expected number of units to be realized. The original cost of the natural assets is readily determinable. It equals the total cost of acquiring the asset plus any other costs associated with retrieving it. However, determining the number of units available is more problematic. At best, a firm can only estimate the quantity of the available resource and periodically adjust its DEPLETION EXPENSE as the estimates change.

FINANCIAL STATEMENT PRESENTATION

Some firms, like The New York Times Company, include DEPRECIATION (and other amortization) EXPENSE in the income statement as part of OPERATING or SELLING, GENERAL, AND ADMINISTRATIVE EXPENSES. This is illustrated in Example 1.

EXAMPLE 1

The New York Times Company

	Year Ended December 31		
	1987	**1986**	**1985**
Revenues	**$1,689,598**	$1,564,663	$1,393,772
Costs and Expenses			
Raw materials cost	**312,649**	285,843	287,046
Operating costs	**602,711**	572,278	521,313
Selling, general and administrative expenses	**482,910**	434,926	372,288
Total	**1,398,270**	1,293,047	1,180,647
Operating profit	**291,328**	271,616	213,125
Interest expense, net of interest income	**22,911**	35,535	19,653
Income before income taxes and equity in earnings of associated companies	**268,417**	236,081	193,472
Income taxes	**126,074**	123,414	98,541
Income before equity in earnings of associated companies	**142,343**	112,667	94,931
Equity in earnings of associated companies	**17,990**	19,560	21,387
Net income	**$ 160,333**	$ 132,227	$ 116,318

Dollars and shares in thousands except per share data

Others, like Cooper Industries, explicitly report them, as illustrated in Example 2.

EXAMPLE 2

	Cooper Industries		
	Year Ended December 31		
	1985	1984	1983
Revenues	$3,067,169	$2,029,915	$1,850,280
Costs and Expenses			
Cost of sales	2,070,992	1,357,949	1,250,359
Depreciation and amortization	105,815	73,636	67,909
Selling and administrative expenses	534,471	368,376	363,101
Interest expense	97,723	20,572	28,460
	2,809,001	1,820,533	1,709,829
Income before income taxes	258,168	209,382	140,451
Income taxes	123,088	102,518	69,282
Net Income	$ 135,080	$ 106,864	$ 71,159

The total accumulated depreciation is reported in the balance sheet either explicitly, like The New York Times Company, as illustrated in Example 3,

EXAMPLE 3

The New York Times Company		
Property, Plant and Equipment (at cost)		
Land	48,543	30,150
Buildings, building equipment, and improvements	279,491	214,973
Equipment	475,971	424,134
Construction and equipment installations in progress	157,884	76,351
Total	961,889	745,608
Less accumulated depreciation	317,636	261,620
Total property, plant and equipment, net	644,253	483,988

or net, like Cooper Industries, as illustrated in Example 4.

EXAMPLE 4

Cooper Industries

Plant and equipment, at cost less accumulated depreciation	973,235	685,548
Intangibles, less accumulated amortization	863,464	231,803
Investments and other assets	51,789	37,255

Major classes of depreciable assets are reported in the footnotes to the financial statements as illustrated in Example 5.

EXAMPLE 5

Cooper Industries

Note 5: Plant and Equipment & Intangibles

	December 31	
	1985	**1984**
	(000 omitted)	
Plant and equipment:		
Land and buildings	$ 433,755	$ 318,691
Machinery and equipment	866,697	656,505
Office furniture and equipment	77,533	51,836
Construction in progress	38,786	29,212
	1,416,771	1,056,244
Accumulated depreciation	(443,536)	(370,696)
	$ 973,235	$ 685,548
Intangibles:		
Goodwill	$ 906,782	$ 261,412
Other	12,580	8,152
	919,362	269,564
Accumulated amortization	(55,898)	(37,761)
	$ 863,464	$ 231,803

A description of the method or methods used in computing depreciation for major classes of depreciable assets is usually disclosed in the footnotes to the financial statements as illustrated in Example 6.

EXAMPLE 6

The New York Times Company

Property, Plant and Equipment. Property, plant and equipment is recorded at cost, and depreciation is computed by the straight-line method over estimated service lives.

For firms presenting the CASH FLOWS FROM OPERATIONS using the indirect method, they adjust NET INCOME to CASH FLOWS FROM OPERATIONS by adding DEPRECIATION EXPENSE to NET INCOME. This is illustrated in Example 7.

EXAMPLE 7

The New York Times Company

	Year Ended December 31		
	1987	**1986**	**1985**
Cash Provided (Applied)	(Dollars in thousands)		
Operating Activities			
Net income	$160,333	$132,227	$116,318
Items not requiring (providing) cash			
Depreciation	62,366	54,943	45,588
Amortization	19,153	20,237	12,835
Equity in earnings of associated companies, net	(19,528)	(21,929)	(20,365)
Deferred income taxes	13,773	5,146	28,068
Decrease (increase) in receivables	2,236	(4,599)	(20,096)
(Increase) decrease in inventories	(3,577)	3,578	2,043
Increase in accounts payable, payrolls and accrued expenses	12,394	6,977	4,690
Increase in other current assets	(9,174)	(3,240)	(6,530)
Other—net	24,230	6,775	6,989
Total from operating activities	262,206	200,115	169,540

USER'S PERSPECTIVE

Differences between accounting quantifications may be either substantive differences or measurement differences. A substantive difference arises from the quantification of different accounting events, and a measurement difference arises from the quantification of the same accounting event using two different accounting methods.

The choice of different depreciation methods for the same asset creates a measurement difference in both the balance sheet and the income statement. For example, suppose firm A uses straight-line (SL) depreciation, and firm B uses double-declining balance (DDB). Each firm owns a single depreciable asset costing $17,000, with a residual value of $0, and a 5-year useful life. Both firms have sales of $50,000, and operating expenses requiring cash of $20,000. Let us compare the income statements of the two firms.

	Income Statements **First Year**	
	Firm A (SL)	**Firm B (DDB)**
Sales	$50,000	$50,000
Operating Expenses	(20,000)	(20,000)
Depreciation Expense	(3,400)	(6,800)
Income Before Taxes	$26,600	$23,200
Cash Flows from Operations Before Taxes	$30,000	$30,000

Examining the balance sheets of the two firms, we see the following differences between them:

	Firm A (SL)	**Firm B (DDB)**
Property, Plant and Equipment (original cost)	$17,000	$17,000
Less: Accumulated Depreciation	(3,400)	(6,800)
Net Property, Plant and Equipment	$13,600	$10,200

We see that the SL firm reports $3,400 more in INCOME BEFORE TAX than the DDB firm because it had $3,400 less in depreciation. Certainly, this difference in INCOME BEFORE TAX is **not** a substantive difference, but a measurement difference. Both firms have utilized identical assets for the same time period, and both firms have the same CASH FLOWS FROM OPERATIONS BEFORE TAXES. Though the events that the firms reported were the same, the accounting numbers describing those events are different because they used different depreciation methods.

The choice of depreciation methods also produced differences in the balance sheet. The DDB firm has $3,400 more in Accumulated Depreciation than the SL firm, and the DDB firm's book value of Property, Plant and Equipment is also less by $3,400. Certainly, these differences are also measurement differences, and not substantive differences.

Let us extend our example to the second year. If both firms report the same sales and operating expenses again, then they will prepare the following income statements:

Income Statements
Second Year

	Firm A (SL)	Firm B (DDB)
Sales	$50,000	$50,000
Operating Expenses	(20,000)	(20,000)
Depreciation Expense	(3,400)	(4,080)
Income Before Taxes	$26,600	$25,920
Cash Flows from Operations		
Before Taxes	$30,000	$30,000

The DDB firm again has less INCOME BEFORE TAX than the SL firm, but this time by $680, and again the difference is a measurement difference. The balance sheets of the two firms would be as follows:

	Firm A (SL)	Firm B (DDB)
Property, Plant and Equipment		
(original cost)	$17,000	$17,000
Less: Accumulated Depreciation	(6,800)	(10,880)
Net Property, Plant and		
Equipment	$10,200	$ 6,120

Notice that the difference between book values of the asset has now grown to $4,080, the cumulative difference in the depreciation recorded for the 2 years.

The distinction between substantive and measurement differences can be important not only when comparing two firms at a point in time, but also when comparing one firm over time. For example, let us compare the events that occurred to the DDB firm in years 1 and 2.

The DDB Firm
Income Statements
First and Second Years

	Year 1	Year 2
Sales	$50,000	$50,000
Operating Expenses	(20,000)	(20,000)
Depreciation Expense	(6,800)	(4,080)
Income Before Taxes	$23,200	$25,920
Cash Flows from Operations		
Before Taxes	$30,000	$30,000

INCOME BEFORE TAX in year 2 was $2,720 greater than INCOME BEFORE TAX in year 1. But was the DDB firm really more profitable in the second year? In a substantive sense, no, since the firm experienced identical events, and had identical cash flows in both years. The increase in INCOME BEFORE TAX was due solely to the choice of the depreciation method. You might argue that since INCOME BEFORE TAX for the two firms differ, the REQUIRED TAX PAYMENTS for the two firms would differ, and therefore substantive differences would result. However, the choice of depreciation methods for financial reports does not influence the amount of taxes that must be paid.

Users of financial statements clearly need to distinguish between substantive and measurement differences. But how can they do this? They may not be able to precisely calculate the measurement effect, but they can approximate it by calculating what straight-line depreciation would have been for the DDB firm.

In our example, we know that the depreciation rate for the DDB firm is $2 \div n$ applied to the remaining book value. From the income statement, we know that DEPRECIATION EXPENSE for the first year is $6,800 which is $(2 \div n) \times \$17,000$. Solving for n, we see that the estimated useful life is 5 years. Therefore, having approximated the useful life of the asset, we can approximate what depreciation would be had the firm used straight-line. If the firm chose straight-line depreciation rather than double-declining balance, DEPRECIATION EXPENSE would have been $3,400 $[(1 \div 5) \times (\$17,000 - \$0)]$.

Since the two firms would have reported the same income had they used the same depreciation method, we know that any differences in income are measurement differences. Similarly, we could show that income for the DDB firm would have been the same in years 1 and 2 had they used the straight-line method. Therefore, any differences in reported income are measurement differences.

Our example is overly simplified, of course, since the firms discussed had only one asset and the salvage value was zero. When firms have multiple assets with nonzero salvage values, then we can only approximate the results.

Another example of measurement and substantive differences is caused by FIFO and LIFO assumptions in inventory. The choice of inventory methods will cause both substantive and measurement differences. As we saw in Exhibit 3 in Chapter 9, the difference in COST OF GOODS SOLD between the FIFO and LIFO firms for years 1, 2, and 11 represent measurement differences because both firms sold the same number of units. Note that the ending balance in inventory for the FIFO firm will be greater than that of the LIFO firm; this, too, is a measurement difference. However, because

LIFO is used for tax purposes, the LIFO firm will have less of a tax liability then the FIFO firm, and therefore will pay less taxes. And as we all know, any difference in taxes paid is a substantive difference.

Thus, the total difference between the FIFO and LIFO firm's net income and net-assets will be a compounded difference consisting of a measurement difference and a substantive difference. The measurement difference, COST OF GOODS SOLD, will be partially offset by the substantive difference in taxes paid. The user of financial statements can gauge the extent of the measurement difference by calculating what COST OF GOODS SOLD **would** have been had the firm used FIFO rather than LIFO, using the technique discussed in Chapter 9.

PROBLEMS

1. On July 1, 19X0, Muldoon Corporation purchased factory equipment for $50,000. Salvage value was estimated at $2,000. The equipment will be depreciated over 10 years using the double-declining balance method. Counting the year of acquisition as one-half year, Muldoon should record 19X1 depreciation expense of
   a. $7,680
   b. $9,000
   c. $9,600
   d. $10,000

2. The Karp Corporation purchased factory equipment that was installed and put into service January 2, 19X0, at a total cost of $32,000. Salvage value was estimated at $2,000. The equipment is being depreciated over 8 years using the double-declining balance method. For the year 19X1, Karp should record Depreciation Expense on this equipment of
   a. $5,625
   b. $6,000
   c. $7,000
   d. $8,000

3. If DEPRECIATION EXPENSE was larger than ACQUISITION OF PROPERTY, PLANT AND EQUIPMENT, then either Property, Plant and Equipment (increased/decreased/remained the same) or Accumulated Depreciation (increased/decreased/remained the same).

4. A firm acquires a machine at a cost of $32,000, with an expected useful life of 5 years, and an estimated salvage value of $2,000.
   a. In the first year, Depreciation Expense using the _____ method will be greater than Depreciation Expense using the _____ method, which will be greater than Depreciation Expense using the _____ method.
   b. In the fourth year, Depreciation Expense using the _____ method will be greater than Depreciation Expense using the _____ method, which will be greater than Depreciation Expense using the _____ method.

5. The following expenditures were among those incurred by Relbut Company during 19X1:

A broken gear on a machine was replaced	$1,500
Replacement of tiles on portion of roof	4,500
Overhaul of machinery that is expected to extend its useful life for another 3 years	7,500

How much should be charged to repairs and maintenance in 19X1?
a. $1,500
b. $4,500
c. $6,000
d. $9,000

6. On January 1, 19X0, the Lacy Company purchased for $264,000 a machine to be depreciated by the straight-line method over the estimated useful life of 8 years, with no salvage value. On January 1, 19X3, Lacy determined that the machine has a useful life of 6 years from the date of acquisition and will have a salvage value of $24,000. An accounting change was made in 1991 to reflect this additional data. The Accumulated Depreciation for this machine should have a balance at December 31, 19X3, of
a. $176,000
b. $160,000
c. $154,000
d. $146,000

7. The Gray Company purchased a machine on January 2, 19X0, for $500,000. The machine has an estimated useful life of 5 years and a salvage value of $50,000. Depreciation was computed by the 150 percent declining balance method. The Accumulated Depreciation balance at December 31, 19X1, should be
a. $180,000
b. $229,500
c. $245,000
d. $255,000

8. A company depreciated its only asset using the double-declining balance method. It presented the following related information:

	Year 1	Year 2
Property, Plant and Equipment	$100,000	$100,000
Accumulated Depreciation	(30,000)	(44,000)
Net Property, Plant and Equipment	$ 70,000	$ 56,000

a. What was depreciation expense for the year?
b. If the salvage value of the equipment was $0, then what would depreciation expense have been had the company used the straight-line method?
c. What is the estimated useful life of the asset?

9. A machine with an expected useful life of 4 years and an estimated 15 percent salvage value was acquired on January 1. Would depreciation expense using the sum-of-the-years'-digits method of depreciation be higher or lower than depreciation expense using the double-declining balance method of depreciation in the first and second years?

First Year	Second Year
a. Higher	Higher
b. Higher	Lower
c. Lower	Higher
d. Lower	Lower

10. At the end of the expected useful life of a depreciable asset with an estimated 15 percent salvage value, the Accumulated Depreciation would equal the original cost of the asset under which of the following depreciation methods?

Straight-Line	Sum-of-the-Years'-Digits
a. Yes	Yes
b. No	No
c. Yes	No
d. No	Yes

11. In January 19X0, Colonus Company purchased equipment for $120,000, to be used in its manufacturing operations. The equipment was estimated to have a useful life of 8 years, with salvage value estimated at $12,000. Colonus considered various methods of depreciation and selected the sum-of-the-years'-digits method. On December 31, 19X1, the related Allowance for Accumulated Depreciation should have a balance of
   a. $15,000 less than under the straight-line method
   b. $15,000 less than under the double-declining balance method
   c. $18,000 greater than under the straight-line method
   d. $18,000 greater than under the double-declining balance method

12. The T-accounts below relate to a merchandising firm. If all of the property, plant and equipment retired was fully depreciated, then
   a. Acquisition of property, plant and equipment was _____.
   b. Depreciation expense was _____.
   c. Loss on retirement of equipment was _____.
   d. Which of your answers above would be questionable if these accounts related to a manufacturing concern? Why?

↑	Property, Plant and Equipment	↓	↓	Accumulated Depreciation	↑
10,000					10,000
	50,000				

13.

A and B Companies
Comparative Post-Closing Trial Balance Sheets
Years Ending December 31, 19X0 and 19X1

Debit Balance Accounts	A Company		B Company	
	12/31/X0	12/31/X1	12/31/X0	12/31/X1
Cash	$ 50,000	$110,000	$ 62,000	$136,000
Accounts Receivable	100,000	195,000	100,000	195,000
Inventory	150,000	200,000	150,000	200,000
Property, Plant and Equipment	?	?	?	?
Total Debit Balance Accounts	$?	$?	$?	$?
Credit Balance Accounts				
Estimated Uncollectibles	$ 10,000	$ 20,000	$ 10,000	$ 20,000
Accumulated Depreciation	?	?	?	?
Accounts Payable Merchandise	30,000	40,000	30,000	40,000
Accounts Payable Services	40,000	60,000	40,000	60,000
Common Stock	260,000	400,000	260,000	400,000
Retained Earnings	?	?	?	?
Total Credit Balance Accounts	$?	$?	$?	$?

Notes

(1) A and B Companies began operations on January 1, 19X0. They both acquired three assets: two on January 1, 19X0, and one on January 1, 19X1. Each asset cost $125,000, had an expected useful life of 10 years, and an estimated salvage value of $25,000.

A and B Companies are identical firms in all respects except that A Company depreciates its assets on a straight-line basis, and B Company depreciates its assets on a double-declining basis.

(2) No property, plant and equipment was retired during the year by either firm.
(3) Assume a tax rate of 40 percent.

A and B Companies
Income Statements
19X1

Revenues		A Company			B Company
Sales Revenue		$600,000			$600,000
Uncollectibility Adjustment		(15,000)			(15,000)
Total Revenues		$585,000			$585,000
Expenses					
Cost of Goods Sold	$215,000			$215,000	
Operating Expenses	120,000			120,000	
Depreciation Expense	?			?	
Tax Expense	?			?	
Total Expenses	$?	(?)	$?		(?)
Net Income		$?			$?

Required:
Fill in the blanks and prepare a statement of cash flows for each firm.

14. From the following information relating to the Sodan Company, a manufacturing concern, prepare
    a. A statement of balance sheet changes
    b. An income statement
    c. A statement of cash flows
    No events not described or derivable from the information below occurred.
    (1) Cost of goods sold was $70,000.
    (2) The balance in Prepaid Services increased by $4,000.
    (3) No property, plant and equipment was retired or sold during the year.
    (4) Operating expenses were $35,000.
    (5) Payments to suppliers of services (including labor) were $73,000.
    (6) The balance in Finished Goods increased by $10,000.
    (7) Payments to suppliers of raw materials were $27,000.
    (8) The balance in Accounts Payable Services decreased by $1,000.
    (9) Input of labor services into Work-in-Process was $40,000.
    (10) The balance in Retained Earnings increased by $25,000.
    (11) The balance in Taxes Payable increased by $2,000.
    (12) Sales revenue was $150,000.
    (13) The balance in Raw Materials decreased by $5,000.
    (14) No dividends were declared during the year.
    (15) The balance in Accounts Payable Raw Materials increased by $3,000.
    (16) The only inputs to Work-in-Process were labor, materials, and depreciation.
    (17) The balance in Work-in-Process increased by $6,000.

15. Depreciable assets X, Y, and Z are acquired at the beginning of year 1. You are given the following information:

Asset	Depreciation Method	Estimated Life	Salvage Value
X	Straight-line	3 years	$2,000
Y	Sum-of-the-years'-digits	4 years	3,000
Z	Double-declining balance	5 years	1,000

For each asset, the Depreciation Expense in year 2 is $12,000.

Required:
Determine
a. Original cost of asset X
b. Original cost of asset Y
c. Original cost of asset Z
d. Depreciation expense in year 3 for asset X
e. Depreciation expense in year 3 for asset Y
f. Depreciation expense in year 3 for asset Z

16. Fill in the account titles for accounts 1 to 8. In addition, for each letter A to L, describe the event and give the journal entry.

Income Accounts	Balance Sheet Accounts		

Income Accounts

(1)

    (A)

    (L)

Balance Sheet Accounts

↑   (4)   ↓

(B) | (E)

(L) | (I)

       (J)

↑   (8)   ↓

(F) | (G)

(2)

(G) |

↓   (5)   ↑

(I) | (D)

Interest

↓   Payable   ↑

(J) | (K)

(3)

(K) |

↑   (6)   ↓

    | (C)

Accounts

↑ Receivable ↓

(A) | (B)

Operating Expenses

(C)

(D) |

↓   (7)   ↑

    | (H)

Accounts

↓   Payable   ↑

(E) | (F)

Depreciation Expense

(H) |

17. From the T-accounts below, determine
   a. Depreciation Expense _____.
   b. What X, Y, and Z represent.
   c. What true statement can you make about the magnitude of X?

Property, Plant

↑   and Equipment   ↓

20,000 |

X | Y

Accumulated

↓   Depreciation   ↑

    | 5,000

Z | 8,000

CHAPTER 11

Income Taxes

INTRODUCTION

A corporation prepares financial reports for creditors, owners, and others for **book purposes**—that is, to help users predict cash flows (see Chapter 1). A corporation also prepares reports for **tax purposes** to enable the Internal Revenue Service to raise revenues for the federal government. Since the objectives of the reports differ, it is not surprising that the income statement, which is a financial report prepared according to GAAP, differs significantly from the tax return, which is prepared in accordance with the Internal Revenue Code.

We will focus here on how to account for income taxes in financial statements, and on the important differences between book and tax reporting.

DEFINITIONS

Although there are many similarities between the income statement and the income tax return, the two reports differ in several important respects. Certain events are treated one way in preparing the income tax return, and differently in preparing the income statement.

To minimize the confusion caused by technical jargon relating to taxes, we will define a few terms. In the income statement, INCOME BEFORE TAX represents the difference between revenues plus gains, and expenses plus losses (excluding taxes, of course). INCOME TAX EXPENSE is generally a percentage of INCOME BEFORE TAX, and is subtracted from INCOME BEFORE TAX to determine NET INCOME.

The analogous terms in the tax report are TAXABLE INCOME and the REQUIRED TAX PAYMENT. TAXABLE INCOME represents the excess of taxable inflows over tax deductible outflows. The REQUIRED TAX PAYMENT is calculated by multiplying TAXABLE INCOME by the applicable tax rate. TAXABLE LOSSES represent the excess of tax deductible outflows over taxable inflows.

TAXABLE LOSSES

Under certain circumstances, a TAXABLE LOSS will result in a TAX REFUND, or in a reduction of a REQUIRED TAX PAYMENT. Current tax law permits TAXABLE LOSSES to be carried back 3 years in order to offset TAXABLE INCOME that was reported, and receive a refund on taxes paid in those years. When these TAXABLE LOSSES offset previously taxed income, they are called *operating loss carrybacks*. Losses may also be carried forward 15 years to offset future TAXABLE INCOME. These losses are called *operating loss carryforwards*.

The losses are applied in chronological order, first to the earliest year, then any excess is applied to the next earliest year, and so on. For example, a company reports net income of $40,000, $70,000, and $50,000 in 1986, 1987, and 1988, respectively, but in 1989 suffers a loss of $170,000. The tax rate was and is 40 percent. The loss is carried back 3 years, first to 1986, then to 1987, and finally to 1988.

Year	Taxable Income or (Loss)	Required Tax Payment or (Refund)
1986	$ 40,000	$16,000
1987	70,000	28,000
1988	50,000	20,000
1989	(170,000)	(68,000)

The *operating loss carryback* offsets all the income recorded in 1986, 1987, and 1988. Therefore, the taxes paid to the IRS in those years will be refunded to the company. Thus, $160,000 of the $170,000 TAXABLE LOSS is carried back to the previous 3 years, and results in a $64,000 refund. The remaining $10,000 TAXABLE LOSS can be carried forward to offset TAXABLE INCOME during the next 15 years.

The *operating loss carryforward* will never be reported as an accounting asset, but the benefits will be recognized in future periods when the operating loss carryforward offsets TAXABLE INCOME, and will result in lower REQUIRED TAX PAYMENTS.

The refund will be presented as follows in the income statement:

Income Before Tax	$(170,000)
Tax Benefit	64,000
Net Loss	$106,000

CALCULATING INCOME TAX EXPENSE

The REQUIRED TAX PAYMENT usually differs from INCOME TAX EXPENSE when INCOME BEFORE TAX differs from TAXABLE INCOME. INCOME BEFORE TAX and TAXABLE INCOME can differ because taxable inflows are not equal to revenues and gains, and tax deductible outflows are not equal to expenses and losses. Differences between revenues (gains) and taxable inflows, and between expenses (losses) and tax deductible outflows, reflect differing quantifications of assets and liabilities for book and tax purposes.

The quantification of assets and liabilities is called *book value* for financial reporting and *tax basis* for tax reporting. If there are no differences between the book value and the tax basis of assets and liabilities, and INCOME BEFORE TAX equals TAXABLE INCOME, then INCOME TAX EXPENSE is equal to the REQUIRED TAX PAYMENT. The journal entry to record INCOME TAX EXPENSE is

Income Tax Expense
    Dr. Income Tax Expense (I/S)
        Cr. Taxes Payable

When the book value and tax basis of assets and liabilities differ, INCOME TAX EXPENSE will equal the REQUIRED TAX PAYMENT plus (minus) any additional tax payment (refund) that will result when the asset or liability is liquidated at a price equal to book value. Such a future tax payment (refund) is called a *deferred tax liability (asset)*.

EVENTS CAUSING DIFFERENCES BETWEEN INCOME BEFORE TAX AND TAXABLE INCOME

There are two reasons why book value and tax basis of assets and liabilities, and INCOME BEFORE TAX and TAXABLE INCOME differ. The first is that events recognized for book purposes are never recognized for tax purposes, and the second is that events recognized for tax purposes are never recognized for book purposes. Such differences are called *permanent differences.*

As a result of permanent differences, INCOME BEFORE TAX and TAXABLE INCOME will never be equal, and the difference between them will never reverse. In addition, these differences will never require a future tax payment, or generate a future tax refund. If the only differences between INCOME BEFORE TAX and TAXABLE INCOME are *permanent differences,* then INCOME TAX EXPENSE will be equal to the REQUIRED TAX PAYMENT, and there will be **no** *deferred tax liability.*

For example, INCOME BEFORE TAX will always be greater than TAXABLE INCOME for a firm that has interest income from tax-free municipal bonds, while it will always be less than TAXABLE INCOME for a firm that pays premiums on life insurance policies on its officers, where the benefits are payable to the firm. In the above examples, the interest income is always a revenue for book purposes but never a taxable inflow, while the insurance premium is an expense but never a tax deductible outflow. Therefore, the interest income and the insurance expense will never be included in determining TAXABLE INCOME.

EVENTS CAUSING DIFFERENCES BETWEEN THE BOOK VALUE AND TAX BASIS OF ASSETS

The *book value* and *tax basis* of assets and liabilities, and consequently INCOME BEFORE TAX and TAXABLE INCOME, can differ because although an event is recognized for both book and tax purposes, either the timing of the recognition or the quantification of the event may differ for book and tax reporting. These differences are called *temporary differences,* because over the life of the asset or liability, the difference between book value and tax basis will be eliminated. If INCOME BEFORE TAX is initially greater than TAXABLE INCOME, it will subsequently become less, and if INCOME BEFORE TAX is initially less than TAXABLE INCOME, then it will subsequently become greater.

Because temporary differences reverse over the life of the related asset, or duration of the related liability, total INCOME BEFORE TAX and total TAXABLE INCOME will be equal over that period. However, **at specific times, or over specific periods,** during the useful life of an asset or duration of a liability, the differences in the timing of the reporting or quantification of the same accounting event will result in a difference between INCOME BEFORE TAX and TAXABLE INCOME, and a difference between the book value and the tax basis of the asset or liability.

Temporary differences causing INCOME BEFORE TAX to be initially greater than TAXABLE INCOME can result from the recognition of more revenues for book purposes than taxable inflows (as in installment sales), or the reporting of more tax deductible outflows than expenses (as in the use of accelerated depreciation methods for tax reporting, and straight-line for financial reporting). These temporary differences cause the book value of net-assets to be greater than their tax basis (book value of assets will be larger than their tax basis, and the book value of liabilities will be less than their tax basis).

Temporary differences causing TAXABLE INCOME to be initially greater than INCOME BEFORE TAX can result from initially reporting more taxable inflows than revenues (as in receiving advances for rented space), or the initial recognition of more expenses than tax deductible outflows (as in warranty liability). These temporary differences will cause the book value of net-assets to be less than their tax basis.

TEMPORARY DIFFERENCES CAUSING BOOK VALUE OF NET-ASSETS TO BE GREATER THAN THEIR TAX BASIS

Book value will be greater than the tax basis of net-assets if tax deductible outflows exceed the related expense, or if revenue exceeds the related taxable inflow. Examples of these events are the use of an accelerated depreciation method to calculate the tax deductible outflow, and a straight-line method to calculate the depreciation expense; or the recognition of profits (book purposes) from installment sales at the time of sale, but the recognition of taxable inflows (tax purposes) only when cash is received.

When the book value of net-assets is greater than their tax basis because of a *temporary difference*, a deferred tax liability must be recognized in an amount equal to the tax rate times the difference between the book value and tax basis of the net-asset. **The INCOME TAX EXPENSE that must be recorded each period in this case is the REQUIRED TAX PAYMENT plus (or minus) any change in the Deferred Tax Liability account.** The entry to record this event initially is

Income Tax Expense
    Dr. Income Tax Expense (I/S)
        Cr. Taxes Payable
        Cr. Deferred Tax Liability

Consider a firm that acquires one asset on January 1, costing $17,000, with an estimated useful life of 5 years and a salvage value of $0. For financial reporting purposes, straight-line depreciation may be used to depreciate the asset over its estimated useful life. For tax purposes, the *modified accelerated cost recovery system (MACRS)* method of depreciation is required.

Recent tax legislation stipulates that the *modified accelerated cost recovery system* (MACRS) must be used in calculating the depreciation deduction for tax returns. Under MACRS, eligible property is depreciated by using a declining balance method over an arbitrarily stated depreciation period. This tax depreciation period is generally shorter than the estimated useful life of the property.

For this asset, the depreciation period is 3 years. Since the asset was acquired on January 1, a full year's depreciation will be charged for financial reporting purposes. However, for tax purposes,

MACRS requires that the depreciation deduction in the first year must be limited to one-half year's depreciation, regardless of when in the year the asset was acquired. Therefore, the first year's straight-line depreciation for book purposes would be $3,400 [($17,000 − $0) ÷ 5]. For tax purposes, a full year's depreciation deduction using MACRS would be $11,334 [($17,000 ÷ 3) × 2], but since only one-half can be taken the first year, the deduction would be $5,667.

The book value and tax basis of the asset would be $13,600 ($17,000 − $3,400) and $11,333 ($17,000 − $5,667), respectively.

	Book		Tax	
Year	Depreciation Expense (S/L)	Asset Book Value	Depreciation Deduction (MACRS)	Asset Tax Basis
1	$3,400	$13,600	$5,667	$11,333

If the company has no other temporary differences, the ending balance in the Deferred Tax Liability account will be $907. The ending balance in the Deferred Tax Liability account is calculated by multiplying the tax rate times the difference between the book value and tax basis of the asset. Thus, the ending balance in the Deferred Tax Liability account of $907 is equal to 40 percent times ($13,600 − $11,333), or 40% × $2,266. The Deferred Tax Liability account represents the amount of taxes that will have to be paid if the asset is liquidated at a price equal to book value.

Should the firm sell (liquidate) its asset at the end of the first year at a price equal to the asset's book value, then, in addition to the entry to record the sale of the asset

Sale of Property, Plant and Equipment
    Dr. Cash   13,600
    Dr. Accumulated Depreciation   3,400
        Cr. Property, Plant and Equipment   17,000

it would have to pay the deferred tax liability, and record it as follows:

Tax Payment on Deferred Taxes
    Dr. Deferred Tax Liability   907
        Cr. Cash   907

From year 2 onward, the difference between the book value and the tax basis of the asset decreases. In our example, the depreciation schedules over the estimated (book) and depreciable (tax) lives for this asset would be

	Book		Tax	
Year	Depreciation Expense (S/L)	Asset Book Value	Depreciation Deduction (MACRS)	Asset Tax Basis
1	$3,400	$13,600	$5,667	$11,333
2	3,400	10,200	7,556	3,777
3	3,400	6,800	2,518	1,259
4	3,400	3,400	1,259	0
5	3,400	0	—	0

and the corresponding ending balance in the Deferred Tax Liability account for each year would be

Year	Balance in Deferred Tax Liability
1	$ 907 [40% × ($13,600 − $11,333)]
2	2,569 [40% × (10,200 − 3,777)]
3	2,216 [40% × (6,800 − 1,259)]
4	1,360 [40% × (3,400 − 0)]
5	0 [40% × (0 − 0)]

In order to attain the ending balances in the Deferred Tax Liability account each year, the following entries would have to be made:

Required Entry	
Credit $ 907	($ 907 − $ 0)
Credit 1,662	(2,569 − 907)
Debit 353	(2,216 − 2,569)
Debit 856	(1,360 − 2,216)
Debit 1,360	(0 − 1,360)

TEMPORARY DIFFERENCES CAUSING BOOK VALUE OF NET-ASSETS TO BE LESS THAN THEIR TAX BASIS

The book value of net-assets will be less than their tax basis if TAXABLE INCOME is greater than INCOME BEFORE TAX because a taxable inflow is recognized before the related revenue, or an expense is recognized before the related tax deductible outflow can be taken. An example of this event is the receipt of advances for rented space, which results in a taxable inflow and a book liability (not a tax liability) when it is received, but results in revenue over the rental period. Another example is the recognition of a warranty expense and a book liability (not a tax liability) at the time a sale is made, and a tax deductible outflow as the warranty repairs are made.

When the book value of net-assets is less than their tax basis because of a temporary difference, a *deferred tax asset* is recognized, but only if a tax refund will be receivable in the future when the asset or liability is liquidated at a price equal to its book value. However, a tax refund does not always result when the asset or liability is liquidated, because even if TAXABLE INCOME is negative (TAXABLE LOSS), a refund will result only if TAXABLE INCOME in the carryback period equals or exceeds the amount of TAXABLE LOSS.

Generally, you may not assume that a firm will have TAXABLE INCOME in the carryforward period. Therefore, a refund is considered receivable only if the firm has reported TAXABLE INCOME during the carryback period, and made the REQUIRED TAX PAYMENTS during those years. If such a refund will be receivable, a deferred tax asset will be recognized. In this case, INCOME TAX EXPENSE will be equal to the REQUIRED TAX PAYMENT minus the increase (or plus the decrease) in the Deferred Tax Asset account.

Thus a temporary difference causing TAXABLE INCOME to exceed INCOME BEFORE TAX will create a deferred tax asset only if a refund will result. The entry to record such an event initially is

Income Tax Expense
    Dr. Deferred Tax Asset
    Dr. Income Tax Expense (I/S)
        Cr. Taxes Payable

Consider the following example. A firm sells 1,000 grabules at a price of $80 apiece, warranting them for 3 years. The firm estimates that they will spend $2 per unit to repair damaged goods. The firm records the sales and warranty as follows:

Sales Revenues
    Dr. Accounts Receivable   80,000
        Cr. Sales Revenue (I/S)   80,000

Warranty Expense
    Dr. Estimated Warranty Provision (I/S)   2,000
        Cr. Warranty Liability   2,000

For financial reporting purposes, the estimated warranty provision is treated as a contra-revenue, and the firm would report $78,000 in revenues. For tax purposes, the actual warranty repairs are deductible, not the estimate of provision. Therefore, until the firm actually repairs a grabule, it will report a $2,000 warranty liability, and no liability for tax purposes.

	Book		Tax	
Year	Warranty Expense	Liability Book Value	Warranty Deduction	Liability Tax Basis
1	$2,000	$2,000	$0	$0

Thus, the ending balance in the Deferred Tax Asset account would be $800 [40% × ($2,000 − $0)]. The ending balance in the Deferred Tax Asset account is determined by multiplying the tax rate by the difference between the tax basis and book value of Net Accounts Receivable. Thus, the ending balance is equal to 40 percent times ($2,000 − $0), or 40% × $2,000.

If warranty repairs are made in the amount of $1,000 in years 2 and 3, then the expense and deduction for warranty repairs over the 3-year warranty period would be

	Book		Tax	
Year	Warranty Expense	Liability Book Value	Warranty Deduction	Liability Tax Basis
1	$2,000	$2,000	$0	$0
2	0	1,000	1,000	0
3	0	0	1,000	0

In years 2 and 3, the ending balance in the Deferred Tax Asset account will be $400 and $0, respectively, and the corresponding ending balance in the Deferred Tax Asset account and related entry to the Deferred Tax Asset account, for each year, would be

Year	Balance in Deferred Tax Asset	Required Entry
1	$800 [40% × ($2,000 − $0)]	Debit $800
2	400 [40% × (1,000 − 0)]	Credit 400
3	0 [40% × (0 − 0)]	Credit 400

When the anticipated repairs are made, the Deferred Tax Asset debit balance is reduced, and the following entry is made:

Income Tax Expense
    Dr. Income Tax Expense (I/S)
        Cr. Taxes Payable
        Cr. Deferred Tax Asset

Notice that as time passes, there will be a tax deductible outflow for warranty repairs, but no expense for book purposes. Therefore, eventually, as the warranty liability is liquidated, INCOME BEFORE TAX will exceed TAXABLE INCOME.

SIMPLIFIED CALCULATION FOR TAX EXPENSE: SINGLE ASSETS

In many situations, the calculation for INCOME TAX EXPENSE and DEFERRED TAXES can be simplified. If a firm only has temporary differences, which cause the book value of assets to be greater than their tax basis (because INCOME BEFORE TAX exceeds TAXABLE INCOME), then the credit to the Deferred Tax Liability account will simply be the tax rate times the difference between tax and book expense, or book and tax revenue. The resulting INCOME TAX EXPENSE that will be reported is the applicable tax rate times INCOME BEFORE TAX, and represents the tax that would have been paid had TAXABLE INCOME not been affected by the temporary difference.

Assume a firm acquires one asset on January 1, costing $17,000, with an estimated useful life of 5 years, and a salvage value of $0. For financial reporting purposes, straight-line depreciation may be used to depreciate the asset over its estimated useful life. For tax purposes, the MACRS method of depreciation is required.

Since the asset was acquired on January 1, for financial reporting purposes, a full year's depreciation will be charged. However, for tax purposes, MACRS requires that the depreciation deduction in the first year is limited to one-half year's depreciation, regardless of when in the year the asset was acquired. The depreciation schedules, over the estimated and depreciable lives for this asset, would be

Year	Book (SL)	Tax (MACRS)
1	$ 3,400	$ 5,667 $[(\frac{1}{2}) \times (\frac{2}{3}) \times \$17,000]$
2	3,400	7,556 $[\qquad (\frac{2}{3}) \times \quad 11,333]$
3	3,400	2,518 $[\qquad (\frac{2}{3}) \times \quad 3,777]$
4	3,400	1,259 [Remainder]
5	3,400	0
	$17,000	$17,000

If the company has no other temporary differences, the increase (decrease) in the Deferred Tax Liability account and, therefore, the amount that must be added (subtracted) from the REQUIRED TAX PAYMENT in calculating INCOME TAX EXPENSE each year will be

Year	Required Entry
1	Credit $ 907 [40% × ($5,667 − $3,400)]
2	Credit 1,662 [40% × (7,556 − 3,400)]
3	Debit 353 [40% × (2,518 − 3,400)]
4	Debit 856 [40% × (1,259 − 3,400)]
5	Debit 1,360 [40% × (0 − 3,400)]

and the entries to the Deferred Tax Liability account would appear as follows:

↓	Deferred Tax Liability		↑
Year 3	353	907	Year 1
Year 4	856	1,662	Year 2
Year 5	1,360		

Consider another example that causes a deferred tax liability. A firm sells goods in year 1, for $900, which cost $600, with payments to be made in three equal annual payments of $300. Since collectibility is ascertainable, profit is recognized for financial reporting at the time of sale. For tax reporting, the installment method can be used, resulting in $100 of TAXABLE INCOME as each $300 payment is received.

EXHIBIT 1

	Year 1		Year 2		Year 3	
	Book	Tax	Book	Tax	Book	Tax
Sales	$900					
Cost of Goods Sold	(600)					
Income Before Tax	$300					
Taxable Income		$100		$100		$100
(a) Required Tax Payment		40		40		40
Quantification of Receivable	600	400	$300	200	0	0
(b) Deferred Tax Liability		80		40		0
(c) Increase (Decrease) in Deferred Tax Liability	80		(40)		(40)	
(d) Tax Expense	120		0		0	

TAX EXPENSE (d) equals the REQUIRED TAX PAYMENT (a) plus (minus) the increase (decrease) in the Deferred Tax Liability (c).

If the company has no other temporary differences, the increase or decrease in the Deferred Tax Liability account, and, therefore, the amount that must be added or subtracted from the REQUIRED TAX PAYMENT in calculating INCOME TAX EXPENSE each year will be

Year	Required Entry
1	Credit $80 [40% × ($300 − $100)]
2	Debit 40 [40% × (0 − 100)]
3	Debit 40 [40% × (0 − 100)]

and the entries to the Deferred Tax Liability account would appear as follows:

	↓	Deferred Tax Liability	↑	
Year 2	40		80	Year 1
Year 3	40			

Thus, at the end of year 5 for the first firm, and the end of year 3 for the second firm, the ending balance in the Deferred Tax Liability account will be zero.

ILLUSTRATION OF CALCULATING TAX EXPENSE FOR MULTIPLE ASSETS

A multiple-asset firm, which acquires one additional asset on January 1 of each year, each at a cost of $17,000, with an estimated useful life of 5 years, a salvage value of $0, and a tax depreciation period of 3 years, will report the following book and tax depreciation each year:

Year	Book (SL)	Tax (MACRS)
1	$ 3,400	$ 5,667
2	6,800	13,223
3	10,200	15,741
4	13,600	17,000
5	17,000	17,000

If the company has no other temporary differences, the increase (decrease) in the Deferred Tax Liability account, and, therefore, the amount that must be added (subtracted) from the REQUIRED TAX PAYMENT in calculating INCOME TAX EXPENSE each year will be

Year	Required Entry
1	Credit $ 907 [40% × ($ 5,667 − $ 3,400)]
2	Credit 2,569 [40% × (13,223 − 6,800)]
3	Credit 2,216 [40% × (15,741 − 10,200)]
4	Credit 1,360 [40% × (17,000 − 13,600)]
5	0 [40% × (17,000 − 17,000)]

and the entries to the Deferred Tax Liability account would appear as follows:

↓	Deferred Tax Liability	↑
		907 Year 1
		2,569 Year 2
		2,216 Year 3
		1,360 Year 4

In year 5, and subsequent years, since tax depreciation will equal book depreciation, there will be neither increases nor decreases in the Deferred Tax Liability account. Therefore, the Deferred Tax Liability account will add up to $7,052 by the end of year 4, and will remain at that amount unless the dollar amount of depreciable assets declines. Should the firm increase the dollar amount of depreciable assets, the Deferred Tax Liability account will also increase.

If a firm has INSTALLMENT SALES each year of $900, that cost them $600, then the book and tax reports of this firm will be as follows:

	Year 1		Year 2		Year 3	
	Book	**Tax**	**Book**	**Tax**	**Book**	**Tax**
Sales	$900		$900		$900	
Cost of Goods Sold	(600)		(600)		(600)	
Income Before Tax	$300		$300		$300	
Taxable Income		$100		$200		$300

Therefore, in years 1 and 2, when book revenues exceed taxable profit on INSTALLMENT SALES, there will be a credit to the Deferred Tax Liability account of $80 and $40, respectively; and in year 3 and subsequent years, the taxable profit on INSTALLMENT SALES and the book revenue will be the same, and there will be no debit or credit to the Deferred Tax Liability account. Thus, the Deferred Tax Liability account increases to $120 at the end of year 2, and remains at that level unless the amount of INSTALLMENT SALES declines. Should the volume of INSTALLMENT SALES increase, the Deferred Tax Liability account will increase.

The principal assumptions underlying accounting for income taxes are that a firm **cannot** anticipate that it will earn income in future years, and that existing assets and liabilities can always be liquidated for a price equal to their book value. Under these assumptions, the benefit of a TAXABLE LOSS will not be recognized unless the TAXABLE LOSS can be carried back or unless TAXABLE INCOME is reported in the carryforward period.

As a result, when the book value of net assets is greater than their tax basis, taxes will have to be paid when the assets and liabilities are liquidated. On the other hand, if the tax basis exceeds the book value of assets and liabilities, the liquidation of assets and liabilities at a price equal to their book value will create a TAXABLE LOSS, and **may** result in a tax benefit—a tax refund or a reduction of a future tax liability. The tax benefit is subject to the limitations of carryback and carryforward, of course.

FINANCIAL STATEMENT PRESENTATION

INCOME TAX EXPENSE is reported in the income statement as an expense. If the indirect method of determining CASH FLOWS FROM OPERATIONS is used, then credit (debit) changes in Deferred Tax Liabilities and Assets are added to (or subtracted from) NET INCOME in determining CASH FLOWS FROM OPERATIONS as illustrated in Example 1.

EXAMPLE 1

Warner Communications Inc.			
Years ended December 31 (thousands) **Sources of funds**	**1981**	**1980**	**1979**
Net Income (includes gain on sale of 50% of cable operations in 1979)	$226,493	$137,091	$200,747
Income charges (credits) not affecting working capital:			
Depreciation and amortization	63,858	42,272	30,337
Deferred income taxes	(15,412)	8,775	16,772
Working capital provided from operations	274,939	188,138	247,856

Deferred Tax Liabilities and Assets and any unpaid REQUIRED TAX PAYMENTS are reported in the balance sheet as Deferred Tax Liabilities, Deferred Tax Assets, and Taxes Payable, respectively. This is illustrated in Example 2.

EXAMPLE 2

Warner Communications Inc.
Consolidated Balance Sheet

Assets

As of December 31 (dollars in thousands)	1981	1980
Current assets:		
Cash and short-term investments	$ 135,055	$226,304
Accounts and notes receivable, less allowances for doubtful receivables and returns (1981—$317,768; 1980—$204,280)	645,107	445,868
Inventories	507,351	228,705
Deferred income taxes	81,810	—
Advance royalties	54,701	53,217
Other current assets	44,096	32,127
Total current assets	$1,468,120	$986,221

Liabilities and Shareholders' Equity

As of December 31 (dollars in thousands)	1981	1980
Current liabilities:		
Accounts payable and accrued expenses	$ 904,696	$552,663
Long-term debt due within one year	4,907	12,794
Accrued income taxes	56,309	16,354
Total current liabilities	$ 965,912	$581,811
Long-term liabilities:		
Long-term debt due after one year	187,457	209,652
Accounts payable due after one year	296,866	161,226
Deferred income taxes	72,671	69,121

In addition, firms report the events that caused the Deferred Tax Liability or Asset as a schedule in the footnotes to the financial statements (see Example 3).

EXAMPLE 3

Warner Communications Inc.
7. Income Taxes:

Details of domestic and foreign pretax income are as follows:

Years ended December 31 (thousands)

	1981	1980	1979
Domestic	$239,132	$140,130	$120,895
Foreign	126,061	51,061	44,128
Total	$365,193	$191,191	$165,023

Deferred income taxes result from timing differences in the recognition of revenue and expense for tax and financial statement purposes. The source of these differences and the tax effect of each was as follows:

Details of the provision for income taxes currently payable and amounts deferred are as follows:

Years ended December 31 (thousands)

	1981	1980	1979
Federal:			
Current	$137,340	$40,538	$28,563
Deferred	(83,703)	(24,560)	(12,412)
Foreign:			
*Current	62,100	33,183	32,017
Deferred	5,957	(3,081)	(1,015)
State and local:			
Current	15,217	7,991	9,129
Deferred	1,789	29	(317)
Provision for income taxes	$138,700	$54,100	$55,965

*Includes foreign withholding taxes.

Years ended December 31 (thousands)	**1981**	**1980**	**1979**
Capitalized items which are amortized, depreciated, or expensed for financial statement purposes in a year different from the year reported for tax purposes	$(52,394)	$ (6,465)	$ (9,481)
Income from sales reported in a different period for financial statement purposes than for tax purposes	(112)	11,458	2,354
Sales returns reflected for financial statement purposes in a year different from the year reported for tax purposes	(26,741)	(11,380)	2,962
Income from sales reported on the installment basis for tax purposes	(9,434)	(19,660)	(8,212)
Other items, net	12,724	(1,565)	(1,367)
Total	$(75,957)	$(27,612)	$(13,744)

USER'S PERSPECTIVE

Users of financial statements will find it difficult to assess the significance, or lack thereof, of deferred taxes. Superficially, the treatment of deferred taxes seems appropriate in that it measures the taxes that will have to be paid, or the refunds that will be received in the future. But this is too simplistic a notion.

Consider the effects of depreciating a single asset over its useful life. If an accelerated method is used for tax purposes and straight-line for book purposes, then in the early years there will be an increase in the Deferred Tax Liability account, and in the latter years a decrease. At the end of the asset's useful life the balance in the Deferred Tax Liability account will be zero, and the total REQUIRED TAX PAYMENTS will equal the total INCOME TAX EXPENSE. However, the firm will have benefited, in present value terms, from having delayed paying the liability.

For a stable firm, the deferred tax liability will increase and then level off, maintaining a credit balance in the Deferred Tax Liability account. As a result, the liability will never have to be paid unless the firm liquidates its assets. Even if the firm liquidates its assets and pays its tax liability, it will have benefited, in present value terms, from having delayed paying the liability.

> ### *Thought Question*
> Is a Deferred Tax Liability that will never be paid
> really a liability?

For a growing firm, the Deferred Tax Liability account will continue to increase. Unless the firm liquidates its assets, it will continually defer an increasing amount of taxes. Even if it does liquidate its assets, the delay in paying taxes will result in a present value advantage. The magnitude of the present value advantage will be a function of the duration of the deferred tax liability.

Finally, it is possible that two firms, with identical assets and liabilities, will pay the same amount in taxes but will report different INCOME TAX EXPENSES. Consider the following example: Two firms acquire a depreciable asset for $17,000, with an expected useful life of 5 years, and a salvage value of zero. One firm depreciates its asset for book and tax purposes using an accelerated method (an A/A firm); the other firm uses an accelerated method for tax but straight-line for book (an A/S firm).

Since both firms use an accelerated method (MACRS) for tax purposes, they will deduct the same amount for depreciation for tax purposes, and therefore they will pay the same amount of taxes. However, the A/A firm's INCOME TAX EXPENSE will equal its REQUIRED TAX PAYMENT, while the A/S firm's INCOME TAX EXPENSE will be greater than its REQUIRED TAX PAYMENT, resulting in a deferred tax liability.

Recall that a deferred tax liability represents the tax liability due when the asset is liquidated at a price equal to the asset's book value. But because of the measurement differences in depreciating their assets, it is assumed that the A/A firm can liquidate its asset at a lower price than the A/S firm.

> *Thought Question*
>
> Is it logical to assume that two identical firms liquidate identical assets at the same point in time at different prices?

Given these complexities, the only thing that the user of financial statements can do is to try to estimate the probability that the Deferred Tax Liability or Asset will result in a TAX PAYMENT or REFUND. For most firms, the probability is minimal. If this is so, then the user should recalculate INCOME TAX EXPENSE and NET INCOME, ignoring the Deferred Tax Liability or Asset.

PROBLEMS

1. Light Company had interest income on municipal obligations of $150,000 in 19X1. For financial statement reporting, Light included the $150,000 in the other income section of its income statement. For income tax reporting, the $150,000 was exempt income. Assuming an income tax rate of 50 percent, what should be reported in the provision for deferred income taxes in Light's income statement for the year ended December 31, 19X1?
   a. $0
   b. $75,000 credit
   c. $75,000 debit
   d. $150,000 debit

2. In 19X1 Nest Corporation received $300,000 in royalties under a licensing agreement. Royalties are reported as taxable income in the year received, but in the financial statements, royalties are recognized as income in the year earned and amounted to $200,000 for the year ended December 31, 19X1. Nest's effective income tax rate is 40 percent. By what amount would the balance in the Deferred Tax Liability account change in 19X1?
   a. $20,000 increase
   b. $20,000 decrease
   c. $40,000 increase
   d. $40,000 decrease

3. A machine with a 10-year useful life is being depreciated on a straight-line basis for financial statement purposes, and over 5 years for income tax purposes under the modified accelerated cost recovery system. Assuming that the company is profitable and that there are and have been **no** other temporary differences, the related deferred income taxes would be reported in the balance sheet at the end of the first year of the estimated useful life as a

a. Current liability
b. Current asset
c. Noncurrent liability
d. Noncurrent asset

4. Tarim Company began operations on January 1, 19X0, and a substantial part of its sales are made on an installment basis. For financial reporting Tarim recognizes revenues from all sales under the accrual method. However, on its income tax return, Tarim reports revenues from INSTALLMENT SALES under the installment method. Information concerning gross profit from installment sales under each method is as follows:

Year	Accrual Method	Installment Method
1990	$400,000	$150,000
1991	650,000	350,000

For both years, assume the effective income tax rate is 40 percent and there are no other temporary differences. In its December 31, 19X1, balance sheet, Tarim should report a liability for deferred taxes of
a. $220,000
b. $200,000
c. $180,000
d. $120,000

5. (*AICPA adapted*) WeeBee Corp. prepared the following reconciliation between book income and taxable income for the year ended December 31, 19X1:

Income before taxes	$500,000
Taxable income	300,000
Difference	$200,000
Permanent difference—interest on municipal bonds	$ 50,000
Temporary difference—lower depreciation per books	150,000
Total differences	$200,000

WeeBee's effective income tax rate for 19X1 is 40 percent. WeeBee reported the following information in its annual report:

Income before income taxes		$500,000
Provision for income taxes:		
Current	$?	
Deferred	?	?
Net income		$?

What amount should WeeBee report as the current portion of its provision for income taxes?

a. $120,000
b. $140,000
c. $180,000
d. $200,000

What amount should WeeBee report as the deferred portion of its provision for income taxes?

e. $20,000
f. $60,000
g. $80,000
h. $120,000

6. For calendar year 19X1 Neri Corporation reported depreciation of $300,000 in its income statement. On its 1991 income tax return Neri reported depreciation of $500,000. Additionally, Neri's income statement included interest income of $50,000 on municipal obligations. Assuming an income tax rate of 40 percent, the amount of deferred taxes reported on Neri's 19X1 income statement should be

a. $60,000
b. $80,000
c. $100,000
d. $120,000

7. On January 1, 19X1, Ron Company purchased a building for $1,500,000. The building will be depreciated $50,000 per year by the straight-line method for financial statement reporting. For income tax reporting, Ron uses the MACRS and will be allowed a depreciation deduction of $180,000 for 19X1. Assuming an income tax rate of 40 percent, what amount of deferred income taxes should be added to Ron's deferred income tax liability at December 31, 19X1?

a. $52,000
b. $72,000
c. $78,000
d. $130,000

8. You are the president of the LuBer Company and are responsible for choosing accounting methods. You have a bonus plan which pays you 10 percent of the difference between net income and 15 percent of total assets at the beginning of the period. In other words, your bonus is equal to [0.10 (net income − 0.15 × total assets)]. Assume that prices will increase over the next 2 years and then remain stable, and that you can invest all of your assets at 12 percent.

Required:
a. If you want to maximize your bonus in year 1, will you choose A/A, S/S, or A/S depreciation methods for tax/books?
b. If you want to maximize your bonus over 5 years, will you choose A/A, S/S, or A/S depreciation methods for tax/books?

9. For each of the following questions, fill in the blank space with **less, more,** or **the same.** Assume that a company has a substantial and increasing amount of property, plant and equipment at the end of each year, and there has been a long period of gradually increasing prices.
a. Using an accelerated depreciation method for both tax and book purposes will result in _____ NET INCOME and _____ CASH

FLOWS FROM OPERATIONS than if the straight-line method of depreciation had been used for both tax and book purposes.

b. Using an accelerated method of depreciation for tax purposes and straight-line for book purposes will result in _____ NET INCOME and _____ CASH FLOWS FROM OPERATIONS than if the straight-line had been used for both tax and book purposes.

10. If the PAYMENT OF TAXES was less than TAX EXPENSE during a period, then either

> Account _____ must have increased/decreased
> or Account _____ must have increased/decreased
> or Account _____ must have increased/decreased.

11. There were once three companies identical in all respects except that the first used an accelerated method of depreciation for tax purposes and straight-line for book (A/S); the second used straight-line for both tax and book purposes (S/S); and the third used an accelerated method for both tax and book purposes (A/A). The tax rate for all three companies was 40 percent.

Year 1 was a year of heavy acquisitions of property, plant and equipment, year 2 was a year of no acquisitions of property, plant and equipment, and year 3 was a year of heavy acquisitions of property, plant and equipment. All assets acquired had an expected useful life of 10 years.

Required:
Fill in the blanks with **less** or **more**.

a. In year 1, the A/A firm reported _____ net income than the S/S firm, which reported _____ net income than the A/S firm.

b. Taxes paid in year 2 by the A/A firm were _____ than taxes paid by the S/S firm, which were _____ than taxes paid by the A/S firm.

c. The differences in (a) above are _____ than the differences in (b) above.

d. The net-assets of the A/A firm at the end of year 3 were _____ than the net-assets of the S/S firm, which were _____ than the net-assets of the A/S firm.

e. CASH FLOWS FROM OPERATIONS for the A/A firm were _____ in year 3 than in year 2, which were _____ than in year 1.

12. From the information below relating to the Sonda Company, determine
   a. INCOME TAX EXPENSE for the year
   b. PAYMENT OF TAX for the year
   (1) The REQUIRED TAX PAYMENT is $100,000.
   (2) The balance in the Deferred Tax Asset account increased by $5,000.
   (3) The balance in the Taxes Payable account decreased by $25,000.
   (4) The balance in the Deferred Tax Liability account increased by $75,000.

13. The Dysan Company recognizes revenues from installment sales at the time the sale is made for book purposes, but is only taxed on the portion that is collected. The company reported the following SALES and COST OF GOODS SOLD:

	19X0	19X1	19X2	19X3	19X4
Sales	$100,000	$150,000	$200,000	$100,000	$130,000
Cost of Goods Sold	60,000	75,000	100,000	60,000	65,000

Collections are made as follows:

25 percent in the year the sale is made

50 percent in the year following the sale

25 percent in the third year

Assume that there are no other tax and book differences and that the tax rate is 40 percent. Calculate the balance in the Deferred Tax Liability account each year and the amount by which the REQUIRED TAX PAYMENT is greater or less than the INCOME TAX EXPENSE each period.

14. The Drof Motor Company sells vehicles with a 4-year warranty. Estimated warranty costs are 5 percent of the price of each vehicle and are expected to be expended in the fourth year. In 19X1 the Drof Company sold vehicles for $15,000,000 and recognized INCOME BEFORE TAX of $2,000,000.

Assume a tax rate of 40 percent and that TAXABLE LOSSES can be carried back 3 years.

Required:
a. Determine TAXABLE INCOME, INCOME TAX EXPENSE, the REQUIRED TAX PAYMENT, and the balance in the Deferred Tax Asset account for 19X1.
b. Assume that everything that occurred in 19X1 recurred in 19X2. Determine TAXABLE INCOME, INCOME TAX EXPENSE, the REQUIRED TAX PAYMENT, and the balance in the Deferred Tax Asset account for 19X2.
c. How would your answer to (a) and (b) differ if TAXABLE LOSSES could be carried back for 4 years instead of for 3?

15. The Vidon Company had a deferred tax liability of $400,000 on January 1, 19X1, and $420,000 on December 31, 19X1. Assume that the deferred tax liability is due solely to Vidon's use of double-declining depreciation for tax purposes and straight-line depreciation for book purposes. If the tax depreciation was $100,000, the rate at which they depreciate assets for tax purposes is 10 percent, the tax rate 40 percent, and there were no retirements of property, plant and equipment, then calculate
a. Depreciation expense for book purposes during 19X1
b. The balances in Property, Plant and Equipment, and Accumulated Depreciation at the end of 19X1

16.

The Malach Company
Comparative Balance Sheets
Years Ending December 31, 19X0 and 19X1

Assets	12/31/X0	12/31/X1
Cash	$100,000	$150,000
Accounts Receivable	115,000	165,000
Estimated Uncollectibles	(25,000)	(30,000)
Inventory	150,000	165,000
Prepaid Services	5,000	0
Property, Plant and Equipment	300,000	460,000
Accumulated Depreciation	(120,000)	(140,000)
Total Assets	$525,000	$770,000

Liabilities and Owners' Equities		
Accounts Payable Merchandise	$ 50,000	$ 40,000
Accounts Payable Services	62,000	70,000
Taxes Payable	0	20,000
Dividends Payable	10,000	8,000
Deferred Taxes	0	10,000
Common Stock	100,000	300,000
Retained Earnings	303,000	322,000
Total Liabilities and Owners' Equities	$525,000	$770,000

Notes

(1) Receipts from credit customers were $700,000.
(2) $4,000 of Accounts Receivable was written off as uncollectible.
(3) $180,000 of services were utilized.
(4) Inventory of $200,000 was purchased during the year.
(5) Property, plant and equipment was sold for $10,000, incurring a loss of $11,000.
(6) No common stock was retired during the year.
(7) Income tax expense was $75,000.
(8) Depreciation expense for the year was $80,000.
(9) Dividends declared during the year were $195,000.

Required:
a. Prepare an income statement for 19X1.
b. Prepare a statement of cash flows for 19X1.

17.

A/S and S/A Companies
Comparative Post-Closing Trial Balance Sheets
Years Ending December 31, 19X0 and 19X1

	A/S Company		S/A Company	
Debit Balance Accounts	12/31/X0	12/31/X1	12/31/X0	12/31/X1
Cash	$150,000	$?	$150,000	$?
Accounts Receivable	200,000	195,000	200,000	195,000
Inventory	350,000	400,000	350,000	400,000
Deferred Tax Asset	0	?	0	?
Property, Plant and Equipment	0	240,000	0	240,000
Total Debit Balance Accounts	$700,000	$?	$700,000	?
Credit Balance Accounts				
Estimated Uncollectibles	$ 10,000	$ 20,000	$ 10,000	$ 20,000
Accumulated Depreciation	0	40,000	0	80,000
Accounts Payable Merchandise	20,000	60,000	20,000	60,000
Accounts Payable Services	30,000	90,000	30,000	90,000
Deferred Tax Liability	0	?	0	?
Common Stock	290,000	400,000	290,000	400,000
Retained Earnings	350,000	310,000	350,000	286,000
Total Credit Balance Accounts	$700,000	$?	$700,000	$?

Thought Question

Under what circumstances can a firm recognize a Deferred Tax Asset?

Notes

(1) The A/S and S/A Companies are identical in all respects except that the A/S Company depreciates its assets using double-declining balance for tax purposes and a straight-line basis for book purposes, and the S/A Company depreciates its assets on a straight-line basis for tax purposes and double-declining balance for book. Each asset cost $240,000, had an expected useful life of 6 years, and an estimated salvage value of $0.
(2) No property, plant and equipment was retired during the year for either firm.
(3) Assume a tax rate of 40 percent.

A/S and S/A Companies
Income Statements
19X1

	A/S Company		S/A Company	
Revenues				
Sales Revenue		$600,000		$600,000
Uncollectibility Adjustment		(15,000)		(15,000)
Total Revenues		$585,000		$585,000
Expenses				
Cost of Goods Sold	$215,000		$215,000	
Operating Expenses	120,000		120,000	
Depreciation Expense	?		?	
Tax Expense	?		?	
Total Expenses	$?	(?)	$?	(?)
Net Income		$?		$?

Required:
a. Fill in the blanks and prepare a statement of cash flows for each
   firm.
b. What affect would the following changes have on the A/S
   Company's financial statements if they depreciated their assets
   on:
   (1) A straight-line basis for tax purposes;
   (2) Or an accelerated basis for book purposes?

Financing Events

Part Three of this book deals with the financing events of a firm. A firm can obtain financing from various sources. As we saw in Part Two, the operating activities of a firm are financed by obtaining short-term financing from its vendors and suppliers in the form of Accounts Payable Merchandise and Accounts Payable Services, and from cash flows from operations. Long-term financing generally comes from two sources: debt and equity. Debt financing can come either from banks or bondholders, and equity financing can come either from common or from preferred stockholders.

Debt financing events consist of the issue of long-term debt and bonds, their repayment, and the payment for having used the cash (interest). Equity financing events are the issue and repurchase of equity securities, and the related payments to owners (dividends).

In Part Three, we will describe how these events are recorded and show the differing effects on the financial statements between debt and equity financing. We will also present the obvious differences in the financial statements that result from the alternative financing techniques, and the consequences that these alternatives have on the amount and variability of cash flows and on widely used financial ratios.

CHAPTER 12

Accounting for Long-Term Debt: *Loans*

INTRODUCTION

Long-term debt arises when an economic resource is received in exchange for payments in the future. The borrower (debtor) promises to pay cash over an extended period of time, in exchange for cash or other assets provided by the lender (creditor). The borrower promises to repay the original borrowing, usually called *principal* or *proceeds*, and the accrued interest (the cost of using the cash or other asset) by making one or more lump-sum payments at a specified time or times, or by making a series of periodic payments for a specified period of time, or by a combination of the two. The particular timing and combinations of payments is a result of the interaction between the borrower and the lender(s), and reflects the cash-generating prospects and preferences of both parties.

Examples of a borrower's promise to repay long-term debt are an installment loan or mortgage, where the only payments are equal periodic payments; a discounted note or zero-coupon bond where the only payment is a lump-sum payment; a long-term bank loan or bond, where the payments are a combination of periodic **and** lump-sum payments.

In this chapter, we will discuss accounting for the borrowing and repayment of *long-term loans*. A long-term loan represents a source of financing available to a firm from lenders (creditors) of the firm. Common lenders are mortgage banks (mortgages) and commercial banks (loans).

CHARACTERISTICS OF DEBT

Accounting for the *proceeds of a long-term loan* is straightforward; accounting for the *repayment of a long-term loan* is a bit more difficult. The terms and conditions of the contract will determine the amount, timing, and sequencing of the RECLASSIFICATION OF

LONG-TERM LOAN, INTEREST EXPENSE, and REPAYMENT OF LOAN, and how they will be recorded and reported. However, the effects of borrowing will always have the following conditions:

1. The present value of the cash inflows (*proceeds*) equals the present value of the cash outflows (repayment), at the effective interest rate. The **effective interest rate** is that rate of interest at which the present value of **all** payments (periodic and lump-sum) is equal to the proceeds.

2. The balance of debt (long-term **and** current portion) equals the present value of all of the remaining payments at that point in time (**discounted** at the effective interest rate at the time of borrowing).

3. Interest cost for the period equals the effective interest rate multiplied by the balance of the debt at the beginning of the period. Interest expense equals interest cost less any interest associated with long-term construction, during a period.

4. Reclassification of a long-term loan to the current portion of debt always occurs in the period **prior** to the scheduled payment.

In this chapter, we will illustrate and compare the accounting for the borrowing and repayment of $85,000 for 4 years, at 10 percent compounded annually, when the contract calls for (*a*) *periodic payments* only, (*b*) a *lump-sum payment* only, and (*c*) various combinations of periodic and lump-sum payments. In case *a*, the four equal periodic payments to pay back the $85,000 are $26,815. In case *b*, the lump-sum payment at the end of 4 years required to pay back the $85,000 is $124,449. In case *c*, if the four equal periodic payments are $8,500 (or $5,100, $20,400), the lump-sum payment will be $85,000 (or $100,779, $29,772, respectively).

> ### Thought Question
> Assuming the periodic payments above were given,
> how were the lump-sum payments determined?

ACCOUNTING FOR THE PROCEEDS OF A LONG-TERM LOAN: PERIODIC PAYMENTS ONLY

Assume that a firm borrowed $85,000, agreeing to repay the loan plus interest accrued at an annual rate of 10 percent, in equal periodic payments made at the end of each year, for 4 years. The event would be recorded as follows:

Long-Term Borrowing
> Dr. Cash   85,000
> > Cr. Long-Term Loan   85,000

The event is quantified by the amount of cash received, which is also the present value of the required payments, discounted at the effective (market) rate of interest. That is, the **present value of the proceeds** (inflows) **always equals** the **present value of the payments** (outflows).

ACCOUNTING FOR THE REPAYMENT OF A LONG-TERM LOAN: PERIODIC PAYMENTS ONLY

Consider a contract that requires periodic payments only. Each required payment would be $26,815, which would repay the entire *principal* of $85,000, plus all of the interest at 10 percent, compounded annually, for 4 years. In the appendix to Chapter 1, we discussed the technique of determining the required periodic payment in order to repay a loan. In our example, the periodic payment, $26,815, equals $85,000 ÷ 3.169865; where 3.169865 is the present value of an annuity of $1.00, at $n = 4$ and $r = 10$ percent.

The *debt constant* represents the ratio (percentage) of the periodic payment to the original proceeds. The debt constant, in our example, is 0.315471 ($26,815 ÷ $85,000). Notice that the *debt constant* 0.315471 is greater than the *effective interest rate* of 0.100000 (10 percent). That means that the periodic payment is larger than the periodic interest cost, and includes not only all of the interest expense associated with this loan, but also part of the principal. The part of each periodic payment in excess of the interest cost is considered repayment of the original proceeds, thus reducing or amortizing the amount of the outstanding debt. Since interest expense is the cost of using borrowed cash (or other assets), interest expense will decrease as the remaining debt, and therefore, the cash (or other asset) borrowed, decreases. And, since the dollar amount of the periodic payment is constant each period, the amount of debt repaid (amortized) each period increases.

During the first year, the firm owed and had the use of $85,000. At the end of year 1, it paid $26,815: $8,500 (10% × $85,000) is payment of interest, and the remaining $18,315 is a repayment of principal. Therefore, during the second year, the firm only owed and had the use of $66,685 ($85,000 − $18,315) of borrowed money. At the end of year 2, it paid $26,815, a $6,668 (10% × $66,685) payment of interest, and the remaining $20,147 ($26,815 − $6,668), a repayment of principal. During the third year, the firm only owed and had the use of $46,538 ($66,685 − $20,147). At the end of year

3, it paid $26,815, a $4,654 (10% × $46,538) payment of interest, and the remaining $22,161 ($26,815 − $4,654), a repayment of principal. Finally, during the fourth year, the firm only owed and used $24,377 ($46,538 − $22,161), it paid $26,815, a $2,438 (10% × $24,377) payment of interest, and the remaining $24,377 ($26,815 − $2,438), a repayment of principal, thereby repaying the entire loan, and having no further debt. At the time of the final payment, the debt is said to *mature*.

The method of calculating INTEREST EXPENSE discussed above is called the **effective interest method**. Table 1 shows in tabular form the results discussed above, the INTEREST EXPENSE and the REDUCTION (AMORTIZATION) of the loan over the 4-year period.

> ### Thought Question
> Could the balances in Table 1
> have been determined without using the table?

At the **end** of each year, an entry is made for INTEREST EXPENSE, debiting INTEREST EXPENSE and crediting Interest Payable for the amount shown in column *b*; and an entry is made for the REPAYMENT OF DEBT, debiting Interest Payable for the amount shown in column *b*, debiting Current Portion of Debt for the amount shown in column *d*, and crediting Cash for the amount shown in column *c*. For example, the entries for year 1 would be

TABLE 1

Amortization of a Loan
Case (a): Periodic Payments Only

Year	Beginning Balance (a)	Interest Expense (b)	Periodic Payment (c)	Amortization (d)	Ending Balance (e)
1	$85,000	$ 8,500	$ 26,815	$18,315	$66,685
2	66,685	6,668	26,815	20,147	46,538
3	46,538	4,654	26,815	22,161	24,377
4	24,377	2,438	26,815	24,377	0
Totals		22,260	107,260	85,000	

(a) The present value of all of the remaining payments, as of the **beginning** of the year.
(b) Column *a* multiplied by the effective interest rate (10 percent).
(c) The required periodic payment, $26,815.
(d) The amount of the debt repaid (column *c* − column *b*).
(e) The present value of all of the remaining payments, as of the **end** of the year (column *a* − column *d*).

Interest Expense

Dr. Interest Expense (I/S)	8,500	
Cr. Interest Payable		8,500

Periodic Payment

Dr. Interest Payable	8,500	
Dr. Current Portion of Debt	18,315	
Cr. Cash		26,815

ACCOUNTING FOR THE RECLASSIFICATION OF LONG-TERM LOAN: PERIODIC PAYMENTS ONLY

From line 1 in year 1 of Table 1 above, $8,500 of the $26,815 payment will go to pay interest, and the remaining $18,315 will be a repayment of principal. The repayment of debt occurring during the first year should be reported as a current liability. Since the firm recorded the $85,000 it originally borrowed as Long-Term Loan, $18,315 of the original $85,000 of the long-term loan must be classified as Current Portion of Debt (current liability) during the first year. This event is referred to as the RECLASSIFICATION OF LONG-TERM LOAN and is recorded, immediately after the borrowing takes place, as follows:

Reclassification of Long-Term Loan

Dr. Long-Term Loan	18,315	
Cr. Current Portion of Debt		18,315

> ### Thought Question
> How would you calculate the Current Portion of Debt, and the beginning and ending balance in debt for any year, without preparing an amortization schedule?

Recall that the present value of all payments equals the balance sheet quantification of the debt. This will be true at all times throughout the life of the debt. Therefore, the balance sheet quantification at any point in time is the present value of all remaining payments discounted at the effective (market) interest rate at the inception of the loan. Accordingly, if the beginning balance is greater than the ending balance, then the difference is the amount of principal that became current **prior to the beginning** of the period, to be repaid **during** the period.

At the beginning of the first year (the inception of the loan), the present value of the four annual payments was $85,000 ($26,815

× 3.169865 at $n = 4$, $r = 10\%$). At the end of the first year, the present value of the remaining three annual payments was $66,685 ($26,815 × 2.486852 at $n = 3$, $r = 10\%$). Since the remaining balance at the end of the first year was $66,685, and the original loan amount was $85,000, then $18,315 must have become current, and was paid back during the first year.

> ### Thought Question
> Why is the balance in the Current Portion of Debt only $18,315 if the periodic payment is $26,815?

At the end of the first year, the portion of the long-term loan to be repaid during the second year had to be reclassified as Current Portion of Debt from Long-Term Loan. Since the present value of the remaining three payments at the beginning of the second year was $66,685, and the remaining balance at the end of the second year was $46,538 ($26,815 × 1.735537 at $n = 2$, $r = 10\%$), the difference of $20,147 must have become current at the end of the first year, and was paid back at the end of the second year. The entry to record this is

Reclassification of Long-Term Loan (for year 2)
    Dr. Long-Term Loan   20,147
        Cr. Current Portion of Debt   20,147

Similarly, the present value of the remaining payments at the beginning of the third year was $46,538 and at the end of the third year $24,377 ($26,815 × 0.909091 at $n = 1$, $r = 10\%$), therefore $22,161 must have become current at the end of the second year, and was paid back at the end of the third year. Finally, the present value of the remaining payments at the beginning of the fourth year was $24,377, and at the end of the fourth year, $0, so $24,377 must have become current at the end of the third year, and was paid back at the end of the fourth (and last) year.

Notice two relationships: One, that the dollar amount of the debt at the beginning of the final year 4 is the same as the dollar amount that became current during the prior year 3; and two, that the payment at the end of the loan will be equal to the beginning balance in year 4 plus the interest on that amount **during** year 4.

Compare the results of the exercise above, and that of Table 1. You can readily see that the two methods yield the same results. In addition to the entries made during the first year, the firm would make the following entries at the **end** of each of years 2, 3, and 4:

Year 2 Interest Expense
         Dr. Interest Expense (I/S)   6,668
                Cr. Interest Payable   6,668

         Periodic Payment
         Dr. Interest Payable   6,668
         Dr. Current Portion of Debt   20,147
                Cr. Cash   26,815

         Reclassification of Long-Term Loan (for year 3)
         Dr. Long-Term Loan   22,161
                Cr. Current Portion of Debt   22,161

Year 3 Interest Expense
         Dr. Interest Expense (I/S)   4,654
                Cr. Interest Payable   4,654

         Periodic Payment
         Dr. Interest Payable   4,654
         Dr. Current Portion of Debt   22,161
                Cr. Cash   26,815

         Reclassification of Long-Term Loan (for year 4)
         Dr. Long-Term Loan   24,377
                Cr. Current Portion of Debt   24,377

Year 4 Interest Expense
         Dr. Interest Expense (I/S)   2,438
                Cr. Interest Payable   2,438

         Periodic Payment
         Dr. Interest Payable   2,438
         Dr. Current Portion of Debt   24,377
                Cr. Cash   26,815

ACCOUNTING FOR THE PROCEEDS OF A LONG-TERM LOAN: LUMP-SUM PAYMENT ONLY

Assume that a firm borrowed $85,000 at the beginning of the year promising to make only one payment at the end of the fourth year, for the principal ($85,000) and any interest accrued, with interest compounded at 10 percent annually. In this case, the contract calls for no periodic payments (a debt constant of zero), and just one *lump-sum payment* to be made at the end of the loan. The entry to record this event is

Long-Term Borrowing
         Dr. Cash   85,000
                Cr. Long-Term Loan   85,000

ACCOUNTING FOR THE REPAYMENT OF A LONG-TERM LOAN: LUMP-SUM PAYMENT ONLY

Since the firm will not make any payments **during** the 4 years, at the end of the fourth year the firm will pay back not only the entire principal, but **all** of the cumulative (compounded) interest too. That is, they will pay $124,449, the original $85,000, and the cumulative (compounded) interest ($124,449 = $85,000 × 1.461000, where 1.461000 is the future value of $1.00 at $n = 4$, $r = 10\%$).

We can look at this in two other ways. First, since the firm will not be making any periodic payments during the first 4 years, at *maturity* they will owe the entire principal and the cumulative (compounded) value of all interest payment deficiencies. A deficiency in interest payments is the difference between the interest cost (effective interest rate × the beginning balance of the debt each period) and the periodic payment (debt constant × original proceeds).

Second, at maturity, the firm will owe the entire principal and the future value of an annuity of the first period's deficiency. In our example, the cumulative (compounded) interest for 4 years is $39,449, calculated as follows:

[(Effective interest rate − debt constant) × original proceeds]
× future value of an annuity of $1.00 in arrears
= cumulative interest, where

$$\text{Effective interest rate} = 0.100000$$
$$\text{Debt constant} = 0.000000$$
$$\text{Original proceeds} = \$85,000$$
$$\text{Future value of annuity at } n = 4, r = 10\% = 4.641000$$

$$(0.100000 - 0.000000) \times \$85,000 \times 4.641000 = \$39,449$$

Therefore, the total amount to be paid at the end of the fourth year is $124,449 ($85,000 + $39,449). The last payment will **always** be the original proceeds plus the **future value of the annuity** of the proceeds multiplied by the difference between the effective interest rate and the debt constant.

Thought Question
Why will these two methods produce the same results?

If the difference between the effective interest rate and the debt constant is negative (when the effective interest rate is less than the debt constant), we still add the future value of the deficiency in interest payments to the original proceeds to calculate the final payment. On page 301 we had just such a case. The effective interest rate was 0.100000, the debt constant was 0.315471, and the difference, −0.215471. In multiplying −0.215471 × $85,000 × 4.641000, we get −$85,000. And now when we add −$85,000 to the original proceeds, $85,000, we get $0!

ACCOUNTING FOR THE RECLASSIFICATION OF A LONG-TERM LOAN: LUMP-SUM PAYMENT ONLY

Unlike the accounting treatment for the reclassification of a long-term loan when the promise to repay includes periodic payments, the reclassification of a long-term loan, when the repayment is a lump-sum, occurs, only once, at the end of the next-to-last year. To calculate the amount that will become current ($113,135), multiply the $124,449 (the final lump-sum payment) by 0.909091 (the present value of $1.00, at $n = 1$, $r = 10\%$). Below is the entry to record this event:

Reclassification of Long-Term Loan
    Dr. Long-Term Loan   113,135
        Cr. Current Portion of Debt   113,135

During the first 3 years, there will be no cash disbursements related to this borrowing. But this does not mean that there is no cost of using borrowed money during these years. Since the money was used, there must be an interest expense, and accounting rules require that the INTEREST EXPENSE associated with this debt be recognized each period.

In order to calculate the INTEREST EXPENSE for the first period, the balance of Long-Term Loan (the $85,000 available to be used) is multiplied by the effective interest rate (10 percent). Thus, INTEREST EXPENSE for the first year is $8,500 ($85,000 × 0.10), and the entry to record the INTEREST EXPENSE is

Interest Expense
    Dr. Interest Expense (I/S)   8,500
        Cr. Long-Term Loan   8,500

You might be wondering why the credit (Cr.) effect of the entry above did not go to Interest Payable. Interest Payable is a current liability. Since there are **no** expected cash outflows until the end of the fourth year, there cannot be a current liability until the fourth year. Therefore, the balance of Long-Term Loan is increased (***negatively amortized***) by the amount of interest expense. At the end of the first year the balance of Long-Term Loan is $93,500 ($85,000 + $8,500). For the second, third, and fourth years, INTEREST EXPENSE will be $9,350 (10% × $93,500), $10,285 (10% × $102,850), and $11,314 (10% × $113,135), respectively.

TABLE 2

Amortization of a Loan
Case (b): Lump-Sum Payment Only

Year	Beginning Balance (a)	Interest Expense (b)	Lump-Sum Payment (c)	Amortization (d)	Ending Balance (e)
1	$ 85,000	$ 8,500	$0	$ (8,500)	$ 93,500
2	93,500	9,350	0	(9,350)	102,850
3	102,850	10,285	0	(10,285)	113,135
4	113,135	11,314	124,449	113,135	0
Totals		39,449	124,449	85,000	

(a) The present value of all of the remaining payments, as of the **beginning** of the year.
(b) Column a multiplied by the effective interest rate (10 percent).
(c) The final lump-sum payment of $124,449.
(d) The amount of the debt repaid (column c − column b). The negative amount is called *negative amortization*, and increases the loan balance.
(e) The present value of all of the remaining payments, as of the **end** of the year (column a − column d).

Thought Question
Is $93,500 the amount of cash available for use during the second year?

Table 2 is the **amortization schedule** for this long-term loan.

The remaining entries relating to this borrowing, recorded at the **end** of each of the remaining 3 years, are

Year 2 Interest Expense

Dr. Interest Expense (I/S)	9,350	
Cr. Long-Term Loan		9,350

Year 3 Interest Expense

Dr. Interest Expense (I/S)	10,285	
Cr. Long-Term Loan		10,285

Reclassification of Long-Term Loan

Dr. Long-Term Loan	113,135	
Cr. Current Portion of Debt		113,135

Year 4 Interest Expense

Dr. Interest Expense (I/S)	11,314	
Cr. Current Portion of Debt		11,314

Repayment of Debt

Dr. Current Portion of Debt	124,449	
Cr. Cash		124,449

ACCOUNTING FOR THE PROCEEDS OF A LONG-TERM LOAN: PERIODIC AND LUMP-SUM PAYMENTS

Consider the possibility that the contract calls for a periodic payment such that the debt constant is somewhere between zero, where there is no periodic payment, and 0.315471, where all of the principal is repaid through the periodic payments. Consider the effects of the following debt constants:

c-1 0.10, or in our example, a periodic payment of $8,500

c-2 0.06, or in our example, a periodic payment of $5,100

c-3 0.24, or in our example, a periodic payment of $20,400

Clearly, all three cases require both periodic payments **and** a lump-sum payment. Nevertheless, the recording of the effect of the proceeds from long-term borrowing will always have a debit (Dr.) to Cash for the amount of cash received, and always have a credit (Cr.) to Long-Term Loan. The journal entry would be

Long-Term Borrowing
    Dr. Cash   85,000
        Cr. Long-Term Loan   85,000

ACCOUNTING FOR THE REPAYMENT OF A LONG-TERM LOAN: PERIODIC AND LUMP-SUM PAYMENTS

In case c-1 (Table 3), the firm had the use of $85,000 during the first year. At the end of year 1, it paid $8,500. Since the interest was $8,500 (10% × $85,000) no principal was repaid. Therefore, during the second year, the firm still owed $85,000. At the end of year 2, it paid $8,500. The interest was $8,500 (10% × $85,000) and again no principal was repaid. From the pattern that is developing, you can see that all that is being paid each period is the interest, and the original proceeds will be repaid as the lump-sum payment at the end of the fourth year. We call this type of loan an *interest only loan*. This arises when the effective interest rate equals the debt constant.

At the **end** of each of the 4 years, the firm would record the following journal entries:

Interest Expense
    Dr. Interest Expense (I/S)   8,500
        Cr. Interest Payable   8,500

Periodic Payment
    Dr. Interest Payment   8,500
        Cr. Cash   8,500

TABLE 3

Amortization of a Loan
Case c-1: Periodic and Lump-Sum Payments
(Debt Constant of 0.10)

Year	Beginning Balance (a)	Interest Expense (b)	Payment (c)	Amortization (d)	Ending Balance (e)
1	$85,000	$ 8,500	$ 8,500	$0	$85,000
2	85,000	8,500	8,500	0	85,000
3	85,000	8,500	8,500	0	85,000
4	85,000	8,500	93,500	85,000	0
Totals		34,000	119,000	85,000	

(a) The present value of all of the remaining payments, as of the **beginning** of the year.
(b) Column a multiplied by the effective interest rate (10 percent).
(c) The required periodic payments of $8,500, plus the final lump-sum payment of $85,000.
(d) The amount of the debt repaid (column c − column b).
(e) The present value of all of the remaining payments, as of the **end** of the year (column a − column d).

In case c-2 (Table 4), the firm had the use of $85,000 during the first year. At the end of year 1, it paid $5,100. Since interest expense amounted to $8,500 (10% × $85,000), the periodic payment didn't cover $3,400 of interest. So, in addition to the principal that still needs to be repaid at the end of the fourth year, the cumulative (compounded) effect of not having paid all of the interest will also have to be repaid at the end of the fourth year.

During the second year, the firm owed $88,400 ($85,000 + $3,400). At the end of year 2, it paid $5,100. This time the periodic payment did not cover $3,740 of the $8,840 interest expense ($8,840 = 10% × $88,400). During the third year, the firm owed $92,140 ($88,400 + $3,740). At the end of the third year, the firm paid $5,100, continuing to pay only part of the interest cost. During the fourth year, the firm owed $96,254 ($92,140 + $4,114). At the end of the fourth year, the firm paid $105,879, consisting of the periodic $5,100 payment, $4,325 less than the $9,625 interest, plus the lump-sum $100,779 payment ($96,254 + $4,325).

Put in other terms, the $100,779 represents the original proceeds, $85,000, plus the cumulative (compounded) unpaid interest, $15,779 ($15,779 = $3,400 × 4.641000, where 4.641000 represents the future value of an annuity of $1.00 in arrears, at $n = 4$, $r = 10\%$). The $3,400 annuity is the difference between the effective interest rate, 10 percent, and the debt constant, 6 percent, multiplied by the original proceeds, $85,000 (see page 306).

TABLE 4

Amortization of a Loan
Case c-2: Periodic and Lump-Sum Payments
(Debt Constant of 0.06)

Year	Beginning Balance (a)	Interest Expense (b)	Payment (c)	Amortization (d)	Ending Balance (e)
1	$85,000	$ 8,500	$ 5,100	$ (3,400)	$88,400
2	88,400	8,840	5,100	(3,740)	92,140
3	92,140	9,214	5,100	(4,114)	96,254
4	96,254	9,625	105,879	96,254	0
Totals		36,179	121,179	85,000	

(a) The present value of all of the remaining payments, as of the **beginning** of the year.
(b) Column a multiplied by the effective interest rate (10 percent).
(c) The required periodic payments of $5,100, plus the final lump-sum payment of $100,779.
(d) The amount of the debt repaid (column c − column b).
(e) The present value of all of the remaining payments, as of the **end** of the year (column a − column d).

Thought Question
What journal entries would have to be made for this loan?

Finally, in case c-3 (Table 5), the firm had the use of $85,000 for the first year. At the end of year 1, it paid $20,400, $8,500 (10%

TABLE 5

Amortization of a Loan
Case c-3: Periodic and Lump-Sum Payments
(Debt Constant of 0.24)

Year	Beginning Balance (a)	Expense (b)	Payment (c)	Amortization (d)	Ending Balance (e)
1	$85,000	$8,500	$20,400	$11,900	$73,100
2	73,100	7,310	20,400	13,090	60,010
3	60,010	6,001	20,400	14,399	45,611
4	45,611	4,561	50,172	45,611	0
Totals		26,372	111,372	85,000	

(a) The present value of all of the remaining payments, as of the **beginning** of the year.
(b) Column a multiplied by the effective interest rate (10 percent).
(c) The required periodic payment, $20,400, plus the final lump-sum payment of $29,772.
(d) The amount of the debt repaid (column c − column b).
(e) The present value of all of the remaining payments, as of the **end** of the year (column a − column d).

× $85,000) of interest, and the remaining $11,900, principal. Therefore, during the second year, the firm only owed and used $73,100
($85,000 − $11,900). At the end of year 2, it paid $20,400, $7,310
(10% × $73,100) of interest, and the remaining $13,090 ($20,400
− $7,310), principal. During the third year, the firm only owed and
used $60,010 ($73,100 − $13,090). At the end of year 3, it paid
$20,400, $6,001 (10% × $60,010) of interest, and the remaining
$14,399 ($20,400 − $6,001), principal. Finally, during the fourth
year, the firm only owed and used $45,611 ($60,010 − $14,399). At
the end of the fourth year, the firm paid $50,172 consisting of the
periodic $20,400 payment, $4,561 (10% × $45,611) of interest, and
the remaining $15,839 ($20,400 − $4,561), principal, plus the lump-
sum $29,772 payment of the remaining principal, for a total of
$50,172.

ACCOUNTING FOR THE RECLASSIFICATION OF A LONG-TERM LOAN: PERIODIC AND LUMP-SUM PAYMENTS

In case c-1, the present value of the remaining payments of
$93,500—consisting of the last periodic payment of $8,500, and the
lump-sum payment of $85,000—is $85,000 at the beginning of the
fourth year ($93,500 × 0.909091, where 0.909091 is the present
value of $1.00 at $n = 1$, $r = 10\%$), and $0 at the end of the fourth
year. Therefore, $85,000 must have become current at the end of
the third year. The journal entry to record this event is

Reclassification of Long-Term Loan
    Dr. Long-Term Loan   85,000
        Cr. Current Portion of Debt   85,000

In case c-2, the present value of the remaining payments of
$105,879, consisting of the last periodic payment of $5,100 and a
lump-sum payment of $100,779, at the beginning of the fourth year,
is $96,254 ($105,879 × 0.909091, where 0.909091 is the present
value of $1.00 at $n = 1$, $r = 10\%$), and is $0 at the end of the fourth
year. Thus, $96,254 must have become current at the end of the
third year. The journal entry to record this event is

Reclassification of Long-Term Loan
    Dr. Long-Term Loan   96,254
        Cr. Current Portion of Debt   96,254

In case c-3, the present value of all payments at the beginning
of the first year (the inception of the loan), is $85,000 [$20,400 ×
3.169865 (where 3.169865 is the present value of an annuity of $1.00
at $n = 4$, $r = 10\%$) + $29,772 × 0.683013 (where 0.683013 is the
present value of $1.00 at $n = 4$, $r = 10\%$)]. At the end of the first
year, the present value of the remaining three annual payments is

$73,100 [$20,400 × 2.486852 (at $n = 3$, $r = 10\%$) + $29,772 × 0.751315 (at $n = 3$, $r = 10\%$)].

Just as in case *a*, a reclassification entry must be made each year, because a current portion of the remaining principal must be repaid each year. The amounts to be reclassified prior to the year in which they will be paid are listed in Table 5, column *d*. Thus, the reclassification at the beginning of the first year is $11,900, and at the end of the first, second, and third years is $13,090, $14,399, and $45,611, respectively.

SUMMARY

Let us review some of the concepts associated with accounting for a long-term loan where the payments are either periodic, or lump-sum, or a combination of both periodic and lump-sum. The rate at which we accrue interest is called the effective interest rate, and the rate at which we make payments is called the debt constant. We have seen that when the debt constant is **less than** the effective interest rate

1. The cash proceeds will be **less than** the lump-sum payment.
2. There will be *negative amortization.*
3. The average borrowings will be **greater than** the original proceeds.

> *Thought Questions*
> How would the results above change
> if the debt constant was **greater than** the effective interest rate?
> **Equal to** the effective interest rate?

When the debt constant is **greater than** the effective interest rate

1. The cash proceeds will be **greater than** the lump-sum payment.
2. The debt will amortize partially if there is a lump-sum payment, or completely if there is not.
3. The average borrowings will be **less than** the original proceeds.

When the debt constant is **equal to** the effective interest rate

1. The cash proceeds will be **equal to** the lump-sum payment.
2. There will be no amortization of the debt.
3. The average borrowings will be **equal to** the original proceeds.

FINANCIAL STATEMENT PRESENTATION

INTEREST EXPENSE is reported explicitly in the income statement, and INTEREST PAYMENTS in the statement of cash flows. INTEREST PAYMENTS will be reported directly if the direct method of reporting CASH FLOWS FROM OPERATIONS is used. If the indirect method is used, then the credit (debit) change in the Interest Payable account and any deficiencies will be added to (substracted from) NET INCOME to determine CASH FLOWS FROM OPERATIONS. In addition, the amount of interest paid, less any interest associated with long-term construction projects, must be disclosed in the footnotes to the financial statements.

BORROWING AND REPAYMENT OF DEBT will also be reported as financing events in the statement of cash flows, and the effects of borrowing (increasing Long-Term Loan), reclassifying (decreasing Long-Term Loan and increasing Current Portion of Debt), and repaying (decreasing Current Portion of Debt) will be reported in the balance sheet.

Note that the portion of the periodic payment representing INTEREST EXPENSE is reported as an operating cash outflow, and the portion of the periodic payment that represents the REPAYMENT OF DEBT is reported as a financing cash outflow.

In addition, in the footnotes to the financial statements, the firm will present a schedule of long-term borrowings, detailing maturities and interest rates as illustrated by footnote 7 relating to the 1987 financial statements of The New York Times Company in Example 1.

EXAMPLE 1

The New York Times Company
7. Debt

Long-term debt consisted of the following:

December 31	1987	1986
	Dollars in thousands	
Notes payable due 1995 (net of unamortized discount: 1987, $11,591,000; 1986, $12,069,000) (a)	$150,709	$150,231
8.80% notes due 1992 (b)	50,000	—
9.35% notes due 1990 (b)	50,000	—
Commercial paper (c)	29,525	29,675
6.58% bank loan due 1988 (d)	25,000	25,000
9.57% notes due 1987 (e)	—	30,000
Partnership retirement obligation (f)	43,612	—
Other notes payable, due through 2005 at a weighted average interest rate of 9.3% in 1987 and 9.8% in 1986	12,412	14,731
Total	361,258	249,637
Less current portion	25,518	34,041
Total long-term debt	$335,740	$215,596

Long-term debt, exclusive of amounts due within one year, matures as follows: 1989, $30,089,000; 1990, $50,564,000; 1991, $46,026,000; 1992, $50,564,000; and $158,497,000 thereafter.

(a) In connection with the 1985 acquisition of certain newspapers (See Note 2), the Company issued 10-year notes with an aggregate stated value of $162,300,000 which have been discounted at an interest rate of 11.85% for financial reporting purposes. Interest on certain of the notes is payable semi-annually. The original difference of $12,600,000 between the stated value of the notes and the amount that results from discounting the notes at 11.85% is being amortized as interest expense over the term of the notes.

(b) The Company issued notes totaling $100,000,000 to an insurance company with interest payable semi-annually. In August 1987, $50,000,000 of five-year notes were issued at a rate of 8.8% and the remaining $50,000,000 were issued as three-year notes in November 1987 at a rate of 9.35%.

(c) In December 1985, the Company established a $100,000,000 commercial paper program in the European market. Borrowings are in the form of non-interest bearing unsecured notes of $500,000 denomination sold at discounts with maturities ranging up to 180 days. The $30,000,000 in aggregate face value of such notes outstanding at December 31, 1987 and 1986 were issued at weighted average interest rates of 7.99% and 6.35%, respectively, and are included in long-term debt since the Company intends to refinance these obligations for at least one year. The outstanding commercial paper is supported by the Company's revolving credit and term loan agreements.

(d) In November 1985, the Company negotiated a $25,000,000 loan with a Japanese bank. Interest, payable semi-annually, and the principal, due November 1988, are payable in Japanese yen. As of November 1985 the Company entered into forward exchange contracts for delivery of sufficient yen to meet all interest and principal payments. Interest on the hedged loan approximates 8.99% per annum in United States dollars. The notes are included in current portion of long-term debt at December 31, 1987.

(e) In September 1985, the Company issued notes totaling $30,000,000 to an insurance company. Interest was payable semi-annually and the notes matured in August 1987. The notes are included in current portion of long-term debt at December 31, 1986.

(f) In the fourth quarter of 1987, the Partnership (See Note 2) entered into revolving credit agreements whereby the Partnership can borrow, at any time through April 30, 1991, up to $85,000,000. The agreements permit borrowings which bear interest, at the Partnership's option, (i) for domestic borrowings: based on the certificates of deposit rate, or a prime rate, or (ii) for Eurodollar borrowings: on the London interbank rate. The Partnership must pay a commitment fee of $\frac{1}{8}$th of 1% on the unused commitment. Borrowings under the agreement may be prepaid without penalty at any time and at the Partnership's discretion may be converted into term loans which mature on April 30, 1991. In January 1988, the Partnership borrowed $55,000,000 under these agreements, of which $43,612,000 was used to retire the remaining partnership interest and the remainder for working capital and other purposes.

The Company has available a $100,000,000 revolving credit and term loan agreement with a group of banks. The commitment terminates in July 1990. Commencing in July 1990, then outstanding borrowings would be payable quarterly, aggregating 5%, 22.5%, 35% and 37.5% annually from 1990 to 1993. The agreement permits borrowings which bear interest, at the Company's option, (i) for domestic borrowings: based on the certificates of deposit rate, the Federal funds rate, a prime rate, or money market quotes; or (ii) for Eurodollar borrowings: on the London interbank rate.

The Company also has available a $30,000,000 revolving credit and term loan agreement. The commitment terminates November 1989. Commencing in February 1990, then outstanding borrowings would be payable quarterly, aggregating 20%, 30% and 50% annually from 1990 to 1992. The agreement permits borrowings which bear interest, at the Company's option, (i) for domestic borrowings: based on the certificates of deposit rate or a prime rate; or (ii) for Eurodollar borrowings: on the London interbank rate. Both revolving and term loan agreements also provide for an annual commitment fee of $\frac{1}{8}$th of 1% on the unused commitment. Borrowings under both agreements may be prepaid without penalty and, at the Company's discretion, may be converted into term loans at any time.

Certain of the agreements also include provisions which require, among other matters, specified levels of stockholders' equity. At December 31, 1987, approximately $530,000,000 of stockholders' equity was unrestricted.

At December 31, 1986, accounts and notes payable included $3,500,000 of short-term bank borrowings. There were no such borrowings at December 31, 1987.

Interest expense, net of interest income as shown in the accompanying Consolidated Statements of Income consisted of the following:

	1987	1986	1985
Dollars in thousands			
Interest expense	$25,821	$37,582	$24,490
Interest income	(2,910)	(2,047)	(4,837)
Net	$22,911	$35,535	$19,653

In connection with various construction projects, interest of approximately $6,052,000, $5,795,000 and $1,065,000 was capitalized as property, plant and equipment for 1987, 1986 and 1985, respectively.

USER'S PERSPECTIVE

Financial ratios are used in analyzing accounting data. All ratios compare numbers with a specific objective in mind. Three of the more common ratios are the *current ratio*, used to assess the liquidity of a firm; the *return on assets*, used to assess how effectively assets are utilized by a firm; and the *return on equity*, used to determine the benefits stockholders derive from their investment. To determine the usefulness of any ratio, we must see whether the comparison of the numbers is valid in terms of the objective.

For example, refer to the accounts and related information listed below, and consider the firm's *current ratio*, a ratio generally used to measure the ability of a firm to pay its bills.

Current Assets and Current Liabilities

Cash	$128,630
Accounts Receivable	75,000
Inventory (*a*)	100,000
Total Current Assets	$303,630
Accounts Payable	$125,000
Interest Payable (*b*)	8,500
Current Portion of Debt (*b*)	18,315
Total Current Liabilities	$151,815

Notes

(*a*) The firm uses LIFO for inventory valuation. Had the firm used FIFO, ending inventory would have been $150,000.

(*b*) The firm borrowed $85,000 from the bank on January 1, 19X1, promising to pay $26,815 each January 1 thereafter. The $26,815 payment due on January 1, 19X2, will include $8,500 of interest and $18,315 of principal, and the $26,815 payment due on January 1, 19X3, will include $6,668 of interest and $20,147 of principal.

First, we must determine the extent to which these accounting numbers result from substantive events, rather than from descriptive changes, because descriptive changes have no relevance in assessing a firm's ability to pay its bills. Referring to our example above, the current ratio, which is equal to current assets divided by current liabilities, is 2:1 ($303,630 ÷ $151,815). Had the firm used FIFO instead of LIFO, the current ratio would have been 2.33:1 ($353,630 ÷ $151,815) instead of 2:1, but with exactly the same liquidity!

The current ratio is determined from balance sheet data that represent the cumulative effects of events at a point in time. For this ratio to be correctly calculated, the point in time must be representative of a typical point in time. If it is not, then the firm's current ratio will differ. For instance, if the loan payment in our example above was due and paid on December 31 instead of January 1, then the ending balance in Cash would have been $101,815 ($128,630 − $26,815), the ending balance in Interest Payable would have been $0, and the ending balance in Current Portion of Debt would have been $20,147. Therefore, the current assets would have been $276,815 instead of $303,630, the current liabilities would have been $145,147 instead of $151,815, and the current ratio would have been 1.91:1 instead of 2:1.

The ability of a firm to pay its bills also depends upon the timing of its cash inflows and cash outflows. Refer back to our discussion of the duration dimension on page 199, and recall that the current ratio does not reflect the impact of the duration dimension on cash flows. Moreover, many current assets are quantified at cost, and therefore in terms of a past cash flow, while most current liabilities are quantified in terms of the future cash flow. In assessing liquidity, or for that matter anything, how could it make sense to compare a past cash flow with a future cash flow?

As a result of all of the factors above, a comparison of two firms with identical current ratios may have different liquidities. For instance, compare the current assets and current liabilities of another firm with those presented above. If the second firm had Cash of $153,630; Accounts Receivable of $125,000; Inventory of $25,000; and Accounts Payable of $151,815, then its current ratio would also be 2:1. Both firms have current ratios of 2:1 ($303,630 ÷ $151,815), but are they equally "liquid"? In other words, do both firms have the same ability to pay their bills?

> ### Thought Questions
> Why would the two firm's liquidity differ?
> Could they be the same?

Should these limitations preclude us from ever using this ratio? Clearly not. But in order to use this or any other ratio intelligently, the limitations of ratios and the accounting numbers must be clearly understood. One thing that should not be done is to assign value judgments to ratios in a vacuum. For instance, you will often hear that the current ratio should be 2:1, but such statements are much too simplistic. The comparisons presented in *financial ratios* can often generate insights, particularly when compared with ratios of other firms in the same industry, but the conclusion about whether a ratio is good or bad will vary with the firm and the times, and must be made by the user.

PROBLEMS

1. On September 1, 19X0, a company borrowed cash and signed a 2-year interest-bearing note on which both the principal and interest are payable on September 1, 19X2. At December 31, 19X1, the liability for accrued interest should be
   a. Zero
   b. For 4 months of interest
   c. For 12 months of interest
   d. For 24 months of interest

2. On September 1, 19X1, a company borrowed cash and signed a 1-year interest-bearing note on which both the principal and interest are payable on September 1, 19X2. How will the note payable and the related interest be classified in the December 31, 19X1, balance sheet?

Note Payable	Accrued Interest
a. Current liability	Noncurrent liability
b. Noncurrent liability	Current liability
c. Current liability	Current liability
d. Noncurrent liability	No entry

3. On May 1, 19X1, the Juice Loan Co. lends $30,000 for 1 year to the Risky Retail Co. The borrower promises to pay interest of $500 per month with the payments to be made in two $3,000 installments: one on September 1, 19X1, and the other on January 1, 19X2. The principal will be repaid on May 1, 19X2.

   The borrower prepares financial statements on the last day of each month. Prepare the lender's journal entries for the loan on the following dates:
   a. May 1, 19X1
   b. May 31, 19X1
   c. September 1, 19X1
   d. October 31, 19X1
   e. May 1, 19X2

4. On November 1, 19X1, the Stanton Company borrowed $45,000 for 1 year at 18 percent. Interest is payable every 3 months.

   What journal entries does the Stanton Company record in connection with this loan (principal and interest) on
   a. November 1, 19X1
   b. December 31, 19X1
   c. January 31, 19X2
   d. April 30, 19X2
   e. October 31, 19X2

5. The Romen Company borrowed $100,000 on January 1, 19X1, at an interest rate of 12 percent. They intend to repay the entire amount in one lump-sum on December 31, 19X6.

   Prepare the journal entries that the Romen Company would make on
   a. December 31, 19X3
   b. December 31, 19X4
   c. December 31, 19X5
   d. December 31, 19X6

6. The Liew Company borrowed $200,000 on January 1, 19X1, promising to pay $5,000 each June 30 and December 31 for 5 years, at which time it would make a lump-sum payment. Assume an interest rate of 15 percent.

   Prepare the journal entries that the Liew Company would make on
   a. June 30, 19X1
   b. June 30, 19X2
   c. June 30, 19X3
   d. December 31, 19X4
   e. December 31, 19X5

7. The Manor Company made the following entries on December 31, 19X3:

Dr. Interest Expense	10,000	
Cr. Long-Term Debt		10,000
Dr. Long-Term Debt	110,000	
Cr. Current Portion of Debt		110,000

   The money was originally borrowed on January 1, 19X0, to be repaid on December 31, 19X4.
   a. How much was originally borrowed?
   b. How much will be repaid on December 31, 19X4?

8. From footnote 7 of the financial statements relating to The New York Times Company (page 315)
   a. Calculate the stated interest rate (periodic payment ÷ stated value of note) relating to the notes that are due in 1995.
   b. What was the PERIODIC PAYMENT on all debt during 1987?

9. If the Current Portion of Long-Term Debt increased by **less** than Long-Term Debt increased, and Interest Payable did not change, and Long-Term Borrowing was equal to Repayment of Debt, then Interest Expense was (greater than/less than/equal to) Payment of Interest.

10. If payments associated with **all forms** of long-term debt were greater than Interest Expense associated with **all forms** of long-term debt, and no new long-term debt was incurred, then either

> Account _____ must have increased/decreased
> or Account _____ must have increased/decreased
> or Account _____ must have increased/decreased
> or Account _____ must have increased/decreased.

11. The Slovo Company borrowed $1,000,000 from the bank at an interest rate of 12 percent, with repayment to be made in one lump-sum at the end of 5 years. The Slovo Company can retire the debt at any time by making a payment equal to the accounting quantification on the date of repayment **plus** a prepayment penalty of 5 percent of that accounting quantification. At the end of the third year, the company can borrow money at 10 percent.

    Should the Slovo Company pay off the original loan at the end of year 3?

12. If equal amounts of money are initially borrowed for equal periods of time:
    Total interest expense over the entire loan period will be larger if
    a. There are only periodic payments.
    b. There is only one lump-sum payment.

    CASH FLOWS FROM OPERATIONS will be larger if
    c. There are only periodic payments.
    d. There is only one lump-sum payment.

13. From the following T-accounts relating to the Rowe Company, prepare all of the journal entries associated with their bank loans.

Current Portion of	
↓ Long-Term Debt ↑	
	400
700	

↓ Long-Term Debt ↑	
	1,000

↓ Interest Payable ↑	
	300
	400

Interest Expense	
500	

14.

The L, P, and IO Company
Comparative Balance Sheets
Years Ending December 31, 19X0 and 19X1

Assets	12/31/X0	12/31/X1
Cash	$150,000	$?
Net Accounts Receivable (note 1)	200,000	300,000
Inventory	250,000	275,000
Property, Plant and Equipment	300,000	500,000
Accumulated Depreciation	(100,000)	(165,000)
Total Assets	$800,000	$?

Liabilities and Owners' Equities		
Accounts Payable	$175,000	$195,000
Long-Term Debt	0	?
Common Stock	250,000	250,000
Retained Earnings	375,000	?
Total Liabilities and Owners' Equities	$800,000	$?

Notes
(1) Bad debt expense was $5,000 during the year.
(2) The effective tax rate was 40 percent.
(3) The company arranged a 5-year, $350,000 loan with the local
bank when the interest rate was 10 percent. They had the option
to either make equal annual payments at the end of each year,
one lump-sum payment at the end of the 5 years, or interest-only
payments at the end of each year and the principal at the end of
the fifth year.

The L, P, and IO Company
Statement of Cash Flows
19X1

Cash Flows from Operations

Collections from Customers		$800,000
Payments to Suppliers of Services	$150,000	
Payments to Suppliers of Merchandise	250,000	
Payment of Interest	?	
Payment of Taxes	?	(?)
Cash Flows from Operations		$?

Cash Flows from Financing Events

Long-Term Borrowing (note 3)	$?	
Total Financing Cash Flows	$?	?

Cash Flows from Investing Events

Purchase of Property, Plant and Equipment	$300,000	
Total Investing Cash Flows	$300,000	(300,000)
Increase (Decrease) in Cash		$?

Required:
For each of the three different options listed in note 3
a. Prepare an income statement.
b. Fill in all of the question (?) marks.

15. From the following information relating to the MaMo Company, prepare
    a. A statement of balance sheet changes
    b. An income statement
    c. A statement of cash flows
    No events not described or derivable from the information below occurred.
    (1) The firm borrowed $50,000 from the bank. They did not repay any loans during the period.
    (2) The company had operating expenses.
    (3) Payments to suppliers of services were $90,000.
    (4) The balance in Inventory decreased by $6,000.
    (5) The balance in Accounts Receivable increased by $20,000.
    (6) Income tax expense was $22,000.
    (7) The balance in Property, Plant and Equipment increased by $80,000.
    (8) The balance in Interest Payable increased by $2,000.
    (9) The balance in Taxes Payable increased by $5,000.
    (10) Property, plant and equipment, with book value of $5,000, was sold for $2,000.
    (11) Collections from customers were $275,000.
    (12) Interest expense was $12,000.
    (13) The balance in Estimated Uncollectibles increased by $7,000.
    (14) The balance in Accounts Payable Merchandise decreased by $4,000.
    (15) Payment of interest was $8,000.
    (16) The balance in Retained Earnings increased by $16,000.
    (17) The balance in Dividends Payable decreased by $1,000.
    (18) There were no writeoffs during the year.
    (19) Net sales revenue (sales minus the uncollectibility adjustment) were $300,000.
    (20) Payment of dividends was $10,000.
    (21) The balance in Prepaid Services decreased by $3,000.
    (22) Purchases of inventory were $75,000.
    (23) Payment of taxes was $11,000.
    (24) The balance in Accumulated Depreciation increased by $17,000.
    (25) Property, plant and equipment was purchased for $100,000 in cash.

CHAPTER 13

Accounting for Long-Term Debt: Bonds

INTRODUCTION

A bond is a source of financing. It is a form of long-term debt similar in every respect to a loan except that bonds are financed by investors in the marketplace, whereas long-term debt, as discussed in the previous chapter, is generally financed by banks. As a result, the accounting for the issuance of bonds is slightly different than that for other forms of long-term debt.

HOW BONDS ARE ISSUED IN THE MARKETPLACE

A *bond* is a formal contract, evidenced by a certificate, between the issuer and the investor. Once issued, a bond is typically traded in a securities market. The most common bond contract is one that obligates the firm to make periodic as well as lump-sum payments in exchange for cash borrowed from the investor. The lump-sum payment per bond is usually $1,000, payable when the bond *matures*, and is referred to as the *face value* of the bond. Each periodic payment, called the *coupon* or *coupon payment*, is a fixed percentage of the face value of the bond; this percentage is called the *coupon rate*.

The coupon rate, and therefore the amount of the coupon payment per bond (periodic payment), is determined by the issuing firm. The amount that the investor is willing to pay for each bond (the cash proceeds to the issuer) is determined by the market, and will equal the present value of the periodic payments plus the present value of the lump-sum payment per bond, discounted at the *market rate* of interest.

There are three rates that we must consider in discussing bonds: the market rate, the coupon rate, and the *debt constant*. The *market rate*, also called *yield-to-maturity*, is the prevailing rate that investors (the market) are demanding; the *coupon rate* is the *coupon payment* divided by the *face value*; and the *debt constant*, usually referred to as the **cash yield rate**, is the *coupon payment* divided by the quantification of the bonds.

When the coupon rate is equal to the market rate at the time the bond is issued, the face value is equal to the cash proceeds, and the cash yield equals both the coupon rate and the market rate. When this situation exists, we say that the bond was issued at *par*.

When the coupon rate is less than the market rate, the face value is greater than the cash proceeds, and the cash yield is greater than the coupon rate but less than the market rate. In this case we say that the bond was issued at a *discount*. Finally, when the coupon rate is greater than the market rate, the face value is less than the cash proceeds, the cash yield is greater than the market rate but less than the coupon rate, and we say that the bond was issued at a *premium*.

> ### Thought Question
> In terms of what we discussed in Chapter 12,
> what are discounts and premiums?

We said above that a discount is a result of the coupon rate being less than the market rate. In other words, a discount arises when the periodic payment that the firm promises is less than the market rate of interest times the proceeds. The firm will make up the deficiency in interest payments by paying back more at the end of the life of the bond than it received when it issued the bond. The cumulative (compounded) amount of the **deficiency** is called a *discount*.

Suppose that a firm wishes to borrow $85,000 by issuing 85, $1,000 face value bonds when the market rate is 10 percent. It can do so only if it establishes the coupon rate at 10 percent. If the firm establishes the coupon rate at less than 10 percent, the bonds will be issued at a discount, and proceeds from issuing the 85 bonds will be less than $85,000. The firm, therefore, will either have to increase the coupon rate to 10 percent, issue more than 85 bonds, or content itself with receiving less than $85,000. The decision as to what coupon rate to establish and how many bonds to issue will depend on the amount the firm wishes to borrow and the prevailing market rate of interest. This decision is usually arrived at with the help of investment advisors or investment bankers.

Similarly, when the firm establishes a coupon rate higher than the market rate, the firm can either borrow more money than it had originally intended, or issue fewer bonds. As a result of the excess in periodic payments, the firm will pay back less at the end of the life of the bond than it received when it issued the bond. The cumulative (compounded) amount of the **excess** of periodic payments is called a *premium*. In other words, a premium arises when the periodic payment that the firm promises is greater than the market rate of interest times the proceeds.

ACCOUNTING FOR THE PROCEEDS OF A BOND ISSUE: PERIODIC AND LUMP-SUM PAYMENTS, WHERE THE COUPON RATE IS *EQUAL TO* THE MARKET RATE

A firm wants to receive $85,000 upon issuing bonds, assuming a market rate of 10 percent, compounded annually, and will make $8,500 coupon (periodic) payments at the end of each year, for 4 years, as well as a lump-sum payment at the end of the fourth year. The lump-sum payment will be $85,000, calculated as follows:

$$\text{Proceeds} = \text{present value of the lump-sum } (L) +$$
$$\text{present value of the periodic payments}$$

$$85,000 = \text{present value of the lump-sum } (L), \text{ at } n = 4, r = 10\% +$$
$$\text{present value of the coupons, at } n = 4, r = 10\%$$

$$85,000 = L \times 0.683013 + \$8,500 \times 3.169865$$

$$L = \$85,000$$

Therefore, in order to receive $85,000, the firm would have to issue bonds with a face value of $85,000. To record the issue of these bonds, the firm would make the following journal entry:

Issue of Bonds

Dr. Cash	85,000	
Cr. **Bonds Payable** (face value)		85,000

The firm would make the following journal entries at the **end** of each of the next 4 years:

Interest Expense

Dr. Interest Expense (I/S)	8,500	
Cr. Interest Payable		8,500

Periodic Payment

Dr. Interest Payable	8,500	
Cr. Cash		8,500

the following journal entry at the **end** of the third year:

Reclassification of Bonds

Dr. Bonds Payable	85,000	
Cr. Current Portion of Debt		85,000

and the following journal entry at the **end** of the fourth year:

Lump-Sum Payment
      Dr. Current Portion of Debt   85,000
            Cr. Cash   85,000

Table 1 shows in tabular form the results discussed above.

TABLE 1

Amortization of Bonds Issued at Par
(Coupon Rate *and* Market Rate are 10 Percent)

Year	Face Value (a)	Interest Expense (b)	Payment (c)	Amortization (d)	Ending Balance of Net Bonds Payable (e)
1	$85,000	$8,500	$ 8,500	0	$85,000
2	85,000	8,500	8,500	0	85,000
3	85,000	8,500	8,500	0	85,000
4	85,000	8,500	93,500	85,000	0
Totals		$34,000	$119,000	85,000	

(a) The present value of all of the remaining payments,
    as of the **beginning** of the year.
(b) Column *a* multiplied by the market rate (10 percent).
(c) The required periodic payments of $8,500.
(d) The amount of the debt repaid (column *c* − column *b*).
(e) The present value of all of the remaining payments,
    as of the **end** of the year (column *a* − column *d*).

We have shown that the effects of borrowing from the bank and of issuing bonds are effectively the same. However, while the term for repaying borrowed money from the bank is usually less than 10 years, the term for bonds is generally longer. For the remaining two examples, we will assume a term of 20 years.

ACCOUNTING FOR THE PROCEEDS OF A BOND ISSUE: PERIODIC AND LUMP-SUM PAYMENTS, WHERE THE COUPON RATE IS *LESS THAN* THE MARKET RATE

A firm wants to receive $85,000 upon issuing bonds, assuming a market rate of 10 percent, compounded annually, but will pay only $8,300 coupon payments instead of $8,500 at the end of each year, for 20 years, as well as a lump-sum payment at the end of the twentieth year. The lump-sum payment ($96,455) will be greater than the original proceeds ($85,000) because of the deficiencies in the periodic payments, calculated as follows:

Proceeds = present value of the lump-sum (L) +
present value of the periodic payments

$85,000$ = present value of lump-sum (L) at $n = 20$, $r = 10\%$ +
present value of the coupons, at $n = 20$, $r = 10\%$

$85,000 = L \times 0.148644 + \$8,300 \times 8.513564$

$L = \$96,455$

Therefore, in order to receive $85,000, the firm would have to issue bonds with a face value of $96,455 and a coupon rate of 8.61 percent. To record the issue of these bonds, the firm would make the following journal entry:

Issue of Bonds

Dr. Unamortized Bond Discount	11,455	
Dr. Cash	85,000	
Cr. Bonds Payable (face value)		96,455

The **Unamortized Bond Discount** account is a *contra-liability*, and its balance represents the compounded interest deficiency remaining until *maturity*. By subtracting the balance in this account from the balance in the Bonds Payable account, you determine **Net Bonds Payable**. Net Bonds Payable is also the present value of the remaining payments associated with the bonds.

Since the firm has the use of $85,000 ($96,455 − $11,455) during the first year, interest expense amounted to $8,500 (10% × $85,000). At the end of year 1, it paid $8,300. The periodic payment didn't cover $200 of interest. So, in addition to the principal that still needs to be repaid at the end of the twentieth year, the cumulative (compounded) effect of not having paid all of the interest will also have to be repaid at the end of the twentieth year.

To record the first year's deficiency, the Unamortized Bond Discount account is credited for $200, the difference between the interest expense ($8,500) and the periodic payment ($8,300). By crediting the Unamortized Bond Discount account, the balance is reduced by $200, to a new balance of $11,255. As a result, Net Bonds Payable is increased to $85,200 ($96,455 − $11,255). The journal entry to record this event is

Interest Expense

Dr. Interest Expense (I/S)	8,500	
Cr. Interest Payable		8,300
Cr. *Unamortized Bond Discount*		200

During the second year, the firm owed $85,200. At the end of year 2, it paid $8,300. This time the periodic payment did not cover $220 of the $8,520 interest expense (10% × $85,200). By crediting the Unamortized Bond Discount account, the balance is further reduced by $220 to a new balance of $11,035 ($11,255 − $220), and Net Bonds Payable is increased to $85,420 ($96,455 − $11,035).

This process continues each year in a similar and familiar manner. At the beginning of the twentieth year, Net Bonds Payable is equal to $95,232.

Thought Question

How would you determine that
the beginning balance in Net Bonds Payable was $95,232,
without amortizing the bond year by year?

At the end of the nineteenth year, the next to last year, the balance in the Bonds Payable account would still be $96,455, and the balance in the Unamortized Bond Discount account would be $1,223. Since the bonds will be repaid during the following year, they would be reclassified from noncurrent to current debt. This reclassification would be recorded by the following journal entry:

Reclassification of Bonds
Dr. Bonds Payable	96,455	
Cr. Unamortized Bond Discount		1,223
Cr. Current Portion of Debt		95,232

During the last year, the firm owed $95,232. At the end of the year, the firm made its final periodic payment of $8,300, plus the lump-sum payment of $96,455. The INTEREST EXPENSE, $9,523 (10% × $95,232), would be recorded by the following journal entry:

Interest Expense
Dr. Interest Expense (I/S)	9,523	
Cr. Interest Payable		8,300
Cr. Current Portion of Debt		1,223

Thought Question

Why wasn't Unamortized Bond Discount credited
for the difference between interest expense ($9,523)
and the periodic payment ($8,300)?

Table 2 shows in tabular form the results discussed above.

TABLE 2

Amortization of Bonds Issued at Discount
(The Coupon Rate is 8.61 Percent and the Market Rate is 10 Percent)

Year	Face Value (a)	Unamortized Bond Discount (b)	Beginning Balance of Net Bonds Payable (c)	Interest Expense (d)	Coupon Payment (e)	Amortization of Discount (f)	Ending Balance of Net Bonds Payable (g)
1	$96,455	$11,455	$85,000	$ 8,500	$ 8,300	$ 200	$85,200
2	96,455	11,255	85,200	8,520	8,300	220	85,420
.	.	.	.	.	.	.	.
.	.	.	.	.	.	.	.
19	96,455	2,335	94,120	9,412	8,300	1,112	95,232

(a) Face value of the bonds.
(b) Balance in the Unamortized Bond Discount account.
(c) The present value of all of the remaining payments,
    as of the **beginning** of the year (column a − column b).
(d) Column c multiplied by the market rate (10 percent).
(e) The required periodic payments of $8,300.
(f) The amount of the interest not paid (column d − column e).
(g) The present value of all of the remaining payments,
    as of the **end** of the year (column c + column f).

At the beginning of this section, we calculated the lump-sum payment to be made when the bond matures. There are two interpretations of the total amount of unamortized bond discount: the first, as a future value of an annuity of interest deficiencies that will be paid at the time the bonds mature. In this case, the unamortized bond discount of $11,455 is the future value of the $200 annuity, the difference between the interest cost in year 1 ($8,500) and the periodic payment ($8,300), at $n = 20$, $r = 10\%$.

The second interpretation of the unamortized bond discount is the amount that the investors subtract from the face value because the coupon rate of the bonds is less than the market rate of interest. Had the coupon rate been equal to the market rate of interest, and $96,455 of bonds had been issued at par, then the coupon payment would have been $9,645. Since the firm is only paying $8,300 periodically, the proceeds are $11,455 less than the face value, which is the present value of the $1,345 annuity, the difference between the market rate (10 percent) and the coupon rate (8.61 percent), multiplied by the face value of the bonds ($96,455), at $n = 20$, $r = 10\%$.

Compare the effects of amortizing the unamortized bond discount in the example above, and the effects of amortizing the loan in case c-2 in Chapter 12 (page 310). The deficiency in the interest payments in the case of the loan directly increased the balance in the Long-Term Loan account, while the deficiency in the case of the bonds issued at discount indirectly increased the balance in the Net Bonds Payable (face value less unamortized bond discount) by decreasing the Unamortized Bond Discount.

ACCOUNTING FOR THE PROCEEDS OF A BOND ISSUE: PERIODIC AND LUMP-SUM PAYMENTS, WHERE THE COUPON RATE IS *GREATER THAN* THE MARKET RATE

Now consider a firm that wants to receive $85,000 upon issuing bonds, assuming a market rate of 10 percent, compounded annually, and willing to pay $8,700 coupon payments instead of $8,500 at the end of each year, for 20 years, as well as a lump-sum payment at the end of the twentieth year. The lump-sum payment ($73,545) will be less than the original proceeds ($85,000) because of the greater periodic payments, and is calculated as follows:

Proceeds = present value of the lump-sum (L) +
present value of the periodic payments

85,000 = present value of lump-sum (L) at $n = 20$, $r = 10\%$ +
present value of the coupons, at $n = 20$, $r = 10\%$

85,000 = L × 0.148644 + $8,700 × 8.513564

L = $73,545

Therefore, in order to receive $85,000, the firm would have to issue bonds with a face value of $73,545, and a coupon rate of 11.83 percent. To record the issue of these bonds, the firm would make the following journal entry:

Issue of Bonds
    Dr. Cash   85,000
        Cr. Bonds Payable (face value)   73,545
        Cr. Unamortized Bond Premium   11,455

The *Unamortized Bond Premium* account is an *adjunct liability* and its balance represents the compounded excess periodic payments remaining until maturity. By adding the balance in this account to the balance in the Bonds Payable account, you determine *Net Bonds Payable*. Net Bonds Payable is also the present value of the remaining payments associated with the bonds.

Since the firm had the use of $85,000 ($73,545 + $11,455) during the first year, interest expense amounted to $8,500 (10% × $85,000). At the end of year 1, it paid $8,700. The periodic payment exceeded the interest expense by $200. To record this excess, the Unamortized Bond Premium account is debited for $200, reducing its balance to $11,255 ($11,455 − $200), and reducing the balance of Net Bonds Payable to $84,800 ($73,545 + 11,255). The journal entry to record this event is

Interest Expense		
Dr. *Unamortized Bond Premium*	200	
Dr. Interest Expense (I/S)	8,500	
Cr. Interest Payable		8,700

During the second year, the firm only owed and used $84,800. At the end of year 2, the interest expense was $8,480 (10% × $84,800) and it paid $8,700. The periodic payment exceeded the interest expense by $220 ($8,700 − $8,480). The balance in the Unamortized Bond Premium account will be debited, reducing its balance to $11,035 ($11,255 − $220) and reducing Net Bonds Payable to $84,580 ($73,545 + $11,035).

This process continues each year in a similar and familiar manner. At the beginning of the twentieth year, Net Bonds Payable is equal to $74,768. At the end of the nineteenth year, the next to last year, the balance in the Bonds Payable account would still be $73,545, and the balance in the Unamortized Bond Premium account would be $1,223. Since the bonds will be repaid during the following year, they would be reclassified from noncurrent to current debt. This reclassification would be recorded by the following journal entry:

Reclassification of Bonds		
Dr. Bonds Payable	73,545	
Dr. Unamortized Bond Premium	1,223	
Cr. Current Portion of Debt		74,768

During the last year, the firm owed $74,768. At the end of the year, the firm made its final periodic payment of $8,700, plus the lump-sum payment of $73,545. The INTEREST EXPENSE, $7,477 (10% × $74,768), would be recorded as follows:

Interest Expense		
Dr. Current Portion of Debt	1,223	
Dr. Interest Expense (I/S)	7,477	
Cr. Interest Payable		8,700

Table 3 shows in tabular form the results discussed above.

TABLE 3

Amortization of Bonds Issued at Premium
(The Coupon Rate is 11.83 Percent and the Market Rate is 10 Percent)

Year	Face Value (a)	Unamortized Bond Premium (b)	Beginning Balance of Net Bonds Payable (c)	Interest Expense (d)	Coupon Payment (e)	Amortization of Premium (f)	Ending Balance of Net Bonds Payable (g)
1	$73,545	$11,455	$85,000	$ 8,500	$ 8,700	$ 200	$84,800
2	73,545	11,255	84,800	8,480	8,700	220	84,520
.	.	.	.	.	.	.	.
19	73,545	2,335	75,880	7,588	8,700	1,112	74,768

(a) Face value of the bonds.
(b) Balance in the Unamortized Bond Premium account.
(c) The present value of all of the remaining payments,
  as of the **beginning** of the year (column a + column b).
(d) Column c multiplied by the market rate (10 percent).
(e) The required periodic payments of $8,700.
(f) The excess amount of interest paid (column e − column d).
(g) The present value of all of the remaining payments,
  as of the **end** of the year (column c − column f).

At the beginning of this section, we calculated the lump-sum payment to be made when the bond matures. There are two interpretations of the total amount of unamortized bond premium: the first, as a future value of an annuity of the excess of periodic payments that will not be paid at the time the bonds mature. In this case, the unamortized bond premium of $11,455 is the future value of the $200 annuity, the difference between the periodic payment ($8,700) and the interest cost in year 1 ($8,500), at $n = 20$, $r = 10\%$.

The second interpretation of the unamortized bond premium is the amount that the investors pay in excess of face value because the coupon rate of the bonds is greater than the market rate of interest. Had the coupon rate been equal to the market rate of interest, and $73,545 of bonds had been issued at par, then the coupon payment would have been $7,355. Since the firm is paying $8,700 periodically, the proceeds are $11,455 greater than the face value, which is the present value of the $1,345 annuity, the difference between the coupon rate (11.83 percent) and the market rate (10 percent), multiplied by the face value of the bonds ($73,545), at $n = 20$, $r = 10\%$.

Compare the effects of amortizing the unamortized bond premium in the example above, and the effects of amortizing the loan in case *c*-3 in Chapter 12 (see page 311). The excess in the interest payments in the case of the loan directly decreased the balance in the Long-Term Loan account, while the excess in the case of the bonds issued at premium indirectly decreased the balance in the Net Bonds Payable (face value plus unamortized bond premium) by decreasing the Unamortized Bond Premium.

SUMMARY

Let us review some of the terms and concepts associated with bonds. The market rate is the prevailing rate that investors (the market) are demanding; the coupon rate is the COUPON PAYMENT divided by the face value; and the case yield rate is the COUPON PAYMENT divided by the quantification of the bonds. The face value of bonds is the lump-sum payment at the end of the life of the bond, and cash proceeds is the amount of money received upon issuance of the bonds. The COUPON PAYMENT is the periodic payment made by the firm, and INTEREST EXPENSE is the cost of using the money.

When the coupon rate is **less than** the market rate:

1. The bonds were issued at a discount.
2. The cash proceeds will be **less than** the face value of the bonds (lump-sum payment).
3. The coupon payment will be **less than** interest expense.

When the coupon rate is **greater than** the market rate:

1. The bonds were issued at a premium.
2. The cash proceeds will be **greater than** the face value of the bonds (lump-sum payment).
3. The coupon payment will be **greater than** interest expense.

When the coupon rate is **equal to** the market rate:

1. The bonds were issued at par.
2. The cash proceeds will be **equal to** the face value of the bonds (lump-sum payment).
3. The coupon payment will be **equal to** interest expense.

We assumed in our discussion of bonds above, that the face value and the coupon rate are dependent upon a firm's cash requirements: cash proceeds and coupon payments. This assumption is correct for firms that issue *zero-coupon bonds*—bonds issued with a promise to make one lump-sum payment, and no periodic payments.

In general, the face value and coupon rate of a bond are fixed. The face value is usually a multiple of $1,000, and approximates the expected cash proceeds, and the coupon rate is in multiples of eighths of a percentage point, and approximates the market rate of interest. Since bond certificates are preprinted, and the market rate constantly changes, it is improbable that the coupon rate will ever equal the market rate at the time the bonds are issued.

When bonds are issued, the difference between the coupon rate and market rate causes discounts and premiums, and causes a difference between face value and cash proceeds. Cash proceeds are calculated as the present value of the face value and the coupon payments, discounted at the market rate of interest. The formula is the same as that shown on page 327.

$$\text{Proceeds} = \text{present value of the lump-sum } (L) + \\ \text{present value of the periodic payments}$$

The only difference now is that we solve for proceeds instead of for L.

Finally, if a bond is issued and the cash proceeds do not meet the firm's needs, the firm can either reprint the certificates with a new coupon rate, or issue a different amount of certificates: more for discounts, less for premiums.

RETIREMENT OF BONDS BEFORE MATURITY

When bonds are retired before *maturity*, a gain is recognized for financial reporting purposes if the book value of the bond [face value minus (plus) unamortized discount (premium)] exceeds the cash paid to retire the bonds, while a loss is recognized if the book value of the bonds is less than the cash paid to retire them.

The book value of bonds is a function of the prevailing interest rate at the time of issue, while the amount to be repaid is a function of the prevailing interest rate at the time of retirement. Therefore, when bonds are retired after interest rates have increased, then a gain will be recognized, and if the interest rate decreases, a loss will be recognized.

Thought Questions
When interest rates increase and bonds are retired,
we recognize a gain. Why?
If interest rates increase and bonds are not retired,
can we recognize a gain?

Consider the following example: A firm issued $85,000 of 5-year, 10 percent annual coupon bonds when the market rate was 10 percent. They recorded the issue of bonds as

Issue of Bonds
Dr. Cash	85,000	
Cr. Bonds Payable		85,000

Two years later, when the market rate of interest increased to 15 percent, the firm retired its bonds by paying $75,296, and recorded the retirement as follows:

Retirement of Bonds (before maturity)
Dr. Bonds Payable	85,000	
Cr. Cash		75,296
Cr. Gain on Retirement of Bonds (I/S)		9,704

Had the interest rate decreased from 10 to 8 percent, then the firm would have recorded a loss on retirement of the bonds as follows:

Retirement of Bonds (before maturity)
Dr. Loss on Retirement of Bonds (I/S)	4,381	
Dr. Bonds Payable	85,000	
Cr. Cash		89,381

CONVERSION OF BONDS INTO SHARES OF COMMON STOCK

Many companies issue convertible bonds. The bondholders may exchange their bonds into a specified number of shares of common stock, usually for a limited period of time. Upon conversion, the net accounting quantification of the debt is eliminated, and the Contributed Capital accounts are increased by an equal amount. For example, a convertible bond, with a face value of $1,000 and an unamortized discount of $40, is converted into 60 shares of common stock. The journal entry to record this conversion would be

Conversion of a Bond into Shares of Common Stock
Dr. Bonds Payable	1,000	
Cr. Unamortized Bond Discount		40
Cr. Common Stock		960

Thought Questions

At what minimum market value of the stock
will the bondholder convert?
Would you be willing to pay more for convertible bonds
than for nonconvertible bonds? Why?

FINANCIAL STATEMENT PRESENTATION OF BONDS

The issue, repayment, and retirement of bonds are reported as financing events in the statement of cash flows. The PAYMENT OF INTEREST is reported as an operating event in the statement of cash flows either directly, or indirectly by adjusting net income as follows: NET INCOME, plus AMORTIZATION OF DISCOUNT, minus AMORTIZATION OF PREMIUM, plus (minus) the increase (decrease) in the Interest Payable account. The effect on the balance sheet accounts is to report the portion of bonds that will be repaid within the next period as Current Portion of Debt, and the remaining book value of bonds [face value minus (plus) unamortized discount (premium)] as Net Bonds Payable. As in the case with long-term debt, firms, like General Foods, present a schedule of bonds in the footnotes to their financial statement as illustrated in Example 1.

EXAMPLE 1

General Foods Corporation
5. Long-Term Debt

(In thousands)	1984	1983
13.8% Notes, due in four annual payments beginning March 1988	$150,000	$150,000
14¾% Notes, $150,000 due March 1989 net of unamortized discount (14½% effective rate)	149,331	149,256
7½% Notes, due March 1984	—	100,000
10½% Debentures, $100,000 due January 1995, net of unamortized discount (10.6% effective rate)	99,550	99,509
7% Debentures, $200,000 due June 2011 net of unamortized discount (13.8% effective rate)	104,073	103,743
6% Debentures, $150,000 due June 2001 net of unamortized discount (13.75% effective rate)	74,027	72,969
11⅝% Debentures, due May 2010 with minimum annual sinking fund payments of $2,500 beginning 1991	50,000	50,000
8⅞% Debentures, due July 1990 with minimum annual sinking fund payments of $4,500	17,393	23,143
7.85% Debentures, $19,433 due January 1996, net of unamortized discount with minimum annual sinking fund payments of $2,000	18,184	18,421
Other international debt	46,018	63,240
Other domestic debt	70,332	21,816
	778,908	852,097
Less current portion of long-term debt	28,939	115,666
Long-term debt	$749,969	$736,431

Minimum annual payments on long-term debt for the four fiscal years beginning fiscal 1986 through fiscal 1989 are: $55.1 million; $14.3 million; $44.7 million; and $198.4 million, respectively.

USER'S PERSPECTIVE

Consider the elements of the following income statement for a firm that issued $500,000 of 10 percent annual coupon bonds, at par, at the beginning of the year:

Income Statement 19X1		
Revenues		
Sales Revenue		$900,000
Total Revenues		$900,000
Expenses		
Cost of Goods Sold	$300,000	
Operating Expense	150,000	
Interest Expense	50,000	
Tax Expense	160,000	
Total Expenses	$660,000	(660,000)
Net Income		$240,000

At any level of sales, INTEREST EXPENSE will remain fixed at $50,000. But COST OF GOODS SOLD and most OPERATING EXPENSES will vary directly with the level of SALES REVENUE, an operating event, while INCOME TAX EXPENSE, which is a hybrid effected by both operating and financing events, will vary directly with INCOME BEFORE TAX. As a result, any variation in SALES REVENUES will result in proportional changes to COST OF GOODS SOLD and OPERATING EXPENSES, and a disproportional change to INCOME TAX EXPENSE and NET INCOME.

Consider what would happen if SALES REVENUE, and COST OF GOODS SOLD, and OPERATING EXPENSES, and as a result, INCOME BEFORE INTEREST AND TAX, increased or decreased by 40 percent. We see that a 40 percent increase in INCOME BEFORE INTEREST AND TAX increases NET INCOME from $240,000 to $348,000, a 45 percent increase, and that a 40 percent decrease in INCOME BEFORE INTEREST AND TAX would decrease NET INCOME from $240,000 to $132,000, a 45 percent decrease.

The volatility created by fixed amounts, such as INTEREST EXPENSE, is called leverage. Leverage results from the interaction of elements that vary in response to a stimulus with other elements that do not vary. The degree of volatility is determined by the relationship of the fixed and variable elements. Earnings that are more volatile are considered riskier because the volatility increases the likelihood of a large decrease in earnings, and increases the probability that the firm will be unable to meet its obligations, and possibly face bankruptcy. When debt is incurred, two costs result: INTEREST EXPENSE and increased risk. INTEREST EXPENSE reduces net income and is readily determinable from the income statement. The increased volatility, and the resulting increased riskiness of earnings, is not as readily determinable. However, it must be considered by users of financial statements because of their concern not only with the amount and timing of cash flows, but also with the riskiness of those cash flows.

A ratio often used to assess the extent of financial leverage is called the *debt-equity ratio*. The debt-equity ratio is determined by

$$\frac{\text{Long-term debt}}{\text{Owners' equities}}$$

where long-term debt includes, but is not limited to BORROWING FROM THE BANK and the ISSUE OF BONDS.

Everything else being equal, the greater the debt-equity ratio, the greater the financial leverage and the riskier the earnings are. However, the *debt-equity ratio* is a comparison of two balance sheet amounts; it does not directly reflect the increased volatility resulting from debt. There is no consensus as to whether there is an optimal debt-equity ratio, but those who think there is an optimal debt-equity ratio differ as to what it should be.

Another ratio often used to weigh the impact of financial leverage is called *times interest earned*. The times interest earned ratio is equal to INCOME BEFORE INTEREST AND TAX divided by INTEREST EXPENSE. The purpose of this ratio is to determine how much income is available for INTEREST EXPENSE.

Only cash, not income, can be used to meet interest obligations. Since cash flow and income are generally quite different from each other, the *times interest earned ratio* may not be well suited for its purpose. Thus, while this ratio measures the risk of bankruptcy to some degree, it does not measure the volatility of earnings.

Volatility, as measured by the *volatility index*, is

$$\frac{\text{Net income plus after-tax fixed costs}}{\text{Net income}}$$

By comparing NET INCOME PLUS AFTER-TAX FIXED COSTS with NET INCOME, we measure the volatility of net income as a result of changes in sales. Some expenses vary directly with the level of sales (*variable costs*), some remain constant (*fixed costs*), and others are both variable and fixed (hybrid). Sales minus related variable costs is equal to net income plus after-tax fixed costs. Refer to the income statement on page 340. NET INCOME ($240,000) PLUS AFTER-TAX FIXED COSTS ($30,000) divided by NET INCOME equals 1.125. This means that NET INCOME will increase 1.125 times the rate that SALES REVENUES increase. For example, if SALES REVENUES increase by 100 percent, NET INCOME will increase by 112.5 percent.

In other terms, if SALES REVENUES increased from $900,000 to $1,800,000 (COST OF GOODS SOLD would increase from $300,000 to $600,000; OPERATING EXPENSES from $150,000 to $300,000; and INCOME TAX EXPENSE from $160,000 to $340,000), then NET INCOME will increase from $240,000 to $510,000, an increase of 112.5 percent.

The *volatility index* can be applied to cash flows in the same manner. The volatility ratio for cash flows would be

$$\frac{\text{Cash flows from operations plus after-tax fixed costs}}{\text{Cash flows from operations}}$$

You can readily see that fixed costs affect risk and volatility. The greater the fixed cost, the riskier the income and cash flows and the greater the volatility index. That is, the greater the fixed costs, the greater the risk of bankruptcy, and the more NET INCOME and CASH FLOWS FROM OPERATIONS will change as a result of changes in sales.

Similarly, the less the fixed cost, the less risky the cash flows and the less NET INCOME and CASH FLOWS FROM OPERATIONS will change as a result of changes in sales.

PROBLEMS

1. The market price of a bond is the
   a. Present value of its maturity amount plus the present value of all future interest payments
   b. Maturity amount plus the present value of all future interest payments
   c. Maturity amount plus all future interest payments.
   d. Present value of its maturity amount only

2. On April 1, 19X1, Phela Corporation issued 200 of its 10 percent, $1,000 bonds at a 2 percent discount. The bonds were dated January 1, 19X1, and mature in 10 years. Interest is payable semiannually on January 1 and July 1. From the bond issuance, Phela would realize net cash receipts of
   a. $191,000
   b. $196,000
   c. $198,500
   d. $201,000

3. The issuer of a 10-year term bond sold at par 3 years ago with interest payable May 1 and November 1 each year, should report on its December 31 balance sheet a(an)
   a. Liability for accrued interest
   b. Addition to Bonds Payable
   c. Increase to deferred charges
   d. Contingent liability

4. How would the amortization of discount on Bonds Payable affect each of the following?

Accounting Quantification	Net Income
a. Increase	Decrease
b. Increase	Increase
c. Decrease	Decrease
d. Decrease	Increase

5. How would the amortization of premium on Bonds Payable affect each of the following?

Accounting Quantification	Net Income
a. Increase	Decrease
b. Increase	Increase
c. Decrease	Decrease
d. Decrease	Increase

6. For the issuer of a 10-year term bond, the amount of amortization would increase each year if the bond was sold at a

Discount	Premium
a. No	No
b. Yes	Yes
c. No	Yes
d. Yes	No

7. On January 1, 19X1, Handwerk Inc., issued for $939,000, 1,000 of its 9 percent, $1,000 bonds. The bonds were issued to yield 10 percent. The bonds are dated January 1, 19X1, and mature in 10 years. Interest is payable annually on December 31. In its December 31, 19X1, balance sheet, Handwerk should report unamortized bond discount of
   a. $57,100
   b. $54,900
   c. $51,610
   d. $51,000

8. On January 1, 19X1, when the market rate for bond interest was 14 percent, Frank Corporation issued bonds in the face amount of $500,000, with interest at 12 percent payable semiannually. The bonds mature in 10 years, and were issued at a discount of $53,180. How much of the discount should be amortized at July 1, 19X1?
   a. $1,277
   b. $2,659
   c. $3,191
   d. $3,723

9. (AICPA adapted) On January 1, 19X1, Debbs Corporation issued $1,000,000 in 5 year, 5 percent serial bonds to be repaid in the amount of $200,000 on January 1, 19X2, 19X3, 19X4, 19X5, and 19X6. Interest is payable at the end of each year. The bonds were sold to yield a rate of 6 percent. Information on present value and future amount factors is as follows:

	Present Value of an Ordinary Annuity of $1 for 5 years		Future Amount of an Ordinary Annuity of $1 for 5 years	
	5%	6%	5%	6%
	4.3295	4.2124	5.5256	5.6371

Number of Years	Present Value of $1		Future Amount of $1	
	5%	6%	5%	6%
1	.9524	.9434	1.0500	1.0600
2	.9070	.8900	1.1025	1.1236
3	.8638	.8396	1.1576	1.1910
4	.8227	.7921	1.2155	1.2625
5	.7835	.7473	1.2763	1.3382

Required:
   a. Prepare a schedule showing the computation of the total amount received from the issuance of the serial bonds.
   b. Assume the bonds were originally sold at a discount of $26,247. Prepare a schedule of amortization of the bond discount for the first 2 years after issuance.

10. The following T-accounts were taken from the ledger of the Disaster Company, a merchandising concern. Fill in the account titles for accounts 1 to 16. In addition, for each letter A to P (excluding "O"), describe the event and give the journal entry. An event having more than two effects is marked by an asterisk(*).

Income Accounts **Balance Sheet Accounts**

(1)		↑ (7) ↓		(12)	
(B)			(E)		(N)*

(2)		↓ (8) ↑		(13)	
(C)			(F)	(K)	(C)

(3)		(9)		(14)	
(D) (E) (F)		(A)	(J) (L)	(I)	(G)*

(4)		(10)		(15)	
	(G)*	*(G) (L) *(M)	(H) (I)	*(M)	(P)*

(5)		(11)		(16)	
*(P)		(J)	(B)		(M)*

Accounts Payable Merchandise		**Accumulated Depreciation**	
(6)			
*(N)		(H)	(K)	*(G)	(D)

Sales		**Interest Payable**		**Taxes Payable**	
	(A)		(P)*		(N)*

11. If the Current Portion of Bonds Payable decreased by more than Bonds Payable and all bonds had been issued at par, then the REPAYMENT OF BONDS (as reported in the statement of cash flows) was (larger than/equal to/less than) the cash received from the ISSUE OF BONDS (as reported in the statement of cash flows).

12. Refer to footnote 5 of The General Foods Annual Report on page 339.
    a. What entries did General Foods make during 1984 in connection with these bonds (assume periodic interest payments are due on December 31 each year)?
    b. What was the average market rate of interest when these bonds were issued?
    c. What entries will General Foods make in 1985 in connection with these bonds?

13. The Y Company has bonds outstanding as of December 31, 19X0 with face value of $1,000,000 and a coupon rate of 10 percent. The bonds mature in 10 years. If the market rate at the time these bonds were issued was 8 percent, and 9 percent on December 31, 19X0, then
    a. What is the balance in the Unamortized Bond Premium (or Discount) account as of December 31, 19X0?
    b. If the bonds were retired (repurchased) on December 31, 19X0, how much will be recognized as a gain (or loss)?

14. The X Company has bonds outstanding that mature at the end of the year 2001. As of December 31, 19X0, the Net Bonds Payable is $1,900,000. The COUPON PAYMENT is $190,000. The market rate of interest at the time the bonds were issued was 12 percent. The market rate of interest on December 31, 19X0 is 10 percent.
    a. What is the balance in the Unamortized Bond Premium (or Discount) account as of December 31, 19X0?
    b. If the bonds were retired (repurchased) on December 31, 19X0, how much will be recognized as a gain (or loss)?

15. Firm A borrowed $1,000,000 from a bank promising to make a lump-sum payment at the end of 10 years. Firm B mortgaged its plant and equipment, receiving $1,000,000, promising to repay its debt in 10 equal annual installments. Firm C issued $1,000,000 of 10-year annual coupon bonds at par.
    Assuming that the effective interest rate for the three companies was the same, and that the borrowings took place on January 1, and that the firms are identical in all other respects, compare their
    a. Current ratio
    b. Debt-equity ratio
    on January 2, of the first, ninth, and tenth years.

16. From the following information relating to the MEG Company, prepare

   a. A statement of balance sheet changes
   b. An income statement
   c. A statement of cash flows

   No events not described or derivable from the information below occurred.

   (1)   The balance in Deferred Tax Asset decreased by $2,000.
   (2)   The balance in Dividends Payable increased by $15,000.
   (3)   Writeoffs were $10,000.
   (4)   Operating expenses exclusive of depreciation were $100,000.
   (5)   The balance in Inventory decreased by $7,000.
   (6)   Collections of accounts receivable were $700,000.
   (7)   The balance in Retained Earnings increased by $50,000.
   (8)   Bonds, with face value of $100,000 and coupon rate of 10 percent, were issued for $120,000 at the beginning of the year.
   (9)   The balance in Estimated Uncollectibles increased by $3,000.
   (10) Net Income for the year was $160,000.
   (11) The balance in Prepaid Services decreased by $6,000.
   (12) The balance in Accounts Payable Merchandise increased by $8,000.
   (13) Taxes paid during the year were $80,000.
   (14) The balance in Unamortized Bond Premium increased by $19,000 during the year, and the balance in Unamortized Bond Discount decreased by $4,000.
   (15) Depreciation for the year was $50,000; no property, plant and equipment was bought or retired during the year.
   (16) The balance in Taxes Payable decreased by $12,000.
   (17) The balance in Interest Payable increased by $5,000.
   (18) The balance in Accounts Receivable increased by $20,000.
   (19) Operating cash flows before interest and taxes was $310,000.
   (20) The balance in Accounts Payable Services decreased by $11,000.
   (21) The balance in Deferred Tax Liability increased by $4,000.
   (22) A principal payment of $50,000 was made to bondholders when their bonds matured.
   (23) The balance in Current Portion of Bonds Payable increased by $10,000.

17.

The Parred Company
Comparative Balance Sheets
Years Ending December 31, 19X4 and 19X5

Assets	12/31/X4	12/31/X5
Cash	$120,000	$?
Accounts Receivable	140,000	185,000
Estimated Uncollectibles	(40,000)	(45,000)
Inventory	35,000	38,000
Property, Plant and Equipment	400,000	450,000
Accumulated Depreciation	(175,000)	(185,000)
Total Assets	$480,000	$?

Liabilities and Owners' Equities		
Accounts Payable Services	$ 7,000	$ 9,000
Accounts Payable Merchandise	8,000	10,000
Interest Payable	?	?
Bonds Payable	?	?
Unamortized Bond (Premium or Discount)	?	?
Common Stock	40,000	40,000
Retained Earnings	?	?
Total Liabilities and Owners' Equities	$480,000	$?

Notes:
(1) The Parred Company issued $100,000 of 20-year face value bonds on January 1, 19X1 when the market rate of interest was 12 percent. This was the company's only bond issue.
(2) The book value of property, plant and equipment disposed of was $7,000.
(3) The tax rate is 40 percent.

The Parred Company
Income Statement
19X5

Revenues

Sales Revenue		$600,000
Uncollectibility Adjustment		(10,000)
Net Sales Revenue		$590,000
Gain on Disposal of Property, Plant and Equipment		3,000
Total Revenues		$593,000

Expenses

Cost of Goods Sold	$200,000	
Operating Expenses	141,000	
Depreciation Expense	30,000	
Interest Expense	?	
Tax Expense	?	
Total Expenses	$?	(?)
Net Income		$?

Required:

Consider the possibility that the bonds were issued with a coupon rate of either 12 percent, 10 percent, or 15 percent. For each possibility

a. Prepare a statement of cash flows.
b. Fill in the question (?) marks in the balance sheet and income statement.

18.

The Inmar Company
Comparative Balance Sheets
Years Ending December 31, 19X0 and 19X1

Assets	12/31/X0	12/31/X1
Cash	$100,000	$?
Property, Plant and Equipment	500,000	800,000
Accumulated Depreciation	(200,000)	(298,000)
Total Assets	$400,000	$?

Liabilities and Owners' Equities		
Bonds Payable	$ 0	$?
Unamortized Bond (Premium or Discount)	0	?
Common Stock	100,000	100,000
Retained Earnings	300,000	?
Total Liabilities and Owners' Equities	$400,000	$?

Notes:
(1) The gross margin (sales minus cost of goods sold) is $360,000. Sales are 160 percent of cost of goods sold.
(2) The Inmar Company issued 12 percent semiannual coupon bonds on July 1, 19X1. Coupon payments of $24,000 are due each June 30 and December 31, to yield 10 percent semiannually.
(3) The tax rate is 40 percent.
(4) There were no changes in the current operating accounts.

The Inmar Company
Income Statement
19X1

Revenues

Net Sales Revenue		$?
Total Revenues		$?

Expenses

Cost of Goods Sold	$?	
Depreciation Expense	?	
Interest Expense	?	
Tax Expense	?	
Total Expenses	$?	(?)
Net Income		$114,000

Statement of Cash Flows

Cash Flows from Operating Events		$260,000
Cash Flows from Financing Events		
Payment of Dividend	$ (35,000)	
Issue of Bonds	440,000	
Total Financing Events	$405,000	405,000
Cash Flows from Investing Events		
Purchase of Property, Plant and Equipment	$(350,000)	
Total Investing Events	$(350,000)	(350,000)
Increase in Cash		$315,000

Required:
a. Determine all of the events that occurred during the year.
b. Fill in the question (?) marks.

19. What is the market rate of interest for a bond issue which sells for more than its par value?
   a. Less than rate stated on the bond
   b. Equal to rate stated on the bond
   c. Higher than rate stated on the bond
   d. Independent of rate stated on the bond

20. If the amount paid to holders of a company's bonds during a period was larger than the INTEREST EXPENSE reported during a period, and no new bonds were issued during the period, then either

   Account ———— must have increased/decreased
   or Account ———— must have increased/decreased
   or Account ———— must have increased/decreased
   or Account ———— must have increased/decreased.

21. From the T-accounts below, answer the following questions:
   a. Cash received from issuing the bonds was ————.
   b. Interest expense for the period was ————.
   c. Total payments to bondholders during the period were ————.

↓ Interest Payable ↑	↑ Unamortized Bond Discount ↓	↓ Unamortized Bond Premium ↑
10,000	35,000	58,000
200,000	40,000	60,000

↓ Bonds Payable ↑	↓ Current Portion of Bonds Payable ↑
990,000	160,000
	210,000

22. Calculate the *volatility index* from the following income statement:

Revenues		
Sales Revenue		$180,000
Total Revenues		$180,000
Expenses		
Cost of Goods Sold	$ 60,000	
Operating Expenses	20,000	
Depreciation Expense	20,000	
Interest Expense	30,000	
Tax Expense	20,000	
Total Expenses	$150,000	(150,000)
Net Income		$ 30,000

CHAPTER 14

Financing Events with Owners

INTRODUCTION

We have discussed how firms finance their growth and expansion by borrowing from suppliers (credit purchases), from banks (loans), and from investors (bonds). In all three examples, the sources of financing are unrelated parties. Alternatively, firms can finance their growth and expansion from related parties, the present and prospective equity investors known as owners.

The basic financing events between a firm and its owners consist of the receipt of cash from owners, and the subsequent payment of cash to owners. The accounting problems consist of how to describe the original cash contribution from owners and to determine whether the subsequent payments to owners reflect the return of amounts originally contributed, or represent a distribution of cash which has been generated by the operations of the firm.

CONTRIBUTIONS BY INVESTORS

All corporations issue shares of stock when owners contribute assets (usually cash) to them. These shares, represented by stock certificates, are evidence of ownership and of the rights and privileges associated with ownership. The rights and privileges of ownership, established by the corporate charter and applicable state law, will vary between types and classes of investors. In general, there are two types of investors: *common stockholders* and *preferred stockholders.* If the corporation deems it necessary, there also may be different classes of common stockholders and preferred stockholders.

All corporations issue common stock, and *common stockholders* are usually entitled to the following:

1. *The right to participate in management* by electing the board of directors and voting on other matters at shareholders' meetings.

2. *The right to participate in profits* by receiving dividends when declared by the board of directors; the amount of dividends re-

ceived is proportionate to the number of shares held by each owner.

3. Upon liquidation, *the right to a proportionate share of assets* remaining after all prior obligations are met.

4. *The preemptive right* to purchase a proportionate share of new stock issues, because without this right, the proportional ownership position would be decreased by the issuance of additional shares of stock.

Preferred stockholders invest in a security that combines certain features of both common stock and bonds. *Preferred stockholders* are usually entitled to the following rights:

1. *To receive a stated dividend* As described on the stock certificate, each preferred stockholder receives a stated dividend if such a dividend is voted by the board of directors. Failure to vote a dividend for preferred stockholders in a period prohibits the company from paying a dividend to common stockholders during the same period. If the preferred stock is noncumulative, the investor may never receive that period's dividend. When the preferred stock is cumulative, such dividends are accumulated and must be paid in full before common stockholders receive any dividends.

2. *To receive assets upon liquidation* Each holder of a preferred share receives an equal share of assets, up to a predetermined level, when a corporation is liquidated. Preferred stockholders are paid after creditors, but before common stockholders.

Certain kinds of **preferred stock** include additional features such as:

1. *Convertible* Many issues of preferred stock provide that the owner, at the owner's option, may convert each preferred share into a specific number of common shares.

2. *Redeemble* Many issues of preferred stock may be sold back to the corporation at a specified price whenever the investor chooses to do so.

3. *Callable* Preferred stock may be repurchased by the corporation at its option.

4. *Participatory* Shareholders may receive additional dividends once common and preferred shareholders have received their normal dividends.

The corporate charter authorizes the issue of a stated number of common and preferred shares. The amount of authorized shares to be issued (sold) to the public is determined by the board of directors. Most shares have a nominal *par value,* generally far less than fair market value and totally unrelated to it. For example, if 1,000 shares, par value $15 per share, are issued at par, the journal entry to record this event would be

Issue of Common Stock (1,000 shares for $15)
Dr. Cash	15,000	
Cr. Common Stock (par $15)		15,000

If the same shares were issued for $100 per share, the journal entry would be

Issue of Common Stock (1,000 shares for $100)
Dr. Cash	100,000	
Cr. Common Stock (par $15)		15,000
Cr. Additional Paid-in Capital		85,000

The effect in the Cash account is always for the amount of cash received; the effect in the Common Stock (at par) account is always for the par value of the issue (the product of the number of shares issued times the par value). The effect in the **Additional Paid-in Capital** account is for the excess of cash received over the par value of the issue (the difference between the fair market value and the par value, times the number of shares issued).

Sometimes stock is issued at a *stated value* rather than at a par value, but this difference will not affect the accounting for the issue. Finally, it is possible for a firm to issue *no par* shares. When the shares are no par, the debit (Dr.) would be to Cash for the cash received, the credit (Cr.) would be to Common Stock (no par) for the same amount, and the firm would not have an Additional Paid-in Capital account.

The issue of all types and classes of stock will be reported by the firm as a financing event in the statement of cash flows.

CONVERSIONS TO COMMON STOCK

Many companies issue convertible bonds and convertible preferred stock. The bondholders or preferred stockholders may convert their bonds into common stock, for a limited period of time, at a predetermined price. The conversion rate is chosen so that immediate conversion is unattractive. The interest rate on convertible bonds, and the dividend rate on the convertible preferred stock, is less than the interest rate on other debt securities. From the issuer's point of view, the conversion feature of bonds serves to reduce interest cost in exchange for offering the investor the opportunity to buy the stock at a price less than market price in the future. For the investor, the conversion feature provides the security of a fixed rate of return combined with the possibility of sharing in the company's future prosperity.

Upon conversion, the net accounting quantification of the debt is eliminated, and contributed capital is increased by an equal amount. The journal entry to record the conversion of a bond, with a face value of $1,000 and an unamortized discount of $20, to 60 shares of common stock, par value of $15 per share, is

Conversion of a Bond to Common Stock

Dr. Bonds Payable	1,000	
Cr. Unamortized Bond Discount		20
Cr. Common Stock (par $15)		900
Cr. Additional Paid-in Capital		80

The conversion of bonds for any type or any class of stock will be reported by the firm as **two** noncash significant financing events in the statement of cash flows' schedule of significant noncash financing and investing events.

DISTRIBUTIONS TO EQUITY INVESTORS

A company may at times consider it beneficial to decrease its assets and its stockholders' equities. This can be accomplished in two ways: by declaring and paying a cash dividend, or by repurchasing shares of stock. When a firm repurchases shares of stock, it can either retire the shares or hold them for future distribution.

> *Thought Question*
> Under what circumstances is such an action advisable?

A firm which has 1,000 shares of common stock outstanding wishes to distribute assets to its owners and not alter their proportional interests; it can do so by declaring a cash dividend of $10 per share. When the board of directors declares a cash dividend on the *declaration date,* it establishes two other dates: the *date of record* and the *payment date.* The board, in declaring the cash dividend, determines how much will be distributed, who will receive it, and when it will be paid. PAYMENT OF THE CASH DIVIDEND will be made on the payment date to those stockholders who still own their shares as of the date of record. The DECLARATION OF THE CASH DIVIDEND would be recorded as of the *declaration date*, with the following journal entry:

Declaration of Cash Dividend
    Dr. Retained Earnings   10,000
        Cr. Dividends Payable   10,000

The DECLARATION OF THE CASH DIVIDEND established a legally enforceable responsibility to distribute the $10,000 of cash to the equity investors. When cash dividends are declared, stockholders of record are entitled to receive the cash dividend even if they sell their shares before the *payment date*. However, for companies whose stock is traded on a stock exchange, shares trade *ex dividend* 3 days before the *date of record*. That is, an investor who buys shares after the ex dividend date will not receive the cash dividend. Accordingly, the market price per share declines approximately by the amount of the cash dividend per share while the shares trade *ex dividend*.

On the payment date, the cash dividend is distributed, and the following journal entry is made:

Payment of Dividend
    Dr. Dividends Payable   10,000
        Cr. Cash   10,000

The net result of declaring and paying a cash dividend of $10,000 is to reduce the net-assets and stockholders' equities of the firm by $10,000. If, prior to the dividend, the firm had net-assets of $100,000, each share of stock represented 1/1,000 interest in the $100,000 firm, or $100. After the dividend, the firm had net-assets of $90,000, so that each share of stock represented 1/1,000 of a $90,000 firm, or $90. In addition to the $90 per share interest in the firm, the stockholder has $10 of cash per share from the dividend. The payment of cash dividends is reported as a financing event in the statement of cash flows.

The other way for the firm to reduce its net-assets and stockholders' equities is to repurchase shares of its stock. Suppose the firm repurchases $10,000 of stock in the open market, and retains it for further distribution. If, before the repurchase, the firm had $100,000 in assets and 1,000 shares of stock issued and outstanding with a market value of $100 per share, the firm would have to repurchase 100 shares in the open market. There are two ways of accounting for the acquisition of these shares, commonly called *treasury shares,* depending on the applicable state laws: the *cost method* and the *par value method.*

Assume that 100 shares, with a par value of $15 per share, and originally issued for $100 per share, were repurchased for $70. To record this event using the cost method, the following journal entry would be made:

Repurchase of Common Stock (100 shares for $70)

Dr. Treasury Stock	7,000	
Cr. Cash		7,000

or, using the par value method, the following journal entry would be made:

Repurchase of Common Stock (100 shares for $70)

Dr. Additional Paid-in Capital	5,500	
Dr. Treasury Stock (par $15)	1,500	
Cr. Cash		7,000

Had the original issue price per share for the shares that were repurchased been $50 instead of $100, the journal entry to record the repurchase using the cost method would have been the same, but the journal entry using the par value method would have been

Repurchase of Common Stock (100 shares for $70)

Dr. Retained Earnings	2,000	
Dr. Additional Paid-in Capital	3,500	
Dr. Treasury Stock (par $15)	1,500	
Cr. Cash		7,000

The **Treasury Stock** account is a **contra-equity** account, not an asset account. Using the cost method, the Treasury Stock account is contra to Total Stockholders' Equities, reducing Total Stockholders' Equities. Using the par value method, the Treasury Stock account is contra to the Common Stock (at par) account, reducing the Common Stock (at par) account.

Like the DECLARATION OF THE DIVIDEND, the REPURCHASE OF TREASURY SHARES reduces the net-assets and stockholders' equities of the firm by $10,000. Continuing with our example, prior to the repurchase of the shares each share of stock represented a $100 interest in the firm. After the repurchase, each remaining share still represented a $100 interest in the firm because each share represented a greater interest ($\frac{1}{900}$) in a smaller firm ($100,000 minus $10,000).

Thought Question

If *treasury stock* is purchased,
each remaining share has a $100 interest in the firm.
If a dividend is paid,
each share has a $90 interest in the firm.
What accounts for the difference?

The subsequent REISSUE OF TREASURY SHARES would be accounted for differently depending upon the treatment used for the repurchase, cost or par value method. Suppose that a firm issued 1,000 shares of common stock, par value of $15 per share, for $100 per share. They repurchased 100 shares for $70, and are now reissuing them for $90 per share. The three events would require the following journal entries using the *cost method:*

Issue of Common Stock (1,000 shares for $100)
Dr. Cash	100,000	
Cr. Common Stock (par $15)		15,000
Cr. Additional Paid-in Capital		85,000

Repurchase of Common Stock (100 shares for $70)
Dr. Treasury Stock	7,000	
Cr. Cash		7,000

Reissue of Treasury Stock (100 shares for $90)
Dr. Cash	9,000	
Cr. Treasury Stock		7,000
Cr. Additional Paid-in Capital		2,000

Had the *par value method* been used, the firm would have recorded it as

Issue of Common Stock (1,000 shares for $100)
Dr. Cash	100,000	
Cr. Common Stock (par $15)		15,000
Cr. Additional Paid-in Capital		85,000

Repurchase of Common Stock (100 shares for $70)
Dr. Additional Paid-in Capital	5,500	
Dr. Treasury Stock (par $15)	1,500	
Cr. Cash		7,000

Reissue of Treasury Stock (100 shares for $90)
Dr. Cash	9,000	
Cr. Treasury Stock (par $15)		1,500
Cr. Additional Paid-in Capital		7,500

Had the reissue price been $50 rather than $90, the entries for the cost method and the par value method, respectively, would have been

Reissue of Treasury Stock (100 shares for $50)
Dr. Retained Earnings	2,000	
Dr. Cash	5,000	
Cr. Treasury Stock		7,000

Reissue of Treasury Stock (100 shares for $50)
Dr. Cash	5,000	
Cr. Treasury Stock (par $15)		1,500
Cr. Additional Paid-in Capital		3,500

The cost method treats the repurchase and subsequent reissue of *treasury shares* as related events, while the par value method treats the repurchase as a retirement of stock, and the subsequent reissue in the same way as any other stock issue.

Just as original issues of all types and classes of stock are reported as financing events in the statement of cash flows, so are any repurchases and subsequent reissues.

EMPLOYEE COMPENSATION PLANS

Many companies have stock option plans, designed to provide additional compensation to company executives and employees. Such plans are called compensatory stock option plans.

The option plan includes a measurement date, which is the date when the company will announce the number of shares to be granted and the price at which the option can be exercised. The amount of additional compensation to be recognized as an expense is the difference between the market price and the option price at the measurement date. This amount is allocated as an expense over the periods to which the additional compensation applies. For instance, a firm grants executives the option to purchase 3,000 shares of stock, $15 par value, for $40 per share, when the market price is $50 per share, and considers these options as additional compensation for a 5-year period. The journal entry to record this event would be

Deferred Compensation [3,000 shares × ($50 − $40)]

Dr. Deferred Compensation	30,000	
Cr. Stock Options		30,000

The Stock Options account is considered a stockholders' equity account. Each year, one-fifth of the deferred compensation is recorded as an expense by the following journal entry:

Compensation Expense (⅕ × $30,000)

Dr. Compensation Expense (I/S)	6,000	
Cr. Deferred Compensation		6,000

If and when the options are exercised, the following journal entry would be made:

Exercise of Stock Options (3,000 shares for $40)

Dr. Cash	120,000	
Dr. Stock Options	30,000	
Cr. Common Stock (par $15)		45,000
Cr. Additional Paid-in Capital		105,000

DESCRIPTIVE CHANGES TO STOCKHOLDERS' EQUITIES ACCOUNTS

Some entries are made to the stockholders' equity accounts but do not represent a significant change in stockholders' equities. The most common example of such an event is a *stock dividend* to existing equity investors. When a firm declares a stock dividend, it records the event by debiting (Dr.) Retained Earnings, and crediting (Cr.) the Contributed Capital account(s). Thus, this event has no impact on the net-assets of the firm.

Accounting rules require that the distribution of stock in an amount less than 25 percent of the outstanding shares be treated as a stock dividend, and should be quantified in terms of the market values of the shares issued. The market value of the shares issued as dividends increases the contributed capital accounts (Common Stock and Additional Paid-in Capital) and decreases Retained Earnings.

Returning to our previous example, assume that instead of declaring a cash dividend or repurchasing shares, the firm declared a 10 percent stock dividend. If the par value of each share was $15, the market value of each share $100, and there were 1,000 shares outstanding, the declaration of the dividend would result in the issuance of 100 shares, and would be recorded by the following journal entry:

Declaration of Stock Dividend (100 shares for $100)
    Dr. Retained Earnings   10,000
        Cr. Common Stock (par $15)   1,500
        Cr. Additional Paid-in Capital   8,500

A stock dividend increases the number of shares on the market without increasing stockholders' equity interests or the net-assets of the firm, and therefore does not alter the total market value of the firm. Since more shares are now outstanding, the price per share falls proportionately on the payment date, unless other events occur that influence the market price.

A *stock split* is a descriptive change to stockholders' equities, but is not an accounting event. A stock split is a distribution of new stock certificates to existing stockholders, representing an increase (or decrease) in the number of issued and outstanding shares and a proportionate decrease (or increase) in the *par value* (or *stated value*) of each share. Thus, a stock split is **not** an accounting event, and therefore no accounting entry is made.

Neither *stock dividends* nor *stock splits* are reported in either the statement of cash flows or the income statement. However, they will be reported in the accompanying notes to the statements.

FINANCIAL STATEMENT PRESENTATION
OF STOCKHOLDERS' EQUITY ACCOUNTS

The changes in the various stockholders' equity accounts are generally presented in a separate schedule as illustrated by the footnote to the 1987 financial statements of the Philip Morris Companies Inc., in Example 1.

EXAMPLE 1

Capital Stock
Philip Morris Companies, Inc.

Shares of authorized common stock are 1 billion; issued and outstanding were as follows:

	Issued	Treasury	Outstanding
Balance, January 1, 1985	126,371,774	(4,976,484)	121,395,290
Exercise of stock options and stock units	214,491	285,256	499,747
Purchased		(2,543,800)	(2,543,800)
Retirement of treasury stock	(7,234,528)	7,234,528	
Balance, December 31, 1985	119,351,737	(500)	119,351,237
Exercise of stock options and stock units prior to stock split-up	222,457	500	222,957
Two-for-one stock split-up	119,574,194		119,574,194
Exercise of stock options and stock units after stock split-up	470,560	168,741	639,301
Purchased		(1,930,150)	(1,930,150)
Balance, December 31, 1986	239,618,948	(1,761,409)	237,857,539
Exercise of stock options and stock units		768,946	768,946
Purchased		(2,000,000)	(2,000,000)
Balance, December 31, 1987	239,618,948	(2,992,463)	236,626,485

At December 31, 1987, 10,661,862 shares of common stock were reserved for stock options, stock units and other stock awards and 10,000,000 shares of Serial Preferred Stock, $1 par value, were authorized, none of which have been issued.

EARNINGS PER SHARE

Earnings per share is a required disclosure in financial statements. In the simplest case, the earnings per share calculation is equal to the earnings of the period available per share of common stock outstanding. This earnings per share calculation is made for firms that only have shares of common stock and preferred stock outstanding, and consists of net income minus dividends on preferred stock, divided by the weighted number of shares of common stock outstanding. For example, consider a firm that began the year on January 1 with 10,000 shares of common stock outstanding, and issued an additional 2,000 shares on July 1. If they reported $46,000 of net income, and declared a dividend to preferred stockholders of $2,000, then *earnings per share* would be $4.00, calculated as follows:

$$10,000 \times 12 = 120,000 \text{ share-months outstanding since January 1}$$
$$2,000 \times 6 = \underline{12,000} \text{ share-months outstanding since July 1}$$
$$132,000 \div 12 = 11,000 \text{ weighted number of}$$
$$\text{shares outstanding}$$

and ($46,000 − $2,000) ÷ 11,000 = $4.00.

For firms with complex capital structures, there are two other earnings per share calculations: primary earnings per share and fully-diluted earnings per share. A complex capital structure consists of financial instruments other than common and preferred stock such as stock options, stock warrants, convertible debt, and convertible preferred stock. These instruments give the holder the right to receive shares of common stock. The intricacies of primary and fully-diluted earnings per share are beyond the scope of this book, but the fundamentals of their calculations are presented next.

PRIMARY EARNINGS PER SHARE

Primary earnings per share represents the effects of the hypothetical exercise of all dilutive *common stock equivalents. Stock options* and *stock warrants* are always common stock equivalents if the market value of the common stock exceeds the exercise price. Convertible preferred stock and convertible debt are common stock equivalents if their *yield to maturity* (market rate) at the time of their issue was less than two-thirds of the yield on AA corporate bonds. The rationale behind this condition for convertible instruments is to determine if the value of the financial instrument is primarily the result of its conversion feature or of its yield.

Returning to our example, assume that the firm also issued $20,000 in convertible debt at an interest rate of 5 percent when the AA corporate bond rate was 9 percent, and that 50 shares of common stock would be exchanged for each $1,000 of debt. As a result of the conversion, earnings available would increase by $600. The $600 increase in net income represents the $1,000 reduction in INTEREST EXPENSE, and the $400 increase in TAX EXPENSE (assuming a tax rate of 40 percent). However, the weighted number of shares outstanding will increase to 12,000, such that primary earnings per share will be $3.72, calculated as follows:

$$10,000 \times 12 = 120,000 \text{ share-months outstanding since January 1}$$
$$2,000 \times 6 = 12,000 \text{ share-months outstanding since July 1}$$
$$1,000 \times 12 = \underline{12,000} \text{ share-months assumed issued on January 1}$$
as a result of the conversion
$$144,000 \div 12 = 12,000 \text{ weighted average shares}$$
outstanding

and ($46,000 − $2,000 + $600) ÷ 12,000 = $3.72 (rounded). Since the primary earnings per share is less than earnings per share, the convertible debt is dilutive.

However, if the AA corporate bond rate had been 7 percent rather than 9 percent at the time of issuing the convertible debt, then the security would not have been a common stock equivalent, and would not have been included in the calculation of primary earnings per share.

FULLY-DILUTED EARNINGS PER SHARE

Fully-diluted earnings per share represents the effects of the hypothetical exercise of **all** dilutive financial instruments. The fully-diluted earnings per share calculation is required to determine the maximum **dilution** (reduction) of earnings per share caused by any dilutive security or financial instrument. In addition to convertible securities, stock options, and stock warrants that are not *common stock equivalents*, **stock subscriptions, participating securities,** and different classes of common stock must be considered in calculating fully-diluted earnings per share.

Returning to our example once more, and assuming that the 5 percent convertible debt was issued when the AA corporate bond rate was 7 percent, the security would not have been a common stock equivalent and would not have been included in the primary earnings per share calculation. However, since the effect of including this security dilutes earnings per share it must be included in the fully-diluted earnings per share calculation.

However, if five shares are converted for every $1,000 in debt, instead of 50 shares, then the earnings per share assuming conversion would be $4.02. Thus, the effect of the conversion would have been to increase earnings per share from $4.00 to $4.02, and the convertible debt would not have been included in the earnings per share calculation because it would not have been a dilutive security.

REPORTING EARNINGS PER SHARE IN THE FINANCIAL STATEMENTS

Firms, like Philip Morris, that have issued only common stock and preferred stock are required to report only earnings per share as

EXAMPLE 2

Philip Morris Companies, Inc.
Consolidated Statements of Earnings
(in millions of dollars, except per share data)

	For the years ended December 31		
	1987	1986	1985
Operating revenues	$27,695	$25,409	$15,964
Cost of sales:			
Cost of products sold	11,264	11,039	6,318
Excise taxes on products sold	5,416	4,728	3,815
Gross profit	11,015	9,642	5,831
Marketing, administration and research costs	6,844	5,935	3,121
Amortization of goodwill	104	111	32
Equity in net earnings of unconsolidated subsidiaries and affiliates	126	111	82
Income from operating companies	4,193	3,707	2,760
Corporate expense	160	126	123
Interest and other debt expense, net	685	770	308
Earnings before income taxes	3,348	2,811	2,329
Provision for income taxes	1,506	1,333	1,074
Net earnings	$ 1,842	$ 1,478	$ 1,255
Earnings per share	$ 7.75	$ 6.20	$ 5.24

shown in Example 2. Firms, like Cooper Industries, with more complex capital structures are required to report primary and fully-diluted earnings per share if both primary earnings per share and fully-diluted earnings per share are at least 3 percent less than earnings per share (see Example 3).

If in our example above, the conversion was to 10 shares of common stock rather than five shares, primary earnings per share would have been $4.00, and fully-diluted earnings per share would have been $3.98, neither of which are 3 percent less than earnings per share. In that event, the firm reports only earnings per share.

USER'S PERSPECTIVE

We have discussed two different methods of financing: debt (loans and bonds) and equities. The returns that debtholders expect from their investments are appreciation and interest, and the returns that

EXAMPLE 3

Cooper Industries
Consolidated Results of Operations

(000 omitted except per share data)

	Year Ended December 31,		
	1985	1984	1983
Revenues	$3,067,169	$2,029,915	$1,850,280
Costs and Expenses			
Cost of sales	2,070,992	1,357,949	1,250,359
Depreciation and amortization	105,815	73,636	67,909
Selling and administrative expenses	534,471	368,376	363,101
Interest expense	97,723	20,572	28,460
	2,809,001	1,820,533	1,709,829
Income before income taxes	258,168	209,382	140,451
Income taxes	123,088	102,518	69,282
Net Income	$ 135,080	$ 106,864	$ 71,169
Net Income per Common Share			
Primary	$ 2.79	$ 2.13	$ 1.29
Fully diluted	2.77	2.12	1.28
Dividends per Common Share	1.52	1.52	1.52

equityholders expect from their investments are appreciation and dividends. Let us compare the differences, from the firm's perspective, between issuing debt and issuing common stock.

We saw in Chapter 13 the effects of leverage on net income. Now, let us explore the effects of issuing equity securities rather than debt by comparing a firm that issues $500,000 of common stock to the firm that issued $500,000 in bonds on page 340.

Income Statement
19X1

Revenues

Sales Revenue		$900,000
Total Revenues		$900,000

Expenses

Cost of Goods Sold	$300,000	
Operating Expense	150,000	
Tax Expense	180,000	
Total Expenses	$630,000	(630,000)
Net Income		$270,000

COST OF GOODS SOLD, INCOME TAX EXPENSE, and to a large degree OPERATING EXPENSES will vary directly with the level of SALES REVENUE, an operating event. As a result, any variation in SALES REVENUE will result in proportional changes to COST OF GOODS SOLD, INCOME TAX EXPENSE, and OPERATING EXPENSES.

For example, consider what would happen if SALES REVENUE increased or decreased by 40 percent. COST OF GOODS SOLD, OPERATING EXPENSES, and INCOME TAX EXPENSE would also increase or decrease by 40 percent. As a result, net income would also increase or decrease by 40 percent. We see that a 40 percent increase in SALES REVENUE increases NET INCOME from $270,000 to $378,000, also a 40 percent increase; and a 40 percent decrease in SALES REVENUE would decrease NET INCOME from $270,000 to $162,000, a 40 percent decrease.

Let's compare the results of issuing $500,000 of common stock (equity) with issuing $500,000 of bonds (debt), as shown on page 340. First, net income would be larger ($270,000) if stock is issued than if debt is issued ($240,000). Second, the net income is less volatile if stock is issued than if debt is issued. Thus, the firm enjoys three benefits from issuing stock: a greater amount of net income, less risky income, and less risk of bankruptcy. This represents the good news about issuing stock. The bad news is that although the pie available to stockholders is greater, the pie must be cut into more pieces. This effect is called *dilution*.

Thought Question
Why would a firm ever issue debt instead of common stock?

Suppose that before the issue of either the debt or the common stock, the firm had 50,000 shares of common stock outstanding. After the issue of $500,000 in debt, net income and earnings per share would be $240,000 and $4.80, respectively, and after the issue of 50,000 additional shares of common stock, net income and earnings per share would be $270,000 and $2.70, respectively. While the net income is greater if the firm issues stock rather than debt, earnings per share is significantly less, and therefore diluted. Although a lesser earnings per share results by issuing shares of stock, these lesser earnings are less volatile, hence less risky.

Another negative effect of issuing common stock is reflected on the *return on equity* (ROE) ratio. Return on equity is a measure of the efficiency of utilizing net-assets for the benefit of the stockholders. This ratio is calculated as follows:

$$\text{Net income} \div \text{average net-assets}$$

This ratio is materially affected by the choice of issuing debt or common stock. Referring to our example above, if $500,000 of additional stock is issued, ROE would be 27 percent ($270,000 ÷ $1,000,000). If $500,000 of debt had been issued instead, ROE would be 48 percent ($240,000 ÷ $500,000). Thus the return on equity is generally larger, but riskier, for firms that issue debt rather than common stock.

PROBLEMS

1. The Debrasi Corporation was organized on January 3, 19X1, with authorized capital of 50,000 shares of $10 par value common stock. During 19X1 Debrasi had the following transactions affecting stockholders' equity:

January 7	Issued 20,000 shares at $12 per share
December 2	Purchased 3,000 shares of treasury stock at $13 per share

The cost method was used to record the treasury stock transaction. Debrasi's net income for 19X1 is $150,000. What is the amount of stockholders' equity at December 31, 19X1?

a. $320,000
b. $351,000
c. $354,000
d. $360,000

2. The stockholders' equity section of Smaller Corporation as of December 31, 19X0, was as follows:

Common stock, $20 par value, authorized 150,000 shares, issued and outstanding 100,000 shares	$2,000,000
Capital in excess of par value	400,000
Retained earnings	200,000

On March 1, 19X1, Smaller reacquired 10,000 shares for $240,000. The following transactions occurred in 19X1 with respect to treasury stock acquired:

June 1	Sold 3,000 shares for $84,000
August 1	Sold 2,000 shares for $42,000
September 1	Retired remaining 5,000 shares

Smaller accounts for treasury stock on the cost method. As a result of these transactions
a. Stockholders' equity remained unchanged.
b. Common Stock decreased $100,000 and Retained Earnings decreased $14,000.
c. Common Stock decreased $100,000 and Capital in Excess of Par decreased $14,000.
d. Common Stock decreased $126,000.

3. When treasury stock accounted for by the cost method is subsequently sold for more than its purchase price, the excess of the cash proceeds over the carrying value of the treasury stock should be recognized as
a. Extraordinary gain
b. Income from continuing operations
c. Increase in Additional Paid-in Capital
d. Increase in Retained Earnings

4. As a result of acquiring $100,000 of treasury shares on December 31, 19X0, a company will report (more/less/the same) earnings per share and (more/less/the same) return on equity on 19X1 than if it had declared and paid a
a. Cash dividend of $100,000 on December 31, 19X0
b. Stock dividend of $100,000 on December 31, 19X0

5. For numerous reasons a corporation may reacquire shares of its own capital stock. When a company purchases treasury stock, it has two options as to how to account for the shares: (1) cost method, and (2) par value method.

Required:
Compare and contrast the cost method with the par value method for each of the following:
a. Purchase of shares at a price less than par value
b. Purchase of shares at a price greater than par value
c. Subsequent resale of treasury shares at a price less than purchase price, but more than par value

    d. Subsequent resale of treasury shares at a price greater than both purchase price and par value

    e. Effect on net income

6. On June 30, 19X1, Swintec Inc., declared and issued a 10 percent common stock dividend. Prior to this dividend, Swintec had 20,000 shares of $10 par value common stock issued and outstanding. The market price of Swintec's common stock on June 30, 19X1, was $24 per share. As a result of this stock dividend, by what amount should Swintec's total stockholders' equity increase (decrease)?

    a. $ 0

    b. $ 20,000

    c. $ 28,000

    d. $(48,000)

7. As a result of declaring a **stock dividend** rather than a **cash dividend**, earnings per share will be (more/less/the same) and return on equity will be (more/less/the same) if cash can be profitably invested.

8. How would the declaration and subsequent issuance of a 10 percent stock dividend by the issuer affect each of the following when the market value of the shares exceeds the par value of the stock?

Common Stock	Additional Paid-in Capital
a. No effect	No effect
b. No effect	Increase
c. Increase	No effect
d. Increase	Increase

9. How would the declaration of a 10 percent stock dividend by a corporation affect each of the following on its books?

Retained Earnings	Stockholders' Equity
a. Decrease	Decrease
b. Decrease	No effect
c. No effect	Decrease
d. No effect	No effect

10. In determining earnings per share, interest expense, net of applicable income taxes, on convertible debt which is both a common stock equivalent and dilutive should be

    a. Added back to net income for both primary earnings per share and fully-diluted earnings per share

    b. Added back to net income for primary earnings per share and ignored for fully-diluted earnings per share

    c. Deducted from net income for both primary earnings per share and fully-diluted earnings per share

    d. Deducted from net income for primary earnings per share, and ignored for fully-diluted earnings per share

11. On January 1, 19X1, Iches Inc., had 120,000 shares of common stock outstanding. A 10 percent stock dividend was issued on April 1, 19X1. Iches issued 40,000 shares of common stock for cash on July 1, 19X1. What is the number of shares that should be used in computing earnings per share for the year ended December 31, 19X1?
    a. 146,000
    b. 149,000
    c. 152,000
    d. 172,000

12. When computing primary earnings per share, common stock equivalents are
    a. Recognized only if they are dilutive
    b. Recognized only if they are antidilutive
    c. Recognized whether they are dilutive or antidilutive
    d. Ignored

13. The Sank Company had 300,000 shares of common stock issued and outstanding at December 31, 19X0. No common stock was issued during 19X1. On January 1, 19X1, Sank issued 200,000 shares of nonconvertible preferred stock. During 19X1 Sank declared and paid a $150,000 cash dividend on the common stock and $120,000 on the preferred stock. Net income for the year ended December 31, 19X1, was $660,000. What should be Sank's 19X1 earnings per common share?
    a. $1.30
    b. $1.70
    c. $1.80
    d. $2.20

14. At December 31, 19X1 and 19X0, the Marinas Corporation had 90,000 shares of common stock and 20,000 shares of convertible preferred stock outstanding, in addition to 9 percent convertible bonds payable in the face amount of $2,000,000. During 19X1, Marinas paid dividends of $2.50 per share on the preferred stock. The preferred stock is convertible into 20,000 shares of common stock, and is considered a common stock equivalent. The 9 percent convertible bonds are convertible into 30,000 shares of common stock, but are not considered common stock equivalents. Net income for 19X1 was $970,000. Assume an income tax rate of 40 percent.

    How much is the primary earnings per share for the year ended December 31, 19X1?
    a. $ 7.70
    b. $ 8.36
    c. $ 8.82
    d. $10.78

    How much is the fully-diluted earnings per share for the year ended December 31, 19X1?
    a. $7.70
    b. $8.21
    c. $9.35
    d. $10.22

15. On July 1, 19X1, the Bird Corporation split its common stock 4 for 1, when the market value was $80 per share. Prior to the split, Bird had 50,000 shares of $12 par value common stock issued and outstanding. After the split, the par value of the stock
   a. Remained the same
   b. Was reduced by $3 per share
   c. Was reduced to $3 per share
   d. Was reduced by $4 per share

16. Antidilutive common stock equivalents would generally be used in the calculation of

Primary Earnings per Share	Fully-diluted Earnings per Share
a. Yes	Yes
b. No	Yes
c. No	No
d. Yes	No

17. The stockholders' equity section of Paul Corporation's balance sheet at December 31, 19X0, was as follows:

Common stock ($10 par value, authorized 1,000,000 shares, issued and outstanding 900,000 shares)	$9,000,000
Additional paid-in capital	2,700,000
Retained earnings	1,300,000

On January 2, 19X1, Paul purchased and retired 100,000 shares of its stock for $1,800,000. Immediately after retirement of these 100,000 shares, the balances in the Additional Paid-in Capital and Retained Earnings accounts should be

	Additional Paid-in Capital	Retained Earnings
a.	$ 900,000	$1,300,000
b.	$1,400,000	$ 800,000
c.	$1,900,000	$1,300,000
d.	$2,400,000	$ 800,000

18. From the following information, fill in the blanks below.
   (1) Common stock was issued for $100,000 in cash and no common stock was repurchased.
   (2) The combined Common Stock and Additional Paid-in Capital accounts increased by $120,000.
   (3) Dividends of $250,000 were paid in cash.
   (4) The balance in Dividends Payable increased by $50,000.
   (5) The balance in Retained Earnings increased by $100,000.

a. Net income for the period was _____.
b. Dividends declared during the period were _____.

19. The excess of the issue price over the par value should be recorded as additional paid-in capital for

Common Stock	Preferred Stock
a. No	No
b. No	Yes
c. Yes	No
d. Yes	Yes

20. (*CPA adapted*) At December 31, 19X0, GRQ Inc., had 6,000,000 authorized shares of $10 par value common stock, of which 2,000,000 shares were issued and outstanding. The stockholders' equity accounts at December 31, 19X0, had the following balances:

Common stock	$20,000,000
Additional paid-in capital	7,500,000
Retained earnings	6,500,000

Transactions during 19X1 and other information relating to the stockholders' equity accounts were as follows:

(1) On January 5, 19X1, GRQ issued, at $54 per share, 100,000 shares of $50 par value, 9 percent cumulative convertible preferred stock. Each share of preferred stock is convertible, at the option of the holder, into two shares of common stock. GRQ had 600,000 authorized shares of preferred stock. The preferred stock has a liquidation value equal to its par value.

(2) On February 1, 19X1, GRQ reacquired 20,000 shares of its common stock for $16 per share. GRQ uses the cost method to account for treasury stock.

(3) On April 30, 19X1, GRQ sold 500,000 shares (previously unissued) of $10 par value common stock to the public at $17 per share.

(4) On June 18, 19X1, GRQ declared a cash dividend of $1 per share of common stock, payable on July 12, 19X1, to stockholders of record on July 1, 19X1.

(5) On November 10, 19X1, GRQ sold 10,000 shares of treasury stock for $21 per share.

(6) On December 14, 19X1, GRQ declared the yearly cash dividend on preferred stock, payable on January 14, 19X2, to stockholders of record on December 31, 19X1.

(7) Net income for 19X1 was $4,500,000.

Required:
a. Prepare a statement of retained earnings for the year ended December 31, 19X1.
b. Prepare the stockholders' equity section of GRQ's balance sheet at December 31, 19X1.
c. Compute the book value per share of common stock at December 31, 19X1.

21.

Common Stock
and Additional

↓ Paid-in Capital ↑		↑ Treasury Stock ↓
	?	200,000
0	?	70,000	

↓ Dividends Payable ↑		↓ Retained Earnings ↑
	10,000	100,000
40,000	?	?	?

Required:
From the T-accounts above, determine all the information you can
which would be reported in the financing section of the statement of
cash flows if proceeds from the issuance of treasury shares was
$280,000, and net income for the period was $200,000.

22.

↓ Dividends Payable ↑		↓ Retained Earnings ↑
=	50,000	

Required:
From the T-accounts above, determine
a. The minimum dividends that were paid
b. The minimum that net income could have been

23. From the following information relating to the GEM Company, prepare

a. A statement of balance sheet changes

b. An income statement

c. A statement of cash flows

No events not described or derivable from the information below occurred.

(1) Common stock was issued by the company for $50,000.

(2) The balance in Dividends Payable decreased by $9,000.

(3) The uncollectibility adjustment was $15,000.

(4) Purchases of inventory were $300,000.

(5) The balance in Inventory increased by $15,000.

(6) Collections from customers were $670,000.

(7) The balance in Retained Earnings increased by $45,000.

(8) Bonds, with face value of $100,000 and coupon rate of 10 percent, were issued for $120,000 at the beginning of the year.

(9) The balance in Estimated Uncollectibles increased by $5,000.

(10) Net income for the year was $135,000.

(11) The balance in Prepaid Services did not change.

(12) The balance in Accounts Payable Merchandise increased by $7,000.

(13) Interest paid during the year was $16,000.

(14) The balance in Unamortized Bond Premium increased by $18,000 during the year.

(15) Depreciation for the year was $40,000; no property, plant and equipment was bought or retired during the year.

(16) The balance in Taxes Payable decreased by $6,000.

(17) The balance in Interest Payable increased by $13,000.

(18) The balance in Accounts Receivable decreased by $10,000.

(19) Operating cash flows before interest and taxes was $285,000.

(20) The balance in Accounts Payable Services increased by $8,000.

(21) The balance in Deferred Tax Liability increased by $1,000.

(22) Dividends paid during the year were $84,000.

24.

The Ivid Company
Comparative Post-Closing Trial Balance Sheets
Years Ending December 31, 19X0 and 19X1

Debit Balance Accounts	12/31/X0	12/31/X1
Cash	$110,000	$130,000
Accounts Receivable	100,000	150,000
Prepaid Services	13,000	11,000
Inventory	90,000	120,000
Property, Plant and Equipment	200,000	342,000
Total Debit Balance Accounts	513,000	$753,000

Credit Balance Accounts		
Estimated Uncollectibles	$ 10,000	$ 15,000
Accumulated Depreciation	30,000	40,000
Accounts Payable Merchandise	20,000	38,000
Accounts Payable Services	40,000	21,000
Taxes Payable	28,000	60,000
Dividends Payable	25,000	45,000
Deferred Tax Liability	15,000	16,000
Bonds Payable	50,000	80,000
Unamortized Bond Premium	5,000	9,000
Common Stock	100,000	150,000
Retained Earnings	190,000	279,000
Total Credit Balance Accounts	$513,000	$753,000

Notes
(1) Writeoffs of accounts receivable were $10,000.
(2) Collections from credit customers were $500,000.
(3) Taxes paid during the year were $50,000.
(4) Cost of goods sold plus payments to suppliers of merchandise
    equaled $500,000.

The Ivid Company
Income Statement
19X1

Revenues

Sales Revenue		$?
Uncollectibility Adjustment		(?)
Net Sales Revenue		$?
Total Revenues		$?

Expenses

Cost of Goods Sold	$?		
Operating Expenses	65,000		
Interest Expense	5,000		
Loss on Disposal of Property, Plant and Equipment	3,000		
Tax Expense	?		
Total Expenses	$?	(?)	
Net Income		$?	

Statement of Cash Flows

Cash Flows from Operating Events		$?

Cash Flows from Financing Events

Issue of Common Stock	$ 40,000	
Issue of Bonds	35,000	
Payment of Dividends	(?)	
Total Financing Events	$?	?

Cash Flows from Investing Events

Purchase of Property, Plant and Equipment	$(162,000)	
Disposal of Property, Plant and Equipment	12,000	
Total Investing Events	$(150,000)	(150,000)
Increase in Cash		$ 20,000

Required:
Fill in the question (?) marks.

25.

The Labyrinth Company
Comparative Post-Closing Trial Balance Sheets
Years Ending December 31, 19X0 and 19X1

Debit Balance Accounts	12/31/X0	12/31/X1
Cash	$100,000	$?
Accounts Receivable	300,000	200,000
Inventory	150,000	100,000
Property, Plant and Equipment	?	350,000
Total Debit Balance Accounts	$?	$?
Credit Balance Accounts		
Estimated Uncollectibles	$ 11,000	$ 8,000
Accumulated Depreciation	50,000	35,000
Accounts Payable Services	75,000	85,000
Accounts Payable Merchandise	40,000	?
Taxes Payable	38,000	42,000
Dividends Payable	20,000	5,000
Deferred Tax Liability	?	60,000
Common Stock	?	200,000
Retained Earnings	259,000	?
Total Credit Balance Accounts	$?	$?

Notes

(1) Taxes paid were $92,000.
(2) Writeoffs were $13,000 during the year.
(3) The tax rate is 40 percent.

The Labyrinth Company
Income Statement
19X1

Revenues

Sales Revenue		$713,000
Uncollectibility Adjustment		(?)
Net Sales Revenue		$?
Total Revenues		$?

Expenses

Cost of Goods Sold	$310,000	
Operating Expenses	?	
Depreciation Expense	30,000	
Loss on Disposal of Property, Plant and Equipment	8,000	
Tax Expense	106,000	
Total Expenses	$?	(?)
Net Income		$?

Statement of Cash Flows

Cash Flows from Operating Events $407,000

Cash Flows from Financing Events

Issue of Common Stock	$ 50,000	
Payment of Dividends	(20,000)	
Total Financing Events	$ 30,000	30,000

Cash Flows from Investing Events

Purchase of Property, Plant and Equipment	$(300,000)	
Disposal of Property, Plant and Equipment	10,000	
Total Investing Events	$(290,000)	(290,000)
Increase in Cash		$147,000

Required:
a. Determine all the events that occurred during the year.
b. Fill in the question (?) marks.

Investing Events

Part Four of this book deals with the investing events of a firm. A firm can invest in long-lived assets that it intends to utilize in its operations, or invest in the securities of other firms.

An investing event requires the outlay of cash, with the expectation of generating more cash from the investment. We will discuss the investment in long-lived assets to be utilized in a firm's operations, such as the acquisition and disposition of owned and leased assets, and the acquisition and sale of securities of other firms, and their related returns (dividends and earnings).

In Chapter 15, we will discuss how owned and leased assets differentially affect cash flows, financial statements, and ratios, and in Chapter 16, we will look at the differences that result from owning securities of other firms, whether they are controlled or influenced by the investor or not.

Accounting for Investments in Long-Lived Assets

INTRODUCTION

Investment assets are long-lived assets utilized in operations and other nonoperating assets. Long-lived assets utilized in operations include property, plant and equipment, patents, trademarks, and franchises. Nonoperating assets held for sale are investments in securities of other firms, and loans to other firms.

In this chapter, we will discuss the accounting for the acquisition and disposition of long-lived assets utilized in operations. Most assets of this kind are either depreciable or amortizable since the duration of their useful life is limited. Buildings, machinery, furniture and fixtures, office equipment, and trucks are examples of depreciable assets. Patents, trademarks, and franchises are examples of amortizable assets. (The utilization of these assets was the topic of Chapter 10.) Land has an unlimited duration, hence it is **not** subject to depreciation. (Natural resources qualify as limited duration noncurrent assets.)

ELEMENTS OF ACQUISITION COST: MONETARY TRANSACTIONS

Fixed assets may be purchased, constructed, or leased, but no matter how the right to utilize the asset is acquired, the firm pays for the right to utilize the asset in future periods. The cost of the asset includes all reasonable and necessary expenditures to acquire the physical object and prepare it for use. The cost of an operational asset, such as a machine, includes:

1. The net invoice price plus sales tax
2. Transportation and insurance while in transit
3. Installation, handling charges, and break-in costs

The firm is not interested in the machine as such, but in the services provided by that machine. Since a machine cannot be utilized if it has not been delivered or installed, acquisition cost must include costs of transportation and installation. Additional expenditures due to careless installation or tardy payment (causing the firm to lose available discounts) are charged to income of the period, and are not considered part of the asset cost.

> ### Thought Question
> Why would costs of tardy payments
> not be considered part of the asset costs?

Acquisition cost of land includes all incidental costs paid by the purchaser including sales commissions and broker's fees, legal fees, title search and insurance, delinquent taxes, surveying fees, and costs of permanent improvements such as draining, filling, grading, and landscaping.

The cost of a building constructed by a firm for its own use includes all incremental expenditures directly related to the building, such as:

1. Direct materials and direct labor

2. Related costs for building permits, engineering studies, architects' fees, and insurance during construction

3. Interest on money borrowed to finance construction

A problem may arise when two or more assets are acquired for a single, lump-sum payment. (This is called a "basket purchase.") The cost is divided among the assets acquired in proportion to their fair market values at the time of acquisition.

For example, a firm buys a building and the surrounding tract of land for the bargain price of $80,000. Independent appraisers value the land separately at $40,000, and the building separately at $60,000. The total appraised value is $100,000, of which 40 percent is due to the land, and 60 percent to the building. We apply these same percentages to the cash paid, in order to calculate the cost of the individual assets:

	Cost
Land:	40% × $80,000 = $32,000
Building:	60% × $80,000 = $48,000

RETIREMENTS

When an item of property, plant or equipment is retired, the remaining capacity, quantified by its original cost minus accumulated depreciation, must be removed from the books. If cash proceeds exceed book value of the equipment (original cost minus accumulated depreciation), the difference is called a GAIN ON DISPOSAL. If cash proceeds are less than book value, the difference is called LOSS ON DISPOSAL. Such gains and losses are reported in the income statement, and the proceeds are reported in the statement of cash flows as an investing event.

For example, a building that originally cost $100,000 and had $70,000 of accumulated depreciation associated with it, is sold. If the proceeds upon sale were $30,000 (fair market value), the event would be recorded as follows:

Sale of Property, Plant and Equipment
Dr. Cash	30,000	
Dr. Accumulated Depreciation	70,000	
Cr. Property, Plant and Equipment		100,000

If, instead of receiving $30,000, the seller received $20,000 ($40,000), the event would have been recorded as follows:

Loss on Sale of Property, Plant and Equipment
Dr. Loss on Sale of Equipment (I/S)	10,000	
Dr. Cash	20,000	
Dr. Accumulated Depreciation	70,000	
Cr. Property, Plant and Equipment		100,000

Gain on Sale of Property, Plant and Equipment
Dr. Cash	40,000	
Dr. Accumulated Depreciation	70,000	
Cr. Property, Plant and Equipment		100,000
Cr. Gain on Sale of Equipment (I/S)		10,000

In other words, when the book value of an asset equals the proceeds (fair market value), there will be no gain or loss upon its sale. But if the proceeds are less (or more) than its book value, then it would be correct to say that the asset was insufficiently (or excessively) depreciated, and that the loss (or gain) represents a correction of prior years' depreciation charges.

Thought Question
If there are no proceeds, can there be a gain or a loss on disposal?

GROUP METHOD OF DEPRECIATION

The main difference between unit depreciation and group depreciation is in the treatment of the retirement of property, plant and equipment. Under the unit method of depreciation, if there is a difference between book value and fair market value of the equipment when the equipment is retired, the difference would be recorded as a gain or loss in the income statement.

Under the group method, gains and losses upon sale of equipment are not recognized. Instead of recognizing the difference between **book value** and the **proceeds** in the income statement as a gain or a loss, the difference between the **original cost** and the **proceeds** is debited to the Accumulated Depreciation account and no gain or loss is recognized.

Consider the previous example of the equipment that originally cost $100,000, with $70,000 of accumulated depreciation associated with it, that was sold for $20,000. Under the unit method of depreciation, the entry to record the sale would be

Loss on Sale of Property, Plant and Equipment

Dr. Loss on Sale of Equipment (I/S)	10,000	
Dr. Cash	20,000	
Dr. Accumulated Depreciation	70,000	
Cr. Property, Plant and Equipment		100,000

Under the group method of depreciation, the entry would be

Sale of Property, Plant and Equipment

Dr. Cash	20,000	
Dr. Accumulated Depreciation	80,000	
Cr. Property, Plant and Equipment		100,000

In general, then, when using the unit method, the excess (deficit) of book value over market value is treated as a loss (gain), and reported in the income statement. Thus, the loss (gain) can be thought of as a catch-up of depreciation.

Under the group method, the excess (deficit) of book value over market value decreases (increases) the balance in the Accumulated Depreciation account for the group of assets, thereby adjusting the future depreciation charges. This method accomplishes two things: By treating assets as a group, it smooths the variations in net income caused by recording the retirement of individual assets, and defers any recognition of gains and losses until the group is retired.

ELEMENTS OF ACQUISITION COST: NONMONETARY TRANSACTIONS

In nonmonetary exchanges of dissimilar assets, accounting and tax rules require the exchange to be treated as if the exchange was a sale of the asset surrendered, recognizing gains and losses if necessary, and a purchase of the asset received.

For example, suppose a firm received a tract of land in exchange for a used truck and a cash payment of $12,000. The truck, which originally cost $16,000 and had $10,000 of accumulated depreciation associated with it, had a fair market value of $5,000. The journal entries to record this exchange as if it were a sale and a purchase would be

Hypothetical Sale of Truck

Dr. Loss on Sale of Truck (I/S)	1,000	
Dr. Cash (as if sold at fair market value)	5,000	
Dr. Accumulated Depreciation	10,000	
Cr. Truck		16,000

Hypothetical Purchase of Land

Dr. Land	17,000	
Cr. Cash ($5,000 + $12,000)		17,000

Combining these two entries into one entry:

Exchange of Truck and Cash for Land

Dr. Land	17,000	
Dr. Loss on Exchange (I/S)	1,000	
Dr. Accumulated Depreciation	10,000	
Cr. Truck		16,000
Cr. Cash		12,000

However, in nonmonetary exchanges of similar assets, both the accounting and tax rules change. The accounting rules require that in the exchange of similar assets, the asset received should be quantified at the **lesser** of the book value (original cost minus accumulated depreciation) of the asset surrendered and the asset's fair market value at the time of the exchange, plus any cash paid. The tax rules, on the other hand, require that the asset received should be quantified at the book value of the asset surrendered plus any cash paid. Thus, for accounting purposes a loss, but not a gain can be recognized, and for tax purposes, neither a loss nor a gain can be recognized.

For example, suppose that a firm exchanges one truck and $12,000 for another truck. The truck surrendered, which originally cost $16,000 and had $10,000 of accumulated depreciation associated with it (book value of $6,000), had a fair market value of $8,000.

The journal entry to record this exchange would be

Exchange of Trucks

Dr. New Truck	18,000	
Dr. Accumulated Depreciation	10,000	
Cr. Old Truck		16,000
Cr. Cash		12,000

The new truck would have a book value and tax basis of $18,000. Had the fair market value of the asset surrendered been $5,000, then a loss would have been recognized for book purposes, and the exchange would have been recorded as follows:

Exchange of Trucks

Dr. New Truck	17,000	
Dr. Loss on Exchange of Old Truck (I/S)	1,000	
Dr. Accumulated Depreciation	10,000	
Cr. Old Truck		16,000
Cr. Cash		12,000

In this situation, a loss of $1,000 would have been reported for book purposes and the book value of the asset would be $17,000. For tax purposes, a loss would not be recorded, and the tax basis of the truck would be $18,000.

As a result of the differences in recording this event for book and tax purposes, the book value and tax basis of the truck differ. The book value of the asset is $17,000, but the tax basis is $18,000, the tax basis of the old truck ($6,000) plus the cash paid ($12,000). At the time of the exchange, TAXABLE INCOME would be greater than INCOME BEFORE TAX, and a Deferred Tax Asset may result (see Chapter 11).

FINANCIAL STATEMENT PRESENTATION OF PROPERTY, PLANT AND EQUIPMENT

The acquisition of property, plant and equipment for cash is reported in the statement of cash flows as an investing event, and in the schedule of significant noncash events as **both** an investing event and a financing event, if acquired with debt and/or equity securities. The sale or disposition of property, plant and equipment is reported in the statement of cash flows as an investing event. The cumulative effects of **all** acquisitions and dispositions appears in the balance sheet account, Property, Plant and Equipment, with details provided in the notes to the financial statements, as shown in Example 1.

EXAMPLE 1

General Foods Corporation
3. Land, Buildings, Equipment

(In Thousands)	1984	1983
Land	$ 65,174	$ 68,983
Buildings	792,172	776,618
Machinery and Equipment	1,585,939	1,468,748
Construction in Progress	96,875	69,290
	2,540,160	2,383,639
Less Accumulated Depreciation	925,540	837,916
	$1,614,620	$1,545,723

Estimated useful lives of the major classes of depreciable physical properties range from 20 to 50 years for buildings and 2 to 20 years for machinery and equipment.

LEASES

Every tangible asset is a source of services. The purchase of such an asset entitles the owner to make use of **all** the services available from that asset. However, a company can acquire the right to utilize an asset for a specified period of time, thereby using the services available from it, without purchasing the asset. Such an arrangement is called a *lease*.

A lease is an *executory contract* between the owner of the asset (lessor) and the user of the asset (lessee) conveying the right to use the asset from the lessor to the lessee for a stated period of time, and for a stated dollar amount. This contract is an exchange of promises. Therefore, it does not meet the criteria that we set out in Chapters 2 and 7 for recording accounting events, unless substantially all of the risks and rewards of ownership have been transferred to the lessee. In such cases, the leased asset has, in essence, been sold by the lessor and purchased by the lessee, and the lease is called a *capital lease*. All other leases are called *operating leases*.

RECORDING THE EFFECTS OF A LEASE: THE OPERATING LEASE

Consider a firm that has signed a lease (contract) for the use of a new computer for 4 years. The computer has an expected useful life of 6 years, and has a fair market value of $120,000. The lease requires four equal periodic payments of $26,815, each to be made at the end of the year.

The only events that will be recorded with respect to this lease are the annual utilization of the rented computer (LEASE EXPENSE), and the annual payment for the computer (LEASE PAYMENT). At the end of each year the entries would be

Lease Expense
    Dr. Operating Expenses (I/S)   26,815
        Cr. Current Lease Payable   26,815

Lease Payment
    Dr. Current Lease Payable   26,815
        Cr. Cash   26,815

RECORDING THE EFFECTS OF A LEASE WHEN THE RISKS AND REWARDS OF OWNERSHIP ARE TRANSFERRED

Consider the terms and conditions of the lease discussed above, except for one difference. Suppose that the expected useful life of the computer is 5 years instead of 6 years. Would the accountant record this lease any differently?

The FASB has released many statements addressing the issue of recording the effects of leases. In general, any lease satisfying at least one of the following criteria must be classified by the lessee as if they had acquired the asset and incurred the liability:

1. The lease transfers ownership of the property to the lessee by the end of the term of the lease.

2. The lease contains a bargain purchase option. This means that the lessee has the option to buy the property for a nominal price at some time in the future.

3. The lease term is 75 percent or more of the estimated economic life of the leased property.

4. At the beginning of the lease, the present value of the minimum lease payments is 90 percent or more of the leased asset's fair market value.

In other words, the firm would be required to record the effects of the signing of the lease in a manner similar to the acquisition of property, plant and equipment financed by issuing long-term debt. In order to record the effect of acquiring property, plant and equipment and the issue of long-term debt, the firm would make the following entry:

Acquisition of Property, Plant and Equipment
    Dr. Property, Plant and Equipment
        Cr. Long-Term Debt

Upon signing a lease whose conditions convey the risks and rewards to the lessee, which in substance is equivalent to purchasing the asset through the issue of long-term debt, the firm would record the signing of the lease as follows:

Inception of a *Capital Lease*
    Dr. Leasehold Asset
        Cr. Leasehold Liability

where the debit (Dr.) entry is to **Leasehold Asset** (instead of to Property, Plant and Equipment), and the credit (Cr.) entry is to **Leasehold Liability** (instead of to Long-Term Debt).

The journal entries associated with property, plant and equipment subsequent to its acquisition with long-term debt are

(1) Depreciation Expense
  Dr. Depreciation Expense (I/S)
   Cr. Accumulated Depreciation

(2) Reclassification of Debt
  Dr. Long-Term Debt
   Cr. Current Portion of Debt

(3) Interest Expense
  Dr. Interest Expense (I/S)
   Cr. Interest Payable

(4) Interest Payment
  Dr. Interest Payable
   Cr. Cash

(5) Debt Payment
  Dr. Current Portion of Debt
   Cr. Cash

Entries 4 and 5 above are usually combined into one entry as follows:

Periodic Payment
  Dr. Interest Payable
  Dr. Current Portion of Debt
   Cr. Cash

The analogous entries for a capital lease subsequent to its signing are

(1) Amortization of *Leasehold Asset*
  Dr. Amortization Expense (I/S)
   Cr. Leasehold Asset

(2) Reclassification of Debt
  Dr. *Leasehold Liability*
   Cr. Current Portion of Debt

(3) Interest Expense
  Dr. Interest Expense (I/S)
   Cr. Interest Payable

(4) Periodic Payment
  Dr. Interest Payable
  Dr. Current Portion of Debt
   Cr. Cash

In general, AMORTIZATION EXPENSE is included as part of OPERATING EXPENSES in the income statement, or as part of DEPRECIATION EXPENSE, if depreciation is reported separately in the income statement.

Referring to our example of the computer with an expected useful life of 5 years, four required annual payments made at the **end** of each year, and a market rate of interest of 10 percent, the firm would make the following entries at the inception of the lease:

Inception of Lease

Dr. Leasehold Asset	85,000	
Cr. Leasehold Liability		85,000

The $85,000 represents the present value of the four lease payments, each of $26,815, discounted at 10 percent. Of the first $26,815 payment, $8,500 represents interest on the leasehold liability (10% × $85,000). The remaining $18,315 represents the amount of principal that will be repaid in the current period (year). Since $18,315 is currently payable, that amount is reclassified from long-term to current portion of debt, and recorded by the following journal entry:

Reclassification of Leasehold Liability

Dr. Leasehold Liability	18,315	
Cr. Current Portion of Debt		18,315

The Current Portion of Debt is the amount of the principal that will be repaid in the current period (year).

The leasehold asset would be amortized over the life of the lease (4 years) using the straight-line method. Amortizing the leasehold asset is the same as depreciating property, plant and equipment. The annual AMORTIZATION EXPENSE relating to this asset would be $21,250 ($85,000 ÷ 4), and would be recorded by the following entry at the **end** of each year:

Amortization of Leasehold Asset

Dr. Operating Expenses (I/S)	21,250	
Cr. Leasehold Asset		21,250

In addition to the entries above, the firm would make the following entries at the **end** of each of the 4 years:

Year 1 Interest Expense

Dr. Interest Expense (I/S)	8,500	
Cr. Interest Payable		8,500

Periodic Payment

Dr. Interest Payable	8,500	
Dr. Current Portion of Debt	18,315	
Cr. Cash		26,815

Reclassification of Leasehold Liability
  Dr. Leasehold Liability   20,147
    Cr. Current Portion of Debt   20,147

Year 2 Interest Expense
  Dr. Interest Expense (I/S)   6,668
    Cr. Interest Payable   6,668

Periodic Payment
  Dr. Interest Payable   6,668
  Dr. Current Portion of Debt   20,147
    Cr. Cash   26,815

Reclassification of Leasehold Liability
  Dr. Leasehold Liability   22,161
    Cr. Current Portion of Debt   22,161

Year 3 Interest Expense
  Dr. Interest Expense (I/S)   4,654
    Cr. Interest Payable   4,654

Periodic Payment
  Dr. Interest Payable   4,654
  Dr. Current Portion of Debt   22,161
    Cr. Cash   26,815

Reclassification of Leasehold Liability
  Dr. Leasehold Liability   24,377
    Cr. Current Portion of Debt   24,377

Year 4 Interest Expense
  Dr. Interest Expense (I/S)   2,438
    Cr. Interest Payable   2,438

Periodic Payment
  Dr. Interest Payable   2,438
  Dr. Current Portion of Debt   24,377
    Cr. Cash   26,815

Table 1 shows in tabular form the results discussed above, the reduction (amortization) of the leasehold liability over the 4-year period.

COMPARING OPERATING AND CAPITAL LEASES

The differences in the accounting treatment for operating and capital leases are substantial, and produce material differences in financial statements. While the inception of a lease is not recorded for an operating lease, a capital lease is recorded as a significant noncash financing and investing event, increasing an asset (Leasehold Asset) and a liability (Leasehold Liability). For the duration of

TABLE 1

Amortization of a Leasehold Liability

Year	Beginning Balance (a)	Interest Expense (b)	Payment (c)	Amortization (d)	Ending Balance (e)
1	$85,000	$ 8,500	$ 26,815	$18,315	$66,685
2	66,685	6,668	26,815	20,147	46,538
3	46,538	4,654	26,815	22,161	24,377
4	24,377	2,438	26,815	24,377	0
Totals		$22,260	$107,260	$85,000	

(a) The present value of all of the remaining payments,
    as of the **beginning** of the year.
(b) Column a multiplied by the market rate (10 percent).
(c) The required periodic payment, $26,815.
(d) The amount of the debt repaid (column c − column b).
(e) The present value of all of the remaining payments,
    as of the **end** of the year (column a − column d).

the lease, for a capital lease the Leasehold Asset and Leasehold
Liability are amortized resulting in the recognition of AMORTIZATION
and INTEREST EXPENSE, while only the LEASE PAYMENTS are recognized as expenses for an operating lease. Though the LEASE PAYMENT
is the same for an operating lease and a capital lease, the payment
is reported differently in the statement of cash flows. For an operating lease, the LEASE PAYMENT is a CASH OUTFLOW FROM OPER-
ATIONS, but for a capital lease, only the INTEREST is a CASH OUTFLOW
FROM OPERATIONS, and the REPAYMENT OF PRINCIPAL is reported as
a financing event.

Let us consider our previous examples for operating and capital
leases. Assume that a firm leases an asset, agreeing to make four
equal annual payments, the present value of which is equal to
$85,000. Comparing the income effects of accounting for operating
and capital leases:

Year	Operating Lease Total Expense	Capital Lease Total Expense	Interest Expense	Amortization of Asset
1	$ 26,815	$ 29,750	$ 8,500	$21,250
2	26,815	27,918	6,668	21,250
3	26,815	25,904	4,654	21,250
4	26,815	23,688	2,438	21,250
Totals	$107,260	$107,260	$22,260	$85,000

it is clear that total expenses over the lease period will be equal for both methods, but net income for the capital lease firm would be less than that for the operating lease firm in the earlier years, and greater in the latter years.

Though the cash flows are identical because the LEASE PAYMENT in both cases is the same ($26,815), the OPERATING LEASE PAYMENT is a CASH OUTFLOW FROM OPERATIONS, while the interest and principal portions of the CAPITAL LEASE PAYMENT are OPERATING and FINANCING CASH OUTFLOWS, respectively.

	Operating Lease		Capital Lease		
Year	Payment	Operations	Payment	Operations	Financing
1	$ 26,815	$ 26,815	$ 26,815	$ 8,500	$18,315
2	26,815	26,815	26,815	6,668	20,147
3	26,815	26,815	26,815	4,654	22,161
4	26,815	26,815	26,815	2,438	24,377
Totals	$107,260	$107,260	$107,260	$22,260	$85,000

Therefore, though NET INCOME is less for the capital lease firm in the earlier years than the operating lease firm, CASH FLOWS FROM OPERATIONS is always greater since the total operating cash outflows for an operating lease will be $107,260, while only $22,260 for the capital lease.

FINANCIAL STATEMENT PRESENTATION OF LEASES

The financial statement presentation for operating and capital leases differ. Operating lease expenses are reported in the income statement as either OPERATING EXPENSES or RENT EXPENSE, and the payment is reported in the statement of cash flows as CASH FLOWS FROM OPERATIONS. A schedule of the amount and timing of future operating lease payments is provided in the footnotes as illustrated in footnote 11 relating to the 1987 financial statements of The New York Times Company in Example 2.

AMORTIZATION OF LEASEHOLD ASSETS is generally included as part of OPERATING EXPENSES (or DEPRECIATION EXPENSE), and the interest portion of the debt obligation is generally included as part of INTEREST EXPENSE in the income statement. The lease payment has two parts: interest and principal. The interest portion is reported in the statement of cash flows as part of CASH FLOWS FROM OPERATIONS, and the AMORTIZATION OF PRINCIPAL is reported in the statement of cash flows as a financing event. A schedule of the amount and timing of future capital lease payments is provided in

EXAMPLE 2

The New York Times Company
11. Lease Commitments

Capital Leases:

In connection with the Capital Investment Program (See Note 3), the
Company entered into a long-term lease for a building and site in
Edison, New Jersey. The lease provides the Company with certain
early cancellation rights, as well as renewal and purchase options.
For financial reporting purposes, the lease has been classified as a
capital lease; accordingly, an asset of approximately $57,000,000
(included in construction and equipment installations in progress)
has been recorded.

The following is a schedule of future minimum lease payments under
all capitalized leases together with the present value of the net
minimum lease payments as of December 31, 1987:

Year Ending December 31	Amount
	Dollars in thousands
1988	$ 7,395
1989	6,548
1990	6,434
1991	6,400
1992	6,400
Later years	91,202
Total minimum lease payments	124,379
Less: amount representing interest	67,651
Present value of net minimum lease payments including current maturities of $1,838,000	$ 56,728

Operating Leases:

Such lease commitments are primarily for office space and equipment.
Certain office space leases provide for adjustments relating to
changes in real estate taxes and other operating expenses.

Rental expense amounted to $18,845,000 in 1987, $20,311,000 in 1986
and $18,839,000 in 1985. The approximate minimum rental
commitments under noncancelable leases (exclusive of minimum
sublease rentals of $3,589,000) at December 31, 1987 were as
follows: 1988, $12,816,000; 1989, $10,233,000; 1990, $6,989,000;
1991, $4,425,000; 1992, $7,571,000 and $5,561,000 thereafter.

the footnotes as illustrated in footnote 11 relating to the financial
statements of The New York Times Company in Example 2.

Leasehold assets are usually included in the Property, Plant
and Equipment account, and the Leasehold Liability with Long-
Term Debt and Current Portion of Debt accounts in the balance
sheet. Details about capital leases are generally provided in the

notes to the financial statements which detail the timing for making capital lease payments.

USER'S PERSPECTIVE

There are two ratios that are used to assess the efficiency of a firm: *return on assets* (ROA) and *return on equity* (ROE). In Chapter 14, we discussed return on equity. In this chapter, we will discuss return on assets. ROA is a measure of the efficiency of utilizing individual assets, or a group of assets that constitute the whole firm. This ratio is calculated by

$$\frac{\text{Net income plus after-tax interest expense}}{\text{Average total book value of assets}}$$

The use of the book value of assets in the denominator of this ratio creates problems. Consider a firm that acquires an additional depreciable asset for $15,000, with an expected useful life of 5 years and a salvage value of $0, and as a result, increases its net income by $2,700 per year. If the firm depreciates this asset on a straight-line basis, then the annual depreciation expense and remaining book value at the end of each year would be

Year	Depreciation Expense	Remaining Book Value
0	$ 0	$15,000
1	3,000	12,000
2	3,000	9,000
3	3,000	6,000
4	3,000	3,000
5	3,000	0

The return on assets for this newly acquired asset is

Year	Return on Asset	Net Income	Average Asset		
1	20%	$2,700	$13,500 [($15,000 +	$12,000) ÷ 2]
2	26	2,700	10,500 [(12,000 +	9,000) ÷ 2]
3	36	2,700	7,500 [(9,000 +	6,000) ÷ 2]
4	60	2,700	4,500 [(6,000 +	3,000) ÷ 2]
5	180	2,700	1,500 [(3,000 +	0) ÷ 2]

These results suggest that the return on assets will increase as assets depreciate and their book value declines as long as the firm has a steady income stream, and thus the apparent efficiency of the asset increases over time.

Thought Question
Is the return on assets calculation, as presented,
a realistic measure?

This erroneous interpretation results because book value of an asset is a function of the original cost of the asset and its remaining useful life. A reduction in book value reflects a decrease in the remaining duration of the asset, but does not necessarily reflect a decrease in the efficient utilization of an asset for any given period. You can readily see that if the firm is able to employ its fully depreciated asset in the sixth year, then the return on its asset would be infinite.

We can extend our example of calculating returns for a single asset to the total assets of a firm. Because the remaining duration of the depreciable assets declines as the assets age, ROA will increase each period if the efficiency with which the assets are utilized does not decline. The real measure of efficiency per period should be in terms of capacity per period; measures of efficiency should not be influenced by the remaining duration of the asset.

The cash generated from that acquisition should be compared to the price of the asset acquired ($15,000). Thus, a better measure of operating efficiency would be

$$\frac{\text{Cash flows from operations}}{\text{Original cost of the asset}}$$

ROA is a ratio used to measure the efficiency of utilizing assets. ROE, on the other hand, is used to measure the efficiency with which net-assets are utilized for the benefit of stockholders. The difference between ROA and ROE is caused by utilizing debt instead of equity. ROE will be larger and more volatile than ROA whenever the return on assets is larger than the after-tax interest rate of debt.

Finally, the return on assets is significantly affected by the determination that a lease is either an operating lease or a capital lease. The return on assets for an operating lease is initially greater than that for a capital lease because total assets and LEASE EXPENSE will be less, and NET INCOME greater.

In addition, ROA will remain constant for the duration of the operating lease because total assets and net income remain the same, but for a capital lease, the rate of return will increase, because both the book value of the asset and the LEASE EXPENSE decrease over time, causing the numerator to increase and the denominator to decrease.

> *Thought Question*
>
> Should the return on assets differ for identical assets
> with different accounting quantifications?

Return on assets is not the only ratio affected by the difference between an operating lease and a capital lease. As a result of having recorded a Leasehold Liability for a capital lease, total debt—current and long-term—will increase. Therefore, the *debt-equity* ratio will be smaller for operating lease firms than for capital lease firms, and the *current ratio* (current assets ÷ current liabilities) for capital lease firms will be less than that for operating lease firms.

PROBLEMS

1. On June 1, 19X0, Bastine Company entered into a 10-year noncancelable lease with Garavan Inc., for a machine owned by Garavan. The machine had a fair value of $180,000 at inception of the lease. Ownership of the machine will be transferred to Bastine upon expiration of the lease. The present value of the ten $30,000 annual lease payments, based on Bastine's incremental borrowing rate of 12 percent, is $190,000. The lease agreement specifies that all executory costs are assumed by Bastine. How much should Bastine record as an asset and corresponding liability at the inception of the lease?
   a. $0
   b. $180,000
   c. $190,000
   d. $300,000

2. On January 3, 19X0, Roach Company signed a 10-year noncancelable lease for new equipment, requiring annual payments of $25,000 starting at the beginning of the first year, with title passing to Roach at the expiration of the lease. The equipment has a useful life of 15 years, with no salvage value. Roach uses straight-line depreciation for all of its fixed assets. Aggregate lease payments were determined to have a present value of $158,000, based on implicit interest of 12 percent. For 19X0 Roach should record depreciation expense of
   a. $10,533
   b. $15,800
   c. $15,960
   d. $18,960

3. The Breecher Co. traded its old computer for a new model. The following information is pertinent to this transaction:

Cost of old computer	$60,000
Accumulated depreciation—old computer	20,000
Fair value of old computer	30,000
List price of new model	80,000
Trade-in allowance for old computer	45,000

How much loss should Breecher immediately recognize on this trade-in?

a. $0
b. $5,000
c. $10,000
d. $15,000

4. At its inception, the lease term of lease D is 80 percent of the estimated remaining economic life of the leased property. However, the lease term falls within the last 40 percent of the total estimated economic life of the leased property. The lessee should record lease D as a(an)

a. Asset and a liability
b. Asset but **not** a liability
c. Neither an asset **nor** a liability
d. Expense

5. On December 31, 19X0, the Fern Company leased a machine from Tern Company for a 10-year period. Equal annual payments under the lease are $50,000 and are due on December 31 of each year. The first payment was made on December 31, 19X0, and the second payment was made on December 31, 19X1. The present value at December 31, 19X0, of the ten lease payments over the lease term discounted at 10 percent was $338,000. The lease is appropriately accounted for as a capital lease by Fern. In its December 31, 19X1, balance sheet Fern should report the capitalized lease liability at

a. $243,000
b. $259,200
c. $266,800
d. $400,000

6. The A. Rothchild Company leased a new machine from Booper Company on December 31, 19X0, under a lease with the following pertinent information:

Lease term	8 years
Annual rental payable at the beginning of each lease year	$50,000
Useful life of the machine	10 years
Present value of the eight lease payments at December 31, 19X0	$258,000
Machine reverts to Booper at lease expiration date	

The machine has a fair value of $280,000 at the inception of the lease. A. Rothchild uses the straight-line method of depreciation. For the year ended December 31, 19X1, how much depreciation (amortization) should A. Rothchild record for the capitalized leased machine?

a. $35,000
b. $32,350
c. $28,000
d. $25,800

7. On December 30, 19X1, The Maber Company traded in an old machine with a book value of $10,000 for a similar new machine having a list price of $32,000, and paid a cash difference of $19,000. Maber should record the new machine at

a. $32,000
b. $29,000
c. $22,000
d. $19,000

8. The lessee's net carrying value of an asset arising from the capitalization of a lease would be periodically reduced by the
   a. Total lease payment
   b. Portion of lease payment allocable to interest
   c. Portion of lease payment allocable to reduction of principal
   d. Amortization of the asset

9. On June 30, 19X1, a fire in the Mighty Company's plant caused a total loss to a production machine. The machine had a book value of $80,000 at December 31, 19X0, and was being depreciated at an annual rate of $10,000. The machine had a fair value of $110,000 at the date of the fire, and Mighty received insurance proceeds of $100,000 in October 19X1. The same month Mighty purchased a replacement machine for $130,000. Ignoring income taxes, what amount should Mighty report on its 19X1 income statement as involuntary conversion gain or loss?
   a. $0
   b. $10,000 loss
   c. $20,000 gain
   d. $25,000 gain

10. The Elk Company leased a new machine from Zone Company on July 1, 19X1, under a lease with the following pertinent information:

Lease term	10 years
Annual rental payable at the beginning of each lease year	$30,000
Useful life of the machine	12 years
Implicit interest rate	14%
Present value of an annuity of $1 in advance for 10 periods at 14 percent	5.95
Present value of $1 for 10 periods at 14 percent	0.27

Elk has the option to purchase the machine in 10 years by paying $40,000, which approximates the expected fair value of the machine on the option exercise date. The cost of the machine on Zone's accounting records is $150,000. On July 1, 19X1, Elk should record a capitalized leased asset of
   a. $150,000
   b. $178,500
   c. $189,300
   d. $190,000

11. A purchased patent has a remaining legal life of 15 years. It should be
   a. Expensed in the year of acquisition
   b. Amortized over 15 years regardless of its useful life
   c. Amortized over its useful life if less than 15 years
   d. Amortized over 40 years

12. On September 1, 19X1, Vicon Inc., exchanged 2,000 shares of its $25 par value common stock held in treasury for a parcel of land to be held

for a future plant site. The treasury shares were acquired by Vicon at a cost of $60 per share. Vicon's common stock had a fair market value of $80 per share on September 1, 19X1. Vicon received $9,000 from the sale of scrap when an existing building on the site was razed. The land should be carried at
a. $111,000
b. $120,000
c. $151,000
d. $160,000

13. Audpek Inc., purchased certain plant assets under a deferred payment contract on December 31, 19X1. The agreement was to pay $20,000 at the time of purchase and $20,000 at the end of each of the next 5 years. The plant assets should be valued at
a. The present value of a $20,000 ordinary annuity for 5 years
b. $120,000
c. $120,000 less imputed interest
d. $120,000 plus imputed interest

14. For a 6-year capital lease, the portion of the lease payment in the third year applicable to the reduction of the obligation should be
a. Less than in the second year
b. More than in the second year
c. The same as in the fourth year
d. More than in the fourth year

15. Heleva Inc., leased equipment under a capital lease for a period of 7 years, contracting to pay $100,000 rent in advance at the start of the lease term on December 31, 19X0, and $100,000 annually on December 31, of each of the next 6 years. The present value at December 31, 19X0, of the seven rent payments over the lease term discounted at 10 percent (the implicit interest rate) was $535,000. Heleva amortizes its liability under capital lease using the effective interest method. In its December 31, 19X1, balance sheet, Heleva should report a liability under capital lease of
a. $378,500
b. $391,500
c. $437,350
d. $500,000

16. The Emilena Company purchased a patent on January 1, 19X0, for $178,500. The patent was being amortized over its legal life of 15 years. During 19X3, Emilena determined that the economic benefits of the patent would not last longer than 10 years from the date of acquisition. What amount should be charged to patent amortization expense for the year ended December 31, 19X3?
a. $10,500
b. $17,850
c. $20,400
d. $35,700

17. On January 2, 19X1, Farrel Machine Shops, Inc., signed a 10-year noncancelable lease for a heavy-duty drill press, stipulating annual payments of $15,000 starting at the end of the first year, with title passing to Farrel at the expiration of the lease. Farrel treated this transaction as a capital lease. The drill press has an estimated useful

life of 15 years, with no salvage value. Farrel uses straight-line depreciation for all of its fixed assets. Aggregate lease payments were determined to have a present value of $92,170, based on implicit interest of 10 percent. For 19X1, Farrel should record

	Interest Expense	Depreciation Expense
a.	$ 0	$ 0
b.	$7,717	$6,145
c.	$9,217	$6,145
d.	$9,217	$9,217

18. On July 1, 19X1, the Myshelf Corporation entered into a 10-year noncancelable lease with Tow Inc., for a machine owned by Tow. The machine had a fair value of $200,000 at inception of the lease, and an estimated useful life of 13 years. Present value of the lease payments is $123,000. Myshelf is obligated to return the machine to Tow upon expiration of the lease. No bargain purchase option is provided. How much should Myshelf record as an asset and corresponding liability at the inception of the lease?
    a. $0
    b. $120,000
    c. $123,000
    d. $200,000

19. In a lease that is recorded as an operating lease by the lessee, the equal monthly rental payments should be
    a. Allocated between interest expense and depreciation expense
    b. Allocated between a reduction in the liability for leased assets and interest expense
    c. Recorded as a reduction in the liability for leased assets
    d. Recorded as rental expense

20. On January 1, 19X1, the Georgios Corporation signed a 10-year noncancelable lease for certain machinery. The terms of the lease called for Georgios to make annual payments of $30,000 for 10 years with title to pass to Georgios at the end of this period. The machinery has an estimated useful life of 15 years and no salvage value. Georgios uses the straight-line method of depreciation for all of its fixed assets. Georgios accordingly accounted for this lease transaction as an installment purchase of the machinery. The lease payments were determined to have a present value of $201,302 with an effective interest rate of 10 percent. With respect to this capitalized lease, Georgios should record for 19X1
    a. Lease expense of $30,000
    b. Interest expense of $16,580 and depreciation expense of $13,420
    c. Interest expense of $20,130 and depreciation expense of $13,420
    b. Interest expense of $13,420 and depreciation expense of $16,580

21. Refer to footnote 11 of The New York Times Company (page 396) relating to leases. Calculate
    a. The average rate of interest on their capital lease commitments
    b. What their total lease payments for 1988 will be

22. If depreciation expense minus gain on disposal of property, plant and equipment is **less** than purchases of property, plant and equipment **minus** the proceeds from the disposal of property, plant and equipment, then

    Account _____ must have increased/decreased
    or Account _____ must have increased/decreased.

23. Suppose that a footnote to a firm's financial statements disclosed the following:

Capital Lease Obligations

Payable in 19X1	$ 60,000,000
Payable in 19X2	23,000,000
Payable in 19X3	37,000,000
Subsequent Payments	30,000,000
Total	$150,000,000
Less Interest	(70,000,000)
Capital Lease Obligations	$ 80,000,000

---

and that the average interest rate on their lease obligations is 7.9 percent. From the information above, determine the current portion of lease obligations.

24. *Required:*
    If all of the information relating to a firm's lease obligations is represented by the T-accounts below, and if **all** lease-related expenses were $75,000, what was the lease payment made during the year?

Current Portion of ↓ Leasehold Liability ↑		↓ Leasehold Liability ↑		↑ Leasehold Asset ↓	
	4,000			40,000	
	30,000	30,000		0	

25. No lease prepayments were made. Interest expense associated with the leasehold liability was $30,000, and total lease payments were $300,000.

| Current Portion of | | | | | |
↓ Leasehold Liability ↑		↓ Leasehold Liability ↑		↑ Leasehold Asset ↓	
	10,000		470,000	500,000	
				600,000	

Required:
a. What was the total lease-related expense?
b. What impact did the leases have on operating cash flows? Financing cash flows? Investing cash flows?
c. Can you determine if the company had leases other than capital leases? Why? Why not?

26. From the following information relating to the Fabriz Company, prepare
a. A statement of balance sheet changes
b. An income statement
c. A statement of cash flows
No events not described or derivable from the information below occurred.
   (1) Sales revenue was $230,000.
   (2) The balance in Dividends Payable increased by $1,000.
   (3) Tax expense was $33,000.
   (4) Property, plant and equipment was acquired for $100,000 in cash.
   (5) The balance in Retained Earnings increased by $5,000.
   (6) Writeoffs were $7,000.
   (7) The balance in Accounts Receivable increased by $15,000.
   (8) Purchases of inventory were $80,000.
   (9) The balance in Taxes Payable did not change.
   (10) Property, plant and equipment was sold for $2,500. The company uses the group method for depreciating its assets.
   (11) The balance in Accounts Payable Merchandise increased by $2,000.
   (12) Required lease payments of $13,000 were made in a timely fashion. All leases were capital leases.
   (13) The balance in Accumulated Depreciation (which **does not** include amortization of leasehold asset) increased by $7,000.
   (14) Dividends of $6,000 were paid.
   (15) The balance in Inventory decreased by $8,000.
   (16) Operating expenses (exclusive of depreciation) were $25,000.
   (17) The balance in Property, Plant and Equipment (which does not include Leasehold Asset) increased by $60,000.
   (18) A 10-year capital lease was entered into at the beginning of the year. The present value of the lease payments, at 15 percent, was $70,000. This is the first lease the company ever entered into.
   (19) The balance in Estimated Uncollectibles increased by $3,000.
   (20) The balance in Prepaid Services decreased by $11,000.

27.

The CandO Company
Comparative Balance Sheets
Years Ending December 31, 19X0 and 19X1

Assets	12/31/X0	12/31/X1
Cash	$100,000	$?
Accounts Receivable	80,000	82,000
Estimated Uncollectibles	(6,000)	(8,000)
Inventory	50,000	49,000
Various Other Assets	0	?
Total Assets	$224,000	$670,000

Liabilities and Owners' Equities		
Accounts Payable Services	$ 4,000	$ 3,500
Accounts Payable Merchandise	15,000	16,000
Various Other Liabilities	0	?
Common Stock	50,000	50,000
Retained Earnings	155,000	?
Total Liabilities and Owners' Equities	$224,000	$?

Notes

(1) The CandO Company entered into a lease on January 1, 19X1. The lease required annual lease payments of $20,000 on December 31 of each year, for 20 years.

(2) The market rate of interest at the time of signing the lease was 10 percent.

(3) The company depreciates (amortizes) its fixed assets (property, plant and equipment as well as capital leases) on a straight-line basis for book purposes.

The CandO Company
Income Statement
19X1

Revenues

Sales Revenue	$550,000
Uncollectibility Adjustment	(11,000)
Net Sales Revenue	$539,000
Total Revenues	$539,000

Expenses

Cost of Goods Sold	$270,000	
Operating Expenses	20,000	
Lease-Related Expenses	?	
Tax Expense	?	
Total Expenses	$?	(?)
Net Income		$?

Required:
Consider the possibility that the lease could be accounted for as either an operating lease or a capital lease for book purposes, but **only** as an operating lease for tax purposes. Then for each possibility

a. Prepare a statement of cash flows.

b. Fill in the question (?) marks in the balance sheet and income statement.

c. What accounts are lumped into Various Other Assets and Various Other Liabilities?

d. What assumptions did you make regarding income taxes in the financial statements in the case of the capital lease? Describe the consequences of alternative assumptions.

28.

The Janel Company
Comparative Balance Sheets
Years Ending December 31, 19X0 and 19X1

Assets	12/31/X0	12/31/X1
Cash	$ 50,000	$ 75,000
Net Accounts Receivable	158,000	200,000
Inventory	202,000	175,000
Leasehold Asset	0	?
Total Assets	$410,000	$?

Liabilities and Owners' Equities		
Accounts Payable Services	$ 10,000	$ 15,000
Accounts Payable Merchandise	20,000	30,000
Dividends Payable	30,000	0
Current Portion of Debt	0	?
Deferred Tax Liability	0	?
Leasehold Liability	0	?
Common Stock	140,000	140,000
Retained Earnings	210,000	265,000
Total Liabilities and Owners' Equities	$410,000	$?

Notes

(1) The Janel Company has decided to lease a building, agreeing to pay $7,500 per month, for 25 years, and a lump-sum payment at the end of the lease in the amount of $156,346. The building has a fair market value of $775,000, an expected useful life of 40 years, and an estimated salvage value of $30,000.

(2) Assume a tax rate of 40 percent and an interest rate of 12 percent, compounded monthly.

The Janel Company
Income Statement
19X1

Revenues

Net Sales Revenue	$650,000
Revenues	$650,000

Expenses

Cost of Goods Sold	$300,000	
Operating Expenses	200,000	
Amortization Expense	?	
Interest Expense	?	
Tax Expense	?	
Total Expenses	$?	(?)
Net Income		$?

Statement of Cash Flows

Cash Flows from Operating Events		$?

Cash Flows from Financing Events

Payment of Dividends	$?	
Lease Payment	?	
Total Financing Cash Flows	$?	(?)
Increase in Cash		$ 25,000

Schedule of Significant Noncash Financing and Investing Events

Inception of Lease	$?

Required:
a. What effects would this lease have on the firm's financial statements if the lease was to begin December 1, 19X1? December 31, 19X1?
b. For each date above
   (1) Determine all the events that occurred during the year.
   (2) Fill in all of the question (?) marks.

CHAPTER 16

Accounting for Investments in Other Firms

INTRODUCTION

Firms invest in the growth and expansion of their own operating capacity by acquiring property, plant and equipment and other long-lived assets. The purpose of these investments, taken as a whole, is to increase the cash-generating ability of the firm.

Firms (***investors***) can also benefit from the cash-generating ability of other firms (***investees***) by purchasing their securities. These securities can be debt securities (bonds) or equity securities (common or preferred stock). When an investor acquires either debt securities or a small equity percentage of an investee, the investor can benefit as a result of the cash-generating ability of the investee because of the resulting cash flows from interest (for debt securities) and dividends (for equity securities) it receives from the investee, and the proceeds from the sale of the securities. If the investment in equity securities is sizable the investor has gained significant influence or control over the investee. Because of this influence or control, the investor can **directly** benefit from the cash-generating ability of the firm it controls.

CLASSIFICATION OF INVESTMENTS

Accounting for investments in securities of other corporations depends upon the extent to which an investor can significantly influence or control an investee. An investment in debt securities is never considered to give the investor significant influence, and is accounted for by the *cost method.* For equity investments, significant influence or control is determined by the percentage of the stock of an investee acquired. For example, an investor acquiring less than 20 percent of an investee's stock is assumed to have **no significant influence** over the investee, and must account for the investment by the cost method. Such investments are further differentiated as current, if management acquired the securities with the intention of selling them within 1 year, or noncurrent, if the intention was to hold them for more than 1 year.

However, an investor acquiring more than 50 percent of an investee is assumed to have gained **control** over the investee. Though the firms might continue to operate as separate legal entities, financial statements must be prepared presenting the two firms as if they were one entity. Such a set of statements is called *consolidated financial statements.*

Finally, an investor acquiring between 20 percent and 50 percent is assumed to have **significant influence, but no control** over the investee, and must account for the investment by the *equity method.* In such cases, the investment will be accounted for as a noncurrent asset called Investment in Affiliated Company.

ACCOUNTING FOR AN INVESTMENT BY AN INVESTOR, WITHOUT SIGNIFICANT INFLUENCE OVER THE INVESTEE: DEBT SECURITIES

In Chapter 13, we discussed accounting for the financing event, ISSUE OF BONDS. We showed that if the issuer's coupon rate was less than, equal to, or greater than the market rate, then bonds were said to be issued at discount, par, or premium, respectively, and each case would result in a different accounting effect.

In this section, we will discuss the investing event, INVESTMENT IN BONDS. The investor would quantify its investment in terms of the cash disbursed. Consider our three examples from Chapter 13 in which the firm issued annual coupon bonds in order to receive $85,000 when the market rate was 10 percent. Although the issuer would have recorded those issues differently, the investor would have recorded all three exactly the same. The journal entry for all three cases is

Investment in Bonds
>   Dr. Investment in Bonds   85,000
>   Cr. Cash   85,000

In accounting for an INVESTMENT IN BONDS, only one account is used to report the investment, Investment in Bonds, without the contra and adjunct accounts, Unamortized Bond Discount and Unamortized Bond Premium, respectively.

As time passes, the entries made to record the INTEREST REVENUE by the investor are the opposite of the entries made by the issuer for the INTEREST EXPENSE associated with the bonds. INTEREST REVENUE on bonds is accrued at the market rate of interest at the time of acquisition. If the periodic interest payments to be received are equal to the INTEREST REVENUE, the entry made is

Interest Revenue
    Dr. Interest Receivable
        Cr. Interest Revenue (I/S)

If the periodic payments to be received are less than the INTEREST REVENUE, the entry is

Interest Revenue
    Dr. Investment
    Dr. Interest Receivable
        Cr. Interest Revenue (I/S)

If the periodic payments to be received are greater than INTEREST REVENUE, the entry is

Interest Revenue
    Dr. Interest Receivable
        Cr. Interest Revenue (I/S)
        Cr. Investment

IMPAIRMENT OF DEBT SECURITIES

Debt securities are said to be impaired when the investor (creditor) modifies its requirements from the debtor (borrower) as a result of the debtor's inability to meet its debt obligations. The excess of the original investment over the fair market value of the assets received is treated as a loss for the investor, and as a gain for the debtor.

If the issuer cannot meet its debt obligation, the investor and debtor can agree to modify either the interest rate, the timing of the repayments, or both. The new debt will be recorded at the lesser of the quantification of the old debt or the sum of the future payments. If the sum of the payments of the new debt is less than the quantification of the old debt, then the debtor will recognize a gain and the investor a loss.

Reconsider the $85,000 investment in another firm's bonds, with four annual periodic payments of $8,500 to be received at the end of each year, and a lump-sum payment also to be received at the end of the fourth year. If the terms of the new debt required a lump-sum payment of $75,000 at the end of the fourth year, then the new debt would be quantified as $75,000. The investor and debtor would record this event as follows:

Loss from Debt Impairment (for the investor)
    Dr. Loss on Debt Impairment (I/S)   10,000
    Dr. Investment in Bonds (New)   75,000
        Cr. Investment in Bonds (Old)   85,000

Gain from Debt Impairment (for the debtor)

Dr. Net Bonds Payable (Old)	85,000	
Cr. Bonds Payable (New)		75,000
Cr. Gain from Debt Impairment (I/S)		10,000

If the required lump-sum payment was $85,000 or greater, nothing would have been recorded.

ACCOUNTING FOR AN INVESTMENT BY AN INVESTOR, WITHOUT SIGNIFICANT INFLUENCE OVER THE INVESTEE: EQUITY SECURITIES

Consider a firm that acquires 10 percent of an investee. The firm would record their acquisition with the following journal entry:

Acquisition of Marketable Securities
Dr. Marketable Securities (at cost)
Cr. Cash

Since it is assumed that the investor cannot significantly influence the investee, the investment will be accounted for using the *cost method*. The investor recognizes revenue from the investee when the investee declares a dividend. At the time of the dividend declaration, the investor would make the following journal entry:

Dividend Revenue
Dr. Dividends Receivable
Cr. Dividend Revenue (I/S)

And when the investee distributes its dividend, the investor would record the receipt of the cash with the following journal entry:

Collection of Dividend
Dr. Cash
Cr. Dividends Receivable

If the firm sells its securities, the proceeds (market price of the shares sold minus the commissions paid to sell them) will either be less than, equal to, or greater than the original cost (market price of the shares acquired plus the commissions paid to acquire them). The corresponding journal entries for each of the three cases above are

Sale of Marketable Securities (below cost)
Dr. Realized Loss on Sale of Marketable Securities (I/S)
Dr. Cash
Cr. Marketable Securities (at cost)

Sale of Marketable Securities (at cost)
Dr. Cash
Cr. Marketable Securities (at cost)

Sale of Marketable Securities (above cost)
> Dr. Cash
>> Cr. Marketable Securities (at cost)
>> Cr. Realized Gain on Sale of Marketable Securities (I/S)

IMPAIRMENT OF MARKETABLE SECURITIES

The firm's investments in marketable securities are grouped (aggregated) into current or noncurrent portfolios, depending upon how long the firm intends to hold onto them. If the firm intends to sell the securities within 1 year, they are classified as current, and if not, noncurrent.

A permanent decline in the market value of any marketable security is recorded by debiting (Dr.) a Realized Loss, and crediting (Cr.) the actual security, reducing the Marketable Securities account.

For reporting purposes, **the total market value of each portfolio is compared to its total adjusted cost** on the balance sheet date. The total adjusted cost is the original cost of the securities less any permanent declines in market value. If the total market value is **greater than** or **equal to** the total adjusted cost of its portfolio, we do not record anything. But, if the total market value is **less than** the total cost of the portfolio, we **do** record the decline. However, the decline (and subsequent recovery) of total market value of current portfolios is treated differently from noncurrent portfolios.

A temporary decline in the market value of a portfolio of Current Marketable Securities is recorded by debiting (Dr.) an Unrealized Loss reported in the income statement, and crediting (Cr.) the Valuation Allowance for Current Marketable Securities account, a *contra-asset* account, contra to Current Marketable Securities. A temporary decline in the market value of a portfolio of Noncurrent Marketable Securities is recorded by debiting (Dr.) Net Unrealized Loss in Noncurrent Marketable Securities, a *contra-equity* account, contra to Stockholders' Equities, and by crediting (Cr.) the Valuation Allowance for Noncurrent Marketable Securities, a contra-asset account, contra to Noncurrent Marketable Securities.

If the market value of either portfolio recovers after a previously recorded decline, a reversal will be recorded. Since the *lower-of-cost-or-market* (*LCM*) rule applies to marketable securities, only declines can be reversed. Consequently, a Valuation Allowance account can only have a credit (or zero) balance. A balance in the account means that the total market value of the portfolio is less than the total cost of the portfolio, by the amount of the balance. The balance, which represents the temporary decline in the market value of the portfolio, is recognized as an impairment.

ACCOUNTING FOR INVESTMENTS IN MARKETABLE SECURITIES BY THE COST METHOD

Suppose a firm acquired marketable securities during the month of January 19X1. At the end of the month, they reported their investments as follows:

Security	Purchase Date	Cost	Market	Difference
Alpha	January 4, 19X1	$10,000	$15,000	$5,000
Gamma	January 6, 19X1	15,000	12,500	(2,500)
Delta	January 7, 19X1	20,000	13,500	(6,500)
Total		$45,000	$41,000	$(4,000)

If the firm prepared financial statements at the end of January 19X1, they would report the total cost of the portfolio and its total market value. Since the total market value ($41,000) of the portfolio is less than its total cost ($45,000) by $4,000, the firm would make the following journal entry if the portfolio was classified as current:

Net Unrealized Loss in Current Marketable Securities
 Dr. Net Unrealized Loss in
   Current Marketable Securities (I/S)   4,000
   Cr. Valuation Allowance for
     Current Marketable Securities   4,000

or, if the portfolio was classified as noncurrent:

Net Unrealized Loss in Noncurrent Marketable Securities
 Dr. Net Unrealized Loss in
   Noncurrent Marketable Securities   4,000
   Cr. Valuation Allowance for
     Noncurrent Marketable Securities   4,000

Assume that on February 4, 19X1, the firm sold their investment in The Gamma Company for $11,500. The sale would be recorded as follows:

Sale of Marketable Securities (Gamma)
 Dr. Realized Loss on Sale of
   Marketable Securities (I/S)   3,500
 Dr. Cash   11,500
   Cr. Marketable Securities (at cost)   15,000

After the sale of the Gamma securities, the accounting quantification of the remaining portfolio, Alpha and Delta, would continue to be described by the balances in two accounts, Marketable Securities ($30,000) and Valuation Allowance for Marketable Securities ($4,000), until the next balance sheet date.

> ### *Thought Question*
> What is the significance of the $4,000 balance
> in the Valuation Allowance account?

If at the end of February 19X1, you were to prepare financial statements, you would still report the difference between the original cost of the entire portfolio, and its total market value. Consider five possibilities for the total market value of the remaining marketable securities in the portfolio

(a)	(b)	(c)	(d)	(e)
$32,000	$30,000	$28,000	$26,000	$24,000
	Original Cost			

For each possibility, the Valuation Allowance account would have to have a balance of (a) $0; (b) $0; (c) $2,000; (d) $4,000; and (e) $6,000, respectively. In case *a*, the market value of the portfolio exceeds its total cost, and the balance in the Valuation Allowance account will be zero. Since the Valuation Allowance account has a balance of $4,000 from the previous month, the balance would have to be adjusted in case *a* by decreasing (debiting) it for $4,000 (from $4,000 to $0). If the portfolio was current, the adjustment would be recorded as follows:

Net Unrealized Gain in Current Marketable Securities
  Dr. Valuation Allowance for
      Current Marketable Securities   4,000
      Cr. Net Unrealized Gain in
          Current Marketable Securities (I/S)   4,000

or, if the portfolio was classified as noncurrent:

Net Unrealized Gain in Noncurrent Marketable Securities
  Dr. Valuation Allowance for
      Noncurrent Marketable Securities   4,000
      Cr. Net Unrealized Loss in
          Noncurrent Marketable Securities   4,000

> *Thought Question*
> Why is the credit for the current portfolio
> above to Net Unrealized **Gain**,
> and the credit for the noncurrent
> portfolio above to Net Unrealized **Loss**?

For the remaining four cases, the adjustments to the Valuation Allowance account would be

(*b*) A debit (Dr.) entry of $4,000 (a decrease from $4,000 to $0)

(*c*) A debit (Dr.) entry of $2,000 (a decrease from $4,000 to $2,000)

(*d*) No entry necessary (the balance is already at $4,000)

(*e*) A credit (Cr.) entry of $2,000 (an increase from $4,000 to $6,000)

At the end of February 19X1, the total market value of the portfolio, the balances in the Marketable Securities account and its associated Valuation Allowance account, and the book value (accounting quantification) of the portfolio for each of the five possibilities would be

	Market Value	Marketable Securities	Valuation Allowance	Book Value
(*a*)	$32,000	$30,000	$ 0	$30,000
(*b*)	30,000	30,000	0	30,000
(*c*)	28,000	30,000	2,000	28,000
(*d*)	26,000	30,000	4,000	26,000
(*e*)	24,000	30,000	6,000	24,000

ACCOUNTING FOR AN INVESTMENT BY AN INVESTOR, *WITH* CONTROL OVER THE INVESTEE

Consider a firm that acquires 100 percent of an investee on December 31, 19X0, when both firms continue to operate as separate legal entities. The consolidated entity, however, is not a legal entity; it does not have journals or ledgers from which financial statements can be prepared. Therefore, the required consolidated statements are prepared by combining the accounts of the individual legal entities, and adjusting the combined accounts to reflect what they would have been had the consolidated entity kept its own books. Though these required adjustments are sometimes called consolidated adjusting entries or elimination entries, we will simply refer to them as **adjusting entries**. Whatever term is used, however, they are not really entries because no journal for the consolidated entity exists.

In general, a consolidation is the sum of all of the investor's and investee's events (accounts), with adjustments made to reflect

1. Any difference between the reporting of events (accounts) had the two firms been one entity, and the sum of the events (accounts) that were recorded by each of the separate entities. The adjective used to describe events (accounts) that would have been reported by the two firms had they been one is **consolidated**, and the adjective used to describe the sum of the events (accounts) that were recorded by each of the separate entities is **combined**.

2. Any difference between the cost of the investment, and the prorata share (if less than 100 percent was acquired) of the book value of the investee acquired, at the time of the acquisition.

3. The percentage of the investee acquired by others.

> ### Thought Question
> Consider the following two events:
> The investee borrows $15,000 from the investor,
> and the investor sells one grabule, which cost $11,
> to the investee for $51.
> Under what conditions would these events
> be adjusted for in consolidation?

The financial statements for each entity for 19X0 (the year of the investment) and 19X1 (the first year after the investment), as well as the consolidated statements for both entities for 19X1, are presented on the following three pages.

Comparative Balance Sheets

	Investor		Investee	
Assets	1/1/X0	12/31/X0	1/1/X0	12/31/X0
Cash	$ 75,000	$ 35,000	$ 0	$ 20,000
Accounts Receivable	45,000	65,000	25,000	30,000
Inventory	60,000	90,000	20,000	40,000
Investment in Affiliated Company	0	160,000	0	0
Property, Plant and Equipment	300,000	300,000	200,000	200,000
Accumulated Depreciation	(20,000)	(30,000)	(50,000)	(60,000)
Total Assets	$460,000	$620,000	$195,000	$230,000

Liabilities and Owners' Equities

Accounts Payable Merchandise	$ 50,000	$ 60,000	$ 9,000	$ 20,000
Long-Term Debt	0	120,000	50,000	50,000
Common Stock (par $10)	50,000	50,000	10,000	10,000
Additional Paid-in Capital	150,000	150,000	30,000	30,000
Retained Earnings	210,000	240,000	96,000	120,000
Total Liabilities and Owners' Equities	$460,000	$620,000	$195,000	$230,000

19X0 Income Statements

	Investor		Investee	
Revenues				
Sales Revenue		$200,000		$100,000
Total Revenues		$200,000		$100,000
Expenses				
Cost of Goods Sold	$100,000		$ 40,000	
Operating Expenses	50,000		14,000	
Interest Expense	0		6,000	
Tax Expense	20,000		16,000	
Total Expenses	$170,000	(170,000)	$ 76,000	(76,000)
Net Income		$ 30,000		$ 24,000

19X0 Statements of Cash Flows

	Investor		Investee	
Cash Flows from Operating Events		$ 0		$ 20,000
Cash Flows from Financing Events				
Borrowing from the Bank	$120,000		$0	
Total Financing Events	$120,000	120,000	$ 0	0
Cash Flows from Investing Events				
Investment in Affiliated Company	$160,000		$0	
Total Investing Events	$160,000	(160,000)	$ 0	0
Increase (Decrease) in Cash		$ (40,000)		$ 20,000

Comparative Balance Sheets

Assets	Investor 1/1/X1	Investor 12/31/X1	Investee 1/1/X1	Investee 12/31/X1
Cash	$ 35,000	$ 60,000	$ 20,000	$ 40,000
Accounts Receivable	65,000	110,000	30,000	30,000
Inventory	90,000	140,000	40,000	65,000
Investment in Affiliated Company	160,000	160,000	0	0
Property, Plant and Equipment	300,000	300,000	200,000	200,000
Accumulated Depreciation	(30,000)	(40,000)	(60,000)	(70,000)
Total Assets	$620,000	$730,000	$230,000	$265,000

Liabilities and Owners' Equities

	Investor 1/1/X1	Investor 12/31/X1	Investee 1/1/X1	Investee 12/31/X1
Accounts Payable Merchandise	$ 60,000	$ 60,000	$ 20,000	$ 27,000
Long-Term Debt	120,000	120,000	50,000	50,000
Common Stock (par $10)	50,000	50,000	10,000	10,000
Additional Paid-in Capital	150,000	150,000	30,000	30,000
Retained Earnings	240,000	350,000	120,000	148,000
Total Liabilities and Owners' Equities	$620,000	$730,000	$230,000	$265,000

19X1 Income Statements

	Investor		Investee	
Revenues				
Sales Revenue		$392,000		$110,000
Earnings from Affiliated Company		8,000		0
Total Revenues		$400,000		$110,000
Expenses				
Cost of Goods Sold	$118,000		$ 30,000	
Operating Expenses	50,000		13,000	
Interest Expense	12,000		7,000	
Tax Expense	88,000		24,000	
Total Expenses	$268,000	(268,000)	$ 74,000	(74,000)
Net Income		$132,000		$ 36,000

19X1 Statements of Cash Flows

	Investor		Investee	
Cash Flows from Operating Events		$ 47,000		$ 28,000
Cash Flows from Financing Events				
Payment of Dividends	$ (22,000)		$ (8,000)	
Total Financing Events	$ (22,000)	(22,000)	$ (8,000)	(8,000)
Increase in Cash		$ 25,000		$ 20,000

Comparative Consolidated Balance Sheets

Assets	1/1/X1	12/31/X1
Cash	$ 55,000	$100,000
Accounts Receivable	95,000	140,000
Inventory	130,000	205,000
Investment in Affiliated Company	0	0
Property, Plant and Equipment	500,000	500,000
Accumulated Depreciation	(90,000)	(110,000)
Total Assets	$690,000	$835,000

Liabilities and Owners' Equities

Accounts Payable Merchandise	$ 80,000	$ 87,000
Long-Term Debt	170,000	170,000
Common Stock (par $10)	50,000	50,000
Additional Paid-in Capital	150,000	150,000
Retained Earnings	240,000	378,000
Total Liabilities and Owners' Equities	$690,000	$835,000

19X1 Consolidated Income Statement

Revenues

Sales Revenue		$502,000
Total Revenues		$502,000

Expenses

Cost of Goods Sold	$148,000	
Operating Expenses	63,000	
Interest Expense	19,000	
Tax Expense	112,000	
Total Expenses	$342,000	(342,000)
Net Income		$160,000

19X1 Consolidated Statement of Cash Flows

Cash Flows from Operating Events		$ 67,000

Cash Flows from Financing Events

Payment of Dividends	$ (22,000)	
Total Financing Events	$ (22,000)	(22,000)
Increase in Cash		$ 45,000

ADJUSTING FOR INTERCOMPANY CASH TRANSACTIONS

Suppose that the investor lends $15,000 to the investee. The investor and the investee would record the event as follows:

Lending to the Investee (investor)
      Dr. Loan Receivable   15,000
          Cr. Cash   15,000

Borrowing from the Investor (investee)
      Dr. Cash   15,000
          Cr. Loan Payable   15,000

The consolidated entity would not record this event at all. Doing so would be equivalent to recording the effects of exchanging dimes for nickels, or transferring money from one pocket to another. The combination of the two events can be described by the following entry:

Combined Loan
      Dr. Loan Receivable (investor)   15,000
          Cr. Loan Payable (investee)   15,000

The combined entry would be adjusted to the consolidated entry as follows:

Adjustment for Intercompany Loan
      Dr. Loan Payable   15,000
          Cr. Loan Receivable   15,000

The net effect of this adjusting entry is to eliminate the Loan Receivable from the investee, the Loan Payable to the investor, from the consolidated balance sheets, and to eliminate the financing event (BORROWING FROM THE INVESTOR) and the investing event (LENDING TO THE INVESTEE) from the consolidated statement of cash flows.

> ### *Thought Question*
> Are there any other events or accounts
> that **might** have to be adjusted for
> as a result of this borrowing?

ADJUSTING FOR INTERCOMPANY SALES AND PURCHASES

If the investee **does not** purchase any merchandise from the investor, or vice versa, then operationally, the two firms are independent of one another, and the SALES REVENUE, COST OF GOODS SOLD, and Inventory accounts will be additive and will not require any adjustments. However, if the investee **does** purchase merchandise from the investor, or vice versa, the two firms are not operationally independent, and adjustments will have to be made. In order to simplify the discussion, we will assume that the investee purchases merchandise only from the investor, selling (1) all; (2) none; or (3) half of the merchandise purchased, and that the Accounts Receivable (from the investee), and the Accounts Payable Merchandise (to the investor) remain uncollected (unpaid).

CONSOLIDATED SALES REVENUE is the amount that the consolidated entity sells its product for to unrelated third parties, and CONSOLIDATED COST OF GOODS SOLD is the amount that it cost the consolidated entity to acquire (manufacture or purchase) the product. In our example, the CONSOLIDATED SALES REVENUE is the revenue the investee earns from selling the grabules, and the CONSOLIDATED COST OF GOODS SOLD is the cost to the investor to manufacture the grabules. COMBINED SALES REVENUE is the sum of the investor's and the investee's SALES REVENUE, and COMBINED COST OF GOODS SOLD is the sum of the investor's and the investee's COST OF GOODS SOLD.

Suppose that the investor manufactures grabules at a cost of $11 per unit, and sells 1,000 grabules to the investee for $51 each. They would each record the following events:

Sales Revenue (investor)
    Dr. Accounts Receivable   51,000
        Cr. Sales Revenue (I/S)   51,000

Cost of Goods Sold (investor)
    Dr. Cost of Goods Sold (I/S)   11,000
        Cr. Inventory   11,000

Credit Purchase of Inventory (investee)
    Dr. Inventory   51,000
        Cr. Accounts Payable Merchandise   51,000

If the investee sells all of the grabules that it purchased from the investor for $80 each, then the investee would record the following entries:

Sales Revenue (investee)
    Dr. Accounts Receivable   80,000
        Cr. Sales Revenue (I/S)   80,000

Cost of Goods Sold (investee)
    Dr. Cost of Goods Sold (I/S)   51,000
         Cr. Inventory   51,000

The COMBINED SALES REVENUE, COMBINED COST OF GOODS SOLD, and COMBINED CREDIT PURCHASE OF INVENTORY of the investor and the investee can be represented by

Combined Sales Revenue
      Dr. Accounts Receivable   131,000
             Cr. Sales Revenue (I/S)   131,000

Combined Cost of Goods Sold
      Dr. Cost of Goods Sold (I/S)   62,000
             Cr. Inventory   62,000

Combined Credit Purchase of Inventory
      Dr. Inventory   51,000
             Cr. Accounts Payable Merchandise   51,000

    Since the consolidated entity would have recorded the effects of SALES REVENUE and COST OF GOODS SOLD with the following entries:

Consolidated Sales Revenue (of the investee)
      Dr. Accounts Receivable   80,000
             Cr. Sales Revenue (I/S)   80,000

Consolidated Cost of Goods Sold (of the investor)
      Dr. Cost of Goods Sold (I/S)   11,000
             Cr. Inventory   11,000

the combined entries would be adjusted to the consolidated entries as follows:

Adjustment for Intercompany Sales Revenue
      Dr. Sales Revenue (I/S)   51,000
             Cr. Accounts Receivable   51,000

Adjustment for Intercompany Cost of Goods Sold
      Dr. Inventory   51,000
             Cr. Cost of Goods Sold (I/S)   51,000

Adjustment for Intercompany Sale and Purchase of Inventory
      Dr. Accounts Payable Merchandise   51,000
             Cr. Inventory   51,000

    Aggregating the effects of all of the adjusting entries into one, the adjusting entry for INTERCOMPANY SALES and INTERCOMPANY PURCHASES would be

Adjusting Entry for Intercompany Sales and Purchases
      Dr. Sales Revenue (I/S)   51,000
      Dr. Accounts Payable Merchandise   51,000
             Cr. Accounts Receivable   51,000
             Cr. Cost of Goods Sold (I/S)   51,000

    The net effect of this adjusting entry is to eliminate the Accounts Receivable (from the investee) and Accounts Payable Merchandise (to the investor) from the consolidated balance sheets, and to adjust the consolidated income statement for the SALES REVENUE reported by the investor, the COST OF GOODS SOLD reported by the investee (the same $51,000). No adjustment to the consolidated statement of cash flows would be necessary.

Suppose, that instead of selling all of the grabules, the investee did not sell any. Then the consolidated entity would not have completed the sale, and would have nothing to report. Since the entries for the COMBINED SALES REVENUE, COMBINED COST OF GOODS SOLD, and COMBINED CREDIT PURCHASE OF INVENTORY are

Combined Sales Revenue (of the investor)
Dr. Accounts Receivable	51,000	
Cr. Sales Revenue (I/S)		51,000

Combined Cost of Goods Sold (of the investee)
Dr. Cost of Goods Sold (I/S)	11,000	
Cr. Inventory		11,000

Combined Credit Purchase of Inventory
Dr. Inventory	51,000	
Cr. Accounts Payable Merchandise		51,000

the combined entries would be adjusted to the consolidated entries by reversing the combined entries that were made:

Adjustment for Intercompany Sales Revenue
Dr. Sales Revenue (I/S)	51,000	
Cr. Accounts Receivable		51,000

Adjustment for Intercompany Cost of Goods Sold
Dr. Inventory	11,000	
Cr. Cost of Goods Sold (I/S)		11,000

Adjustment for Intercompany Sale and Purchase of Inventory
Dr. Accounts Payable Merchandise	51,000	
Cr. Inventory		51,000

Aggregating the effects of all of the adjusting entries into one, the adjusting entry for INTERCOMPANY SALES and INTERCOMPANY PURCHASES would be

Adjusting Entry for Intercompany Sales and Purchases
Dr. Sales Revenue (I/S)	51,000	
Dr. Accounts Payable Merchandise	51,000	
Cr. Accounts Receivable		51,000
Cr. Cost of Goods Sold (I/S)		11,000
Cr. Inventory		40,000

The net effect of this adjusting entry is to eliminate the Accounts Receivable (from the investee) and Accounts Payable Merchandise (to the investor), to adjust Inventory in the consolidated balance sheets, and to eliminate the SALES REVENUE and COST OF GOODS SOLD, from the consolidated income statement. There would be no adjustment necessary on the consolidated statement of cash flows.

Finally, suppose that the investee sells only half of the grabules that it purchased from the investor. Then the investee would have recorded the sale with the following journal entries:

Sales Revenue (investee)

Dr. Accounts Receivable	40,000	
Cr. Sales Revenue (I/S)		40,000

Cost of Goods Sold (investee)

Dr. Cost of Goods Sold (I/S)	25,500	
Cr. Inventory		25,500

The COMBINED SALES REVENUE, COMBINED COST OF GOODS SOLD, and COMBINED CREDIT PURCHASE OF INVENTORY of the investor and investee would have been recorded as

Combined Sales Revenue

Dr. Accounts Receivable	91,000	
Cr. Sales Revenue (I/S)		91,000

Combined Cost of Goods Sold

Dr. Cost of Goods Sold (I/S)	36,500	
Cr. Inventory		36,500

Combined Credit Purchase of Inventory

Dr. Inventory	51,000	
Cr. Accounts Payable Merchandise		51,000

Since the consolidated entity would have recorded the sale of half the grabules as follows:

Consolidated Sales Revenue

Dr. Accounts Receivable (investee)	40,000	
Cr. Sales Revenue (I/S)		40,000

Consolidated Cost of Goods Sold

Dr. Cost of Goods Sold (I/S)	5,500	
Cr. Inventory (investor)		5,500

the combined entries would be adjusted to the consolidated entries as follows:

Adjustment for Intercompany Sales Revenue

Dr. Sales Revenue (I/S)	51,000	
Cr. Accounts Receivable		51,000

Adjustment for Intercompany Cost of Goods Sold

Dr. Inventory	31,000	
Cr. Cost of Goods Sold (I/S)		31,000

Adjustment for Intercompany Sale and Purchase of Inventory
Dr. Accounts Payable Merchandise   51,000
  Cr. Inventory   51,000

Aggregating the effects of all of the adjusting entries into one, the adjusting entry for INTERCOMPANY SALES and INTERCOMPANY PURCHASES would be

Adjusting Entry for Intercompany Sales and Purchases
Dr. Sales Revenue (I/S)   51,000
Dr. Accounts Payable Merchandise   51,000
  Cr. Accounts Receivable   51,000
  Cr. Cost of Goods Sold (I/S)   31,000
  Cr. Inventory   20,000

The net effect of this adjusting entry is to eliminate the Accounts Receivable (from the investee) and Accounts Payable Merchandise (to the investor), to adjust Inventory in the consolidated balance sheets, and to adjust SALES REVENUE and COST OF GOODS SOLD, as a result of this sale, in the consolidated income statement. There would not be any adjustment necessary on the consolidated statement of cash flows.

To summarize, in order to adjust from combined financial statements to consolidated financial statements

1. Always debit (Dr.) Accounts Payable Merchandise, and credit (Cr.) Accounts Receivable for unpaid (uncollected) intercompany amounts.

2. Always debit (Dr.) SALES REVENUE for the total INTERCOMPANY SALES REVENUE.

3. Credit (Cr.) Inventory for intercompany profit on the remaining inventory, if any.

4. Always credit (Cr.) COST OF GOODS SOLD for the difference between (2) and (3) above. This credit will be equal to the INTERCOMPANY SALES REVENUE (if all of the units have subsequently been sold), equal to the INTERCOMPANY COST OF GOODS SOLD (if none of the units have subsequently been sold), or somewhere between the two amounts if some of the inventory was sold and some remains to be sold.

ADJUSTING FOR THE INVESTMENT IN CONSOLIDATED BALANCE SHEETS

Suppose that an investor purchases all of the stock of an investee for $160,000, and that at the time of the acquisition, the book value (net-assets or owners' equities) of the investee is also $160,000 (refer to page 420 for the financial statements of the investee). The investor would record the investment as follows:

Investment in Affiliated Company
  Dr. Investment in Affiliated Company   160,000
    Cr. Cash   160,000

The Investment in Affiliated Company by the investor can be represented by the addition of the investee's individual assets and equities to those of the investor's, as recorded by the following journal entry:

Acquisition of Investee's Assets and Equities
  Dr. Individual Assets and Equities   160,000
    Cr. Common Stock   10,000
    Cr. Additional Paid-in Capital   30,000
    Cr. Retained Earnings   120,000

The combined net-assets of the investor and investee can be represented by the following journal entry:

Combined Net-Assets
  Dr. Investment in Affiliated Company   160,000
  Dr. Net-Assets   160,000
    Cr. Cash   160,000
    Cr. Common Stock   10,000
    Cr. Additional Paid-in Capital   30,000
    Cr. Retained Earnings   120,000

Since the consolidated entity would have recorded the effects of the acquisition with the following journal entry:

Consolidated Net-Assets
  Dr. Net-Assets   160,000
    Cr. Cash   160,000

the combined entry would be adjusted to the consolidated entry as follows:

Adjusting Entry
  Dr. Common Stock   10,000
  Dr. Additional Paid-in Capital   30,000
  Dr. Retained Earnings   120,000
    Cr. Investment in Affiliated Company 160,000

The net effect of this adjusting entry is to eliminate the Investment in Affiliated Company (of the investor) and the Owners' Equities (of the investee), from the consolidated balance sheets. No adjustment will be necessary to the consolidated income statement or the consolidated statement of cash flows.

ADJUSTING FOR THE DIFFERENCE BETWEEN THE MARKET VALUE AND BOOK VALUE OF AN INVESTEE AT THE TIME OF ACQUISITION

Suppose that the investor invested $200,000 rather than $160,000 for the same investee. In paying $200,000 for a firm that had net-assets of $160,000, the investor evaluated the investee's net-assets differently than their reported book value. Perhaps the equipment or inventory of the investee was considered worth more than its reported book value. If so, either the Property, Plant and Equipment account and/or the Inventory account would have to be debited in the consolidated financial statements to reflect these increases. If the difference between the market value and the book value of the investee cannot be attributed to particular assets, then the difference will be debited (Dr.) to another asset account. This asset account is called **Goodwill** and is reported in the consolidated balance sheet only!

Assume that in our example above, the $40,000 excess paid for the investee could not be attributed to any particular asset. Then, the goodwill must be amortized (expensed) over the period benefited, not to exceed 40 years, and will be recorded each year by the following journal entry:

Amortization of *Goodwill*

Dr. Amortization of Goodwill (I/S)	1,000	
Cr. Goodwill		1,000

ACCOUNTING FOR AN INVESTMENT BY AN INVESTOR, WITH CONTROL OVER THE INVESTEE: LESS THAN 100 PERCENT

When an investor acquires less than 100 percent, but more than 50 percent of an investee, the investor has gained control of the investee. The remaining percentage of the investee not acquired by the investor is referred to as the **Minority Interest.**

Consider an investor that acquires 60 percent of an investee (refer to page 420 for the financial statements of the investee) at a market price equal to its book value. The investor would record the investment with the following journal entry:

Investment in Affiliated Company

Dr. Investment in Affiliated Company	96,000	
Cr. Cash		96,000

The combined net-assets of the investor and investee can be represented by the following journal entry:

Combined Net-Assets

Dr. Investment in Affiliated Company	96,000	
Dr. Net-Assets	160,000	
Cr. Cash		96,000
Cr. Common Stock		10,000
Cr. Additional Paid-in Capital		30,000
Cr. Retained Earnings		120,000

and the consolidated entry for the two firms would be

Consolidated Net-Assets

Dr. Net-Assets	160,000	
Cr. Cash		96,000
Cr. Common Stock (Minority)		4,000
Cr. Additional Paid-in Capital (Minority)		12,000
Cr. Retained Earnings (Minority)		48,000

In adjusting the combined entry to the consolidated entry, the entire stockholders' equity section is eliminated, and the portion of the minority's interest in stockholders' equities is aggregated in one account as follows:

Adjusting Entry

Dr. Common Stock	10,000	
Dr. Additional Paid-in Capital	30,000	
Dr. Retained Earnings	120,000	
Cr. Investment in Affiliated Company		96,000
Cr. *Minority Interest*		64,000

The $64,000 credit (Cr.) to Minority Interest replaces the minority's interest in Common Stock [$4,000 (40% × $10,000)], Additional Paid-in Capital [$12,000 (40% × $30,000)], and Retained Earnings [$48,000 (40% × $120,000)].

The net effect of this adjusting entry is to eliminate the Investment in Affiliated Company account (of the investor), and the Stockholders' Equities accounts (of the investee), and to present the minority's interest in the consolidated balance sheets. No adjustment will be necessary to the consolidated income statement or to the consolidated statement of cash flows.

> ### *Thought Question*
> On page 423, we discussed INTERCOMPANY SALES
> and INTERCOMPANY PURCHASES
> where the investor sold to the investee.
> What effect, if any, would there be
> in the consolidated financial statements
> if instead of selling,
> the investor purchased from the investee?

ACCOUNTING FOR AN INVESTMENT BY AN INVESTOR, WITH SIGNIFICANT INFLUENCE, BUT NO CONTROL, OVER THE INVESTEE

Consider a firm that acquires 25 percent of an investee. The acquisition would be recorded with the following journal entry:

Investment in Affiliated Company
  Dr. Investment in Affiliated Company (at cost)
    Cr. Cash

When the investor can significantly influence but not control the investee, the investment will be accounted for by the *equity method*. The equity method combines features of both the cost method (where the investor has no significant influence) and the consolidation (where the investor has control).

It is similar to the cost method in that the investment (called Investment in Affiliated Company rather than Marketable Securities) is reported on one line in the balance sheet. In all other respects it is identical to a consolidation. The equity method recognizes the earnings of the investee—the increases or decreases in residual net-assets—as earnings of the investor. Thus, the equity method is often called a **one-line consolidation!**

In other words, the equity method recognizes the investor's pro-rata share of the investee's income by increasing the investor's Investment account, and its pro-rata share of the dividends declared by the investee, by decreasing its Investment account in the investee. When the investee earns income, the investor recognizes its pro-rata share of the investee's income (25 percent) with the following journal entry:

Equity in Earnings of Affiliated Company
  Dr. Investment in Affiliated Company
    Cr. Equity in Earnings of Affiliated Company (I/S)

The investor's share of the investee's income is treated as an increase in the Investment account. Does that make sense? Well, the income of the investee means that the residual net-assets of the investee increased. Since the investor owns 25 percent of the investee, and significantly influences it, the investor's share of the residual net-assets of the investee has increased.

When the investee declares its dividend, the investor will record its pro-rata share (25 percent) of the dividend declaration with the following journal entry:

Dividend to Be Received
    Dr. Dividends Receivable
        Cr. Investment in Affiliated Company

The DECLARATION OF A DIVIDEND by the investee is treated as a decrease in the Investment account. Does that make sense? Obviously the investor is promised cash, but has the investment really decreased? Prior to the DECLARATION OF THE DIVIDEND, the investor owns 25 percent of the investee. After the declaration, the investor still owns 25 percent of a smaller investee (by the amount of the dividend declared), but has the right to receive 25 percent of the dividends.

Finally, the investor would record its pro-rata share (25 percent) of the dividends distributed by the investee with the following journal entry:

Collection of Dividend
    Dr. Cash
        Cr. Dividends Receivable

Unlike accounting for securities by the cost method, any temporary decline in market value of the securities of an investee accounted for by the equity method is not recognized as an accounting event. Only permanent declines will be recognized, by debiting (Dr.) a REALIZED LOSS in the income statement, and crediting (Cr.) the Investment account.

COMPARING THE COST AND EQUITY METHODS

A comparison of the cost and equity methods is presented below.

	Cost Method	Equity Method

Investment in Investee	Dr. Marketable Securities
	    Cr. Cash
		Dr. Investment in Affiliated Company
		    Cr. Cash

Decline in Market Value	Dr. Net Unrealized Loss Cr. Valuation Allowance	No Entry
Earnings of Investee	No Entry	Dr. Investment in Affiliated Company Cr. Equity in Earnings of Affiliated Company (I/S)
Amortization of Goodwill	No Entry	Dr. Equity in Earnings of Affiliated Company (I/S) Cr. Investment in Affiliated Company

Dividends Declared by Investee	Dr. Dividends Receivable
	    Cr. Dividend Revenue (I/S)
		Dr. Dividends Receivable
		    Cr. Investment in Affiliated Company

Dividends Distributed by Investee	Dr. Cash
	    Cr. Dividends Receivable
		Dr. Cash
		    Cr. Dividends Receivable

> *Thought Questions*
>
> Consider the differences in applying the cost and equity methods.
> Which is the more realistic method?
> What arguments can be made for using each method?

COMPARING THE EQUITY METHOD TO CONSOLIDATING AN AFFILIATED COMPANY

In this section we will compare the equity method of accounting for an investee, and the consolidation of an affiliated company, and show why the equity method is referred to as a one-line consolidation.

Consider the possibility that we could account for a wholly owned investee by the equity method. Referring to our previous example (pages 420–421), the investor's journal entries associated with the original investment, and the affiliate's earnings, declaration and payment of dividends would be

Investment in Affiliated Company
Dr. Investment in Affiliated Company	160,000	
Cr. Cash		160,000

Equity in Earnings of Affiliated Company
Dr. Investment in Affiliated Company	36,000	
Cr. Equity in Earnings of Affiliate (I/S)		36,000

Dividends Declared by Affiliated Company
Dr. Dividends Receivable	8,000	
Cr. Investment in Affiliated Company		8,000

Collection of Dividend
Dr. Cash	8,000	
Cr. Dividends Receivable		8,000

The net effect of these journal entries is to increase the net-assets of the investor by $36,000 (an increase in the Investment account of $28,000, and an increase in the Cash account by $8,000), with a corresponding increase in Retained Earnings of $36,000.

Compare the results above with the comparative consolidated balance sheets on page 422. The net-assets (owners' equities) of the investor at the beginning of 19X1 were $440,000 ($620,000 − $180,000), and at the end of 19X1, $578,000 ($835,000 − $257,000), an increase of $138,000. Since $102,000 was unrelated to the investee (NET INCOME minus AFFILIATE'S EARNINGS minus DIVIDEND DECLARED) $36,000 must have been attributable to the investee. Therefore, the effects of accounting for investees by the equity method are identical to the effects of accounting for investees by consolidation. The only difference is the amount of detail that is reported.

In accounting for an investee by consolidation, each event (account) is consolidated and reported separately, and in accounting for an investee by the equity method (one-line consolidation) the net effect of all increases and decreases of all of the events (accounts) is condensed into one line!

FINANCIAL STATEMENT PRESENTATION

Some firms, like Warner Communications, present information about their investments in marketable securities in their footnotes as illustrated in Example 1. Others show the cost of acquiring marketable equity securities over which they have no significant influence as either a current or a noncurrent asset in the balance sheet. The amount by which the market value of the portfolios of current and noncurrent marketable equity securities is below the cost of those portfolios is shown as a contra-account to the cost of those portfolios. This is illustrated by the balance sheet relating to the Ogden Corporation in Example 2 shown on pages 436 and 437.

EXAMPLE 1

Warner Communications Inc.
Marketable Equity Securities

At December 31, 1981, the portfolio of marketable equity securities is carried at its aggregate cost of $93,392,000 (market $100,257,000) and at December 31, 1980, at its aggregate cost of $37,175,000 (market $49,302,000).

Gross unrealized gains and gross unrealized losses pertaining to the marketable equity securities were $10,635,000 and $3,770,000, respectively, at December 31, 1981, and $15,921,000 and $3,794,000, respectively, at December 31, 1980. Realized gains and losses during 1981, 1980, and 1979 are not material.

It is management's present intention to maintain a portfolio of marketable equity securities as a source of capital for long-term investments. Accordingly, the investment in these marketable equity securities has been classified as a noncurrent asset.

EXAMPLE 2

Ogden Corporation and Subsidiaries
Consolidated Balance Sheets

Assets	Dec. 31, 1987	Dec. 31, 1986
Current Assets		
Cash (including restricted funds: 1987, $30,552,000 and 1986, $2,500,000)	$ 60,454,000	$ 23,849,000
Marketable securities—at cost, which approximates market	229,325,000	277,217,000
Receivables (less allowances: 1987, $5,269,000 and 1986, $5,223,000)	224,163,000	195,042,000
Income taxes receivable	15,295,000	
Inventories	8,079,000	7,289,000
Deferred taxes	9,189,000	8,684,000
Prepaid expenses	4,922,000	8,222,000
Total current assets	551,427,000	520,303,000
Property, Plant and Equipment		
Land	5,436,000	3,628,000
Buildings and improvements	77,881,000	66,918,000
Machinery and equipment	113,890,000	102,701,000
Construction in progress	3,855,000	12,008,000
Total	201,062,000	185,255,000
Less accumulated depreciation and amortization	91,964,000	87,055,000
Property, plant and equipment—net	109,098,000	98,200,000
Other Assets:		
Investment in and advances to unconsolidated subsidiaries	10,507,000	32,460,000
Other investments	171,143,000	110,329,000
Noncurrent receivables (less allowances: 1987 and 1986, $46,000)	27,690,000	8,230,000
Goodwill and other intangible assets	17,691,000	16,975,000
Miscellaneous	59,350,000	31,991,000
Total other assets	286,381,000	199,985,000
Total	$946,906,000	$818,488,000

Shareholders' Equity:	Dec. 31, 1987	Dec. 31, 1986
Serial cumulative convertible preferred stock, par value $1 per share; authorized: 1987 and 1986, 4,000,000 shares; outstanding: 1987, 144,000 shares; 1986, 158,000 shares; aggregate involuntary liquidation value 1987, $2,896,000	144,000	158,000
Common stock, par value $.50 per share; authorized, 80,000,000 shares; outstanding: 1987, 39,134,000 shares; 1986, 38,580,000 shares	19,567,000	9,645,000
Capital surplus	26,713,000	29,435,000
Earned surplus	373,486,000	358,870,000
Total	419,910,000	398,108,000
Less:		
Cumulative translation adjustment—net	1,865,000	2,327,000
Net unrealized loss on noncurrent marketable equity securities	2,103,000	
Total shareholders' equity	415,942,000	395,781,000
Total	$946,906,000	$818,488,000

USER'S PERSPECTIVE

If a firm is successful in generating more cash from its operations than it is obligated to spend, it must then decide what to do with this excess cash. Consider a firm that has such excess cash and is considering the following options:

1. Investing the money to expand its current level of operations

2. Investing in securities

3. Prepaying its debt

4. Repurchasing shares of common stock outstanding

5. Distributing a cash dividend

What choice should the company make and how can users of financial statements evaluate these decisions? In theory, the decision criterion is simple—invest (or apply) the money if the firm can earn more for the investor than the investor could earn if the money was distributed. However, the application of the criterion is difficult, and assessing whether the correct choice was made is even more difficult.

Let us consider the possible impacts of the alternatives listed above on a firm's financial statements and financial ratios. Consider a firm that has $100,000 in assets, $50,000 in debt, and $50,000 in owners' equity. If the firm reports NET INCOME and CASH FLOWS FROM OPERATIONS of $10,000, then the return on assets and return on equity will be 10 percent and 20 percent, respectively. If the firm's managers invest the $10,000 in expanding the level of operations, then in the next year, assets, owners' equity, revenues, and expenses will increase. If the expansion is profitable, net income will exceed $10,000, and earnings per share will also increase. However, the return on assets and return on equity might be smaller, larger, or the same as in the previous year, depending upon how profitable the expansion was.

The impact of investing in securities, if the securities are profitable, would be similar, except that there will be no additional expenses and the risks assumed may be different. If they invest in government securities, the risk might be less than investing in their own assets, but investing in another firm's securities might be riskier than investing in their own assets.

If they use the $10,000 to retire the debt, net income, return on equity, and earnings per share will increase, return on assets will remain the same, and earnings will be less risky. If they use the $10,000 to repurchase shares of stock, return on equity and earnings per share will increase, and assets, net income, and return on assets will remain the same. And, if they distribute the $10,000 as a dividend, everything will remain the same.

These various alternative uses for the $10,000 obviously produce widely differing impacts on financial statements and financial ratios. Yet the correctness of the choice cannot be assessed by simply looking at the impact the decision had on the financial data and financial ratios. An increase in any ratio may not necessarily reflect a good decision, and a decrease in any ratio may not reflect a bad decision. For instance, return on assets may decline as a result of the correct decision to expand, while earnings per share may increase as a result of a wrong decision to expand.

This brings us back full circle. We started this book by denying the existence of the tooth fairy—a magic bottom line that will tell us all we need to know to make us rich. By now, you should be very sure of this. We have looked accounting figures in the eye, and have seen what they are and what they are not. But we have also seen how accounting numbers can be used to gain knowledge about what events have occurred, and what risks a firm faces. Accounting does not make decisions or evaluations for users, but it allows users to make more informed decisions. When the weatherman says there is a 40 percent chance of rain, he does not tell us whether to take an umbrella or not. In the same way, accounting provides us with relevant information that helps us make rational economic decisions about a firm.

PROBLEMS

1. On January 1, 19X1, the Myko Company purchased as a long-term investment $500,000 face value of Termac Corporation's 8 percent bonds for $456,200. The bonds were purchased to yield 10 percent interest. The bonds mature on January 1, 19X6, and pay interest annually on January 1. What amount should Myko report on its December 31, 19X1 balance sheet as long-term investment?
   a. $50,580
   b. $456,200
   c. $461,820
   d. $466,200

2. On January 1, 19X0, the Carpel Company purchased Debos Corporation's 9 percent bonds with a face value of $200,000, for $187,800. The bonds were purchased to yield 10 percent. The bonds are dated January 1, 19X0, mature on December 31, 19X9, and pay interest annually on December 31. Carpel uses the interest method of amortizing bond discount. In its income statement for the year ended December 31, 19X0, what total amount should Carpel report as interest income from the long-term bond investment?
   a. $172,000
   b. $202,000
   c. $208,000
   d. $232,000

3. O'Brien Inc., is indebted to VeeLee Finance Company under a $600,000, 10 percent, 5-year note dated January 1, 19X0. Interest, payable annually on December 31, was paid on the December 31, 19X0 and 19X1, due dates. However, during 19X2 O'Brien experienced severe financial difficulties and is likely to default on the note and interest unless some concessions are made. On December 31, 19X2, O'Brien and VeeLee signed an agreement restructuring the debt as follows:

   Interest for 19X2 was reduced to $30,000 payable March 31, 19X3.

   Interest payments each year were reduced to $40,000 per year for 19X3 and 19X4.

   The principal amount was reduced to $400,000.

   What is the amount of loss that VeeLee should report on the debt restructure in its income statement for the year ended December 31, 19X2?
   a. $120,000
   b. $150,000
   c. $200,000
   d. $230,000

4. During 19X0, the Mabol Company purchased marketable equity securities as a short-term investment. At December 31, 19X0, the balance in the Allowance for Decline in Value of Current Marketable Equity Securities was $20,000. There were no security transactions during 19X1. Pertinent data at December 31, 19X1, are as follows:

Security	Cost	Market Value
X	$210,000	$190,000
Y	185,000	207,000
Z	100,000	90,000
	$495,000	$487,000

In its 19X1 income statement, Mabol should report a(an)
a. Recovery of unrealized loss of $12,000
b. Unrealized loss of $12,000
c. Recovery of unrealized loss of $10,000
d. Unrealized loss of $8,000

5. Which of the following conditions generally exists before market value can be used as the basis for valuation of a company's marketable equity securities?
a. Management's intention must be to dispose of the securities within 1 year.
b. Market value must be less than cost for each security held in the company's marketable equity security portfolio.
c. Market value must approximate historical cost.
d. The aggregate market value of a company's marketable equity security portfolio must be less than the aggregate cost of the portfolio.

6. During 19X1, the Kimmy Company purchased marketable equity securities as a long-term investment. Pertinent data are as follows:

Security	Cost	Market Value at 12/31/X1
A	$ 20,000	$ 18,000
B	40,000	30,000
C	90,000	93,000
	$150,000	$141,000

Kimmy appropriately carries these securities at the lower of aggregate cost or market value. The amount of unrealized loss on these securities to flow through Kimmy's income statement for 19X1 should be
a. $0
b. $3,000
c. $9,000
d. $12,000

7. In 19X1, the Grastine Corporation purchased marketable securities, and at December 31, 19X1, had the following marketable equity securities:

	Cost	Market	Unrealized Gain (Loss)
In Current Securities			
Security X	$ 80,000	$ 50,000	$(30,000)
Y	15,000	20,000	5,000
Totals	$ 95,000	$ 70,000	$(25,000)
In Noncurrent Securities			
Security Q	$ 60,000	$ 70,000	$ 10,000
R	90,000	45,000	(45,000)
Totals	$150,000	$115,000	$(35,000)

Valuation allowances at December 31, 19X1, should be established with a corresponding charge against

Income	Stockholders' Equity
a. $ 0	$60,000
b. $25,000	$ 0
c. $25,000	$35,000
d. $60,000	$ 0

8. When the market value of a company's current marketable equity securities portfolio is lower than its cost, the difference should be
   a. Accounted for as a liability
   b. Disclosed and described in a footnote to the financial statements but not accounted for
   c. Accounted for as a valuation allowance deducted from the asset to which it relates
   d. Accounted for separately in the shareholders' equity section of the balance sheet

9. On January 1, 19X1, the L. Jay Miller Company purchased 25 percent of Bluestone Corporation's common stock; no goodwill resulted from the purchase. L. Jay Miller appropriately carries this investment at equity and the balance in Miller's Investment account was $190,000 at December 31, 19X1. Bluestone reported net income at $120,000 for the year ended December 31, 19X1, and paid dividends totaling $48,000 during 19X1. How much did Miller pay for its 25 percent interest in Bluestone?
   a. $172,000
   b. $202,000
   c. $208,000
   d. $232,000

10. On January 4, 19X0, The Roburn Company bought 15 percent of Padiam Corporation's common stock for $60,000. Roburn appropriately accounts for this investment by the cost method. The following data

concerning Padiam are available for the years ended December 31, 19X0 and 19X1:

	19X0	19X1
Net income	$30,000	$90,000
Dividends paid	None	80,000

In its income statement for the year ended December 31, 19X1, how much should Roburn report as income from this investment?
a. $4,500
b. $9,000
c. $12,000
d. $13,500

11. Cash dividends declared out of current earnings are distributed to an investor. How will the investor's Investment account be affected by those dividends under each of the following accounting methods?

Cost Method	Equity Method
a. Decrease	No effect
b. Decrease	Decrease
c. No effect	Decrease
d. No effect	No effect

12. On July 1, 19X1, Staith Inc., paid $1,000,000 for 100,000 shares (40 percent) of the outstanding common stock of Winston Corporation. At that date the net-assets of Winston totaled $2,500,000 and the fair value of all of Winston's identifiable assets and liabilities were equal to their book values. Winston reported net income of $500,000 for the year ended December 31, 19X1, of which $300,000 was for the 6 months ended December 31, 19X1. Winston paid cash dividends of $250,000 on September 30, 19X1. In its income statement for the year ended December 31, 19X1, what amount of income should Staith report from its investment in Winston?
a. $80,000
b. $100,000
c. $120,000
d. $200,000

13. When an investor uses the equity method to account for investments in common stock, the Investment account will be increased when the investor recognizes
a. A proportionate interest in the net income of the investee
b. A cash dividend received from the investee
c. Periodic amortization of the goodwill related to the purchase
d. Depreciation related to the excess of market value over book value of the investee's depreciable assets at the date of purchase by the investor

14. When an investor uses the cost method to account for investments in common stock, cash dividends received by the investor from the in-

vestee should normally be recorded as
a. Dividend income
b. An addition to the investor's share of the investee's profit
c. A deduction from the investor's share of the investee's profit
d. A deduction from the Investment account

15. (*CPA adapted*) At the end of its first year of operations, the Reginas Company had a current marketable equity securities portfolio with a cost of $500,000 and a market value of $550,000. At the end of its second year of operations, Reginas Company had a current marketable equity securities portfolio with a cost of $525,000 and a market value of $475,000. No securities were sold during the first year. One security with a cost of $80,000 and a market value of $70,000 at the end of the first year was sold for $100,000 during the second year.

Required:
How should Reginas report the above facts in its balance sheets and income statements for both years? Discuss the rationale for your answer.

16. On January 1, 19X1, the Brenkin Corp. paid $600,000 for 60,000 shares of Malee Company's common stock which represents a 25 percent investment in Malee. Brenkin has the ability to exercise significant influence over Malee. Brenkin received a dividend of $1 per share from Malee in 19X1. Malee reported net income of $320,000 for the year ended December 31, 19X1. The balance in Brenkin's balance sheet account, Investment in Malee Company, at December 31, 19X1, should be
a. $600,000
b. $620,000
c. $680,000
d. $740,000

17. A parent corporation which uses the equity method of accounting for its investment in a 40 percent owned subsidiary, which earned $20,000 and paid $5,000 in dividends, made the following entries:

Dr. Investment in Affiliated Company	8,000	
Cr. Equity in Earnings of Affiliated Company		8,000
Dr. Cash	2,000	
Cr. Dividend Revenue		2,000

What effect will these entries have on the parent's balance sheet?
a. Investment in Subsidiary understated, Retained Earnings understated.
b. Investment in Subsidiary overstated, Retained Earnings overstated.
c. Investment in Subsidiary overstated, Retained Earnings understated.
d. Financial position will be fairly stated.

18. The Jack Company owns 80 percent of the outstanding common stock of Jill Corporation. On November 1, 19X1, Jack made advances of $100,000 to Jill. In the December 31, 19X1, consolidated balance sheet, the advances should be reported as
a. $0
b. $20,000

    c. $80,000

    d. $100,000

19. Consolidated financial statements are typically prepared when one company has
    a. Accounted for its investment in another company by the equity method
    b. Accounted for its investment in another company by the cost method
    c. Significant influence over the operating and financial policies of another company
    d. The controlling financial interest in another company

20.

Current Marketable		↓ Valuation Allowance ↑	
↑ Equity Securities ↓			
20,000			15,000
100,000			

The T-accounts above refer to year 19X1. On January 1, 19X1, all of the current marketable equity securities were sold for $60,000, the price that prevailed on December 31, 19X0. Give all of the entries that were made regarding current marketable equity securities during 19X1.

21.

Investment in		Dividend Receivable	
↑ Affiliated Company ↓		↑ from Affiliate ↓	
100,000		40,000	
			50,000

Required:
From the T-accounts above, determine
a. The maximum that net investments could have been
b. The minimum that earnings of the affiliated company could have been

22. *Required:*
If A only sells to and **never** buys from B, then
a. What was the minimum/maximum consolidated cost of goods sold?
b. How much did B purchase from A?

↑ A's Inventory ↓		↑ B's Inventory ↓		A and B's Consolidated	
				↑ Inventory ↓	
200,000		50,000			
400,000	?	?	600,000	800,000	

23.

The Rex and Oedipus Companies
Condensed Balance Sheets
Year Ending December 31, 19X0

Assets	Rex	Oedipus
Current Assets	$306,000	$106,000
Net Fixed Assets	360,000	81,000
Investment in Oedipus Company	114,000	0
Total Assets	$780,000	$187,000

Liabilities and Owners' Equities	Rex	Oedipus
Current Liabilities	$150,000	$ 50,000
Common Stock (par $100)	500,000	100,000
Retained Earnings	130,000	37,000
Total Liabilities and Owners' Equities	$780,000	$187,000

Notes

(1) Assume that on January 1, 19X0, the Rex Company purchased 800 shares of the Oedipus Company at a cost of $114,000. On that date, the owners' equity was Common Stock of $110,000, and Retained Earnings of $30,000.

(2) Rex Company owes Oedipus Company $15,000 and has included this debt in its Current Liabilities.

(3) On December 20, Oedipus declared a cash dividend of $10,000. The dividend has not been recorded by Rex nor paid by Oedipus.

(4) During 19X0, Rex sold $15,000 of merchandise to Oedipus for $20,000. None of these goods still remain in Oedipus's inventory.

Required:
From the condensed balance sheets of Rex and Oedipus above, prepare a condensed consolidated balance sheet as of December 31, 19X0.

24.

The JamBo Co.
Comparative Balance Sheets
Years Ending December 31, 19X0 and 19X1

Assets	12/31/X0	12/31/X1
Cash	$100,000	$125,000
Net Accounts Receivable (note 1)	170,000	210,000
Inventory (note 2)	100,000	90,000
Property, Plant and Equipment	200,000	250,000
Accumulated Depreciation	(70,000)	(90,000)
Leasehold Asset	100,000	85,000
Investment in Affiliated Company (note 3)	70,000	90,000
Total Assets	$670,000	$760,000

Liabilities and Owners' Equities		
Accounts Payable Services	$ 20,000	$ 15,000
Accounts Payable Merchandise	30,000	30,000
Interest Payable	0	8,000
Current Portion of Leasehold Liability	0	10,000
Deferred Tax Liability (note 4)	10,000	22,000
Leasehold Liability	100,000	90,000
Common Stock	90,000	100,000
Retained Earnings	420,000	485,000
Total Liabilities and Owners' Equities	$670,000	$760,000

Notes

(1) The balances in Accounts Receivable are net of the balance in the Estimated Uncollectibles account of $8,000 in 19X0, and $9,000 in 19X1. During the year, $11,000 of accounts receivable were written off.

(2) Inventory is quantified at LIFO. Had FIFO been used, the balances in the Inventory account would have been $30,000 and $27,500 more on December 31, 19X0 and 19X1, respectively.

(3) The company has one investment in an affiliated company and exerts significant influence over it.

(4) The deferred tax liability is due solely to the difference between the tax basis and the book value of property, plant and equipment.

(5) The only equipment disposed of was fully depreciated.

(6) The company depreciates its assets by using MACRS for tax purposes and straight-line for book purposes. Depreciation Expense includes Amortization of Leasehold Asset.

(7) Assume a tax rate of 40 percent.

The JamBo Co.
Income Statement
19X1

Revenues

Net Sales Revenue		$900,000
Gain on Sale of Equipment (note 5)		1,000
Earnings of Affiliated Company		22,000
Revenues		$923,000

Expenses

Cost of Goods Sold	$485,000	
Operating Expenses	200,000	
Depreciation Expense (note 6)	40,000	
Interest Expense	8,000	
Tax Expense	36,000	
Total Expenses	$769,000	(769,000)
Net Income		$154,000

Required:
a. Prepare a statement of cash flows.
b. What was the tax advantage (disadvantage) associated with the company's choice of LIFO rather than FIFO this year? What is the cumulative advantage (disadvantage) of having used LIFO over FIFO?
c. What is the tax basis of property, plant and equipment as of December 31, 19X1?
d. What was the depreciation deduction on the company's tax return?
e. The balance in Accounts Payable Merchandise did not change even though the balance in Inventory declined. Can you draw any conclusion from this? Why or why not?

25.

The Rodoth Company
Balance Sheet
Year Ending December 31, 19X0

Assets	12/31/X0
Cash	$100,000
Property, Plant and Equipment (note 2)	800,000
Accumulated Depreciation	(300,000)
Investment in Affiliated Company	50,000
Total Assets	$650,000

Liabilities and Owners' Equities

Common Stock (par $100)	$400,000
Retained Earnings	250,000
Total Liabilities and Owners' Equities	$650,000

Notes
(1) There were 5,500 shares of common stock issued at par, and outstanding at the end of the year.
(2) The Rodoth Company received $10,000 in dividends from its affiliated company.
(3) The company issued $100,000 face value bonds at the beginning of 19X1 and made $7,000 in coupon payments.
(4) The company paid $100,000 in taxes.
(5) Cash receipts exceeded cash disbursements during the year by $30,000.
(6) There were no changes in current operating accounts.

The Rodoth Company
Income Statement
19X1

Revenues

Net Sales Revenue	$700,000
Earnings of Affiliated Company	30,000
Total Revenues	$730,000

Expenses

Cost of Goods Sold	$300,000	
Operating Expenses	134,000	
Interest Expense	6,000	
Tax Expense	116,000	
Total Expenses	$556,000	(556,000)
Net Income		$174,000

Statement of Cash Flows

Cash Flows from Operating Events		$?
Cash Flows from Financing Events		
Issue of Bonds	$110,000	
Issue of Common Stock	100,000	
Payment of Dividends	(50,000)	
Total Financing Events	$160,000	160,000
Cash Flows from Investing Events		
Purchase of Property, Plant and Equipment	$(400,000)	
Total Investing Events	$(400,000)	(400,000)
Increase (Decrease) in Cash		$?

Required:
a. Prepare a balance sheet as of the end of the year.
b. Fill in all of the question (?) marks.

26.

The P and S Companies
Balance Sheets
Year Ending December 31, 19X0

Assets	P Co.	S Co.
Cash	$ 40,000	$ 5,000
Net Accounts Receivable	60,000	7,000
Inventory	20,000	3,000
Net Property, Plant and Equipment	100,000	20,000
Totals Assets	$220,000	$35,000

Liabilities and Owners' Equities	P Co.	S Co.
Accounts Payable	$ 30,000	$ 3,000
Common Stock (par $1)	40,000	6,000
Additional Paid-in Capital	110,000	20,000
Retained Earnings	40,000	6,000
Total Liabilities and Owners' Equities	$220,000	$35,000

Notes

(1) Company S owes company P $1,000.
(2) Company P issues two of its shares (market value of $3) for each of company S's shares.
(3) Company S's property, plant and equipment has a book value of $20,000 and a market value of $22,000. For all other of company S's assets, market value equals book value.

Required:
Prepare acquisition entries and consolidated balance sheets at acquisition assuming
a. 100 percent ownership
b. 90 percent ownership

27. An investor purchases a 20 percent interest in an investee for $50,000 cash. During the year, the investee earns income of $25,000 and pays a cash dividend of $10,000 to its stockholders.

Required:
a. Assuming that the investor can use the *cost method,* how much does the investor earn from its investment in the investee?
b. Assuming that the investor can use the *equity method,* how much does the investor earn from its investment in the investee?
c. Assuming that the investor can use the *cost method,* what is the balance in the Investment account after recognizing income and dividends from the investee?
d. Assuming that the investor can use the *equity method,* what is the balance in the Investment account after recognizing income and dividends from the investee?

Epilogue

INTRODUCTION

Throughout the text and problem material in this book, we have stressed the techniques of determining information from financial statements in order to assess the cash-generating ability of a firm. We illustrated how transactional analysis disaggregates financial statements into the events that occurred, and how the accounting assumptions, conventions, and principles differentially impact accounting numbers.

To apply the concepts and information-gathering techniques from Part One to the material covered in Parts Two, Three, and Four of this book, we summarize the following events reported in financial statements, how they can be used to derive other events and important relationships, and the impact of accounting conventions and assumptions upon these events: operating events derived from SALES REVENUE, COST OF GOODS SOLD, OPERATING EXPENSES, and TAX EXPENSE; financing events derived from INTEREST EXPENSE and PAYMENT OF CASH DIVIDENDS; and investing events derived from DEPRECIATION EXPENSE, LEASE PAYMENT, and EARNINGS FROM AFFILIATED COMPANY.

DERIVATION OF OPERATING EVENTS FROM:

Sales Revenue

The cash events associated with SALES REVENUE and the UNCOLLECTIBILITY ADJUSTMENT (BAD DEBT EXPENSE), as reported in the income statement (IS), are COLLECTIONS FROM CUSTOMERS. The related balance sheet accounts are Accounts Receivable, Estimated Uncollectibles, and Advances from Customers.

Derivation

The sum of COLLECTIONS FROM CUSTOMERS **and** WRITEOFFS can be determined by adding (subtracting) the credit (debit) changes in Accounts Receivable **and** Advances from Customers to (from) SALES REVENUE. If BAD DEBT EXPENSE is reported in the income statement, then WRITEOFFS can be determined by adding (subtracting) the debit (credit) change in the Estimated Uncollectibles account to (from) BAD DEBT EXPENSE. Having determined WRITEOFFS, COLLECTIONS FROM CUSTOMERS is derivable.

Relationships

The time between revenue recognition and cash collection (the duration dimension of Accounts Receivable and Advances from Customers) can be approximated by dividing the average balance in Net Accounts Receivable (Accounts Receivable minus Estimated Uncollectibles minus Advances from Customers) by SALES REVENUE, and multiplying by the number of days in the period.

Cost of Goods Sold

The events associated with COST OF GOODS SOLD (IS) for a merchandising firm are PURCHASES OF INVENTORY and PAYMENTS TO SUPPLIERS OF MERCHANDISE. The related balance sheet accounts are Inventory and Accounts Payable Merchandise.

Derivation

PURCHASES OF INVENTORY can be determined by adding (subtracting) the debit (credit) change in Inventory to (from) COST OF GOODS SOLD, and PAYMENTS TO SUPPLIERS OF MERCHANDISE can be determined by adding (subtracting) the debit (credit) change in Accounts Payable Merchandise to (from) PURCHASES OF INVENTORY.

Effect of Accounting Methods

The accounting quantification of the balance in the Inventory account and the amount of COST OF GOODS SOLD are a direct result of choosing a flow assumption, like FIFO or LIFO, while the PURCHASES OF INVENTORY and PAYMENTS TO SUPPLIERS OF MERCHANDISE are not.

Relationships

The time between the purchase of inventory and its sale (the duration dimension of inventory) can be approximated by dividing the average balance in Inventory by PURCHASES OF INVENTORY, and multiplying by the number of days in the period.

The best approximation of the duration dimension of inventory is to divide the average balance of Inventory at current cost by average PURCHASES OF INVENTORY (which is at current cost). The balance in the Inventory account using the FIFO flow assumption approximates current cost, while the balance in the Inventory account using LIFO flow assumption approximates historical cost. Thus, if the firm uses LIFO, you must adjust the ending balances from LIFO to FIFO.

The time between the purchase of and payment for the inventory (the duration dimension of Accounts Payable Merchandise) can be approximated by dividing the average balance in Accounts Payable Merchandise by PURCHASES OF INVENTORY and multiplying by the number of days in the period.

The time between PAYMENTS TO SUPPLIERS OF MERCHANDISE and COLLECTIONS FROM CUSTOMERS can be approximated by subtracting the duration dimension of Accounts Payable Merchandise from the duration dimension of Inventory, and adding that to the duration dimension of Accounts Receivable and Advances from Customers.

Operating Expenses

The events associated with OPERATING EXPENSES (IS) are PAYMENTS TO SUPPLIERS OF SERVICES. The related balance sheet accounts are Prepaid Services and Accounts Payable Services.

Derivation

PAYMENTS TO SUPPLIERS OF SERVICES can be determined by adding (subtracting) the debit (credit) changes in Prepaid Services **and** Accounts Payable Services to (from) OPERATING EXPENSES.

Relationships

The time between expense recognition and payments to suppliers (the duration dimension of Prepaid Services and Accounts Payable Services) can be approximated by dividing the average balance of Net Services Payable (Accounts Payable Services minus Prepaid Services) by OPERATING EXPENSES, and multiplying by the number of days in the period.

Income Tax Expense

The events associated with INCOME TAX EXPENSE (IS) are the CURRENTLY REQUIRED TAX PAYMENT and the PAYMENT OF TAXES. The related balance sheet accounts are Taxes Payable and Deferred Tax Liability (Asset).

Derivation

The CURRENTLY REQUIRED TAX PAYMENT can be determined by adding (subtracting) the debit (credit) changes in Deferred Tax Liability **and** Deferred Tax Asset to (from) INCOME TAX EXPENSE.

The PAYMENT OF TAXES can be determined by adding (subtracting) the debit (credit) change in Taxes Payable to (from) the CURRENTLY REQUIRED TAX PAYMENT.

DERIVATION OF FINANCING EVENTS FROM:

Interest Expense

The events associated with INTEREST EXPENSE (IS) are the CURRENTLY REQUIRED INTEREST PAYMENT and the PAYMENT OF INTEREST. The related balance sheet accounts are Interest Payable, Unamortized Bond Discount, and Unamortized Bond Premium.

Derivation

In a period when there were no bonds issued, the CURRENTLY REQUIRED INTEREST PAYMENT can be determined by adding (subtracting) the debit (credit) changes in Unamortized Bond Discount **and** Unamortized Bond Premium to (from) INTEREST EXPENSE. In a period when new bonds were issued, the premium (discount) on the issue must also be added (subtracted) to (from) INTEREST EXPENSE.

In a period when bonds were issued and not repaid, the premium (discount) on issue can be determined by subtracting the credit change in Bonds Payable from the proceeds from the ISSUE OF BONDS, as reported in the statement of cash flows (SCF). In a period when bonds were issued and repaid, the premium (discount) on issue can be determined by subtracting (adding) the credit (debit) changes in Bonds Payable and Current Portion of Bonds Payable from net proceeds (issue minus repayment, as reported in the statement of cash flows).

The PAYMENT OF INTEREST can be determined by adding (subtracting) the debit (credit) change in Interest Payable to (from) the CURRENTLY REQUIRED INTEREST PAYMENT.

Payment of Cash Dividends

The accounting event associated with the PAYMENT OF CASH DIVIDENDS (SCF) is the DECLARATION OF DIVIDENDS. The related balance sheet accounts are Dividends Payable, Common Stock, and Additional Paid-in Capital.

Derivation

In a period when there were no issues or repurchases of common stock, the DECLARATION OF DIVIDENDS can be determined by adding (subtracting) the credit (debit) changes in Dividends Payable **and** Common Stock **and** Additional Paid-in Capital to (from) the PAYMENT OF CASH DIVIDENDS (SCF).

In a period when common stock was issued and not repurchased, also subtract the amount received from the ISSUE OF COMMON STOCK (SCF) to the PAYMENT OF CASH DIVIDENDS (SCF). In a period when common stock was repurchased and not issued, also add the amount disbursed (SCF) to the PAYMENT OF CASH DIVIDENDS. In a period when common stock was both issued and repurchased, add (subtract) the net excess disbursements (receipts), as reported in the statement of cash flows, to (from) the PAYMENT OF CASH DIVIDENDS.

DERIVATION OF INVESTING EVENTS FROM:

Depreciation Expense

The accounting events associated with DEPRECIATION EXPENSE (IS) are the ACQUISITION AND DISPOSITION OF PROPERTY, PLANT AND EQUIPMENT. The related balance sheet accounts are Property, Plant and Equipment and Accumulated Depreciation and the related income statement accounts are LOSS AND GAIN ON DISPOSAL OF PROPERTY, PLANT AND EQUIPMENT.

Derivation

In a period when property, plant and equipment for a merchandising firm is not disposed of, the credit change in Accumulated Depreciation represents DEPRECIATION EXPENSE, and is reported in the income statement as either DEPRECIATION EXPENSE or as part of OPERATING EXPENSES. The debit change in Property, Plant and Equipment represents the amount acquired, and the acquisition is reported in the statement of cash flows or in the schedule of significant noncash financing **and** investing events.

In a period when property, plant and equipment for a merchandising firm is disposed of but not acquired, the ACCUMULATED DEPRECIATION ASSOCIATED WITH THE DISPOSED EQUIPMENT can be determined by adding (subtracting) the debit (credit) change in Accumulated Depreciation to (from) DEPRECIATION EXPENSE. The credit change in Property, Plant and Equipment represents the PROPERTY, PLANT AND EQUIPMENT DISPOSED OF AT ORIGINAL COST. The proceeds from the DISPOSITION OF PROPERTY, PLANT AND EQUIPMENT is reported as an investing event in the statement of cash flows. Any excess of proceeds over book value (original cost minus accumulated depreciation) will be reported in the income statement as a gain, and any excess of book value over proceeds will be reported in the income statement as a loss.

In a period when property, plant and equipment is acquired and disposed of, the ACQUISITION AND DISPOSITION OF PROPERTY, PLANT AND EQUIPMENT is reported in either the statement of cash flows or the schedule of significant noncash financing **and** investing events. The original cost of the equipment disposed of can be determined by adding (subtracting) the credit (debit) change in Property, Plant and Equipment to (from) the ACQUISITION OF PROPERTY, PLANT AND EQUIPMENT. Any GAIN ON DISPOSITION in the income statement will indicate if the proceeds from the disposition exceeded the book value, and by how much. Similarly, any LOSS ON DISPOSITION will indicate if the book value exceeded the proceeds, and by how much. Thus, ACCUMULATED DEPRECIATION ASSOCIATED WITH DISPOSED PROPERTY, PLANT AND EQUIPMENT can be readily determined.

Capital Lease Payment

The accounting event associated with a CAPITAL LEASE PAYMENT is LEASE EXPENSE. LEASE EXPENSE is made up of two accounting events: INTEREST EXPENSE and the AMORTIZATION OF LEASEHOLD ASSET. It is common to include the INTEREST EXPENSE associated with the Leasehold Liability with all other INTEREST EXPENSE, and to include AMORTIZATION OF LEASEHOLD ASSET with either AMORTIZATION EXPENSE, DEPRECIATION EXPENSE, or even OPERATING EXPENSES. The related balance sheet accounts are Leasehold Asset, Leasehold Liability, Current Portion of Long-Term Liabilities, and Interest Payable.

Derivation

The LEASE PAYMENT represents the payment of interest and principal. In a period when no new capital lease was entered into, the principal repaid is equal to the net of the debit change in Leasehold Liability increased (decreased) by the credit (debit) change in Current Portion of Long-Term Liabilities (assuming there are no other long-term liabilities).

The remainder (lease payment minus principal repayment) is equal to the PAYMENT OF INTEREST. The INTEREST EXPENSE can be determined by adding (subtracting) the credit (debit) change in Interest Payable to (from) the PAYMENT OF INTEREST. The AMORTIZATION OF LEASEHOLD ASSET is equal to the credit change in Leasehold Asset. Now LEASE EXPENSE can be determined.

In a period when a new capital lease was entered into, the principal repayment can be determined by adding (subtracting) the debit (credit) changes in Leasehold Liability **and** Current Portion of Long-Term Liabilities (assuming there are no other long-term liabilities) from the INCEPTION OF CAPITAL LEASE, as reported in the schedule of noncash financing **and** investing events. The PAYMENT OF INTEREST is determinable again.

The AMORTIZATION OF LEASEHOLD ASSET can be determined by adding (subtracting) the credit (debit) change in Leasehold Asset from the new lease as reported in the schedule of significant noncash financing **and** investing events.

Earnings from Affiliated Company

The cash event associated with EARNINGS FROM AFFILIATED COMPANY (IS) is the COLLECTION OF CASH DIVIDENDS. The related balance sheet accounts are Dividends Receivable and Investment in Affiliated Company.

Derivation

In a period when no investments or disinvestments in an affiliated company are made, the COLLECTION OF CASH DIVIDENDS can be determined by adding (subtracting) the credit (debit) changes in Dividends Receivable **and** Investment in Affiliated Company to (from) the EARNINGS FROM AFFILIATED COMPANY (IS).

In a period when there are investments and/or disinvestments in an affiliated company, also subtract the net INVESTMENT IN AFFILIATED COMPANY (investment minus disinvestment, as reported in the statement of cash flows), from EARNINGS FROM AFFILIATED COMPANY.

CONCLUSION

Financial statements provide information that decision makers can use to **predict, compare, and evaluate,** the **amount, timing, and uncertainty** of a company's future cash flows. But no cursory look at financial statements will provide users with enough information to make sound decisions. Users need: a complete history of all of the accounting events; a way to determine the cash implications of those events; and a way to assess the relationships between those events in terms of their cash significance.

As we have seen, financial statements can provide a history of many of the cash significant events relating to a firm if they are properly understood and analyzed. Such a history, which highlights events and the significant relationships among events, is valuable in assessing the impact of events and conditions as they occur in the economy, industry, and firm.

Glossary

Accounting *(p. 3)* The art of communicating financial information.

Accounting assets *(p. 29)* Also called assets, an *economic asset* recognized by the accountant: a right to utilize an economic resource resulting from *accounting events*.

Accounting equities *(p. 29)* An economic equity recognized by the accountant: an obligation to provide an economic resource resulting from an *accounting event*. Accounting equities include *liabilities, contributed capital,* and *retained earnings*.

Accounting events *(p. 29)* Economic events that are recorded by accountants.

Accounting numbers *(p. 3)* The authors' term used to describe the numbers used to quantify an *accounting event*.

Accounting reports *(p. 3)* Also called financial statements. Reports prepared from the *journals, ledgers,* and other records of *accounting units*.

Accounting units *(p. 5)* All economic units that maintain *journals, ledgers,* and other records, and prepare *accounting reports*.

Accounts *(p. 74)* Also called ledger accounts, they are storage devices used to accumulate the effects of *accounting events* for each category of *asset* and *equity*.

Accounts Payable *(p. 58)* A balance sheet account, classified as a *current liability*. The balance in the Accounts Payable account represents the accounting quantification of the amount still owed for raw materials, supplies, and merchandise purchased.

Accounts Payable Services *(p. 52)* A balance sheet account, classified as a *current liability*. The balance in the Accounts Payable Services account represents the accounting quantification of the amount still owed for services utilized.

Accounts Receivable *(p. 49)* A balance sheet account, classified as a *current asset*. The balance in the Accounts Receivable account represents the accounting quantification of the amount still owed by, and potentially collectible from, credit customers.

Accrual *(p. 49)* A balance sheet account that results from the occurrence of an *accounting event* in anticipation of its cash effect. Accruals can be *liabilities*, such as Rent Payable or Interest Payable, or *assets* such as Accounts Receivable or Interest Receivable (compare with deferral).

Accrual method *(p. 49)* The system of accounting that recognizes *accruals* and *deferrals* as well as cash events (compare with cash method).

Accumulated Depreciation *(p. 51)* A balance sheet account, classified as a noncurrent *contra-asset*. The balance in the Accumulated Depreciation account represents the accounting quantification of the amount of property, plant and equipment utilized to date.

Activity statement *(p. 80)* A financial statement that reports the occurrence of *accounting events* such as the *statement of cash receipts and disbursements,* the *income statement,* and the *statement of cash flows*.

Additional Paid-in Capital *(p. 355)* A balance sheet account, classified as an *equity* account. The balance in the Additional Paid-in Capital account represents the accounting quantification of the amount received for the issuance of shares of stock in excess of *par value.*

Adjunct liability *(p. 332)* A *credit* balance account, that when added to the balance of a related *liability* determines the *book value* of that *liability.*

Adjusting entry *(p. 164) Journal entries* made at the end of the accounting period. The *recording signal* for adjusting entries is the end of the period.

Advances from Customers *(p. 52)* A balance sheet account, classified as a *current liability.* The balance in the Advances from Customers account represents the accounting quantification of the amount received for goods and services to be provided.

Aging-of-receivables *(p. 203)* The direct method of calculating the ending balance in the *Estimated Uncollectibles* account—thus the indirect method of calculating the *estimated uncollectibility adjustment* (compare with percentage-of-sales).

Agreement stage *(p. 33)* The first of two stages of a contract. The agreement stage **never** leads to recording an *accounting event.* (*see* Performance stage.)

Amortization *(p. 241)* In general, the term used for the systematic reduction of an accounting quantification over time. The term specifically applies to the accounting quantification of *tangible assets* like *patents, goodwill,* and *leasehold assets* (compare with depreciation and depletion).

Annuity *(p. 19)* A series of equal periodic amounts, spaced at equal time intervals.

Annuity due *(p. 19) See* Annuity in advance.

Annuity in advance *(p. 19)* Also called an annuity due. It is an annuity whose amounts occur at the beginning of each period.

Annuity in arrears *(p. 19)* Also called an ordinary annuity. It is an annuity whose amounts occur at the end of each period.

Assets *(p. 34) See* Accounting assets.

Average cost *(p. 216)* An inventory flow allocation method that assumes that the cost of an item sold is the average of all items purchased (compare with First-in, First-out and Last-in, First-out).

Bad Debt Expense *(p. 189) See* Estimated Uncollectibility Adjustment.

Balance sheet *(p. 77)* A required financial statement (*see* Accounting reports) that reports the balances in all accounts at a point in time (*see* Comparative balance sheets).

Bank Loan *(p. 53) See* Long-Term Debt.

Basic inventory equation *(p. 216)* Beginning balance plus purchases of inventory equals ending balance plus *Cost of Goods Sold.*

Benefit *(p. 4)* An increase in a right or a decrease in a responsibility (*see* Economic decision).

Bonds *(p. 325)* Bonds represent borrowings from the market by the issue of securities (compare with long-term loans).

Bonds Payable *(p. 327)* A balance sheet account, classified as a *noncurrent liability.* The balance in the Bonds Payable account represents the accounting quantification of the amounts due at *maturity.*

Book value *(p. 51)* The accounting quantification of *assets* and *equities* used in financial statements. It is the difference between the original quantification of *assets* and *liabilities* plus (minus) the balances in their related *adjunct (contra)* accounts (compare with tax basis).

The book value of an *asset* is its original cost minus the balance in its related *contra-asset* account. The book value of a *liability* is its original quantification, minus (plus) its related contra-liability (adjunct) account.

Capital lease *(p. 389)* A *lease* that in essence is considered a purchase of an *asset* (compare with operating lease).

Cash *(p. 49)* A balance sheet account, classified as a *current asset*. The balance in the Cash account represents the accounting quantification of the amount of cash at that point in time.

Cash assets *(p. 130)* Cash, and marketable securities that are readily convertible into cash without risk of loss.

Cash Flows from Operations *(p. 132)* All cash flows related to *accounting events* affecting *net income*.

Cash method *(p. 49)* The system of accounting that recognizes only those events that impact cash (compare with accrual accounting).

Cash yield rate *(p. 326)* The amount of *periodic payment* divided by the *market value* or *proceeds of long-term debt*.

Closing process *(p. 91)* The process by which the balances in all *event accounts* are eliminated, and their effects closed to Retained Earnings.

Collection period *(p. 199)* A *financial ratio* used to calculate the elapsed time between credit sales and collections:

$$\frac{\text{Average accounts receivable}}{\text{Average daily sales}}$$

Common Stock *(p. 53)* A balance sheet account, classified as an *equity* account. The balance in the Common Stock account represents the accounting quantification of the amount received in exchance for shares of common stock issued and outstanding at *par* or *stated value*.

Common stock equivalents *(p. 362)* Any security that is assumed to be converted into shares of common stock for the purposes of calculating *primary earnings per share*.

Common stockholders *(p. 353)* Shareholders of a corporation that own shares of common stock (compare with preferred stockholders).

Comparative balance sheets *(p. 79)* A required financial statement (*see* Accounting reports) that reports the balances in all accounts at two or more points in time (*see* Balance sheet).

Completed-contract method *(p. 194)* The method of recognizing *revenue* upon completion of a long-term project when costs **cannot** be reasonably estimated (compare with percentage-of-completion method).

Compound interest *(p. 16)* The difference between an amount and its future equivalent. Compound interest reflects interest on amounts **plus** interest on interest previously earned (compare with simple interest).

Consolidated financial statements *(p. 412)* Financial statements presenting two or more independent firms as if they were one operating entity. These statements are prepared when an *investor* owns more than 50 percent of an *investee*, and controls it.

Contra-asset *(p. 93)* A *credit* balance account, that when subtracted from the balance of a related *asset* account, determines the *book value* of that *asset*.

Contra-equity *(p. 358)* A *debit* balance account, that when subtracted from the balance of a related *equity* account, determines the *book value* of that *equity*.

Contra-liability *(p. 329)* A *debit* balance account, that when subtracted from the balance of a related *liability* account, determines the *book value* of that *liability*.

Contributed Capital *(p. 53)* A collection of balance sheet accounts, all classified as equity accounts. The Contributed Capital accounts include *Common Stock* and *Additional Paid-in Capital, Preferred Stock* and *Additional Paid-in Capital.*

Cost accounting *(p. 7) See* Management accounting.

Cost method *(p. 357)* The term cost method has many meanings in accounting. One definition relates to the method of accounting for the acquisition and subsequent reissue of treasury shares (compare with par value method).

Another definition relates to the method of accounting for an investment when the *investor* **does not** exercise either significant influence or control over an *investee* (compare with equity method).

Cost of Goods Sold *(p. 88)* The accounting quantification of goods sold.

Cost recovery method *(p. 192)* The method of recognizing income such that no profit is recognized until cash collections equal total costs of the product (compare with installment method).

Coupon *(p. 325) See* Coupon payment.

Coupon payment *(p. 325)* The *periodic payment* associated with a bond. It equals the *coupon rate* times the *face value* of the bond.

Coupon rate *(p. 325)* The stated interest rate that when multiplied by the *face value* of a bond determines the *periodic payment* promised by the issuer.

Credits *(p. 65)* The right side of a *journal entry.* The amounts stored on the right side of *accounts*—increases in *equities,* decreases in *assets, revenues* and *gains* (compare with debits).

Current assets *(p. 35) Assets* that are expected to be utilized within a year or operating cycle, whichever is longer, such as *Cash, Accounts Receivable, Prepaid Services,* and *Inventory.*

Current liabilities *(p. 37) Liabilities* that are expected to be discharged within a year or operating cycle, whichever is longer, such as *Accounts Payable, Wages Payable, Interest Payable, Taxes Payable,* and *Dividends Payable.*

Current ratio *(p. 316)* A *financial ratio* used to assess liquidity:

$$\frac{\text{Current assets}}{\text{Current liabilities}}$$

Date of record *(p. 356)* Shareholders on this date are entitled to receive dividends *(see* Declaration date and Payment date).

Debits *(p. 65)* The left side of a *journal entry.* The amounts stored on the left side of *accounts*—decreases in *equities,* increases in *assets, expenses* and *losses* (compare with credits).

Debt constant *(p. 301)* A *financial ratio:*

$$\frac{\text{Periodic payment}}{\text{Proceeds}}$$

Debt-equity ratio *(p. 340)* A *financial ratio* used to assess financial leverage:

$$\frac{\text{Long-term debt}}{\text{Owners' equities}}$$

Declaration date *(p. 356)* The date that a dividend is declared *(see* Date of record and Payment date).

Deferral *(p. 49)* A balance sheet account that results from the occurrence of a cash flow in anticipation of a future and related event. Deferrals can be *liabilities,* such as *Advances from Customers* or *Unearned Revenues,* or *assets* such as *Prepaid Services* or *Deferred Charges* (compare with accrual).

Deferred Charges *(p. 50) See* Deferred Expenses.

Deferred Expenses *(p. 132)* Cash paid in exchange for goods and/or services to be utilized.

Deferred Revenue *(p. 132)* Cash received in exchange for goods and/or services to be provided.

Deferred Tax Asset *(p. 273)* A balance sheet account, classified as either a *current* or *noncurrent asset*. The balance in the Deferred Tax Asset account quantifies the amount that would be refunded if the difference between the *tax basis* and *book value* of *assets* or *liabilities* was eliminated (compare with Deferred Tax Liability).

Deferred Tax Liability *(p. 273)* A balance sheet account, classified as either a *current* or *noncurrent liability*. The balance in the Deferred Tax Liability account quantifies the amount of taxes that will be paid when the difference between the *tax basis* and *book value* of *assets* or *liabilities* is eliminated (compare with Deferred Tax Asset).

Dependently quantified *(p. 59)* One of two effects of every *accounting event*. It is the effect of an *accounting event* quantified in terms of its other effect (compare with independently quantified).

Depletion *(p. 241)* The accounting quantification of the utilization of natural resources (compare with amortization and depreciation).

Deposits *(p. 132) See* Advances from Customers.

Depreciable assets *(p. 51) Tangible assets* that have limited useful lives, such as *Property, Plant and Equipment*.

Depreciation *(p. 94)* The accounting quantification of the utilization of *depreciable assets* (compare with amortization and depletion).

Dilution *(p. 364)* The reduction of earnings per share by the hypothetical conversion of *common stock equivalents* or other convertible securities.

Direct method *(p. 136)* A method by which *cash flows from operations* is determined by explicitly listing the operating cash inflows and operating cash outflows.

Discount *(p. 326)* The excess of *face value* over *book value* of bonds. When the *coupon rate* is less than the *market rate*, and the *proceeds* are less than the *face value*, we say that bonds are issued at discount (compare with par and premium).

Discounted *(p. 300)* The *present value* of future amounts.

Dividends Payable *(p. 53)* A balance sheet account, classified as a *current liability*. The balance in the Dividends Payable account represents the accounting quantification of the amount still owed for cash dividends declared.

Double T-account *(p. 108) See* T-account.

Double-declining balance method *(p. 242)* An accelerated *depreciation* method of allocating the cost of property, plant and equipment as a fixed percentage of the decreasing book value of the *asset* over its expected useful life (compare with straight-line and sum-of-the-years'-digits).

Double-entry accounting *(p. 54)* A system of *accounting*. Each *accounting event* has two **and only** two effects, both quantified by the same number.

Duration period *(p. 198)* For *assets*, the time elapsed between their recognition and utilization; for *liabilities*, the time elapsed between their incurrence and discharge.

Earnings per share *(p. 362)* A *financial ratio* used to calculate the earnings available per share of common stock outstanding as follows:

$$\frac{\text{Net income} - \text{preferred dividends}}{\text{Weighted number of shares of common stock outstanding}}$$

Economic assets *(p. 29)* A right to utilize an economic resource.

Economic decision *(p. 4)* A choice in which a *sacrifice* is incurred with the expectation of receiving a future *benefit*.

Economic equities *(p. 29)* An obligation to provide an economic resource.

Economic units *(p. 5)* The unit making *economic decisions*.

Effect account *(p. 89)* The authors' term used to describe a balance sheet account.

Effective interest method *(p. 302)* A method of calculating *interest expense*: the *effective interest rate* times the *book value* of the debt at the beginning of the period.

Effective interest rate *(p. 300)* The *interest rate* at which the *present value* of all *periodic payments* and *lump-sum payments* equals the *proceeds*.

Entry *(p. 67)* *See* Journal entry.

Equities *(p. 32)* *See* Accounting equities.

Equity method *(p. 412)* The method of accounting for an investment when the *investor* exercises significant influence but not control over the *investee* (compare with cost method).

Estimable liability *(p. 37)* A *liability* likely to require a provision. The dollar amount is not known but can be estimated. An example of such a *liability* is a Warranty Liability.

Estimated Uncollectibility Adjustment *(p. 189)* Also called Bad Debt Expense, this is an estimate of how much of the credit sales of a period will never be collected (compare with Writeoffs).

Estimated Uncollectibles *(p. 189)* Also called Allowance for Doubtful Accounts, this is a balance sheet account, classified as a *current contra-asset*. The balance in the Estimated Uncollectibles account represents the accounting quantification of the amount of accounts estimated to be uncollectible.

Event account *(p. 89)* The authors' term used to describe a *revenue* or *gain, expense* or *loss* account.

Ex-dividend *(p. 357)* Shares of stock that trade without the right to receive a dividend.

Executory contract *(p. 389)* An *agreement*, exchanging promises, without any *performance*. Hence, executory contracts are not recorded (*see* Lease).

Expenses *(p. 88)* Expenses are the *terminal utilization* of goods and/or services, decreasing *residual net-assets*.

Face value *(p. 325)* The amount to be received when a bond *matures*.

FIFO *(p. 216)* Acronym for *first-in, first-out*.

Financial accounting *(p. 7)* Information useful to reach external decisions, decisions made **about** the firm (compare with management accounting).

Financial ratios *(p. 316)* Relationships amongst accounting data used in analysis.

Financing cash flow *(p. 129)* A cash flow associated with the financing operations of a firm, such as the borrowing and repayment of long-term debt, the issue and repurchase of common stock, and the payment of cash dividends.

Finished Goods *(p. 51)* A balance sheet account, classified as a *current asset*. The balance in the Finished Goods account represents the accounting quantification of the amount of completed goods available for sale.

First-in, first-out *(p. 216)* Also called FIFO, it is an inventory flow allocation method that assumes that the cost of an item sold equals the cost of the first available item purchased (compare with last-in, first-out and average cost).

First-in, still-here *(p. 217)* The authors' term to describe the ending inventory when *LIFO* is used (compare with last-in, still-here).

FISH *(p. 217)* Acronym for *first-in, still-here.*

Fixed cost *(p. 226)* A cost that will not vary over an expected range of production.

Fully-diluted earnings per share *(p. 364)* Earnings per share adjusted for the hypothetical conversion of all *dilutive* securities (compare with primary earnings per share).

Fundamental accounting equation *(p. 54)* *Assets* equal *equities;* or *assets* equal *liabilities* plus *contributed capital* plus *residual equity.*

Future value *(p. 15)* The future equivalent of a present amount.

GAAP *(p. 11)* Acronym for *generally accepted accounting principles.*

Gains *(p. 166)* Gains relating to *assets* are the accounting recognition of the excess of their *market value* over their *book value.*

Gains relating to *liabilities* are the accounting recognition of the excess of their *book value* over their *present value.*

General ledger *(p. 74)* The collection of all *accounts.*

Generally accepted accounting principles *(p. 11)* The rules governing accounting practice, promulgated by the accounting profession, academicians, Congress, and the courts.

Goodwill *(p. 430)* A balance sheet account, classified as a *noncurrent asset.* The balance in the Goodwill account represents the accounting quantification of the excess of the cost of investments in affiliated companies over the *adjusted book value* of the *net-assets* of the affiliate.

Group method *(p. 246)* Depreciation of a group of *assets* as if they were all one asset. *Gains* and *losses* **are not** recognized when individual *assets* are disposed of (compare with unit depreciation).

Historical cost principle *(p. 49)* The measurement of *accounting events* in terms of past or present cash flows.

Income Before Tax *(p. 271)* For financial reporting purposes, the difference between *revenues* and *gains,* and *expenses* and *losses* (compare with Taxable Income).

Income statement *(p. 85)* An *activity statement* that lists all *revenues* and *gains, expenses* and *losses* of an accounting period. This statement is a required financial statement (*see* Accounting reports).

Income Tax Expense *(p. 271)* A percentage of *Income Before Tax* (compare with Required Tax Payment).

Independently quantified *(p. 59)* One of two effects of every *accounting event.* It is an effect of an *accounting event* quantified without regard to its other effect (compare with dependently quantified).

Indirect method *(p. 136)* A method by which *cash flows from operations* is determined by adjusting *net income.*

Installment method *(p. 191)* The method of recognizing income only as cash is received (compare with cost recovery method).

Intangible assets *(p. 36)* All *assets* other than *tangible assets* and *monetary assets.*

Interest Expense *(p. 94)* The accounting quantification of the cost of utilizing borrowed money.

Interest-only loan *(p. 309)* A loan whose *periodic payments* equal the periodic *interest expense,* and whose *lump-sum payment* equals the *proceeds.*

Interest Payable *(p. 52)* A balance sheet account, classified as a *current liability*. The balance in the Interest Payable account represents the accounting quantification of the amount still owed for interest.

Interest rate *(p. 15)* The rate which equates amounts of different *time dimensions*.

Intermediate utilization *(p. 91)* The authors' term used to describe the utilization of goods and/or services that results in a salable product (compare with terminal utilization).

Inventory holding period *(p. 228)* A *financial ratio* used to calculate how many days merchandise remains in inventory:

$$\frac{\text{Average inventory}}{\text{Average daily purchase of inventory}}$$

(Compare with inventory turnover ratio.)

Inventory turnover ratio *(p. 228)* A *financial ratio* used to calculate how many times the entire inventory is sold during a period:

$$\frac{\text{Cost of goods sold}}{\text{Average inventory balance}}$$

(Compare with inventory holding period.)

Investees *(p. 411)* Firms that are invested in (compare with investors).

Investing cash flow *(p. 129)* A cash flow associated with the investing activities of a firm, such as the acquisition and disposition of property, plant and equipment, or securities of other firms.

Investors *(p. 411)* People or firms that invest (compare with investees).

Journal *(p. 74)* The collection of *journal entries*.

Journal entry *(p. 67)* The initial recording of an *accounting event*.

Known liability *(p. 37)* A *liability* requiring a provision of known amount such as *Accounts Payable, Wages Payable, Interest Payable, Taxes Payable,* and *Dividends Payable*.

Last-in, first-out *(p. 216)* Also called LIFO, it is an inventory flow allocation method that assumes that the cost of an item sold equals the cost of the last available item purchased (compare with first-in, last-out and average cost).

Last-in, still-here *(p. 217)* The authors' term to describe the ending inventory when *FIFO* is used (compare with first-in, still-here).

LCM *(p. 224)* Acronym for lower-of-cost-or-market.

Lease *(p. 389)* An *executory contract* conveying the right to utilize an *asset* for a specified period of time.

Lease Expense *(p. 390)* For an *operating lease*, it is the *lease payment*. For a *capital lease*, it is the sum of the *amortization* of the *leasehold asset* **plus** the *interest expense* on the *leasehold liability*.

Lease Payment *(p. 390)* The required cash disbursement as called for in the *lease*.

Leasehold Asset *(p. 391)* A balance sheet account, classified as a *noncurrent asset*. The balance in the Leasehold Asset account represents the accounting quantification of the remaining leased assets.

Leasehold Liability *(p. 391)* A balance sheet account, classified as a *noncurrent liability*. The balance in the Leasehold Liability account represents the accounting quantification of the amount of long-term debt still owed.

Ledger accounts *(p. 74)* *See* Accounts.

Liabilities *(p. 33)* Responsibilities to provide resources of known or estimable amounts.

LIFO *(p. 216)* Acronym for *last-in, first-out*.

LISH *(p. 217)* Acronym for *last-in, still-here*.

Long-Term Debt *(p. 299)* A balance sheet account, classified as a *noncurrent liability*. The balance in the Long-Term Debt account represents the accounting quantification of the amount of long-term borrowings still owed.

Long-term loans *(p. 299)* Also called long-term debt, it represents the borrowings from banks or other financial institutions (compare with bonds).

Losses *(p. 166)* Losses relating to *assets* are the accounting recognition of the excess of their *book value* over their *market value*.

Losses relating to *liabilities* are the accounting recognition of the excess of their *present value* over their *book value*.

Lower-of-cost-or-market *(p. 224)* The principle applied to reduce *assets* to the lower of their cost or market.

Lump-sum payment *(p. 300)* A payment made at one point in time.

MACRS *(p. 275)* Acronym for modified accelerated cost recovery system.

Management accounting *(p. 7)* Information used to make internal decisions, decisions **by** the firm (compare with financial accounting).

Market rate *(p. 325)* The rate at which investors are willing to invest. That is, it is the rate which *discounts* future amounts to *market value*.

Market value *(p. 325)* The amount agreed to by unrelated buyers and sellers.

Marketable Equity Securities *(p. 414)* A balance sheet account, classified as either a *current* or *noncurrent asset*. The balance in the Marketable Equity Securities account represents the original cost of securities owned.

Materiality *(p. 58)* Information significant in making decisions.

Mature *(p. 302)* The total repayment of debt.

Minority Interest *(p. 430)* A balance sheet account, classified as an *equity*. The balance in the Minority Interest account represents the percentage of *Contributed Capital* and *Retained Earnings* allocated to the minority *investors*.

Modified accelerated cost recovery system *(p. 275)* The tax method of depreciating *assets* (compare with straight-line, sum-of-the-years'-digits, and double-declining balance methods).

Monetary assets *(p. 35)* Cash or promises to receive specific dollar amounts in the future.

Monetary liabilities *(p. 37)* An obligation to pay a fixed dollar amount in the future.

Negative amortization *(p. 307)* An increase in the *book value* of debt because the *periodic payments* are less than *interest expense* (compare with amortization and interest-only loans).

Net bonds payable *(p. 329)* *Face value of bonds* plus (minus) *Unamortized Bond Premium (Unamortized Bond Discount)*.

Net income *(p. 98)* The difference between *revenues* and *gains*, and *expenses* and *losses*.

Net-assets *(p. 55)* *Assets* minus *liabilities*.

No par *(p. 355)* *Common stock* without a *par value*.

Noncurrent assets *(p. 35)* All *assets* that are not expected to be utilized within the next year or accounting period, such as *Property, Plant and Equipment*, and *Patents*.

Noncurrent liabilities *(p. 37)* *Liabilities* that are not expected to be discharged within a year or operating cycle, whichever is longer, such as *Long-Term Debt* and *Bonds Payable*.

Nonmonetary assets *(p. 35)* All *assets* other than *monetary assets*.

Nonmonetary liabilities *(p. 37)* An obligation to provide goods and/or services rather than money in the future.

Nonoperating assets *(p. 130)* All *assets*, other than *operating assets*.

Nonoperating equities *(p. 130)* All *equities*, other than *operating equities*.

Operating assets *(p. 130)* *Current assets* that result from or are utilized in the operating activities of a firm, such as *Accounts Receivable*, *Prepaid Services*, and *Inventory*.

Operating cash flows *(p. 129)* Operating cash flows are both *revenues* and *expenses* that directly impact cash flows, and cash events that impact *operating assets* and *operating liabilities*.

Operating equities *(p. 130)* *Current liabilities* that result from or will be discharged by the operating activities of the firm, such as *Accounts Payable* and *Advances from Customers*.

Operating events *(p. 88)* Repetitive events that are part of the principal activities of a firm.

Operating Expenses *(p. 88)* The accounting quantification of the *terminal utilization* of services.

Operating lease *(p. 389)* All *leases* that are not *capital leases*.

Operating loss carrybacks *(p. 272)* *Taxable Losses* that offset previously taxed income (compare with operating loss carryforwards).

Operating loss carryforwards *(p. 272)* *Taxable Losses* that might offset future *Taxable Income* (compare with operating loss carrybacks).

Operating Revenues *(p. 88)* *See* Revenues.

Ordinary annuity *(p. 19)* *See* Annuity in arrears.

Owners' Equity *(p. 33)* The sum of *contributed capital* and *retained earnings*.

Par *(p. 326)* This term refers to both debt and equity securities. For bonds, when the *coupon rate* equals the *market rate*, and the *proceeds* equal the *face value*, we say that bonds are issued at par (compare with discount and premium).

For equity securities, par is an amount listed on each share of stock. Generally, this price has little or no significance.

Par value method *(p. 357)* A method of accounting for the acquisition and subsequent reissue of *treasury shares* based on the *par value* of the shares acquired (compare with cost method).

Participating securities *(p. 364)* Securities of a corporation that receive additional dividends after the *preferred stockholders* and *common stockholders* have received their initial dividends.

Patent *(p. 94)* An *intangible asset*, granting the holder an exclusive right.

Payment date *(p. 356)* The date on which a dividend will be distributed (*see* Date of record and Declaration date).

Percentage-of-completion method *(p. 194)* The method of recognizing *revenue* as a long-term project progresses, and when costs can be reasonably estimated (compare with completed-contract method).

Percentage-of-sales *(p. 203)* The direct method of calculating the *estimated uncollectibility adjustment* (compare with aging-of-receivables).

Performance stage *(p. 33)* The second stage of a contract. Performance **always** leads to recording *accounting events* (*see* Agreement stage).

Period expense *(p. 197)* The *terminal utilization* of goods and/or services that are indirectly related to revenue generation.

Periodic interest rate *(p. 16)* The *interest rate* for a specific period of time, such as a day, a month, a quarter, or a year.

Periodic inventory method *(p. 219)* The allocation of cost of goods available for sale to ending inventory, utilizing *FISH* or *LISH*, when inventory is physically counted (compare with perpetual inventory method). The remainder is *Cost of Goods Sold*.

Periodic payments *(p. 300)* Payments made at equal intervals. When these payments are equal in amount, they are called an *annuity*.

Permanent differences *(p. 273)* Differences in *tax basis* and *book value* of *assets* and *liabilities* caused by events that are either recognized for tax purposes but not for book purposes, or events that are recognized for book purposes and not for tax purposes (compare with temporary differences).

Perpetual inventory method *(p. 219)* The allocation of cost of goods available for sale to *Cost of Goods Sold*, utilizing *FIFO, LIFO*, or *Average Cost*, at the time the sale is made (compare with periodic inventory method). The remainder is ending inventory.

Preferred measurement *(p. 45)* The authors' term used to describe the criteria for quantifying an *accounting event*.

Preferred Stock *(p. 355)* A balance sheet account, classified as an *equity* account. The balance in the Preferred Stock account represents the accounting quantification of the amount received in exchange for shares of preferred stock issued and outstanding at *par* or *stated value*.

Preferred stockholders *(p. 353)* Shareholders of a corporation that own shares of preferred stock (compare with common stockholders).

Premium *(p. 326)* The excess of *book value* over *face value* of bonds. When the *coupon rate* is greater than the *market rate*, and the *proceeds* are greater than the *face value*, we say that bonds are issued at premium (compare with par and discount).

Prepaid Expenses *(p. 50)* *See* Prepaid Services.

Prepaid Services *(p. 50)* A balance sheet account, classified as a *current asset*. The balance in the Prepaid Services account represents the accounting quantification of the amount of services available for use.

Prepayments *(p. 50)* *See* Prepaid Services.

Present value *(p. 15)* A present equivalent of a future amount.

Primary earnings per share *(p. 362)* *Earnings per share* adjusted for the hypothetical conversion of all *dilutive common stock equivalents* (compare with fully-diluted earnings per share).

Principal *(p. 299)* The *proceeds* from borrowing that have not been repaid.

Proceeds *(p. 299)* The amount originally borrowed.

Property, Plant and Equipment *(p. 51)* A balance sheet account, classified as a *noncurrent asset*. The balance in the Property, Plant and Equipment account represents the accounting quantification of the amount of property, plant and equipment on hand.

Raw Materials and Supplies *(p. 50)* A balance sheet account, classified as a *current asset*. The balance in the Raw Materials and Supplies account represents the accounting quantification of the amount of raw materials and supplies available for use in the manufacturing process.

Reclassification of long-term loan *(p. 299)* The classification of long-term debt as current portion of long-term debt one period prior to *repayment*.

Recording signal *(p. 162)* Anything that causes the accountant to record a *journal entry*.

Repayment of a long-term loan *(p. 299)* The required debt repayment.

Required Tax Payment *(p. 271)* The result of multiplying *Taxable Income* by the applicable tax rate (compare with Income Tax Expense).

Residual equity *(p. 39)* *See* Residual net-assets.

Residual net-assets *(p. 39)* The authors' term used to describe *assets* minus *liabilities* minus *contributed capital* (*see* Retained Earnings).

Retained Earnings *(p. 39)* Also referred to as residual net-assets or residual equity. A balance sheet account, classified as an *equity* account. The balance in the Retained Earnings account can be interpreted in three ways. One, as the cumulative effect of all one-sided events (see page 38); two, as the *residual equity* of the firm; and three as the cumulative difference between total earnings and total dividends declared to date.

Return on assets *(p. 316)* A *financial ratio* used to assess the effective utilization of the *assets* of a firm:

$$\frac{\text{Net income} + \text{after-tax interest expense}}{\text{Average total } \textit{book value} \text{ of assets}}$$

Return on equity *(p. 316)* A *financial ratio* used to assess the benefit that stockholders derive from their investment:

$$\frac{\text{Net income}}{\text{Average net-assets}}$$

Revenues *(p. 88)* Revenues are the provision of goods and/or services which increase *residual net-assets*.

Sacrifice *(p. 4)* A decrease in a right or an increase in a responsibility (*see* Economic decision).

Sales Inflow *(p. 88)* The authors' term used to describe Sales Revenue (*see* Revenues).

Sales Outflow *(p. 88)* The authors' term used to describe *Cost of Goods Sold* (*see* Expenses).

Sales Revenue *(p. 88)* The accounting quantification of the provision of goods and/or services resulting from the operating activities of the firm.

Simple interest *(p. 16)* Interest accumulated on monies originally deposited (compare with compound interest).

Stated value *(p. 355)* A nominal amount for a share of *no par* common stock (compare with par value). Generally, this price has little or no significance.

Statement of cash flows *(p. 85)* An *activity statement* that reports all cash inflows and cash outflows in terms of *operating cash flows, financing cash flows*, and *investing cash flows* during an accounting period. This statement is a required financial statement (*see* Accounting reports).

Statement of cash receipts and disbursements *(p. 80)* An *activity statement* that lists all of the cash receipts and disbursements. This statement is not a required *accounting report*.

Stock dividend *(p. 361)* A distribution of additional shares to stockholders which reduces *Retained Earnings*.

Stock options *(p. 362)* A right to acquire shares of *common stock* at a specific price during a specified time period.

Stock split *(p. 361)* An increase (decrease) in the number of shares of a corporation with a proportionate decrease (increase) in *par value*.

Stock subscriptions *(p. 364)* Agreements to purchase shares of stock from a corporation.

Stock warrants *(p. 363)* Rights to acquire shares of *common stock* at a specific price.

Straight-line method *(p. 241)* A *depreciation* method of allocating the cost of property, plant and equipment in equal amounts over its expected useful life (compare with sum-of-the-years'-digits and double-declining balance).

Sum-of-the-years'-digits method *(p. 241)* An accelerated *depreciation* method of allocating the cost of property, plant and equipment by applying a decreasing rate to a fixed amount over its expected useful life (compare with straight-line and double-declining balance).

T-account *(p. 75)* A visual representation of an *account*. A T-account includes the name of the account, its beginning and ending balances, and the *debits* and *credits* that affect the *account*.

A double T-account includes the name of the *account*, the difference between its beginning and ending balances, and the *debits* and *credits* that affect the *account*.

Tangible assets *(p. 36)* Physical resources owned by a firm such as *Property, Plant and Equipment*.

Tax basis *(p. 273)* The quantification of *assets* and *liabilities* for tax purposes (compare with book value).

Taxable Income *(p. 271)* For tax purposes, the excess of taxable inflows over tax deductions (compare with Income Before Tax).

Taxable Losses *(p. 271)* Negative *Taxable Income*.

Temporary differences *(p. 274)* Differences in *tax basis* and *book value* of *assets* and *liabilities* caused by the differences in either the timing of the recognition or the quantification of an accounting event for tax and financial reporting purposes (compare with permanent differences).

Terminal utilization *(p. 92)* The authors' term used to describe expenses—the utilization of goods and/or services that does **not** result in another *asset* (compare with intermediate utilization).

Time dimension *(p. 14)* The date associated with a specific dollar amount.

Times interest earned *(p. 340)* A *financial ratio* used to assess the risks of financial leverage:

$$\frac{\text{Income before interest and taxes}}{\text{Interest expense}}$$

Transactional analysis *(p. 105)* The technique used to disaggregate financial statements into the *accounting events* that occurred during the reporting period that gave rise to these statements.

Treasury shares *(p. 357)* Shares repurchased by a firm and not retired.

Treasury Stock *(p. 358)* A balance sheet account, classified as a *contra-equity* account. The balance in the Treasury Stock account represents either the *par value* of the repurchased shares (if the *par value method* is used), or the total cost of the repurchased shares (if the *cost method* is used).

Unamortized Bond Discount *(p. 329)* A balance sheet account, classified as a *noncurrent contra-liability*. The balance in the Unamortized Bond Discount account represents the excess of *face value* over the *present value* (at the *effective interest rate*) of the remaining *periodic payments* (compare with Unamortized Bond Premium).

Unamortized Bond Premium *(p. 332)* A balance sheet account, classified as a *noncurrent adjunct liability*. The balance in the Unamortized Bond Premium account represents the excess of the *present value* (at the *effective interest rate*) of the remaining *periodic payments* over the *face value* of the bonds (compare with Unamortized Bond Discount).

Uncollectibility Adjustment *(p. 189)* *See* Estimated Uncollectibility Adjustment.

Unearned Revenue *(p. 132)* *See* Deferred Revenue.

Unit depreciation *(p. 246)* *Depreciation* of *assets* on an individual basis. Gains and losses **are** recognized when individual assets are disposed of (compare with group method).

Valuation Allowance *(p. 415)* A balance sheet account, classified as either a *current contra-asset* or *noncurrent contra-asset* account. The balance in the Valuation Allowance account represents the excess of cost over market of the portfolio. Current and Noncurrent Marketable Equity Securities accounts have separate Valuation Allowance accounts.

Variable cost *(p. 226)* A cost that increases (decreases) proportionately as production increases (decreases) (compare with fixed cost).

Volatility index *(p. 341)* A *financial ratio* used to assess the sensitivity of financial leverage:

$$\frac{\text{Net income} + \text{after-tax fixed costs}}{\text{Net income}}$$

Wages Payable *(p. 53)* A balance sheet account, classified as a *current liability*. The balance in the Wages Payable account represents the accounting quantification of the amount still owed for utilizing labor services.

Work-in-Process *(p. 50)* A balance sheet account, classified as a *current asset*. The balance in the Work-in-Process account represents the accounting quantification of the amount of incomplete goods remaining in the manufacturing process.

Working capital *(p. 130)* *Current assets* minus *current liabilities*.

Writeoff *(p. 189)* The accounting recognition that a specific receivable will not be collected (compare with Estimated Uncollectibility Adjustment).

Yield-to-maturity *(p. 325)* *See* Market rate.

Index

Accounting:
  cost, 7
  definition, 3
  double-entry, 54
  financial, 7
  management, 7
Accounting events:
  acquisition of patent for common stock, 94–95, 172
  acquisition of property, plant and equipment, 68, 172, 383–384, 387–388, 455
  advances from customers, 72, 172
  amortization:
    of goodwill, 430
    of patent, 172
  bad debt expense, 189, 451
  borrowing from the bank, 67, 172, 300, 305, 309
  collection of interest, 172
  collections from customers, 72, 172, 190, 451
  completion of manufacturing process, 71, 87, 172
  cost of goods sold, 87–91, 172, 216–218, 452
  currently required interest payment, 453
  currently required tax payment, 453
  declaration of dividends, 172, 357
  depreciation expense, 172, 241–246, 455
  dividend revenue, 414
  earnings from affiliated company, 456
  estimated uncollectibility adjustment, 189, 451
  inception of capital lease, 390
  income tax expense, 172, 271, 453
  input equipment into production, 172
  input labor services into production, 70, 87, 172
  input raw materials into production, 69, 70, 87, 172
  input services into production, 70, 87, 172
  interest expense, 172, 300, 303, 305, 453
  interest revenue, 172, 413
  issue of common stock, 65, 172
  lease expense, 391–393
  lease payment, 391–393
  operating expenses, 172, 196–198, 453
  payment:
    of cash dividends, 172, 356–357, 454
    of interest, 172, 453
    of taxes, 172, 453

Accounting events (Cont.):
  payments to suppliers:
    of labor services, 72, 87, 172
    of merchandise, 172, 452
    of raw materials, 72, 172
    of services, 172, 453
  reclassification of long-term debt, 172, 303–305, 307–308, 312–313
  purchase of inventory, 172, 452
  purchase of raw materials, 67, 86, 172
  repayment of debt, 172, 301–303, 306–307, 309–312
  repurchase of common stock, 172, 357–360
  sale of property, plant and equipment, 172, 385–386
  sales revenue, 87–91, 172, 185–193
  (See also Recognizing accounting events; Recording accounting events; Reporting accounting events)
Accounting reports (see Financial statements)
Accounting systems:
  accrual method, 49
  cash method, 49
Accounts, 74, 174–175
  event, 89
  ledger, 74
  (See also Balance sheet accounts; Contra-accounts)
Accounts payable, 52, 67, 72, 73, 75, 86, 95, 97, 112, 115, 133–134
Accounts payable merchandise, 175, 452
Accounts payable services, 52, 175, 453
Accounts receivable, 49, 90, 95, 97, 112, 115, 134, 174, 451
Accrual, 49
Accrual method, 49
Accumulated depreciation, 51, 96, 112, 115, 134, 174, 455
Activity statement, 80
Addback (indirect) method, 136–142
Additional paid-in capital, 355, 454
Adjunct liability, unamortized bond premium, 332–335, 454
Adjusting entries, 164, 419
Advances from customers, 52, 72, 73, 75, 90, 95, 97, 134, 175, 451
Aging-of-receivables, 203
Allowance accounts (see Contra-accounts)

Amortization:
  of bond discount, 329–332
  of bond premium, 332–335
  definition, 241
  of franchise, 255
  of goodwill, 430
  of lease, 391–393
  negative, 307
  of patent, 172
  of property, plant and equipment (*see*
      Expenses, depreciation)
Annuities:
  in advance or annuity due, 19
  in arrears or ordinary annuity, 19
  definition, 19
Assets:
  book value of, 51, 415
  cash, 130
  contra (*see* Contra-assets)
  current (*see* Current assets)
  definition, 29
  deferred tax, 273, 453
  depreciable, 51
  intangible (*see* Intangible assets)
  leasehold, 390–391, 456
  monetary (*see* Monetary assets)
  noncurrent (*see* Noncurrent assets)
  nonmonetary (*see* Nonmonetary assets)
  nonoperating, 130, 397–399
  return on, 316
  tangible (*see* Tangible assets)
Average cost, 216, 218

Bad debt expense, 189
Balance sheet(s), 77, 174
  comparative, 79
    consolidated, 422
Balance sheet accounts:
  accounts payable, 52, 67, 72, 73, 75, 86, 95,
      97, 112, 115, 133–134
  accounts payable merchandise, 175, 452
  accounts payable services, 52, 175, 453
  accounts receivable, 49, 90, 95, 97, 112, 115,
      134, 174, 451
  accumulated depreciation, 51, 96, 112, 115,
      134, 174, 455
  additional paid-in capital, 355, 454
  advances from customers, 52, 72, 73, 75, 90,
      95, 97, 134, 175, 451
  bank loan, 53, 67, 73, 75, 97, 112, 115, 133
  bonds payable, 327-335
  cash, 49, 65, 73, 75, 86, 95, 97, 112, 115,
      133-134, 173
  common stock, 53, 65, 73, 75, 112, 115,
      133-134, 175
  current portion of debt, 175, 456
  deferred charges, 50
  deferred expenses, 132

Balance sheet accounts (*Cont.*):
  deferred revenue, 132
  deferred tax asset, 273, 453
  deferred tax liability, 273, 453
  deposits, 132
  dividends payable, 53, 101, 112, 115, 175,
      454
  dividends receivable, 414
  estimated uncollectibles, 189, 451
  finished goods, 51, 71, 73, 75, 89, 95-97, 112,
      115, 133-134, 175
  goodwill, 430
  interest payable, 52, 96-97, 112, 115, 134,
      175
  interest receivable, 413
  inventory, 174, 452
  investment in affiliated company, 432
  leasehold asset, 390-391, 456
  leasehold liability, 390-391, 456
  long-term debt, 175, 299
  marketable equity securities, 414
  patent, 94, 96-97, 112, 115, 134, 174
  preferred stock, 354-355
  prepaid services, 50, 68, 70, 73, 75, 87, 92-97,
      112, 115, 133-134, 174, 453
  prepayments, 50
  property, plant and equipment, 51, 68, 75,
      97, 112, 115, 133-134, 174, 455
  raw materials and supplies, 50, 67-68, 70-71,
      73, 75, 86-87, 95, 97, 112, 115, 133, 174
  retained earnings, 39, 101, 112, 115, 175
  taxes payable, 175, 453
  treasury stock, 357-360
  unamortized bond discount, 329-332, 454
  unamortized bond premium, 332-335, 454
  unearned revenue, 132
  valuation allowance, 415
  wages payable, 53, 72, 73, 75, 87, 95-97, 112,
      115, 133-134, 175
  warranty liability, 193
  work-in-process, 50, 70, 71, 73, 75, 87, 95, 97,
      112, 115, 133, 174
Bank loan, 53, 67, 73, 75, 97, 112, 115, 133
Basic inventory equation, 216
Benefit, 4
Bonds, 325–341
  conversion to common stock, 337–338
  effects on financial ratios, 339–341
  financial statement presentation,
      338–339
  interest expense, 327–335
  issuance of, 325
    discount, 328–332
    par, 327–328
    premium, 332–335
  periodic payments, 327, 329, 332
  reclassification, 327, 330, 333
  repayment, 328
  retirement, 336–337
Bonds payable, 327

Book value of assets:
  marketable equity securities, 415
  property, plant and equipment, 51

Capital:
  additional paid-in, 355, 454
  contributed, 53
  working, 130
Capital lease, 389–393
Cash, 49, 65, 73, 75, 86, 95, 97, 112, 115,
    133–134, 173
Cash assets, 130
Cash flows:
  consolidated statement of, 422
    (*See also* Statement of cash flows)
  financing, 129
  from financing events, 132
  from investing events, 133
  from operating events, 130–132
    direct method, 133–136
    indirect (addback) method, 136–142
Cash method, 49
Cash receipts and disbursements, statement of,
    80–81
Cash yield rate, 326
Closing process, 91, 99–100, 170, 173
Collection period, 199
Common stock (*see* Stockholders' equity)
Common stock equivalents, 362
Comparative balance sheets, 79
Completed contract method, 194
Compound interest, 16
Consolidated comparative balance sheets, 422
Consolidated financial statements, 412, 422
Consolidated income statements, 422
Consolidated statement of cash flows, 422
Consolidations, 418–431
  entries:
    adjusting, 419, 423, 425–429
    combined, 419, 423, 425–429
    consolidated, 419, 425–429
  financial statements, 422
  intercompany:
    cash transactions, 423
    purchases, 423–428
    sales, 423–428
Contra-accounts:
  contra-asset, 93
  contra-equity, 358
  contra-liability, 329
Contra-assets:
  accumulated depreciation, 51, 96, 112, 115,
    134, 174, 455
  estimated uncollectibles, 189, 451
  valuation allowance, 415
Contra-equities:
  net unrealized loss in noncurrent marketable
    securities, 416–417
  treasury stock, 357–360

Contra-liability, unamortized bond discount,
    329–332, 454
Contributed capital, 53
Cooper Industries, 259, 260, 366
Cost of goods sold:
  average, 216, 218
  effect on financial statements, 220–224
  effects on financial ratios, 316–318
  financial statement presentation,
    226–227
  first-in, first-out (FIFO), 216–218, 462
  last-in, first-out (LIFO), 216–218, 462
  manufacturer, 225–226
  periodic method, 219–220
  perpetual method, 219–220
  specific identification, 216
Cost accounting, 7
Cost method, 357, 416–418
Cost recovery method, 192
Coupon, 325
Coupon payment, 325
Coupon rate, 325
Credits, 65
Current assets:
  accounts receivable, 49, 90, 95, 97, 112, 115,
    134, 174, 451
  cash, 49, 65, 73, 75, 86, 95, 97, 112, 115,
    133–134, 173
  deferred charge, 50
  deferred expense, 132
  definition, 35
  deposits, 132
  finished goods, 51, 71, 73, 75, 89, 95–97, 112,
    115, 133–134, 174
  inventory, 174, 452
  marketable equity securities, 414, 416–418
  prepaid services, 50, 68, 70, 73, 75, 87,
    92–97, 112, 115, 133–134, 174, 453
  prepayments, 50
  raw materials and supplies, 50, 67–68, 70–71,
    73, 75, 86–87, 95, 97, 112, 115, 133, 174
  work-in-process, 50, 70, 71, 73, 75, 87, 95, 97,
    112, 115, 133, 174
Current liabilities:
  accounts payable, 52, 67, 72, 73, 75, 86, 95,
    97, 112, 155, 133–134
  accounts payable merchandise, 175, 452
  accounts payable services, 52, 175, 453
  advances from customers, 52, 72, 73, 75, 90,
    95, 97, 134, 175, 451
  current portion of debt, 175, 456
  deferred revenue, 132
  definition, 37
  dividends payable, 53, 101, 112, 115, 175, 454
  interest payable, 52, 96–97, 112, 115, 134,
    175
  taxes payable, 175, 453
  unearned revenue, 132
  wages payable, 53, 72, 73, 75, 87, 95–97, 112,
    115, 133–134, 175

Current liabilities *(Cont.)*:
  warranty liability, 193
Current ratio, 316

Debits, 65
Debt, long-term *(see* Long-term debt)
Debt constant, 301
Debt-equity ratio, 340
Deferral, 49
Deferred charges, 50
Deferred expenses, 132
Deferred revenue, 132
Deferred tax asset, 273, 453
Deferred tax liability, 273, 453
Dependently quantified, 59
Depletion:
  definition, 241
  of natural resources, 256
Deposits, 132
Depreciable assets, 51
Depreciation:
  accumulated *(see* Accumulated depreciation)
  changes in estimates, 254–255
  definition, 94
  effect on financial statements, 248–251
  financial statement presentation, 256–259
  group, 248, 386
  methods of:
    double-declining balance, 244–245
    modified accelerated cost recovery system, 275–279
    straight-line, 242–243
    sum-of-the-years'-digits, 243–244
  unit, 248
Dilution, 364
Direct method, 136
Discount, 326
Discounted, 300
Dividends, 356–357
  cash, 53, 172, 357
  date of declaration, 356
  date of record, 356
  ex-dividend, 357
  payment date, 356
  stock, 361
Dividends payable, 53, 101, 112, 115, 175, 454
Double-declining balance method, 242, 244–245
Double-entry accounting, 54
Double T-account, 108
Duration dimension:
  of accounts payable merchandise, 229
  of accounts payable services, 201
  of accounts receivable, 199
  of inventory, 228
  of operating cash cycle, 229
Duration period, 198

Earnings per share, 362–366
  basic, 362

Earnings per share *(Cont.)*:
  common stock equivalents, 363
  dilution, 364
  financial statement presentation, 362–366
  fully-diluted, 364
  primary, 362–363
Effect account, 89
Effective interest method, 302
Effective interest rate, 300
Entry, 67
Equity(ies):
  operating, 130
  residual, 39
  return on, 316, 367–368
  (See also Contra-equities; Owners' equity; Stockholders' equity)
Equity method, 412
Estimated uncollectibility adjustment:
  aging-of-receivables, 189
  percentage-of-sales, 189
Estimated uncollectibles, 189, 451
Event account, 89
Executory contract, 389
Expenses:
  deferred, 132
  definition, 88
  financial statement presentation categories:
    amortization, 172
    bad debt, 189
    cost of goods sold, 88, 172
    depletion, 241
    depreciation, 94, 172
    estimated uncollectibility adjustment, 189
    income taxes, 271, 453
    interest, 94, 172
    lease, 391–393
    operating, 172, 390
    (See also Operating expenses)
    period, 197
    product, 197

Face value, 325
FIFO (first-in, first-out), 216–218, 462
Financial accounting, 7
Financial ratios:
  collection period, 199
  current, 316
  debt constant, 301
  debt-equity, 340
  earnings per share, 362–366
    basic, 362
    fully-diluted, 364
    primary, 362–363
  inventory holding period, 228
  inventory turnover, 228
  return on assets, 316, 397–399
  return on equity, 316, 367–368
  times interest earned, 340
  volatility index, 341

Financial statement presentation:
  bonds, 338–339
  earnings per share, 362–366
  expenses, 199
  income taxes, 284–286
  inventory, 227
  leases, 396
  long-term debt, 315, 339
  marketable equity securities, 435–437
  property, plant and equipment, 256–259
  revenues, 195–196
  stockholders' equity, 362
Financial statements:
  balance sheet, 77, 174
  comparative balance sheets, 79
  consolidated:
    comparative balance sheets, 422
    income statement, 422
    statement of cash flows, 422
  income statement, 85, 173
  statement of cash flows, 85, 173
  statement of cash receipts and disbursements,
    80–81
Financing cash flow, 129
Finished goods, 51, 71, 73, 75, 89, 95–97, 112,
    115, 133–134, 174
First-in, first-out (FIFO), 216–218, 462
First-in, still-here (FISH), 217–218
Fixed cost, 226
Fully-diluted earnings per share, 364
Fundamental accounting equation, 54
Future value, 15

GAAP (generally accepted accounting
    principles), 11
Gains:
  definition, 166
  effect on financial statements, 168–169
General Electric Company, 196
General Foods Company, 339, 389
General ledger (see Accounts)
Generally accepted accounting principles
    (GAAP), 11
Goods sold, cost of (see Cost of goods sold)
Goodwill, 430
Group method, 246

Historical cost principle, 49

Income before tax, 271
Income statement, 85, 173
  closing process, 91, 99–100, 170, 173
  consolidated, 422
  expenses, 88
  gains, 166
  losses, 166
  revenues, 88

Income tax expense, 271
Income taxes, 271–288
  currently required payment, 453
  deferred tax asset, 273, 453
  deferred tax liability, 273, 453
  definitions, 271–272
  expense, 271
  financial statement presentation, 284–286
  operating loss carrybacks, 272
  operating loss carryforwards, 272
  permanent differences, 273
  temporary differences, 274
Independently quantified, 59
Indirect (addback) method, 136–142
Installment method, 191
Intangible assets:
  goodwill, 430
  leasehold asset, 390–391, 456
  patent, 94, 96–97, 112, 115, 134, 174
Interest:
  compound, 16
  coupon payment, 325, 327
  coupon rate, 325
  currently required payment, 453
  definition, 94
  discounting, 300
  expense, 94, 172
  simple, 16
Interest-only loan, 309
Interest payable, 52, 96–97, 112, 115, 134, 175
Interest rate, 15
Intermediate utilization, 91
Inventory holding period, 228
Inventory turnover ratio, 228
Inventory valuation methods:
  average cost, 216, 218
  effect on financial statements, 221, 223
  effects on financial ratios, 316–318
  financial statement presentation, 226–227
  first-in, still-here, 217–218
  FISH, 217–218
  last-in, still-here, 217–218
  LISH, 217–218
  periodic method, 219–220
  perpetual method, 219–220
  specific identification, 216
Investees, 411
Investing cash flow, 129
Investments, 411–439
  accounting treatment:
    consolidations, 418–431
    cost method (LCM), 416–418, 433
    equity method, 432–433
    marketable equity securities, 416–418
  financial statement presentation, 435–437
  investee, 411
  investment in affiliated company, 432–433
  investor, 411
  net unrealized loss in noncurrent marketable
    securities, 416–417

Investments (*Cont.*):
  valuation allowance:
    current, 416–418
    noncurrent, 416–418
Investors, 411

Journal, 74
Journal entry, 67

Last-in, first-out (LIFO), 216–218, 462
Last-in, still-here (LISH), 217–218
LCM (lower-of-cost-or-market), 224, 415–418
Lease, 389–397
  asset, 390–393
  capital, 389–393
    expense, 391–393
    payment, 391–393
  definition, 389
  effect on financial ratios:
    current, 399
    debt-equity, 399
    return on assets, 397
    return on equity, 398
  financial statement presentation, 396
  liability, 390–393
  operating, 389–390
    expense, 389–390
    payment, 389–390
Lease expense, 391–393
Lease payment, 391–393
Leasehold asset, 390–391, 456
Leasehold liability, 390–391, 456
Ledger accounts, 74
Liabilities:
  adjunct, 332
  contra-, 329–332, 454
  current, (*see* Current liabilities)
  definition, 33
  deferred tax, 273, 453
  leasehold, 390–391, 456
  monetary (*see* Monetary liabilities)
  noncurrent (*see* Noncurrent liabilities)
  nonmonetary, 37, 273, 453
LIFO (last-in, first-out), 216–218, 462
LISH (last-in, still-here), 217–218
Loans, long-term, 299
Long-term debt, 299–318, 325–341
  accounting:
    for proceeds:
      lump-sum payment only, 305
      periodic payments and lump-sum
        payment, 309
      periodic payments only, 300
    for reclassification:
      lump-sum payment only, 307–308
      periodic payments and lump-sum
        payment, 312–313
      periodic payments only, 303–305

Long-term debt
  accounting (*Cont.*):
    for repayment:
      lump-sum payment only, 306–307
      periodic payments and lump-sum
        payment, 309–312
      periodic payments only, 301–303
Long-term loans, 299
Losses:
  definition, 166
  effect on financial statements, 168–169
Lower-of-cost-or-market, 224, 415–418
Lump-sum payment, 300

MACRS (modified accelerated cost recovery
    system), 275–279
Management accounting, 7
Market rate, 325
Market value, 325
Marketable equity securities:
  definition, 414
  financial statement presentation,
    435–437
  impairment, 415–416
Materiality, 58
Mature, 302
Minority interest, 430–431
Modified accelerated cost recovery system
    (MACRS), 275–279
Monetary assets, 35
  cash, 49, 65, 73, 75, 86, 95, 97, 112, 115,
    133–134, 173
  accounts receivable, 49, 90, 95, 97, 112, 115,
    134, 174, 451
Monetary liabilities, 37
  accounts payable, 52, 67, 72, 73, 75, 86, 95,
    97, 112, 115, 133–134
  accounts payable merchandise, 175, 452
  accounts payable services, 52, 175, 453
  bonds payable, 327
  current portion of debt, 175, 456
  dividends payable, 53, 101, 112, 115, 175, 454
  interest payable, 52, 96–97, 112, 115, 134,
    175
  leasehold liability, 390–391, 456
  long-term debt, 175, 299
  taxes payable, 175, 453
  wages payable, 53, 72, 73, 75, 87, 95–97, 112,
    115, 133–134, 175

Negative amortization, 307
Net-assets, 55
  residuals, 39
Net bonds payable, 329
Net income, 98
New York Times Company, The, 195–196, 227,
    259–261, 315, 396
No par, 355

Noncurrent assets:
  deferred tax asset, 273, 453
  goodwill, 430
  investment in affiliated company, 432
  leasehold asset, 390–391, 456
  marketable equity securities, 414, 416–418
  patent, 94, 96–97, 112, 115, 134, 174
  property, plant and equipment, 51, 68, 75,
    97, 112, 115, 133–134, 174, 455
Noncurrent liabilities:
  bonds payable, 327
  deferred tax liability, 273, 453
  leasehold liability, 390–391, 456
  long-term debt, 175, 299
Nonmonetary assets, 35
  deferred charge, 50
  deferred expense, 132
  deferred tax asset, 273, 453
  deposits, 132
  finished goods, 51, 71, 73, 75, 89, 95–97, 112,
    115, 133–134, 174
  goodwill, 430
  inventory, 174, 452
  investment in affiliated company, 432
  leasehold asset, 390–391, 456
  marketable equity securities, 414, 416–418
  patent, 94, 96–97, 112, 115, 134, 174
  prepaid services, 50, 68, 70, 73, 75, 87,
    92–97, 112, 115, 133–134, 174, 453
  prepayments, 50
  property, plant and equipment, 51, 68, 75,
    97, 112, 115, 133–134, 174, 455
  raw materials and supplies, 50, 67–68, 70–71,
    73, 75, 86–87, 95, 97, 112, 115, 133, 174
  work-in-process, 50, 70, 71, 73, 75, 87, 95, 97,
    112, 115, 133, 174
Nonmonetary liabilities, 37
  deferred tax liability, 273, 453
Nonoperating assets, 130
Nonoperating equities, 130

Ogden Corporation, The, 436–437
Operating assets, 130
Operating cash flows, 129
Operating equities, 130
Operating events, 88
Operating expenses:
  definition, 88
  financial statement presentation, 199
Operating lease, 389
Operating loss carrybacks, 272
Operating loss carryforwards, 272
Operating revenues, 88
Ordinary annuity, 19
Owners' equity, 33

Par, 326
Par value method, 357

Patent, 94, 96–97, 112, 115, 134, 174
Percentage-of-completion method, 194
Percentage-of-sales, 203
Period expense, 197
Periodic interest rate, 16
Periodic inventory method, 219
Periodic payments, 300
Permanent differences, 273
Perpetual inventory method, 219
Philip Morris Companies, 362, 365
Preferred measurement, 45
Preferred stock, 354–355
Premium, 326
Prepaid expenses, 50
Prepaid services, 50, 68, 70, 73, 75, 87, 92–97,
    112, 115, 133–134, 174, 453
Prepayments, 50
Present value, 15
Primary earnings per share, 362–363
Principal, 299
Proceeds, 299
Property, plant and equipment, 51, 174
  accounting for the acquisition:
    by monetary transactions, 383–384
    by nonmonetary transactions, 387–388
  depreciation, 94
  financial statement presentation, 389
  retirements, 385
  return on assets, 316, 397–399

Raw materials and supplies, 50, 67–68, 70–71,
    73, 75, 86–87, 95, 97, 112, 115, 133, 174
Reclassification of long-term loan, 299
Recognizing accounting events, 155–162
Recording accounting events:
  criteria, 155–163
  by signal, 164–166
    documentation, 163
    inference, 163
  in T-accounts:
    balance sheet, 173–175
    income summary, 173
Recording signal, 162, 164–166
Repairs:
  extraordinary, 253–254
  ordinary, 253–254
  restoration, 253–254
Repayment of long-term loan, 299
Reporting financing events, 168
Reporting investing events, 168–169
Reporting operating events, 167–168
Required tax payment, 271
Residual equity, 39
Residual net-assets, 39
Retained earnings, 39, 101, 112, 115, 175
Return on assets, 316, 397–399
Return on equity, 316, 367–368
Revenue(s):
  deferred, 132

Revenue(s) *(Cont.):*
    definition, 88
    financial statement presentation, 195–196
    recognition methods:
        completed contract, 194
        cost recovery, 192
        installment sales, 191
        percentage of completion, 194

Sacrifice, 4
Sales inflow, 88
Sales outflow, 88
Sales revenue, 88
Schedule of noncash financing and investing
        events, 142–143
Simple interest, 16
Stated value, 355
Statement of cash flows, 129–144
    financing cash flows, 132
    investing cash flows, 133
    operating cash flows, 130–132
        direct method, 133–136
        indirect (addback) method, 136–142
Statement of cash receipts and disbursements,
        80–81
Stock(s):
    preferred, 354–355
    treasury, 357–360
Stock dividend, 361
Stock options, 362
Stock split, 361
Stock subscriptions, 364
Stock warrants, 363
Stockholders' equity:
    additional paid-in capital, 355, 454
    common stock, 53, 65, 73, 75, 112, 115,
        133–134, 175
    compensation plans, 360
    contra-:
        net unrealized loss in noncurrent
            marketable securities, 416–417
        treasury stock, 357–360
    contributed capital, 53
    effect on financial ratios:
        earnings per share, 362–365
        return on equity, 367–368
    financial statement presentation, 362
    preferred stock, 354–355
    repurchase, 357–360
    retained earnings, 39, 101, 112, 115, 175
    stock dividends, 361
    stock options, 362
    stock splits, 361
Straight-line method, 241, 243–244
Sum-of-the-years' digits method, 241
Summary of accounting:
    for bonds, 335

Summary of accounting *(Cont.):*
    for events, 169–175
    for investments in other firms, 433
    for leases, 393–395
    for long-term debt, 313

T-account, 75
    double, 108
Tangible assets, 36
    finished goods, 51, 71, 73, 75, 89, 95–97, 112,
        115, 133–134, 174
    property, plant and equipment, 51, 68, 75,
        97, 112, 115, 133–134, 174, 455
    raw materials and supplies, 50, 67–68, 70–71,
        73, 75, 86–87, 95, 97, 112, 115, 133, 174
    work-in-process, 50, 70, 71, 73, 75, 87, 95, 97,
        112, 115, 133, 174
Tax basis, 273
Taxable income, 271
Taxable losses, 271
Temporary differences, 274
Terminal utilization, 92
Time dimension, 14
Times interest earned, 340
Transactional analysis, 105
Treasury shares, 357–360
Treasury stock, 357–360

Unamortized bond discount, 329–332, 454
Unamortized bond premium, 332–335, 454
Uncollectibility:
    estimate of:
        aging-of-receivables, 204
        percentage-of-sales, 203
    writeoffs, 204
Uncollectibility adjustment, estimated, 189
Uncollectibles, estimated, 189, 451
Unearned revenue, 132
Unit depreciation, 246

Valuation allowance, 415
Variable cost, 226
Volatility index, 341

Wages payable, 53, 72, 73, 75, 87, 95–97, 112,
        115, 133–134, 175
Warner Communications, Inc., 284–286, 435
Work-in-process, 50, 70, 71, 73, 75, 87, 95, 97,
        112, 115, 133, 174
Working capital, 130
Writeoff, 189

Yield-to-maturity, 325